Kinship Ideology and Practice in Latin America

Kinship Ideology and Practice in Latin America

Edited by Raymond T. Smith

The University of North Carolina Press

Chapel Hill and London

Library of Congress Cataloging in
Publication Data

Main entry under title:
Kinship ideology and practice in Latin America.

Papers resulting from meetings held in New
York in Sept. 1980 and in Ixtapan de la Sal,
Mexico in Sept. 1981, both sponsored by the Joint
committee on Latin American Studies.
     1. Family—Latin America—History—
Congresses.   2. Kinship—Latin America—
History—Congresses.   3. Latin America—Social
life and customs—Congresses.   I. Smith,
Raymond Thomas, 1925–   II. Joint
Committee on Latin American Studies.
HQ560.5.L68   1984   306.8'5'098   83-26082

ISBN 0-8078-1607-8

Set in Plantin by G & S Typesetters, Inc.
Designed by Naomi P. Slifkin

Contents

Preface

In October of 1976 a small planning meeting was held at the Social Science Research Council offices in New York, a meeting called by Peter H. Smith, Francesca Cancian, and Louis Wolf Goodman. They wanted the burgeoning research on the family in Latin America, particularly historical research, to be informed by the most sophisticated social theory available and by a due respect for the particularities of Latin American society. As a result of that meeting the Joint Committee on Latin American Studies of the American Council of Learned Societies and the Social Science Research Council agreed to sponsor a workshop to explore further the issues set out in the background paper, "The History of the Family in Latin America: An Interdisciplinary Approach," written by Smith, Cancian, and Goodman.

The project was most successful, especially as it generated some differences of opinion about the factors to be stressed in the analysis of kinship—differences that are apparent in the published results of the workshop, *The Family in Latin America* (1978). With admirable forbearance the joint committee agreed to sponsor a continuation project proposed by Larissa Lomnitz and Raymond T. Smith, both of whom had participated in the first workshop. This was to be devoted to further exploration of the theoretical issues raised there, and especially to discussions of the cultural particularities of the Latin American and Caribbean region.

Two meetings were held—in New York in September 1980 and in Ixtapan de la Sal, Mexico, in September 1981. The result of those meetings is presented here. We are deeply grateful to Louis Wolf Goodman, George Reid Andrews, Elizabeth deG. R. Hansen, and Brooke Larson, staff associates of the Social Science Research Council, who were successively responsible for the planning and organization of the meetings and the subsequent work on preparation of this book. The success of the meetings was also greatly enhanced by the participation of Sylvia Yanagisako, Ronald Inden, Linda Lewin, Susan Lobo, and Arakcy Martins Rodrigues. Although they do not have essays in this book, their influence is apparent throughout. We are most grateful to them, and to Lois Bisek, Michael Sullivan, John Calagione, Kathryn Barnes, and Laura Doan, who helped in various ways with the preparation of the final manuscript.

Larissa A. Lomnitz
Raymond T. Smith

Kinship Ideology and Practice in Latin America

Introduction

Raymond T. Smith

With the bourgeoisie . . . only one *relation is valid on its own account—the relation of exploitation. . . . where he encounters relations which cannot be directly subordinated to the relation of exploitation, he does at least subordinate them to it in his imagination. . . . all the activity of individuals in their mutual intercourse . . . e.g. speech, love, etc., is depicted as a relation of utility and utilisation. . . . one sees at a glance that the category of "utilisation" is first of all abstracted from the actual relations of intercourse which I have with other people . . . and then these relations are made out to be the reality of the category that has been abstracted from them themselves, a wholly metaphysical procedure.*

Marx and Engels, *The German Ideology*

A tradition has grown up in Latin American and Caribbean studies which purports to be in some way "Marxist" and in which all social phenomena are interpreted as being caused by economic factors. Far from being Marxist, many of the writers in this tradition are best described as utilitarians who reduce all social reality to the actions of individuals seeking to maximize their gains, or pleasures, and minimize their losses, or pains. No topic is less suited to the crudities of such an approach than is the family, as Marx himself clearly understood. Of course, bourgeois society does tend to reduce all human relations to this form, and the bloodless categories of life in U.S. suburbia may yield to market analysis; Latin American society will not.

Kinship is not much studied in Latin America, except by anthropologists concerned with "primitive" or "tribal" or "folk" Indian groups. The few scholars dealing with kinship and family life among urban, or more developed rural, groups generally have been concerned to understand the impact of "modernization" on what were supposed to be traditional systems brought from Europe or carried forward from an Indian past. In this concern they have followed the pattern developed for the understanding of European history, a pattern which assumes that economic development erodes kinship as social relations become impersonal, competitive, and calculating, leaving only an isolated nuclear family as a "haven in a heartless world." The family has been more studied in the Caribbean, and although the underlying theoretical assumptions are the same, the supposed pattern of development has been somewhat different. Economic factors in the form of plantation slavery are held to have produced an early disorganization in kinship relations, from which the family has not yet fully recovered.

Historians of Europe are beginning to recognize the variety of responses to industrialization, not all of which have led to the erosion of kinship ties. Anthropologists and sociologists have documented the persisting strength and extension of kinship relations even in large industrial cities. It is tempting to replicate these studies in Latin America, but we need to rethink both theories and methods of research if they are to be adequate for the understanding of this region. Kinship in Latin America and the Caribbean is not just following an evolutionary pattern set by Europe; it has its own structure, its own history, and its own pattern of transformation.

The essays collected here were written expressly for this volume. They deal with the specific cultural features of Latin American societies and explore their relevance for understanding changes in family, kinship, and marriage, although they do so in a variety of ways. Latin America is an area of cultural and historical diversity in which research is still fragmentary, and in which different approaches are being tried. One must avoid premature generalization, and for this reason we speak not of "Latin American kinship" but of kinship in Latin America. The non-Hispanic Caribbean is included because it seems to belong in the same universe of discourse; the Caribbean territories share many historical and structural features with the countries of South and Central America, though I do not wish to minimize the difference (see "Issues and Answers," below).

More attention should be paid to the particularity of the historically generated cultural forms characteristic of this area, and to the social practices through which those forms operate in the specific conditions of contemporary society.

That is the theme around which this book is organized. However, the contributors approach their problems from a range of theoretical perspectives, even though they share a general desire to accord greater than usual weight to cultural, or ideological, factors. The significance of this desire can be appreciated only if it is contrasted with general practice in kinship analysis. Consequently, I begin with a discussion of the shortcomings of what has been called the "standard interpretation" of family history (Cancian, Goodman, and Smith 1978, p. 320), before reviewing some modifications of this interpretation.

Theoretical Problems

The Structural-Functional Paradigm

Standard works on kinship are laden with assumptions, of which the following are the most common.

Since the late eighteenth century, at least, European writers have generally assumed that the family of parents and children is a universal human institution that provides certain functions indispensable for the reproduction of all societies. This assumption has been embodied in developing social theory, and it would be surprising if the contributors to this book did not betray signs of it. Marriage and the formation of a new family, according to this view, provide the proper context for the birth of children who will have a legitimate place in society. The family socializes new members and provides secure refuge for adults and children alike. Even eighteenth-century writers were aware that many societies, including those in Europe, have family units that do not quite fit this description. It was argued that more complex forms are created by the extension of elementary units, and if one looks closely enough one can see that "nuclear" units are there. The solidarity produced within those units is extended outward, and thus new groups that can be used for a variety of political, economic, and ritual purposes are created. All kinship is based, ultimately, upon relationships of consanguinity and affinity (blood and marriage), or so the argument goes. However, each society stresses some genealogical links and ignores others; this process of selection gives to each kinship system a distinctive shape or form. In preindustrial societies kinship is often the most embracing, or privileged, mode of social relationship.

From this base the theory views processes of change. As societies become more complex, it is argued, they become more differentiated in their internal structure. Institutions are now specialized in just one function rather than being loaded with many. Because of this specialization, the family gradually loses functions to other institutions, some of them quite new, until it consists only of husband and wife, who specialize in the rearing of children and in providing for each other's emotional sustenance in an increasingly fragmented and impersonal world.

This curious mélange of folk wisdom and theoretical sophistication has been confronted with all kinds of empirical challenge, but too often it has been met by surface adjustment without reference to the underlying theoretical assumptions that shape the conventional view. What are those assumptions? They derive from the idea that human societies are systems of social relations in which interaction is rendered orderly and predictable by virtue of common adherence to shared values and internalized norms of conduct. The systematicity of social relations is organized around the need for certain functions to be performed in order that societies may continue to exist. Not all societies take the same form, but it is assumed that basic functions can be expressed in abstract, analytical language that transcends the particularity of given societies and enables us to view them all in the same terms—much as we can view all mammals, say, in the general terms of anatomy and physiology. Within this broad conception there is considerable variation that emphasizes different "needs" as primary; and indeed, the extent to which societies stress adaptation, political integration, religious values, or other functions may be made the basis of a system of classification, as in the work of Talcott Parsons (see especially Parsons 1951).

Of the many ironies in the development of structural-functional theory none is more profound than its relation to evolutionism. In its twentieth-century version, functionalism was made to oppose what Radcliffe-Brown (1952) called "conjectural history," a procedure used by evolutionists to construct the hypothetical sequence of stages through which all societies were thought to have passed, or to be going to pass. Structural-functional anthropology, by contrast, advocated the synchronic study of living societies, in which the function of each part could be measured by the contribution it made to the stability and continuity of the whole of which it was a part. Although this model assumed that societies would remain in, or return to, a state of equilibrium, its advocates were always aware of the dynamic elements in social life. Anthony Smith (1973) has shown that structural-functional theory is essentially a disguised form of evolutionary theory with an inherent tendency to fall back into that mode of reasoning via the elaboration of "modernization theory." The concepts of "differentiation" and "specialization of function" become the mechanisms whereby "moving equilibrium" is converted into an evolutionary sequence. Smelser's book entitled *Social Change in the Industrial Revolution* (1959) is an excellent example of the application of these concepts to a well-known period of English history. Talcott Parsons, for all the charges of rigidity that have been leveled against his theories, had a very keen sense of the degree to which conflict, variation, and malintegration can produce what Parsons called strain that leads to changing patterns of integration.

Criticisms of structural-functional theory grew in volume during the 1950s until now one can find very few open advocates (see A. Smith 1973 for an excellent summary). The paradigm has not been totally abandoned, however; rather, there have been attempts to introduce modifications. Even when the theory is repudiated, its principles are often unwittingly incorporated into new positions. I have said that the major concern of this book is to examine the influence of specifically Latin American culture upon kinship and family relations. In order to understand the theoretical import of this concern it is necessary to review the manner in which the limitations of structural-functional theory forced a recognition that problems of meaning must be accorded greater weight. At the end of this review we shall be in a better position to assess the extent to which each essay deals with the problem.

Transactional Analysis

As early as 1947 Raymond Firth suggested that a distinction be made between "social structure" and "social organization" on the grounds that one needs to study variation as well as the continuity implied in the concept of social structure. Variation must be studied because "a structural analysis alone cannot interpret social change," and therefore anthropology should concern itself with social process (Firth 1951, p. 35). He proposed that the term *social organization* be applied to that process in which people act in pursuit of ends, a process that "involves allocation of resources [and] . . . implies within the scheme of value judgments a concept of efficiency" (p. 36). Thus social structure represents the continuity in social life, whereas social organization points to personal choice, variation, and social change, albeit guided by an efficiency principle that Firth clearly derived from economics. These ideas were elaborated in two addresses to the Royal Anthropological Institute in 1954 and 1955 (see Firth 1964, chaps. 3 and 4).

In view of these early works by Firth it is quite surprising to find that Kapferer, in what must be regarded as the definitive statement on transactional analysis, regards the publication of Barth's *Models of Social Organization* (1966) as the event "marking a 'paradigm' shift in British social anthropology" (Kapferer 1976, p. 2). In that short report Barth criticizes the emphasis upon normative consensus in structural-functional theory, but this criticism was hardly new. Even within the British anthropological tradition, Leach (1954, 1961), Gluckman (1955), Bailey (1960), and others in addition to Firth had all proposed substantial modifications to take account of conflict, ambiguity, and personal choice. Less friendly critics such as Kroeber (1952) and Geertz (1957) had suggested even more radical modifications. Barth's essay did provide the form for what came to be known as transactional analysis, a variant of exchange theory, which applies utility models or game theory to social interaction.

The appeal of methodological individualism, and of various forms of utility theory that depict social life as the outcome of the interaction of rational individuals seeking to maximize their own advantage, has been constant since at least the end of the eighteenth century, and the success of economics in developing this paradigm to explain market transactions has always been an inspiration to other social scientists. It is not surprising, then, that a strong pull in that direction was exerted when it appeared that the limits of structural-functional analysis had been reached.

Unfortunately, transactional analysis is a theoretical dead end, although it has been useful in challenging the received wisdom of structural-functionalism, and even in ordering new observations. Kapferer's 1976 essay sets out clearly the problems that arise when one uses "sequences of interaction systematically governed by reciprocity" (p. 3) as the focus of analytical attention. The conventional procedure is to assume that individuals always act rationally in pursuit of profit, self-interest, or utility, making the most efficient use of means available for the pursuit of ends. Kapferer points out that such a reduction of attention to the principles guiding *individual* behavior, even if it results in the development of a more adequate theory of interests, still leaves out of account (or greatly minimizes) the effect of influences external to the individual. It then becomes necessary to create various devices that will restore "the social" to its proper place. Among those devices we find venerable ideas such as "the definition of the situation" and "emergent properties," each of which permits the analyst to pay attention to culture and institutional regularities while ostensibly dealing only with interindividual transactions (see Kapferer 1976, p. 15).

Anthropologists working in societies outside Europe are particularly sensitive to cultural variation, or to deviations from the norms of formal rationality, and this sensitivity leads rapidly to the employment of auxiliary theories. Kapferer himself believes that transactional theory can be salvaged, but it is difficult to see what is left when his prescription is followed:

> Once it is recognized that relationships and systems of relationships can exert an independent effect upon the behavior of individuals, the futility of reducing all study of social behavior to individual components becomes clear. [1976, p. 16]

> It is possible to modify and develop the transactional model so that it is both more closely rooted in the realities of a certain context and capable of wider application. Clearly this can be achieved by examining transactional activity in terms of specific guiding cultural rules rather than constraining it within an abstract principle of gains exceeding or equalling costs; by examining the code within which transactional activity is cast; and by attending to the procedures whereby actors assign symbolic meaning to their transactions. The

model can be developed by drawing on the ideas of phenomenology, symbolic interactionism, linguistics and communication theory. [1976, p. 20]

At the end of that process what is the theoretical significance of *transaction*? From our point of view the interesting development is not the attempt to save transaction theory but the manner in which the logic of its disintegration leads to a recognition of the importance of meaning structures, and the consequent experimentation with phenomenology and symbolic analysis.

Cultural Analysis

British social anthropology was not the only, or even the most important, expression of structural-functional theory. Beginning with *The Structure of Social Action* (1937) and reaching a high point in *The Social System* (1951), the work of Talcott Parsons has had an enormous impact on all the social sciences. Deriving from the same sources in Durkheimian sociology and embodying the same preoccupation with normative consensus as social anthropology, Parsons's theory allowed more space for the cultural tradition. As Parsons grew older he enlarged that space (see for example Parsons 1966), though it was the anthropologists working with him who expanded the role of culture in the developing "Theory of Action" (see Parsons and Shils 1951). Eventually a point was reached where the theory was forced to recognize the autonomy of anthropology as a university discipline specializing in the study of culture. This recognition was sanctified in the famous Kroeber and Parsons declaration of 1958.

Without slighting this broader background (indeed, one could examine the developing importance in American anthropology of a somewhat different concept of culture beginning with Boas), it is convenient to consider an early essay by Clifford Geertz that embodies a series of issues relevant to our theme. In "Ritual and Social Change: A Javanese Example" (1957), Geertz takes as his point of departure exactly the same criticism of structural-functionalism as that which led to transactional analysis: it cannot deal adequately with social change. Geertz's proposed modifications of received wisdom are very different, reflecting the American preoccupation with culture and some new experimentation with theories of meaning.

Geertz's major complaint is that structural-functional anthropology, whether of the Radcliffe-Brown or the Malinowskian variety, is biased in favor of well-integrated systems and emphasizes the functional, rather than dysfunctional, aspects of life. When functionalists deal with change they tend to see disintegration, and here Geertz refers to Redfield's study of Yucatán (1941), in which individualization is presented as being accompanied by secularization and cultural disorganization. According to Geertz:

> It is the thesis of this paper that one of the major reasons for the inability of functional theory to cope with change lies in its failure to treat sociological and cultural processes on equal terms; almost inevitably one of the two is either ignored or is sacrificed to become but a simple reflex, a "mirror image," of the other. Either culture is regarded as wholly derivative from the forms of social organization—the approach characteristic of the British structuralists as well as many American sociologists; or the forms of social organization are regarded as behavioral embodiments of cultural patterns—the approach of Malinowski and many American anthropologists. . . . In such a situation, the dynamic elements in social change which arise from the failure of cultural patterns to be perfectly congruent with the forms of social organization are largely incapable of formulation. [1957:33]

His remedy for this situation is to concentrate upon the wholly different modes of integration that are supposed to characterize culture and social structure respectively: a laying side by side of two antithetical traditions of analysis with a declaration that their relationship is to be discovered empirically.

Geertz draws upon a carefully worded passage from *The Social System* in which Parsons argues that a "completely concrete system of social action" can be viewed, analytically, in three different ways, each of which can be "considered to be an independent focus of the elements of the action system" (Parsons 1951, p. 6). Social system, culture, and personality cannot be reduced to each other; they are independent and interpenetrating systems, but each is theoretically autonomous. Geertz seizes upon this point as the key to a more dynamic form of functionalism in which the disjunction between "causal functional" social structure and "logico-meaningful" culture becomes the means of understanding the relationship between them, and hence of the analysis of social change.

It is not necessary to review the details of the case that Geertz analyzes in order to exemplify his approach. Suffice it to say that a dispute which arises over how a burial should be effected is interpreted as resulting from the "discontinuity between the form of integration existing in the social structural ('causal-functional') dimension and the form of integration existing in the cultural ('logico-meaningful') dimension—a discontinuity which leads not to social and cultural disintegration, but to social and cultural conflict" (Geertz 1957, p. 49). The discontinuity is produced by the fact that the symbols constituting the death ritual are ambiguous; they have both "religious and political significance . . . the same symbols are used in both political and religious contexts" (pp. 49–51).

Although Geertz has continued to view anthropology as a science, he has increasingly viewed it as a science of interpretation, seeking to develop what, in a 1966 essay, he called "a scientific phenomenology of culture" ([1966] 1973, p. 364). That is, he has viewed it as an accurate delineation of the manner in which ordinary people in a particular society at a particular time invest their experience with meaning by virtue of their use of conceptual structures embodied in symbolic forms.

Geertz is a leading practitioner of "cultural analysis," but by no means is he the only anthropologist seeking a more precise, limited, and theoretically exact role for the discipline. Componential analysis, or cognitive anthropology, represents a determined bid to bring mathematical and logical exactitude into the study of "how natives think." There is no need to rehearse the many fallacies of componential analysis here (see Schneider 1965; Geertz 1973, chap. 1; Burling 1964); essentially it is reductionist, attempting to explain social life in terms of the laws of psychology or cognition. Kinship terminologies are a prime focus of attention because they are thought to constitute cognitive maps enabling people to find their way through the maze of otherwise overwhelming genealogical ties that are the assumed basis of kinship (see Romney 1967 for an example of the application of this approach to Latin American materials).

D. M. Schneider's version of cultural analysis is much closer to Geertz's position (they both studied with Parsons and Kluckhohn at Harvard). Because I have recently reviewed the development of Schneider's thinking on kinship (R. Smith, in press) and he has himself provided an up-to-date statement (Schneider [1968] 1980, chap. 7), his position can be summarized briefly here.

Schneider's most insistent concern has been to avoid imposing categories that, while purporting to explain the working of a particular society, actually distort our understanding of its system of social action. Such distortion can arise from an inadequate realization that culture, defined here as a system of symbols and meanings, "has a role in determining that action" (Schneider 1976, p. 197). According to Schneider, kinship is just such an imposed category, "a chimera, an artifact of a bad theory" which he should never have used in the title of his 1968 book, *American Kinship* ([1968] 1980, p. 119). The term *kinship* should not have been used because, according to Schneider, the symbolic structures with which he was dealing are not confined to that domain which Americans call "kinship"; they are also found in areas normally designated "nationality," "religion," "sex roles," "education," and perhaps "community." This diversity, in his view, requires that cultural analysis detach itself from the analysis of social institutions, because complexes of cultural symbols (which he now calls "galaxies") are *not* isomorphic with institutions. This distinction raises in a particularly sharp way the question of the relation between culture and behavior.

When Schneider's book on American kinship was published in 1968, its contents surprised many people. After several years of interviewing and the compilation of detailed genealogies and case studies, the 117-page book contained practically no "data" in the accepted sense of case materials, background information on the informants, or descriptions of the areas in which they spent their daily lives. Some of the interviewers felt that they had wasted their time collecting a mass of detail on the behavior of kin toward each other, and Schneider has described how he decided against including illustrative material assembled for the book by "a close associate" ([1968] 1980, pp. 123–24). Schneider's argument was that data are just as much selected according to a theory as are the generalizations drawn from them, and therefore he was content to give only the cultural principles abstracted from the data. Culture is an abstracted system of symbols and meanings that can be understood quite apart from the details of everyday life.

Many critics were unconvinced. Geertz, for example, referred to "schematicism" in a passage that provoked a long reply from Schneider. The object of anthropological analysis, says Geertz, is to clarify and enhance our understanding of previously strange peoples or customs, and if that goal is to be achieved by describing the constructions that the informants themselves place upon life, then the measure of the adequacy of an ethnographic account is the degree to which it enables us to understand the nuances of the discriminations made by the natives in the flow of behavior. If we begin by paying close attention to the detail of social action, including listening closely to the informants, as advocated by Schneider, are we justified in abstracting subsequently only that part in which we have a special interest (culture, in this case), and ignoring the rest? Geertz is sharply critical of such a procedure, and he explains why:

> Culture is most effectively treated, the argument goes, purely as a symbolic system (the catch phrase is, "in its own terms"), by isolating its elements, specifying the internal relationships among those elements, and characterizing the whole system in some general way —according to the core symbols around which it is organized, the underlying structures of which it is a surface expression, or the ideological principles on which it is based. Though a distinct improvement over "learned behavior" and "mental phenomena" notions of

what culture is, and the source of some of the most powerful theoretical ideas in contemporary anthropology, this hermetical approach to things seems to me to run the danger (and increasingly to
have been overtaken by it) of locking cultural analysis away from its
proper object, the informal logic of actual life. There is little profit
in extricating a concept from the defects of psychologism only to
plunge it immediately into those of schematicism. [1973, p. 17]

Geertz goes on to explain that cultural forms are made manifest in
social action, as well as in consciousness, and that the meaning of a cultural form is to be found not in the relation that cultural items have to one
another but in the part they play in "an ongoing pattern of life":

A further implication of this is that coherence cannot be the major
test of validity for a cultural description. Cultural systems must have
a minimal degree of coherence, else we would not call them systems;
and, by observation, they normally have a great deal more. But
there is nothing as coherent as a paranoid's delusion or a swindler's
story. The force of our interpretations cannot rest, as they are now
so often made to do, on the tightness with which they hold together,
or the assurance with which they are argued. Nothing has done more,
I think, to discredit cultural analysis than the construction of impec-
cable depictions of formal order in whose actual existence nobody
can quite believe. [1973, pp. 17–18]

Although Geertz does not mention him by name, the criticism is directed at Schneider, whose response is a reiteration of his position. The
details of this particular disputation need not concern us here, but at the
end of it we see how these two anthropologists, who share so many assumptions, differ on the question how "culture" is to be studied and analyzed. Schneider excludes "mere behavior" from consideration on the
grounds that it is "not entailed in the symbol and meaning system," and
one must assume that this exclusion covers all behavior that is not norm
governed—not in conformity with "rules for action" (Schneider [1968]
1980, pp. 125–33). For Schneider norms are the meaningful part of an
ongoing pattern of life, and at the same time they constitute the social system. The cultural system is contained within, or is implicit in, norms and
can be abstracted from them. Because he also follows Saussure in arguing
that the meaning of cultural symbols derives from the relation they bear to
each other in a structure of symbols, and not from their use in action,
there is a strong implication that culture is prior to, and constitutive of,
action. Because "mere behavior" is entirely excluded from consideration,
the system appears to be tightly closed.

Geertz, by contrast, is concerned with the behavior generated by changing social circumstance and hence inadequately fitted within the patterns of culture (what Schneider would call, presumably, "mere behavior"). This inadequacy creates conflict, sets up ambiguity within the symbolic structures, and leads to a reverberation of mutual effects. The process is not one-sided. Culture does not merely reflect social structure or respond to social and organizational change, nor does it simply emerge out of praxis; such an interpretation of Geertz's work cannot be sustained. But Geertz is aware that meaning, like structure, must be produced and reproduced in the flow of action. Methodologically, there is no alternative to the painstaking task of observing the detail and checking the interpretation against its ability to illuminate our understanding of the detail.

Precisely the same problems have been dealt with by Marshall Sahlins in a series of works beginning with his protracted criticism of the lingering utilitarian assumptions in anthropological theory (Sahlins 1976), and culminating in a recent essay on the problem of integrating structural analysis with historical inquiry (Sahlins 1981). This latter work is particularly interesting from the point of view of the issues that arise in the study of Latin American kinship and its historical development, though most of Sahlins's essays are taken up with the particularities of Hawaiian history. He adopts Braudel's idea of a "structure of the conjuncture" and modifies and uses it to understand the process by which "the projects of people as social beings" take advantage of situations to produce new structural arrangements (Sahlins 1981, p. 50). He gives many examples of the way in which Hawaiians—men, women, and chiefs—once they came into contact with the British, pursued in that new situation activities that were motivated by their traditional culture but that set them against each other: "The complex of exchanges that developed between Hawaiians and Europeans, the structure of the conjuncture, brought the former into uncharacteristic conditions of internal conflict and contradiction. Their differential connections with Europeans thereby endowed their own relationships to each other with novel functional content. This is structural transformation. The values acquired in practice return to structure as new relationships between its categories" (p. 50). Although Sahlins is careful to stress the fact that individual interests are socially constructed, and his attention to the details of "the flow of life" is exemplary, he is dealing with a very limited period in the early contact of Polynesians and Europeans. Hierarchy, in the form of traditional chieftaincy, is important and gets its due share of attention, but the new hierarchies established by European hegemony are beyond the scope of his analysis. In Latin American studies they are of the essence.

Culture and Science

The approaches to the study of culture that have been discussed so far all seek to bring it within the framework of a scientific theory of society or social action. Not all students of culture share this aim, nor are the varied responses to the problems of structural-functional analysis neatly divided by the Atlantic Ocean.

In 1950 Evans-Pritchard brought into the open a series of profound disagreements that had been simmering beneath the apparently tranquil surface of British social anthropology. The occasion was a series of broadcasts about anthropology intended for an educated, but nonprofessional, audience. As professor at Oxford, and one of the most distinguished students of A. R. Radcliffe-Brown, Evans-Pritchard was expected to avoid dissension and to present the accepted idea that anthropology is "the science of man." Instead he threw down the gauntlet and declared that "social anthropology studies societies as moral, or symbolic, systems and not as natural systems, . . . it is less interested in process than in design, and it therefore seeks patterns and not laws, demonstrates consistency and not necessary relations between social activities, and interprets rather than explains" (Evans-Pritchard 1951, p. 62). This is a more drastic departure from structural-functional theory than the modifications made by Geertz and Schneider. Although Evans-Pritchard made a radical break with the idea of a natural science of society, his analytical practice remained very close to that of other social anthropologists; he argued that the structural-functional paradigm remained useful so long as one regarded it as a "heuristic device."

The aim of this brief exposition has been to show, in the work of a small number of representative scholars, the convergence upon problems of meaning and the increased use of symbolic analysis as the limitations of structural-functional analysis became apparent. Some of the difficulties of cultural analysis have also been touched upon. What lessons can we derive from this overview that are relevant to the study of kinship in Latin America?

Latin America and Kinship Studies

Generalizations about a region as large and complex as Latin America are bound to be either inadequate or uninteresting. In spite of the size and diversity of Latin America there is a common history of colonial domination and exploitation that itself created societies of great internal complexity. A small group of scholars has made a start on the study of the mode of production in these societies, but much remains to be done. We are even further from understanding the cultural dimensions of economic life. But to attempt any analysis of kinship we must formulate some general conception of the social formation as a whole; without it one resorts to the empiricism of small-scale studies or falls back upon generalizations derived from other times and other places.

The most pervasive general structure is that which has been described for the Caribbean under such names as "creole" or "colonial" society (see R. Smith 1967). A hierarchical social order is established by European domination of a native or imported slave population and then maintained —at least partially—through the dissemination of an ideology of relative worthiness. That ideology defines superiority in terms of race, but increasingly substitutes "civilization," education, or achievement as the criteria of esteem. Although the model seems to apply as well to Latin America as to the Caribbean, conditions vary throughout the area and it would be impossible to specify details of the social order here.

In general terms, one finds at the core of Latin American and Caribbean social systems relations of production that derive their key features from "dependency" or, even more specifically, from what Mintz and Wolf (1957) have described as "the hacienda type" of enterprise. Economists such as Best (1968) and Beckford (1972) have referred to "the plantation model" to characterize the economy as a whole. It matters little whether we are talking about actual plantations and their hinterlands in Cuba, Colombia, Brazil, Guyana, Jamaica, and so on, or about tin mines in Bolivia, copper mines in Chile, or oil wells in Venezuela. The point is that a certain type of hierarchical structure of ownership and societal influence comes to be seen as appropriate, even inevitable, a structure that incorporates the experience of hierarchy established originally under colonial or slave regimes.

Associated with these societies, in which immigrant groups have been historically sedimented and involved in complex systems of relations, one finds a diversity of culture that is difficult to grasp. Drummond has suggested that the concept of "cultural continuum" may be useful in describing the manner in which creole culture contains variation within a set of shared beliefs about difference:

Diversity and divisiveness are fundamental to the system. Differences can operate as representations because they take their significance from a pool of shared myth and experience. Individuals are cognisant of much or all the possible range of behaviour and belief in the continuum, although need not behave or act as the other does, just as speakers of a creole language can generally understand utterances at either extreme of the continuum but rarely control both extremes in their own speech. The reality of the system is, therefore, the set of bridges or transformations required to get from one end to the other. [1980, p. 353]

The concept, "cultural system" or "culture," will have to be re-defined so that a particular human population ("society") is no longer thought to possess an ideational component ("culture") char-acterised by uniform rules and invariant relationships. The "ele-mentary structure" of such a cultural system is not an isolated proposition, but an intersystem—the pragmatic residue of persons seeking to define their identity *vis-à-vis* one another. [1980, p. 370]

The notion of "persons seeking to define their identity *vis-à-vis* one an-other" is in need of considerable clarification, but we can certainly agree that the distinctions and divisions within the creole continuum must be related pragmatically to the historical development of the society, a pro-cedure that definitely precludes the "schematicism" to which Geertz re-ferred (see "Cultural Analysis," above).

Most studies of kinship in Latin America have ignored these complex creole structures. Concentrating mainly on the study of American Indians, these studies have used a very different concept of culture. The prevailing concept, derived from Boas, viewed each culture as a unique pattern of learned behavior, historically produced, perpetuated by transmission from one generation to the next, with language as the most important, but not the exclusive, vehicle of that transmission. Change was explained as a pro-cess of "acculturation" in which new elements were learned, usually by subordinate groups, and somehow fitted into the preexisting pattern. With a theory of this kind it was difficult to envisage radical change without the total destruction of the culture in place, though many attempts were made to grasp more gradual processes of change. Herskovits reversed the for-mula of acculturation and asked not what had changed but what had "sur-vived" even when change seemed to be total. The most successful modi-fication of Boasian theory shifted attention to the culture's "adaptation" to its ecological situation as a means of understanding change.

A major study of Puerto Rico was undertaken in the late 1940s by Julian Steward, five of his graduate students, and several field assistants (Steward et al. 1956). Although it attempted to place Puerto Rico in a broad historical and economic context, it was committed to a method that in fact fragmented the society into a series of "socio-cultural segments," each representing a specific mode of cultural-ecological adaptation: a tobacco and mixed crops area, a coffee-growing municipality, a government-owned sugar plantation, and a corporate plantation area. A "prominent families" category was added in an attempt to tie together the other segments, which were further integrated by placement along a time sequence.

The sophistication and regard for holistic analysis that characterized this study was generally absent from most investigations in Latin America. Community studies, and the categorization of community types, have been more common—as they have been in the Caribbean. Carlos and Sellers, in a much-cited review of the literature on kinship, organize their material into studies of "(1) Rural Peasant (Indian); (2) Mestizo Peasant Village; (3) Town Lower Class; (4) Town Upper Class"; and a series of three class "socio-cultural segments" for urban areas (1972, p. 99). Similar distinctions are made in the Caribbean between community types, and once again the categories reflect the assumption that economic type, class position, and ethnic category are probably coterminous with one another and with cultural difference.

It has been demonstrated repeatedly that narrow studies of ecological adaptation leading to the supposed formation of discrete sociocultural segments are misguided (see Forman 1975 and Collier 1975 for only two examples). Although it is difficult to keep the general characteristics and the historical experience of a whole continent within one's field of view, some means must be found to avoid undue preoccupation with discrete segments and their supposed survivals, continuities, and ecological adaptations. It is that "pool of shared myth and experience" (Drummond 1980, p. 353) which gives meaning to the distinctions that are made among territorial, ethnic, class, and other categories. To study these problems of meaning and to arrive at an understanding of the role of ideology in social life requires knowledge of symbolic structures and, more important, knowledge of their use in social practice. This knowledge is as important in the study of kinship as in that of economic relations. One finds virtual dynasties in control of crucial economic resources, using marriage alliances to consolidate holdings and drawing upon kinsmen to man positions in family enterprises (see Lomnitz and Pérez-Lizaur 1978 and in this book). In general, there is only a weak development of impersonal market mechanisms for organizing production. At the other extreme, poverty, the effects of world market conditions, and the efforts of local elites to maintain dominance all have deleterious effects upon those sections of the population which may be powerless to maintain relations based upon kinship values.

The dynamics of the use of symbols can be understood only when social interaction has been mapped. This is not merely the study of what Barnes has called "tactics and strategy" as opposed to "rules of the game"

(1980, p. 301); it is the means by which we arrive at an understanding of the nature of meaningful social action.

Issues and Answers

Once committed to analyze the nature of ideology and its role in social practice, we encounter many new problems, as is evident in the essays presented here. Starting with a common agreement to consider these issues, the authors end up by taking many different positions. The variety of their approaches may be considered in relation to three major propositions that have emerged from the discussion of theoretical development: (1) meaning must be studied if one is to understand social structure; (2) a major problem in analyzing meaning is the pervasiveness of variation and change; (3) kinship is neither an autonomous domain nor a "dependent variable."

The Analysis of Meaning as a Necessary Step in the Study of Social Structure

The history of the social sciences is replete with examples of the way in which "psychology, anthropology, and the social sciences in general, have repeatedly falsified their 'observations' by unrecognized epistemological and ideological closures imposed upon the systems under study" (Wilden 1972, p. 389). This is a particular problem in the study of kinship, where it has generally been assumed that kinship is nothing but the recognition of the "real" facts of consanguinity and affinity. The distortions produced by the imposition of this European concept upon the observations of other societies can be avoided by a careful study of native concepts defining the meaningful units within the domain of kinship and family. The essay in this collection that concentrates most fully—indeed, almost exclusively—upon meaning is that by Alexander on the Jamaican family.

Alexander follows very closely the mode of analysis prescribed by Schneider and discussed in "Theoretical Problems," above. The method gives us an immediate increment in understanding of the Jamaican kinship system; for the first time we have a detailed account of what Jamaicans (or some Jamaicans) think and say about kinship, and of the manner in which it articulates with their conception of race, class, and status. Through painstaking analysis of the voluminous texts created by repeated interviews with a few individuals, Alexander is able to construct a model of the cultural image of kinship (which he believes to be a "collective representation" deeply embedded in the thought processes of his informants). Al-

though he discusses "action" it is really a discussion of the logical consequences for action of certain cultural assumptions, and not close study of
actual social practice. He makes some reference to the activities of his informants and to certain overall characteristics of social behavior, such as
the prevalence of outside unions and illegitimacy, but his major concern is
with the coherence of cultural meaning and the ability of cultural concepts
to represent social reality and guide ideal social action. As he declares at
the outset, "The analysis assumes that culture consists of a pure level of
domains . . . which consist of a set of collective representations that cohere, and that pure domains combine on a conglomerate level to create
domains—such as the family—that are guides for action."

Other essays, notably those by Gudeman and Schwartz and by Ossio,
while not expressing their underlying assumptions in quite the same terms,
nonetheless share Alexander's view of the priority of structures of cultural
meaning. Moreover, these essays raise the question just how meaning is to
be analyzed; what do symbols actually "mean"? Ossio's discussion of Andean *compadrazgo* is a good example of the difficulty that must be faced in
studying deep and persistent structures. In a brilliantly argued essay published in 1972, Stephen Gudeman brought to the discussion of Latin
American *compadrazgo* a concern for meaning that had been noticeably
absent from previous work on this institution. Instead of seeing ritual
co-godparenthood as some kind of functional mechanism for advancing individual material interests or repairing holes in the social fabric, he examined the content of the beliefs and traced the development of the institution from early Christianity. He also brought Latin American *compadrazgo*
into a wider comparative framework with similar practices found in Europe and other parts of the world, showing that the essential structures are
the same in spite of variation in detail. Ossio's essay in this book is a logical
development of Gudeman's analysis; while agreeing that functionalist explanations in fact explain nothing, he asks whether *compadrazgo* in the Andean region actually means what Gudeman says it means—whether it is
not in fact a series of Catholic forms imbued with meanings that predate
the Spanish conquest.

This is a problem of general significance in the New World. It sur-
faced many years ago in the discussion of Afro-American culture, when
Herskovits took exception to the prevailing notion that slavery had stripped
African immigrants of their culture, leaving them with only an impoverished version of European culture. Ossio's analysis is much more sophisticated than Herskovits's attempt to catalog African survivals, but he is
also reacting against a more recent tendency to explain all aspects of life
at the periphery of the modern world system in terms of dependence upon
the center—that is, Europe and North America. Instead of urging us to

recognize the essential Andean nature of this cultural complex as an act of faith, he suggests that analysis of cultural meaning should always be related to its context of use. This is a point that I shall consider again, but it is crucial to be aware of the multivocality of symbols and their capacity to acquire, or carry, different meanings in different contexts—a point well made by Wittgenstein in one of his earliest works ([1921] 1974, p. 15).

Ossio is dealing with contemporary communities and current usage, so that in a longer study than this short essay we would be justified in demanding from him a more detailed body of native exegesis, as well as a wider range of interpretative contexts. It would be unreasonable to make such demands on the authors who deal only with historical materials. But Gudeman and Schwartz may question the relevance of native exegesis to the kind of structural analysis in which they are interested. They examine what they assume must be an inherent conflict between the meaning of godparent and the master-slave relationship in eighteenth-century Brazil, a conflict at the level of belief and the actions that logically would flow from such beliefs. They then test the analysis by examining available baptismal and other records, finding that their hypothesis is amply borne out. The argument is coherent, tight, and persuasive. The only difficulty is that we have no idea whether the actors in that historical situation actually experienced such a conflict of meanings or deployed symbols in that way. Even if data were available on the actors' states of mind, would they be relevant to such a structural analysis? Relevant, perhaps, they might be, but not decisive.

The Pervasiveness of Variation and Change as a Major Problem in Analyzing Meaning

The central issue to have emerged from the differences among those who practice some form of cultural analysis is, ironically, precisely the issue that led to its development away from structural-functionalism: the question how we are to understand change.

A more precise analytical concept of culture arose out of the very success of structural-functional theory among American anthropologists. The old definition of culture dating back to its formulation by Tylor—"that complex whole which includes knowledge, belief, art, morals, law, custom, and any other capabilities and habits acquired by man as a member of society" ([1871] 1958, 1:1)—lost ground after the 1940s as structural-functional theory spread its influence among American anthropologists. For all its seeming empiricism ("I use the term 'social structure' to denote this network of actually existing relations" [Radcliffe-Brown 1952, p. 190]), structural-functional anthropology stressed heavily the determining role of values and moral norms, as evidenced by Fortes's 1949 discussion of the absolute value of the patrilineal principle among the Tallensi. Not only was detailed attention paid to native concepts and native social theory in the work of the best of these anthropologists, but the terms in which they discussed "social structure" bore a striking resemblance to more recent statements about "culture." For example:

> By abstracting the constant features in the patterns of organization of all the activities in which a particular kinship relation is significant, we arrive at a formulation of that relationship as an element of the social structure. Tale kinship relations are embedded in social activities but they are not coterminous with any one category of social activities. They are not reducible to economic relations . . . nor can they be derived exclusively from Tale jural concepts, or ritual beliefs or political institutions. . . . Nor can the Tale kinship system be accounted for on the grounds of utility.
>
> Kinship, in short, among the Tallensi as among many other primitive peoples, is one of the irreducible principles on which their organized social life depends. [Fortes 1949, p. 340]

Fortes's "irreducible principles" are only marginally different from Parsons's categories or the concepts of culture, social system, and personality used by David Schneider.

The major weakness of analyses such as Fortes's was the idea of social structure as a closed, self-regulating system in which values, norms, and actual behavior are all consistent:

> There cannot . . . be gross divergence between the rules governing the ownership and use of land or other productive property, and those governing the application of labour to production or the consumption of the products of labour, since both sets of rules are aspects of the jural relations of a specific group of kinsfolk by birth and marriage. Similarly the religious beliefs of the natives cannot be grossly inconsistent with their actual social behaviour since they have a common context of social organization in relationships determined by kinship. [Fortes 1949, p. 340]

Fortes was not unaware of variation, flexibility, and the like; it is the detailing of variation that makes his books difficult to read. The time dimension was also prominent in his work, and he referred to social structure as the sum of processes in time. But, for him, variation is always contained within the enduring structure (see 1949, pp. 83–4).

Cultural analysis can end up in exactly the same position. Schneider's pursuit of ever more abstract "galaxies" of symbols and meanings produces principles that remain constant in spite of all the variation made necessary by rules for behavior in differentiated societies (see R. Smith, in press). Louis Dumont (1970) has described the most general structure of Hindu ideology (culture), a structure stable through time and pervasive in the varied contexts of actual social life. Inden and Nicholas (1977) abstract a structure of meaning that lies behind the varied forms of Bengali kinship behavior and assert that it has been constant over a long period of time and is widespread in Hindu society. These studies are an important corrective to those that see all social life as a response to immediate self-interest, but, as Sylvia Yanagisako has pointed out, "The question of whether our discovery of cultural uniformity in the midst of social diversity is an artifact of our relative lack of facility in recognizing diversity in symbolic systems can only be answered by further research and by the refinement of our conceptual armature for eliciting and displaying the symbolic components of family and kinship" (1979, p. 193).

Although transactional analysis appears more able to deal with variation and change, it generally advances but little beyond classical structural-functionalism unless it lays primary stress upon meaning. Comaroff's analysis of marriage among the Baralong boo Ratshidi of Botswana shows in a particularly clear way how close attention to native concepts can save an analysis from the errors of imposed categorization (Cohen and Comaroff 1976). All Tswana, of which the Baralong are a subgroup, favor cousin marriages of all kinds. Comaroff shows the futility of just counting up and classifying marriages; of much greater importance is the native theory that agnates compete for power, whereas affines do not. When a man marries a cousin—say, his father's brother's daughter—the question arises whether her kin are really his agnates or his affines. Comaroff demonstrates that there can be no a priori definition based on supposed universal definitions of kinship; everything depends upon the political activities in which the various parties are engaged. Marriages and genealogical relationships are socially constructed, not biologically determined; or, as he puts it, meanings are *managed* in the process of social life.

In spite of the dynamic quality of this analysis, it assumes a common code in terms of which meaning can be managed, and in that sense does not deal with variation and long-term change any more than do the theories of Schneider or Dumont. Parkin, another member of this school, sounds very much like Schneider when, in discussing changes in the meaning of a key cultural concept among the Giriama of Kenya, he says, "The exchange of role terms is therefore not random; it generally follows an underlying cultural template of ideas, a kind of *langue*" (1976, p. 188).

The reference to Saussure's concept of *langue* is significant in that it invokes a whole theory of cultural structure in which meaning is independent of action.

Though few of our contributors address these problems directly, all are aware of their importance, and many of the analyses are relevant to the theoretical issues involved. In his discussion of love, honor, and marriage in New Mexico, Ramón Gutiérrez documents an example of the process by which cultural factors interact with changing social practice to produce a shift in norms. In the period of early settlement of the province of New Mexico, marriage was closely regulated to serve family interest. The sexual behavior of women, in particular, had to be restricted if family honor was to be maintained. Nonetheless, two factors operated in a contrary manner, even when the dominant values prescribed arranged marriages and a total prohibition on sexual activity outside marriage. Men and women, especially of the lower orders, were prone to temptation, and many records exist of cases brought before the ecclesiastical courts where, as Gutiérrez says in the section entitled "The Concept and Practice of 'Love,'" "the egalitarian and subversive notions of natural love" or "love stemming from concupiscence" had quite overwhelmed considerations of honor. More important, the doctrines of the Catholic church also enshrined values antithetical to strong familial control. Coercion of a couple into marriage was considered an impediment, and if the investigation prior to marriage discovered such force, the priest could prohibit the union. It is easy to forget the many ways in which Catholicism opposed familial authority, and this is a useful reminder.

When changing demographic, political, and economic relations in the late eighteenth and early nineteenth centuries created new patterns of social mobility and individual autonomy, a corresponding shift took place in the patterns of marital choice. However, Gutiérrez shows that this change did not require new values to materialize out of thin air; there was a shift in the meaning of cultural symbols that already existed. From being defined as illicit sexual activity, *amor* came to mean individual, heartfelt devotion to another person. Gutiérrez's discussion of the heart, and its subtle shifts of meaning, is a fascinating analysis of the manner in which the cultural system can maintain a core of meaning while undergoing transformations which bring that meaning into conjunction with entirely new forms of social practice.

The essays by De la Peña and by Lomnitz and Pérez-Lizaur both deal with variation in social relations between economically differentiated groups that share a common body of kinship culture or ideology. Both attempt to integrate a basically structural-functional and transactional mode of analysis with a concern for cultural analysis, a procedure that could be cast very nicely into the terms of Talcott Parsons's distinction between culture and social structure.

Fiona Wilson and Verena Stolcke are each directly concerned with the problems that arise in understanding variation over time, and both deal at great length with sex-role differentiation, a topic that has not received proper attention in Latin American studies. Stolcke's account of the effect on family structure of changes in the method of employing labor in the coffee industry of São Paulo is of great comparative interest. The coffee laborers with whom she worked are the descendants of Europeans recruited mostly from Italy, Switzerland, and Germany between 1880 and 1920. Plantations in other parts of the New World also recruited labor, as did those in South Africa, Fiji, and Mauritius, but Brazil is a special case in that these coffee workers were recruited in family units and employed in a special kind of sharecropping system.

The analysis proceeds in three stages. First Stolcke shows that this form of labor system had certain advantages that could be calculated quite rationally, though the calculation rested on a series of cultural assumptions about "the family" and about kinship, assumptions shared by planters and immigrants alike. The family system of the immigrants was essentially nuclear, with a system of sex-role differentiation familiar from nineteenth-century Europe, stressing male authority and responsibility for providing maintenance and female submissiveness and responsibility for mothering. However, this was not a bourgeois family system entirely; everyone had to work according to capacity, under the direction of the male head. In this regard the system bears a striking resemblance to the English family system in the early stages of the development of the textile industry as described by Smelser (1959, pp. 182–88). The transformation from a system of family labor to the eviction of families from the plantations and the recruitment of individuals for strictly temporary paid work is described in detail, and once again there are many resemblances to early industrialization in Europe—both in the destruction of family work teams and in its effect on the family. At this point Stolcke's essay illustrates graphically the third of the propositions that emerged from our discussion of theoretical developments in kinship theory, a matter covered in the following section.

Kinship as Neither an Autonomous Domain nor a Dependent Variable

It would be all too easy for Stolcke to develop a simple causal model in which the family is a dependent variable in a structural-functional system, responding directly to changes in economic factors. While documenting graphically the effects of market forces upon familial and other relations, Stolcke nevertheless stresses the continuity of underlying family values, against which—and often in terms of which—changes take place. One gets the impression that these values, these structures of cultural assumption, are resilient and will survive periods of dislocation, as they did among the working class in Europe and as they did among immigrants to North America who were similarly subject to economic distress and dislocation (see for example Thomas and Znaniecki [1918–20] 1958).

Stolcke does not explicitly draw far-reaching conclusions from her analysis, but they are not difficult to see. The implications of this work for theorizing about the "matrifocal family" are particularly interesting. This term was first used to describe domestic familial relations in an Afro-Guyanese community (R. Smith 1956). The configuration of relations was similar to that described by Stolcke for the contemporary situation of her Brazilian coffee workers, superficially at least: the loss of status and authority of the husband-father, accompanied by a corresponding prominence of the mother's affective centrality and by an increase in illegitimacy, paternal desertion, and the incidence of female-headed households. It is only when we begin to study meaning structures more carefully that we discover we are dealing with quite different systems with a different historical development.

From its inception, the West Indian family was rooted in a dual marriage system in which nonlegal unions (either co-residential or visiting) were an integral part of kinship and family structure (R. Smith 1978, 1982). Neither economic stabilization nor upward social mobility has in itself changed that structure, though both have certainly affected some aspects of social practice. In the case of the immigrant coffee workers in Brazil it would be interesting to see the phases of change in cultural concepts as generations move through the experience of changing economic circumstances in Brazil and as they become increasingly affected by relations with the Afro-Brazilian population. That is the kind of study done by Yanagisako on the Japanese-American population of Seattle (in press), and Stolcke has whetted our appetite for further publications on Brazil.

A number of other essays illustrate graphically that kinship concepts do not stand alone, but have to be understood in their multitudinous relations with class and other bases of social differentiation. Both Cardoso's study on Brazil and the essay by Lomnitz and Pérez-Lizaur on Mexico City demonstrate the manner in which the same basic concepts can take on different significance in varying class contexts. Cardoso's discussion of adoption is particularly interesting in showing how "code for conduct" comes to be foregrounded in the socially fragile conditions of shantytown life, whereas stress upon the continuity of "substance" is much more appropriate to the middle- and upper-class concern with property transmission and the maintenance of close status-group cohesion (see Schneider [1968] 1980 for explication of the concepts of "substance" and "code for conduct").

Conclusion

One of the consequences of the gradual abandonment of the rigidities of structural-functional theory has been a redirection of interest toward process, transformation, history, and evolution. Neo-evolutionary or "modernization" models have been widely used in Latin American studies, and it was partly as a reaction to the uncritical application of such models that the project giving rise to these essays was conceived. Although our approach has been historical, it has tried to avoid both evolutionary generalization and a relativist empiricism. The contributors are variously historians, anthropologists, and sociologists, but at no stage of the discussions did these differences of disciplinary background obtrude, become an issue, or inhibit the exchange of ideas.

Although research methods are not a primary focus of attention, the essays raise, and sometimes explicitly deal with, methodological issues. Thus, Higman, who has always been meticulous in the care with which he has used demographic and other techniques, discusses at length the limitations of household analysis and here experiments with data sources that might begin to provide an understanding of meaning for relatively inarticulate populations in past time. Similarly, Enrique Mayer takes us into the daily lives of peasants in sixteenth-century Peru in a way that is imaginatively informed by historical records, theoretical models, and experience of field research in the same community some four hundred years later. I have already referred to Gutiérrez's analysis of the meaning of "heart" in colonial New Mexico, and it is also clear that Ossio's discussion of Andean *compadrazgo* depends upon subtle imputations of meaning based upon an extensive understanding of both language and ritual.

It must be conceded that neither in this introduction nor in any individual essay has the concept of "meaning" been discussed in any detail or in a rigorous manner. The essays do not present carefully delimited semantic analyses, but attempt to arrive at broad contextualized understandings of native concepts, expanding rather than contracting the range of material considered. Given a theoretical approach that views society as a process in time, structured by principles that are historically constituted, reproduced, and transformed, it is evident that history and social science cease to be distinguishable. It is my hope that these essays indicate the potential of such an approach.

References

Bailey, F. G.

1960   *Tribe, Caste and Nation: A Study of Political Activity and Political Change in Highland Orissa.* Manchester: Manchester University Press.

Barnes, John A.

1980   "Kinship Studies: Some Impressions of the Current State of Play." *Man,* n.s. 15:293–303.

Barth, Frederik

1966   *Models of Social Organization.* Occasional Paper no. 23. London: Royal Anthropological Institute.

Beckford, George L.

1972   *Persistent Poverty.* London: Oxford University Press.

Best, Lloyd

1968   "Outline of a Model of Pure Plantation Economy." *Social and Economic Studies* 17:283–326.

Burling, Robbins

1964   "Cognition and Componential Analysis: God's Truth or Hocus-Pocus?" *American Anthropologist* 66:20–28.

Cancian, Francesca; Goodman, Louis Wolf; and Smith, Peter H.

1978   "Capitalism, Industrialisation and Kinship in Latin America: Major Issues." *Journal of Family History* 3:319–36.

Carlos, Manuel, and Sellars, Lois

1972   "Family, Kinship Structure and Modernization in Latin America." *Latin American Research Review* 7:95–124.

Cohen, A. P. and Comaroff, John L.

1976   "The Management of Meaning: On the Phenomenology of Political Transactions." In *Transaction and Meaning: Directions in the Anthropology of Exchange and Symbolic Behavior,* edited by Bruce Kapferer, pp. 87–107. Philadelphia: Institute for the Study of Human Issues.

Collier, George A.

1975   *Fields of the Tzotzil: The Ecological Bases of Tradition in Highland Chiapas.* Austin: University of Texas Press.

Drummond, Lee

1980   "The Cultural Continuum: A Theory of Intersystems" *Man,* n.s. 15:352–74.

Dumont, Louis

1970   *Homo Hierarchicus: An Essay on the Caste System.* Chicago: University of Chicago Press.

Evans-Pritchard, Edward E.
1951   *Social Anthropology.* London: Cohen and West.
Firth, Raymond
1951   *Elements of Social Organization.* London: Watts and Co.
1964   *Essays on Social Organization and Values.* London: Athlone Press.
Forman, Shepard
1975   *The Brazilian Peasantry.* New York: Columbia University Press.
Fortes, Meyer
1949a   *The Web of Kinship among the Tallensi.* Oxford: Oxford University Press, Clarendon Press.
1949b   "Time and Social Structure: an Ashanti Case Study." In *Social Structure: Studies Presented to A. R. Radcliffe-Brown,* edited by Meyer Fortes, pp. 54–84. Oxford: Oxford University Press, Clarendon Press.
Geertz, Clifford
1957   "Ritual and Social Change: A Javanese Example." *American Anthropologist* 59:32–54.
1973   *The Interpretation of Cultures.* New York: Basic Books.
Gluckman, Max
1955   *Custom and Conflict in Africa.* Glencoe, Ill.: Free Press.
Gudeman, Stephen
1972   "The *Compadrazgo* as a Reflection of the Natural and Spiritual Person." *Proceedings of the Royal Anthropological Institute of Great Britain and Ireland for 1971,* pp. 45–71.
Inden, Ronald B., and Nicholas, Ralph W.
1977   *Kinship in Bengali Culture.* Chicago: University of Chicago Press.
Kapferer, Bruce, ed.
1976   *Transaction and Meaning: Directions in the Anthropology of Exchange and Symbolic Behavior.* Philadelphia: Institute for the Study of Human Issues.
Kroeber, Alfred
1952   *The Nature of Culture.* Chicago: University of Chicago Press.
Kroeber, Alfred L., and Parsons, Talcott
1958   "The Concepts of Culture and of Social System." *American Sociological Review* 23:582.
Leach, Edmund
1954   *Political Systems of Highland Burma.* London: Bell.
1961   *Rethinking Anthropology.* London: Athlone Press.
Lomnitz, Larissa, and Pérez-Lizaur, Marisol
1978   "The History of a Mexican Urban Family." *Journal of Family History* 3:392–409.

Mintz, Sydney, and Wolf, Eric
1957   "Haciendas and Plantations in Middle America and the Antil-
les." *Social and Economic Studies* 6 : 380–412.
Nutini, Hugo G.; Carrasco, Pedro; and Taggart, James M., eds.
1976   *Essays on Mexican Kinship.* Pittsburgh: University of Pittsburgh Press.
Parkin, David
1976   "Exchanging Words." In *Transaction and Meaning: Directions
in the Anthropology of Exchange and Symbolic Behavior,* edited
by Bruce Kapferer, pp. 163–90. Philadelphia: Institute for the
Study of Human Issues.
Parsons, Talcott
1937   *The Structure of Social Action.* New York: McGraw-Hill.
1951   *The Social System.* New York: Free Press.
1966   *Societies: Evolutionary and Comparative Perspectives.* Englewood Cliffs, N.J.: Prentice-Hall.
Parsons, Talcott, and Shils, Edward, eds.
1951   *Toward a General Theory of Action.* Cambridge: Harvard University Press.
Radcliffe-Brown, Alfred R.
1952   *Structure and Function in Primitive Society.* London: Cohen
and West.
Redfield, Robert
1941   *The Folk Culture of Yucatán.* Chicago: University of Chicago
Press.
Romney, A. Kimball
1967   "Kinship and Family." In *Handbook of Middle American Indians,* edited by Robert Wauchope, 6 : 207–37. Austin: University of Texas Press.
Sahlins, Marshall
1976   *Culture and Practical Reason.* Chicago: University of Chicago
Press.
1981   *Historical Metaphors and Mythical Realities: Structure in the
Early History of the Sandwich Islands Kingdom.* Ann Arbor:
University of Michigan Press.
Schneider, David M.
1965   "American Kin Terms and Terms for Kinsmen: A Critique of
Goodenough's Componential Analysis of Yankee Kinship Terminology." *American Anthropologist* 67 : 288–308.
1976   "Notes Toward a Theory of Culture." In *Meaning in Anthropology,* edited by Keith H. Basso and Henry A. Selby, pp.
197–220. Albuquerque: University of New Mexico Press.

1980   *American Kinship: A Cultural Account.* Chicago: University of
[1968]   Chicago Press, [Englewood Cliffs, N.J.: Prentice-Hall].
Smelser, Neil
1959   *Social Change in the Industrial Revolution.* London: Routledge
          and Kegan Paul.
Smith, Anthony
1973   *The Concept of Social Change.* London: Routledge and Kegan
          Paul.
Smith, Raymond T.
1956   *The Negro Family in British Guiana: Family Structure and Social
          Status in the Villages.* London: Routledge and Kegan Paul.
1967   "Social Stratification, Cultural Pluralism and Integration in
          West Indian Societies." In *Caribbean Integration: Papers on So-
          cial, Political and Economic Integration*, edited by Sybil Lewis
          and Thomas G. Mathews, pp. 226–58. Rio Piedras: Institute
          of Caribbean Studies.
1978   "The Family and the Modern World System: Some Observa-
          tions from the Caribbean." *Journal of Family History* 3:337–60.
1982   "Family, Social Change and Social Policy in the West Indies."
          Nieuwe West-Indische Gids 56 (no. 3/4): 111–42.
In press "Kinship and Class in Chicago." In *Urban Anthropology in the
          United States*, edited by Leith Mullings. New York: Columbia
          University Press.
Steward, Julian et al.
1956   *The People of Puerto Rico.* Urbana: University of Illinois Press.
Thomas, William I., and Znaniecki, Florian
1958   *The Polish Peasant in Europe and America.* 2d ed. 2 vols. New
[1918-20] York: Dover Publications.
Tylor, Edward B.
1958   *Primitive Culture: Researches into the Development of Mythology,*
[1871]   *Philosophy, Religion, Art and Custom.* 2 vols. Gloucester,
          Mass.: Peter Smith.
Wilden, Anthony
1972   *System and Structure: Essays in Communication and Exchange.*
          London: Tavistock Publications.
Wittgenstein, Ludwig
1974   *Tractatus Logico-Philosophicus.* London: Routledge and Kegan
[1921]   Paul.
Yanagisako, Sylvia Junko
In press *Transforming the Past: a Cultural History of Japanese American
          Kinship.* Stanford: Stanford University Press.

Kinship Ideology in Slave Societies

Cleansing Original Sin: Godparenthood and the Baptism of Slaves in Eighteenth-Century Bahia

Stephen Gudeman
Stuart B. Schwartz

The practice of Christian baptism dates from the earliest days of the religion; it originated with the immersion of Christ by John. In the intervening two thousand years the theological meaning of the act has been elaborated and transformed, but since the third century at least baptism has signified the cleansing of original sin. The use of godparents to assist, to validate, and to stand for the baptized at the rite is not so ancient as baptism itself, but this custom also has a lengthy history. That the term *sponsor*, for example, also appeared in the third century suggests that sponsors were used prior to this time.

By contrast to the antiquity of baptismal sponsorship, formal studies of godparenthood are recent. The nineteenth-century anthropologist, E. B. Tylor, who observed godparenthood in Mexico, was one of the first to comment upon it (1861, pp. 250–51). But only in the last half century has godparenthood received intensive analysis. Anthropologists have studied the institution in the Philippines, Sri Lanka, Yugoslavia, Latin America, and the Mediterranean world. Their investigations have centered on current patterns as well as the historical evolution of the complex. We now possess many synchronic studies of the institution, some longitudinal studies of godparenthood in the church and particular societies, and a few cross-cultural theories about it (Arantes Neto 1970; Bossy 1973; Coy 1974; Gudeman 1972, 1975; Hart, 1977; Lomnitz 1971; Middleton, 1975; Nutini and Bell 1980; Pitt-Rivers 1973, 1976; Stirrat 1975).

For the historical context of slavery, however, few data have been presented and few analyses offered. This study of godparenthood in eighteenth-century Bahia is designed partially to fill the gap. But it has a second goal, for a study of godparenthood within the context of a slave society also is revealing of aspects of the master-slave relationship and the sociopolitical context itself (Russell-Wood 1968; Freyre 1968, p. 288;

Queiros Mattoso 1979, pp. 149–52). We are led to doubt, for example, that white masters forged strong paternalistic relationships with their slaves; at least, godparenthood did not "function" to reinforce directly the master-slave relationship. But this takes us ahead of the story, and we should consider first the relation between the institution and its functions.

An Anthropological Dualism

Explanations of godparenthood may be divided broadly into two types. For some anthropologists, the central concern is to know how the institution actually functions within a society. In such studies the emphasis falls upon how the relationships are used. Given a historical context, for what goals or to what ends is the complex employed?

Underlying this view is the assumption that institutions fulfill social needs. They "do" something "for" society, whether disruptive or harmonizing. To explicate the purpose, effectiveness, and linkages of a social practice is to understand it. Of course, such functionalist approaches take various forms, from extreme teleological constructions to sensitive contextual analyses; still, the studies are founded on the proposition that to know what a thing does is to know the phenomenon itself. We understand something by seeing it in use—whether the thing is an object of nature, a machine made by humans, or an institution in society.

Anthropologists of this functionalist persuasion have emphasized that godparenthood is cross-culturally variable; in different social constellations, it is set to different purposes. Thus, it is frequently said that the complex is flexible and that this adaptability accounts for its proliferation and persistence (Horstmann and Kurtz 1979).

A contrasting approach to understanding godparenthood focuses more upon form and meaning (Gudeman 1972, 1975; Hammel 1968; Ingham 1970; Pitt-Rivers 1973). The emphasis here falls upon defining the institution's distinctive features as compared to those of other social relationships. For these investigators, the argument that godparenthood functions is insufficient, for the family and other social groupings also "do something." A relationship—whether actively sought, neutrally tolerated, or reluctantly consented to—bears a meaning for its participants. Godparenthood is a construction, a system of signs. The task, by this view, is to elucidate the meaning of godparenthood in relation to its use. Godparenthood is an idiom through which people express themselves and by which they live.

These two approaches to godparenthood themselves represent a broad theoretical fissure in anthropology. Advocates of the first tend to rely on the validity of direct observation and the utility of their own analytic categories, such as adaptation or function. Proponents of the second urge that social life is a construction; we can observe and calibrate, but the data are never "raw" in the sense in which physical occurrences are. Social relationships are "codes" or idioms constructed by people and constituting a reality for them.

Given this schism in the theory about godparenthood, a historical study of the complex in colonial and slave Brazil presents interesting puzzles. Our major sources of information are parish registers from the Bahian Recôncavo dating to the 1780s. (For 1780–81 a one-in-six sample was taken; for 1788–89 all recorded baptisms were used.) Few travelers to Brazil in this period commented on the operation of godparenthood, nor was it a topic that usually entered official correspondence. Ecclesiastical regulations for the institution were provided by the Bahian archdiocese, but the relation between official enunciation and social practice is problematic (Monteiro da Vide 1765). There are, furthermore, no adequate historical studies of godparentage in Portugal, although some preliminary work has been done (Borges Landeiro 1965; Pinheiro Marques 1974; Oliveira Duarte 1974). The studies by Mintz and Wolf (1950) and by Foster (1953) on Spain are suggestive, but they are not based on primary historical data. As for studies on Brazil, there exist Schwartz's 1978 study, an unpublished thesis chapter by Ramos (1972), an unpublished paper by Smith (1973), and a few remarks by Slenes (1978; Slenes and Carvalho de Mello 1978) on work still in progress.

We have, therefore, little direct information about how godparenthood in colonial Brazil was used, not to speak of its meaning. Nonetheless, we shall attend to numerical data on godparent selection. Our thesis is that we can best understand this pattern by looking at the meaning of the institution. An entry point or anchor for cross-cultural analysis is provided by the specifically religious meaning of the complex; the church formulation, however, does not account for the entirety of the complex. A unique dimension of godparenthood is that it is formed in the church between individuals who carry it outside the formal institution. Godparenthood is projected into the social domain. Thus, part of our thesis is that choice of godparents in Bahia was also determined by the social context of slavery. In Bahian society the relationship of master to slave was central, and it too conveyed certain meanings. But this point brings us to the core of the argument. The idiom of godparenthood rests uneasily with that of slavery; we shall show that this disjuncture had a profound impact on the choice of a sponsor.

The Data and Their Setting

Large portions of the Bahian Recôncavo in the eighteenth century were plantation zones devoted to the cultivation of sugar cane and to the processing of sugar for export abroad. Slave labor, in the fields and elsewhere, was the principal form of the human contribution to the productive process. The data here examined derive from four Recôncavo parishes and date from the eighteenth and early nineteenth centuries (ACMS, Saubara, 1723–24, 75 entries; ACMS, Rio Fundo, 1780–81, 1788–89, 131 entries; ACMS, São Gonçalo, 1816–17, 92 entries). We concentrate on the 264 baptisms in the contiguous parishes of Rio Fundo and Monte but make use of the other parishes to verify patterns or illustrate specific points.

The size and distribution of the slave and free population in these parishes were not unusual for the New World. Nossa Senhora do Monte in the township of São Francisco was one of the older and most aristocratic of the Recôncavo parishes. In 1757 it contained nineteen sugar mills (*engenhos*) within a territory of about seventy-five square miles. Its population was 3,884. By 1816 it had twenty mills worked by 1,732 slaves, and another 588 slaves were owned by cane farmers. The parish of São Pedro de Trararipe e Rio Fundo was created in 1718 by dismembering portions of Monte and of Nossa Senhora da Purificação. Rio Fundo lay further inland to the north, but it was watered by a number of small rivers and its lands were also suitable for sugar. By 1757 it had fifteen *engenhos* and 4,252 people, the majority of whom were slaves. In addition to the sugar mills and cane farms, the parish also contained thirty-six *sitios* (places), where a few manioc or tobacco farmers lived. These *sitios* were impermanent, being subject to the vagaries of soil exhaustion, crop diseases, and infestation by insects. By 1816 the parish contained 5,178 slaves distributed among 491 owners. There were thirty-six mills holding 2,218 slaves; cane growers owned another 1,448; and the rest were held by subsistence farmers, artisans, and others (Schwartz 1982). Although the information for both parishes reflects the period of growth for slavery and sugar between 1793 and 1816, and represents a later stage in the region's history than we consider, the patterns of difference between the two parishes were probably the same in the 1780s (see Table 1).

The structure of slaveholding in Monte and Rio Fundo represents patterns typical of the Recôncavo. Monte, older and on the shores of the bay, was characterized by larger *engenhos* and a higher concentration of ownership, fewer cane farmers per mill, and fewer small farmers. Rio Fundo, newer and closer to the sugar frontier, had smaller *engenhos* and more of them; over one-third of the slaves involved in sugar cultivation were owned by cane farmers, and many slaves were owned by artisans,

Table 1. The Structure of Slaveholding in the Parishes of Nossa Senhora do Monte and São Pedro do Rio Fundo in 1816

	No. engenhos	Slaves/ engenho	No. cane farmers	Slaves/ cane farmer	Total slaves in parish	Total owners in parish	$\overline{X}$	Gini
Monte	20	86.6	59	9.9	2,448	135	19.6	.77
Rio Fundo	38	63.4	144	10.1	5,178	491	10.5	.62

Source: Arquivo Publico do Estado da Bahia, Cartas ao Governo 232, 233, 234.

subsistence farmers, and others. Together these two contiguous parishes represent the structural boundaries of sugar plantation parishes in colonial Bahia.

The Baptismal Registers

Traditionally the church has required for its records a minimal amount of information about a baptism. It must have the names of the baptized, the parents, and the godparents. The name bestowed at baptism should be a Christian or a saint's name. Just as important, the church requires that the prospective sponsors have the qualifications for their position; before being permitted to discharge their functions, godparents must state that they have been baptized and are instructed members of the church. Beyond this halo of religious information the church requires little.

Significantly, the information actually contained in the Brazilian baptismal records is more comprehensive. The church registers are not only religious but social documents; the information recorded speaks to the total social persona of the individual. From parish to parish there were slight variations, but the general format was constant. For all the participants—baptized, mother, father, godmother (*madrinha*), godfather (*padrinho*)—legal status, marital status, and color (if not white) usually were recorded. The legal statuses were defined as free, slave, or freed (*liberto, forro*). To this legal position of the individual was often added the person's color, coded not on a binary basis but according to a scale of variations. Color served as an index of ancestry, perhaps also of enculturation in the New World. In some parishes, when Africans were involved, their "nation" was also listed. In addition, for the baptized and often for his or her parents a birth status was entered: legitimate, illegitimate, foundling (*exposto*). Although birth status was not entered for the godparents, their marital status and that of the parents was recorded. For all the participants parish residence was sometimes inscribed.

The registers, of course, often exhibit gaps, especially in the matter of color, and whether a category such as "color" represents an accurate phenotype or the social and personal impressions of a cleric will never be known; but the registers do present information about people in the round. More than that, they are testimony that godparenthood was seen as both a religious and a social phenomenon; it had a meaning and it functioned within a specific social context.

Masters and Slaves

From the census data several interesting patterns emerge, but there is one that was unexpected yet quite comprehensible. We should, however, first sketch the theoretical context. In the anthropological and historical literature it has often been suggested that godparenthood ties serve to unite or connect persons of different classes; it has been argued, for example, that the bonds are used in the context of, or overlie, patron-client ties. Godparents are patrons, godchildren (*afilhados*) and their parents are clients. The religious ties give stability and continuity to what might otherwise be a fragile and uncertain social bond (Horstmann and Kurtz 1979, p. 362). Some historians have argued also that, in the master-slave relationship, godparenthood served as a bond or reinforcement (Slenes 1978). The function of the religious, in this view, was to stabilize the secular.

Our first finding runs contrary to these suppositions. In no instances did masters serve as godparents for their own slaves; slaves invariably had as spiritual protectors persons who were other than their owners. Evidence from the urban parish of Conceição de Praia presented by Smith (1973), in fact, suggests that this choice pattern may have been widespread.

In seeking an understanding of the pattern we would first dispose of a facile but misleading answer. We do not know who was actually choosing godparents. Was it the parents, a friend, an overseer, the master, or the godparents? Did the church cleric himself assign the godparents? We doubt, however, that specifying the persons vested with choice would yield an understanding of the pattern, for individual actors are hardly autonomous; they act on the basis of information, influence, advice, pressure, social expectations, and rules. Indeed, in the anthropological literature it has been found that similar patterns of godparenthood result even when the decision-making role varies (Gudeman 1975). Certainly, the pattern of not selecting masters as godparents was an outcome of individual choices and strategies, but we are less interested in who made the choice than in why it was made.

The church undoubtedly made its own reconciliation with slavery, but we suggest that the nonchoice of masters is a direct outcome of a conflict between the two idioms and institutions of the church and slavery. Each implies a different kind of relationship; when the two meet in the singular event of baptism, there can only be silence and a turning away, not an overlap. Baptism, above all, creates a spiritual relationship; this is the "thought of" bond that unites the baptized and the sponsors. The expressed tie signifies or indicates this unseen dimension. Godparenthood is a bond not of the body or of the flesh or of human volition as expressed in civil law; it represents, rather, a joining or solidarity through the sharing of "spiritual substance." As it was expressed in the time of Justinian, "by God's mediation their souls are united" (Coleman-Norton 1966, pp. 1067–68). Regardless of the functions it may subserve, godparenthood for the church means spiritual relationship.

In this connection it is worth recalling that at least since the Council of Munich in 813, parents have been forbidden to serve as godparents to their own children. Regardless of its origin, this rule is now seen as an expression of the fundamental opposition that obtains between the spiritual bonds of godparenthood and the carnal bonds of paternity.

The master-slave bond offers a striking contrast to that based on spirituality. In Bahia slavery was not only a productive relationship but the dominating social institution. Flourishing in a context of colonization and the spread of a market economy, slavery defined the conditions of production and cast its shadow on all other ties. Masters held the right to the labor effort of their slaves; they had the right to discipline, to sell, to dispose of, and to kill their slaves. A slave was held as a piece of property, a kind of tool, or a piece of equipment, albeit a living one. Masters, in effect, could do away with much of their slaves' humanness, often attributing to them characteristics of animality. Slaves frequently were denied the right to marry or to have official or legitimate families. The master's concern was to keep his slaves in good working condition at the lowest cost. If the bond of godparenthood was a spiritual relationship of protection, the master-slave bond was an asymmetric relationship of property ownership. Where one stood for succor, the other meant servility.

The two complexes could hardly be more opposed. As an event in the life cycle of the individual, baptism represents membership in the church and equality as a Christian and as a person with others. The baptized has been saved from perdition; he has new parents and new relations of "fraternity." The baptized has partaken of the most important of the sacraments and has the right to participate in church ceremonies. Baptism signals or indexes something opposed to slavery: equality, humanity, freedom from sin. The historical crossing of images between these two domains provides some evidence of their differing meanings. One ancient mode of conceptualizing or justifying slavery is that the slave is a sinner; conversely, one argument in Christian ideology has been that sinners are slaves of the Devil (Davis 1966). The metaphoric equivalence of sin and slavery remains today in expressions such as "the wages of sin" or "the wages of the Devil." To be sinless is to be released from bondage.

The baptism of slaves thus represents a threat to slavery, whereas enslavement of the baptized is a potential contradiction for the church. Each relationship stands, in part, for what the other is not. The baptism of slaves brings together incompatible if not contradictory relationships.

The resolution to this incompatibility, we argue, was not to abolish slavery or baptism, although the contradiction eventually contributed to slavery's extinction. Rather, the truly conflicting relationships were kept apart. Slaves were baptized in accord with pressures from the church, but their rebirth from "slavery" was never to their own masters. Others, whether they were slaves or free or the masters of others, served as godparents. The incompatible ties were kept separate. Indeed, we would press the argument to the point of reintroducing individual decisions. Regardless of who chose the godparents, it seems likely that masters refused to serve for their own slaves, for doing so would have indicated a willingness to abrogate some of their own powers. Whether they served for their own recently liberated slaves (*alforriados*) is a different question.

Henry Koster, an Englishman who administered a plantation in Brazil and who observed firsthand the selection of godparents for slaves, caught the essence of the relationship and the contradiction it implied when he stated: "I never heard of the master in Brazil being likewise the god-father; nor do I think that this ever happens; for such is the connection between two persons which this is supposed to produce, that the master would never think of ordering the slave to be chastised" (1817, 2: 199). That baptism and spiritual relations defined part of the slaves' selfhood is illustrated also by the first or Christian names inscribed in the register. Slaves were given the same Christian names as were free persons. In Bahia there was no parallel to the practices in Jamaica or South Carolina, where Graeco-Roman, day and month, or ironic names were bestowed and imposed on slaves. In other parts and times of Brazil the naming practices may have been different. In *Dom Casmurro*, for example, Machado refers to slaves carrying Christian names, but for each owner they are arrayed in alphabetical order, which is to imply that they are not so much names as letters. In Bahia, at least, both slaves and the freeborn named children for

Table 2. Naming Patterns in Baptismal Registers, Rio Fundo
and Monte Parishes

	Same as godparent of same sex	Different	Total	Same as parent of same sex	Different	Total
Boys						
Free	11 (14.4)	65	76	14 (23.7)	45	59
Slave	6 (10.0)	54	60	1 (7.1)	13	14
	17	119	136	15	58	63
Girls						
Free	6 (12.5)	42	48	9 (13.4)	58	67
Slave	3 (9.6)	28	31	2 (4.9)	39	41
	9	70	79	11	97	108

Source: Tables 2–10 are based on the parish registers of Rio Fundo and Monte 1780–1788
Note: Percentages of the total are in parentheses.

parents or godparents at about the same rate; and the names most commonly selected—Maria, José, João, Manoel—indicated a direct kinship
with and rebirth in the mold of the Catholic family (see Table 2). In name,
if not fact, black and white were equal.

By contrast to the pattern in which masters were not selected, it appears that indirect paternalism could be expressed through godparenthood. Such was the case in 1781 when the son of the *senhor* (plantation
owner) of *engenho* Jacuipe sponsored the child of a slave couple owned
by his father, or when in 1788 the child of cane farmer Clemente Nogueira's slave was presented by a *pardo* (colored) carpenter who was himself Nogueira's godchild (ACMS, Rio Fundo baptizados, 7 May 1781,
116; 10 October 1788, 120). But even such indirect forms were relatively
rare. We found only 4 (out of 264) cases in which such a relationship was
overtly stated. Though there may have been others in which the priest
simply failed to note the ties, we doubt that paternalism in the narrow
(master and slave) or expanded (master of another and slave) sense was
commonly expressed through godparenthood. Koster suggested that slave
women sometimes sought distinguished sponsors for their children in
hopes that these sponsors would pay to have their godchildren freed, but
free godparents did not often provide funds to liberate their godchildren

from bondage. One study of Bahia between 1684 and 1745 revealed that less than 1 percent of all manumissions and less than 2 percent of those obtained by purchase were paid for by godparents freeing their godchildren (Koster 1817, 2:195; Schwartz 1974). Whatever the hopes or designs of the slaves, such instances were few.

The Freeborn and Slaves

We have suggested that selection of godparents was guided by two invariable, negative rules. In accord with church law and practice, parents were never chosen as godparents; in the social context of Bahian slavery, masters never served as godparents to their own slaves. These two rules, then, dictated an inner negative circle of choice prohibition. They do not reveal, however, the factors that positively guided choice. We may phrase this point differently. Godparents in relation to their godchildren embodied or signified a complex of elements. The task is to tease apart the characteristics godparents represented. To do this we have distinguished between the normal baptisms of recently born healthy infants and the baptisms of adult African slaves, foundlings, children baptized in the shadow of death, and children born of slave mothers but freed at birth. These latter groups are examined separately, and we turn first to the normal baptisms of 138 children born to free mothers and 107 children born to slave mothers.

Just as the slavery situation had a predominant impact on who was not chosen to be godparent, so also it had an influence on the actual selections. To orient our discussion, we begin with the following propositions, although they will need refinement and qualification:

    1. Slaves served as godparents for slaves.

    2. Slaves did not serve as godparents for the freeborn.

    3. The freeborn served as godparents for slaves.

    4. The freeborn served as godparents for the freeborn.

To express this same point, but from the standpoint of the baptized, we may say that slaves were sponsored either by slaves or by the freeborn; the freeborn were almost always sponsored by the freeborn.

Before proceeding with the analysis, we should observe that this pattern of choice is hardly a given or self-explanatory. Again, the entirety hinges upon what godparenthood represents. If, for example, godparenthood signified impurity or pollution, the pattern would be different; godparents would be chosen from the lowest sectors of society. The meaning of godparenthood is decisive in determining its relation to other social bonds. The church itself has never spoken directly to the issue of the social status a godparent should occupy, yet implicit in many of its laws is the idea that spiritual paternity represents a superior or higher bond than carnal generation. Such reasoning, for instance, was used as early as 692 by the Council of Trullo. Thus, it is a striking fact that, cross-culturally, godparents are almost always of a status equal to, or higher than, that of their godchildren. Let us frame the argument in this manner. The bond of godparent-godchild signifies spiritual relationship. But this bond is always mapped onto or projected into a particular social context. A godparent and a godchild are always something more than relatives of "the spirit." They are actors whose total relationship includes extraecclesiastical characteristics. If sponsor and child were confined in their interactions solely to the realm of the church, relative social status would be irrelevant; but it is precisely the task of godparents to extend the religion to new members and to bring it outside the context of strictly religious occasions and places.

In the social context of slavery, then, we would expect and do discover that one selection pattern is almost never found. A principal consideration in choice was precisely the free or slave status of the child: slaves, with a rare exception, were not godparents for freeborn children. In the one exception a slave godmother was chosen for a free child, the son of a *pardo* carpenter of Rio Fundo (ACMS, Rio Fundo baptismos, 23 October 1780, 106). In all other baptisms of the freeborn, free godparents were selected. If we label the nonchoice of masters a direct impact of slavery upon baptismal choice patterns, we may call this second factor an indirect effect of slavery.

In the case of baptized slaves, however, the godparent category was hardly homogeneous. When godparents were present, free persons filled sponsorship roles in 70 percent of slave baptisms, slaves served in 20 percent, and former slaves (*libertos*) acted in the remainder (see Table 3).

Why should this pattern exist? Some evidence suggests that slaves were using godparenthood to secure a possible ally or protector, a theory that fits the very meaning of the ties. In the plantation zones it was not uncommon for runaway slaves to go to a neighboring estate and seek the intercession of a "sponsor," who would then return the slave and ask that no punishment be given or that the situation causing the flight be ameliorated. A free godparent living nearby had advantages for slaves, advantages that outweighed the close associations or family ties that would lead to the selection of other slaves.

The category "free godparent for baptized slave," however, is not a precise enough designation. In no case was a slave's godfather of a social position equal to, or higher than, that of the slave's owner. The slaves of plantation owners (*senhores de engenho*) had other slaves or cane farmers (*lavradores de cana*) as sponsors; and the slaves of cane farmers had carpenters. This same pattern was noted by Smith (1973) in his study of Con-

Table 3. Godparent Status of Free and Slave Children in the Parishes of Monte and Rio Fundo, 1780–89

	Godfathers				
	Free	Slave	Liberto (freed at birth)	None	Total
Godmothers (free children)					
Free	88[a]	0	0	1	89
Slave	1	0	0	0	1
Liberto	0	0	0	0	0
None	47[b]	0	0	1[c]	48
Total	136	0	0	2	138
Godmothers (slave children)					
Free	48[d]	0	0	3	51
Slave	2	13	4	0	19
Liberto	0	2	5	0	7
None	29[e]	4	1[f]	1	35[g]
Total	79	19	10	4	112

a. Includes 3 *expostos* (foundlings).
b. Includes 2 *expostos*.
c. This entry is for an *exposto*.
d. Includes 3 *libertos*.
e. Includes 2 *libertos*.
f. This entry is for a *liberto*.
g. Includes 1 *liberto*.

ceição de Praia. It seems to indicate a recognition of status distinctions in the selection of godfathers within the context of master-slave relations. It may also underline the social distance that obtained between the role of master and that of slave.

Color was also a factor in selection of godparents. A hierarchy of color from black to *pardo* to white is evident. Of the thirty-two free *pardos*, for example, who served as godparents, almost 70 percent (22/32) sponsored black children. Similarly, free *pardo* children were more likely to have whites as godparents than any other *pardos*, and they hardly ever had blacks as sponsors. The preferences were upward in the somatic scale of this multiracial slave-based society. Whites almost invariably had whites as godparents. *Pardos* usually had whites as godparents, although in a few instances *pardos* or blacks also served. In thirty cases where the color of both the godmother and the godfather of *pardo* children can be ascertained, 88 percent of the godparents (53/60) were white. Blacks also displayed a tendency to have sponsors of lighter color, but they had a higher proportion of black godparents as well. This pattern probably reflects the limitations placed on the ability of slaves to choose freely. Whereas whites were only 41 percent of the children baptized, whites filled about 80 percent of the sponsor positions (see Table 4).

Government officials and planters sometimes intervened directly to impede the free selection of sponsors by slaves. In Minas Gerais in 1719 the governor, the Count of Assumar, a virulent racist, ordered that slaves be prohibited from sponsoring other slaves. He feared that both slave earnings and the respect and deference owed to masters would be diverted to slave godparents, who in turn might feel themselves morally obliged to help co-parents or *afilhados* to escape or rebel (Ramos 1972, p. 211). In Bahia other sorts of restrictions were imposed. The set of instructions issued to the Jesuit administrator of *engenho* Sergipe in about 1699 forbade the selection of either slave or free *padrinhos* from beyond the plantation itself and also prohibited the plantation's slaves from assuming such roles (ARSI, Bras. 11). Such efforts to limit contacts beyond the borders of an individual slaveholding appear to have been standard practice on the *engenhos*. Plantation inventories, for example, almost never list slaves married to spouses off the estate. In seven of the nine cases in Rio Fundo in which the owner of the baptized slave child could be positively identified as a plantation owner, one or both godparents was a slave (see Table 5). But in the world of the Bahian Recôncavo, where large sugar plantations

Table 4. Color Distribution of Godparents

Baptized	Godfathers			Godmothers		
	White	*Pardo* (colored)	Black	White	*Pardo*	Black
White	61	3	0	64	0	0
Pardo	28	1	1	25	2	3
Black	40	12	14	39	18	9
Total	129	16	15	128	20	12

Note: This table includes only those baptisms of children in which a godmother was present.

Table 5. Baptismal Sponsors of Slaves Owned by *Senhores de Engenho* in Rio Fundo Parish

Senhor	Engenho	Slave	Padrinho	Madrinha
João Coelho de Oliveira	Pandalunga	1	*Liberto pardo* carpenter	*Senhor's* slave
		2	Same	*Senhor's* slave
		3	Free man	None
		4	*Senhor's* slave	None
João Pedro Fiuza Barreto	Terra Nova	1	*Senhor's* slave	*Senhor's* slave
Bento José de Oliveira	Aramaré	1	*Senhor's* slave	*Senhor's* slave
		2	*Liberto pardo*	*Senhor's* slave
Francisco Borges de Barros	Jacuipe	1	*Senhor's* slave	*Senhor's* slave
D. Joana Ferreira	Buraco	1	Free man	Free woman

were surrounded by many smaller holdings of cane farmers, tenants, and subsistence farmers, many of whom also owned slaves, the desire to circumscribe the slave's social universe to the productive unit itself was often frustrated.

To summarize, godparenthood choice in Bahia was almost always horizontal or vertical upward, never downward. What defined social directionality was the context of slavery and race.

Gender and Legal Status

The selection of godparents also was influenced by gender in relation to legal status. As shown in Table 2, in some instances one or the other godparent was missing from the baptism; but the difference in sex of the missing godparent is striking. For slaves, godfathers were missing in 3.6 percent of the baptisms (4/112), but godmothers were missing in 31.2 percent of the cases (35/112). The figures are very similar for the free: godfathers for free children were missing in 1.4 percent of the instances (2/138), but godmothers were omitted in 34.8 percent of the cases (48/138). In other words, regardless of the legal status of the baptized, godmothers were missing almost fourteen times as often as godfathers: presence of the male sponsor was deemed to have been more important than presence of the female.

Furthermore, the legal status of the single godparent is relevant. For the free baptized, the single godparent was always free. For slave children, when the godfather was missing the godmother was free; but when the godmother was missing there were at least a few instances in which the godfather was a slave or *liberto*. Again, what seems to have been important was to have a male sponsor present. When both sponsors were present, their legal statuses were nearly always equal (see Table 6). In the case of free children, in only one instance did a slave godmother stand at the baptism; in this case the baptized was a male, and the godfather was free.

In the case of slave children, the evidence for gender symmetry is more striking. Slave godfather was aligned with slave godmother, free godmother with free godfather. Although, as we have noted, asymmetry in the relation of baptized to godparents and in the relation of godparents to masters is present, asymmetry in the relation of the sponsors themselves is

Table 6. Status of Godparents in Relation to the Status and Gender of Godchildren

Godmothers	Godfathers (free male children)		Godfathers (free female children)	
	Slave	Free	Slave	Free
Slave	0	1	0	0
Free	0	48	0	42

	Godfathers (slave male children)			Godfathers (slave female children)		
	Slave	*Liberto*	Free	Slave	*Liberto*	Free
Slave	8	2	2	5	3	0
Liberto	1	0	0	0	4	0
Free	0	0	25	0	1	18

Note: Sign test comparing number of same-status pair to number of different-status pairs: $z = 4.38$, $p < .0001$, two tailed; $z = 3.96$, $p < .0001$, two tailed.

not. The only slight observation that can be made is that when godparents were of unequal statuses, it was the godmother who tended to be lower. (This observation, incidentally, underlines our prior suggestion that in cases of single godparents it was considered important simply to have a godfather, regardless of legal status.)

The data in Table 6 also suggest that the category "baptized slave" may not have been homogeneous. Was there a pattern by which some slaves had free and some slave godparents? Certainly, gender was one element. The combination of *liberto* godmother and *liberto* godfather was used only for females, and *libertos* in general were used more for females than males. Slave boys were more likely to have free sponsors than slave girls: slave boys had free godparents in 67.6 percent of the cases; the comparable statistic for girls was 58.1 percent.

Overall, gender entered into godparent selection in a dual way, in terms of the baptized and in terms of the godparents. We would argue that this distinction was not simply because male slaves were more productive than female slaves in the Brazilian economic context. They may have been of greater economic value, but the total society itself evinced a gender asymmetry. Free males had command over the means of production, and their principal means was the labor of slave men. At the very core of the society was a gender asymmetry, inserted into production. Upon the free male–slave male relationship the entirety was constructed. Thus, for all persons the free male was most sought as a godparent; and it was slave boys who were most in need of this protection. Greater latitude was shown in selection of godparents for slave girls. Indeed, this more intensive identification of slavery with males, evident in the baptismal registers, can be documented in other aspects of slave society. Manumission favored females, producing a ratio of twice as many women freed as men. Although this pattern was especially marked among adults, it was found among children freed as well (Schwartz 1974). Again, this evidence suggests indirectly that a close connection between male slave and master was not fostered, for this connection represented a threat to the political, economic, and social order upon which the society was based. Paternalistic attitudes probably were less characteristic of the relation between slaveowners and male slaves than of that between owners and female slaves.

Deviations

Along with the normal baptisms of healthy slave and free children, the parish registers also contain registrations of foundlings (*expostos*), children *in extremis*, slave children freed at birth, and adult slaves. Each of these groups in our sample from Monte and Rio Fundo exhibited distinct patterns in godparent selection. Children baptized in the face of death almost invariably had no godparents. A few cases were recorded in which a sick child had recovered and, having been baptized originally by a layman as an emergency measure, was then exorcised of that baptism and properly administered the sacrament by a priest. There were seven slave children freed at birth (5 percent of the slave baptisms), all of unknown fathers. In none of these cases did slaves serve as sponsors, and of the fourteen possible godparents only one was a *liberto*. Assuming that all *expostos* were free at birth, they made up 4 percent (6/137) of the free children and displayed roughly the same patterns of godparent selection as other free children, except for one case in which an *exposto* had neither a godfather nor a godmother.

The baptism of adult slaves called for special attention. The regulations of the archdiocese of Bahia, recognizing the difficulty of giving religious instruction to "brute and unacculturated slaves of incomprehensible language," required that six simple questions be put to them before they could be baptized, such as "Will you sin no more?" (Monteiro da Vida 1765). The failure of masters to baptize newly arrived Africans led to complaints by churchmen. In 1697 a royal order required baptism to take place at African ports and religious instruction to be given on the slave ships, but Africans continued to arrive in the Recôncavo unbaptized (APB, Ordens regias, n. 100). Koster (1817) tells us that newly arrived slaves quickly learned the social advantage of baptism, but we can probably assume that in the case of recently arrived Africans the selection of sponsors was made by the master. Hence, the patterns revealed in Table 7 tell us about slaveowners' attitudes.

Of the seventy-six possible godparents in the thirty-eight cases presented here, there were nine instances when either a godmother or a godfather was not present. Of the remainder, slaves filled these positions in 70 percent of the cases (47/67) and *libertos* in another 10 percent. Though there were a few cases of masters' relatives taking on godparent roles, once again there were no instances when masters served as sponsors for their own slaves.

The difference in the godparenthood patterns between children born as slaves and recently arrived African adults is striking. Whereas slaves constituted only 20 percent of the godparents for children, they were found in those roles three and a half times more frequently for adults. No pattern of godparents from the same African "nation" can be seen in the documents, and we believe that masters appointed or "invited" more ac-

Table 7. Baptismal Sponsors for Adult Slaves from Four Recôncavo
Parishes, 1723–1816

	Godmothers				
	Slave	*Liberto*	Free	None	Total
Godfathers					
Slave	20	1	0	3	24
Liberto	1	1	—	1	3
Free	2	1	4	2	9
None	0	0	1	1	2
Total	23	3	5	7	38

culturated slaves to serve as sponsors because of their ability to assist in the
baptized's integration into the work force, their defining role. This theory
might also explain the higher percentage of *libertos* found as sponsors for
adult slaves than for children. If the theory is correct, the institution of
godparenthood was, in a sense, being used in an "appropriate" way: godparents were "instructing" their godchildren, though not entirely in religious matters.

The most common exception to the symmetrical relationship among
baptized, parents, and godparents called for by custom and regulation was
the absence of one or both of the godparents at a baptismal act. The Council of Trent and more specifically the ecclesiastical regulations of the archdiocese of Bahia set down a series of norms and requirements for baptism.
Babies were to be baptized within a week of birth by a parish priest, with a
fine levied by the church if this duty was not done. The church required
that there be only one godfather and one godmother, with minimum ages
of fourteen for the godfather and twelve for the godmother. It also prohibited parents from serving as the godparents to their own children.

In the Bahian Recôncavo these regulations were often bent or ignored. There were many baptisms at which either a godfather or, far more
frequently, a godmother was lacking. In the parish of São Francisco in the
early nineteenth century, there were a number of cases in which the *madrinha* chosen was the Virgin, "Nossa Senhora Protetora"—a practice
often found elsewhere and still used on occasion in the Bahian interior.
Sometimes there would be no godmother but two godfathers. Such was
the case in 1816 when two sugar craters from Engenho do Oasario sponsored a child, "against the rule of the Tridentino," as the priest recorded it
(ACMS, São Francisco baptisms, 3 January 1816).

Table 8. The Absence of Godmothers from Baptismal Acts in Monte and Rio Fundo

	Free godmother[a]		Slave godmother	
	Present	Absent	Present	Absent
Legitimate child	70	11	19	3
Illegitimate child	21	9	52	12
Total	91	20	71	15

a. $X^2 = 3.98, 1\ df, p < .05$.

Legitimacy

In our discussion of gender we noted the large number of slave and free baptisms in which a godparent was absent. For both free and slave children, godparents were missing in 31 percent of the baptismal acts (45/147 for free, 33/108 for slaves). At first glance, there seems to be little difference between slave and free children in this regard. When we examine the legitimacy of the baptized, however, another pattern emerges. Among slaves, the vast majority (75 percent) of whom were illegitimate, legitimacy had no discernible effect on the presence or absence of a godmother. Among the freeborn, however, legitimacy had a definite effect, and illegitimate children were twice as likely as legitimate to be lacking a godmother (see Table 8). As we might expect in a slave society, color and legitimacy affected the freeborn far more than the slaves. Legitimacy was not an important social marker for a slave; outside this all-defining status, however, legitimacy helped define social position.

Locality

We have already seen evidence that slaveowners tried to limit the social universe of their slaves. Conjugal unions beyond the boundaries of a slaveholding unit were discouraged, and other limitations were imposed. Although large slaveowners probably had some success in these efforts and were able to contain contacts to the circle of their own land and slaves, the nature of Bahian slaveholdings, which included many small plantations interspersed among the larger ones, frustrated any attempts to isolate the slaves. When slaves served as godparents for other slaves, there were almost as many who were owned by a master different from him who owned

Table 9. Relationships of Godparents to Baptized Slaves

	Slave of same owner	Slave of different owner	Related to owner
Godfathers	12	13	6
Godmothers	13	11	1

the baptized as who were held by the same owner (twelve godfathers and thirteen godmothers were slaves of the same master; thirteen godfathers and eleven godmothers were slaves of another master).

The geographic catchment area for both the freeborn and slaves was limited, although somewhat more so for the latter. The chances were about five to one that godparents of either slave or free would be residents within the same parish as the baptized. When a godparent came from elsewhere, it was usually a neighboring town or plantation, not more than a few kilometers distant. In this matter, godfathers displayed a broader geographical distribution than godmothers, a pattern somewhat more marked among slave baptisms than among those of free children. In only 8 slave baptisms of 110 did the godfather reside in a different place from the godmother (see Tables 9 and 10).

The geography of godparenthood was somewhat different between slaves and the free. Among the white elite, especially in the more "aristocratic" parish of Monte, godparents sometimes came from as far away as the city of Salvador, some thirty kilometers distant. Such was the case in 1789 when the daughter of the *senhor de engenho*, Lt. Col. José Diogo Gomes Ferrão Catelobranco, was baptized and both her godparents traveled from Salvador to stand for her. Among the white elite, godparents also might be represented by proxies. For slaves, the distances involved in godparent selection were more limited. Almost invariably, godparents lived in the same parish as the baptized, and usually in the same place. Those who did not often resided at another *engenho*. The unwillingness of masters to serve as sponsors for their own slaves and the desire of slaves to choose upward in status and color and perhaps outward to gain support in the face of their slave status appear to have combined to produce the pattern we observe here.

Conclusion

We draw to a close by returning to our encompassing theme. Godparenthood is a way of connecting people. It is a system of spiritual rela-

Table 10. Residential Propinquity of Godparents to the Baptized

	Same residence		Different residence	
	N	%	N	%
Godmothers of:				
Free children	79	86.8	12	13.2
Slave children	52	88.1	7	11.8
Godfathers of:				
Free children	72	81.8	16	18.2
Slave children	56	81.2	13	18.8

tionships that emanates from the church. Although godparenthood is projected into social domains, the institution never loses its fundamental spiritual resonance and rooting. In use, godparenthood is joined to other kinds of ties, and this total complex of the sacred and the secular determines who is selected to enter the relationships.

In Bahia the dominating institution was slavery, and this is the context into which godparenthood was projected. Our task has been to tease apart this context, to dissolve it into specifics, and in doing so we have tried to show how, for this society, factors such as locality, legitimacy, gender, color, and civil status entered into the selection of godparents. We have tried to reveal some of the dynamics that were internal to Bahian slavery. Above all, we have suggested that the very fact of being a slave or free, of being a master or not, directly entered into the pattern of choice. Slavery and godparenthood were two idioms or sets of relationships by which lives were ordered, but they conveyed different, sometimes quite opposite, meanings. In eighteenth-century Bahia we observe both a discordance and an accommodation between the two. The idiom of slavery was dominant, but that of spiritual relationships was not without influence. As we now know, the balance between these two idioms was to change in the following century. One now has disappeared, but people still use the other to express and to order at least a portion of their lives.

References

Arantes Neto, Antonio
1970   "Compadrio in Rural Brazil." Master's thesis, University of São Paulo.

Archivum Romanum Societatis Iesu. Rome (ARSI).

Arquivo da Curia Metropolitana de Salvador (ACMS).

Arquivo Público do Estado da Bahia (APB).

Borges Landeiro, Carlota M. G.

1965   *A vila de Penamacor no primeiro quartel do Século xviii.* Lisbon: Centro de Estudos Demográficos.

Bossy, John

1973   "Blood and Baptism: Kinship, Community and Christianity in Western Europe from the Fourteenth to the Seventeenth Centuries." In *Studies in Church History,* edited by D. Baker, vol. 10. Pp. 129–43. Oxford: Oxford University Press.

Coleman-Norton, Paul R.

1966   *Roman State and Christian Church: A Collection of Legal Documents to A.D. 535,* vol. 3. London: SPCK.

Coy, Peter

1974   "An Elementary Structure of Ritual Kinship: A Case of Prescription in the *Compadrazgo.*" *Man,* n.s. 9:470–79.

Davis, David B.

1966   *The Problem of Slavery in Western Culture.* Ithaca, N.Y.: Cornell University Press.

Foster, George M.

1953   "Cofradía and Compadrazgo in Spain and Spanish America." *Southwestern Journal of Anthropology* 9:1–28.

Freyre, Gilberto

1968   *Sobrados e Mucambos.* 2 vols. Rio de Janeiro: José Olympio.

Gudeman, Stephen

1972   "The *Compadrazgo* as a Reflection of the Natural and Spiritual Person." *Proceedings of the Royal Anthropological Institute of Great Britain and Ireland for 1971,* pp. 45–71.

1975   "Spiritual Relationships and Selecting a Godparent." *Man,* n.s. 10:221–37.

Hammel, Eugene

1968   *Alternative Social Structures and Ritual Relations in the Balkans.* Englewood Cliffs, N.J.: Prentice-Hall.

Hart, Donn V.

1977   *Compadrinazgo: Ritual Kinship in the Philippines.* DeKalb: Northern Illinois University Press.

Horstmann, Connie, and Kurtz, Donald V.

1979   "*Compadrazgo* and Adaptation in Sixteenth Century Central Mexico." *Journal of Anthropological Research* 35:361–72.

Ingham, John M.
1970   "The Asymmetrical Implications of Godparenthood in Tlaya-capan, Morelos." *Man*, n.s. 5:281–89.
Koster, Henry
1817   *Travels in Brazil*. 2 vols. Philadelphia: M. Carey and Son.
Lomnitz, Larissa
1971   "Reciprocity of Favors in the Urban Middle Class of Chile." In *Studies in Economic Anthropology*, edited by G. Dalton, pp. 93–106. American Anthropological Studies, no. 7. Washington, D.C.: American Anthropological Association.
Middleton, DeWight R.
1975   "Choice and Strategy in an Urban *Compadrazgo*." *American Ethnologist* 2:461–75.
Mintz, Sidney W., and Wolf, Eric R.
1950   "An Analysis of Ritual Co-parenthood (Compadrazgo)." *Southwestern Journal of Anthropology* 6:341–68.
Monteiro da Vide, Sebastião
1765   *Constituições primeiras do arcebispado da Bahia*. Lisbon: Paschoal da Silva.
Nutini, Hugo, and Bell, Betty
1980   *Ritual Kinship*. Princeton: Princeton University Press.
Oliveira Duarte, Maria Celeste dos Santos Duarte
1974   *A freguesia de S. Martinho de Arrifana de Sousa de 1760–1784*. Lisbon: Centro de Estudos Demográficos.
Pinheiro Marques, Maria Lucia de Sousa
1974   *A freguesia de S. Martinho de Arrifana de Sousa de 1730–1759*. Lisbon: Centro de Estudos Demográficos.
Pitt-Rivers, Julian
1973   "The Kith and the Kin." In *The Character of Kinship*, edited by Jack Goody, pp. 89–105. Cambridge: Cambridge University Press.
1976   "Ritual Kinship in the Mediterranean: Spain and the Balkans." In *Mediterranean Family Structures*, edited by J. G. Peristiany, pp. 317–34. Cambridge: Cambridge University Press.
Queiros Mattoso, Katia M. de
1979   *Etre esclave au Bresil xvie–xixe siècle*. Paris: Hachette.
Ramos, Donald
1972   "A Social History of Ouro Preto: Stresses of Dynamic Urbanization in Colonial Brazil." Ph.D. diss., University of Florida.

Russell-Wood, A. J. R.
1968   *Fidalgos and Philanthropists: The Santa Casa da Misericordia of Bahia, 1550–1755.* Berkeley and Los Angeles: University of California Press.
Schwartz, Stuart B.
1974   "The Manumission of Slaves in Colonial Brazil: Bahia, 1684–1745." *Hispanic American Historical Review* 54:603–35.
1978   "Indian Labor and New World Plantations: European Demands and Indian Responses in Northeastern Brazil." *American Historical Review* 83:43–79.
1982   "Patterns of Slaveholding in the Americas: New Evidence From Brazil." *American Historical Review* 87:55–86.
Slenes, Robert
1978   "Coping with Oppression: Slave Accommodation and Resistance in the Coffee Regions of Brazil, 1850–1888." Paper presented to the Southern Historical Association, St. Louis.
Slenes, Robert, and Carvalho de Mello, Pedro
1978   "Paternalism and Social Control in a Slave Society: The Coffee Regions of Brazil, 1850–1888." Paper presented to the Ninth World Congress of Sociology, Uppsala, Sweden.
Smith, David
1973   "Cor. ilegitimidade e compradrio na Bahia seiscentista: os livros de batizado da Conceicao da Praia." Paper presented to the Third Congress of Bahian History, Bahia.
Stirrat, R. L.
1975   "*Compadrazgo* in Catholic Sri Lanka." *Man,* n.s. 10:589–606.
Tylor, Edward B.
1861   *Anahuac.* London: Longmans, Green, Reader, and Dyer.

Terms for Kin in the British West Indian Slave Community: Differing Perceptions of Masters and Slaves

B. W. Higman

Introduction

Within slave societies, the recognition of kinship served quite different functions for slaves and masters. In the first place, it was a distinguishing feature of the institution of slavery that the slave was not accepted into the kinship group of the master (Watson 1980, p. 8; but compare Miers and Kopytoff 1977, p. 23). There were significant differences between slave societies in the ease with which individuals could move from the status of slave to kin, and even in the British Caribbean, where the line was clearly drawn, occasional cases occurred of persons' being defined in law as the slaves of nonwhite consanguines or affines. But the masters of the British Caribbean were concerned above all with jural relationships. Any child born to a slave woman inherited the status of slave, regardless of other relationships within or without the slave community. Although paternity might be recognized, the relationship of father and mother was not important to defining the jural relationship of the child, even when the father was the master himself or when the father was a slave belonging to another master. Some masters formed long-lasting relationships with slave mistresses and favored the children of such unions in a variety of ways, but they rarely endowed these relationships with the meaning they applied to white kinship, and they failed to recognize ramifications within the slave kinship network. Again, although the masters might perceive the existence of a much broader network of relationships within the slave community, they rarely intervened to modify this network internally to match any particular model (as the missionaries did) but regularly shattered it through the separation of recognized kin by sale or removal. The masters isolated themselves from incorporation in the slave community's kinship network and observed the jural mother-child relationship exclusively as a basis for action.

The slaves were forced to recognize the significance of this jural mother-child relationship, and to act within the limits it imposed. But they also recognized the importance of a wider range of bilateral relationships between generations. The masters, of course, were not always unaware of the existence of such relationships, and in certain circumstances they made use of them as tools of social control; but whereas the masters could ignore these relationships whenever it suited, the slaves recognized them as basic determinants of behavior within the slave community, the cosmos created by the slaves themselves, with its own rules and mechanisms of social control.

Attempts to understand the structure and function of social relations within the slave community must confront a number of crucial theoretical and methodological problems. How was the definition and recognition of kinship affected by the institution of slavery? How were power relationships within the slave community related to kinship? How were the roles of father and mother affected by the jural and economic bases of slave society? Precisely which kin relationships were regarded as important by the slaves themselves? Are the observed patterns to be explained in structural-functional terms, or by reference to African, European, or American models? Or are they to be explained as a unique system, developed within the specific circumstances of Caribbean slave society? From a methodological point of view, how are kin relationships to be established from the available historical data, most of it the product of the master class? Is it possible to understand exactly what the slaves meant when they used specific words or terms?

Much of the recent literature concerned with slave family and kinship organization in the British Caribbean has been focused on structural questions. Work has been concentrated on the study of family and household composition and has concluded that the earlier tendency to emphasize the matrifocal unit (Patterson 1967, p. 167; Goveia 1965, p. 235) needs to be balanced by a greater emphasis on the nuclear family household (Higman 1973, 1975, 1978; Craton 1979; Bolland 1977). This new interpretation depends, to a large extent, on a shift from the jural perspective to that of the slave household. But it is a perspective founded on the composition of family households rather than on the functions or sentiments of such units. In this it mirrors trends in European and North American historical demography, and it is not surprising that the two types of studies have shown similar strengths and weaknesses (Anderson 1980).

Two basic problems limit the value of such studies. In the first place, household composition provides only partial clues to the nature of rights and obligations within the unit, while the simple definition of the unit remains problematic. Further, as Yanagisako argues, it is necessary to notice that families "are as much about production, exchange, power, inequality, and status" as about procreation and socialization (1979, p. 199). Secondly, the shift to the analysis of family and household composition has failed to provide a true slave perspective, for the reason that all of the studies have depended for their source materials on official or informal listings created by the masters or the colonial governments (Higman 1977). These data, however valuable, cannot be expected to yield an authentic slave vision.

The lists of slave births kept by the masters can readily be used to create quite detailed pedigrees, even when the masters themselves demonstrated a recognition of no more than the jural mother-child relationship (Gutman 1976; Bolland 1977). This fact has led some historians to conclude that slave communities possessed close-knit kinship networks. Craton, for example, argues that "many a slave plantation population, after four or five generations must have been virtually one huge extended family" (1978, p. 167). The problem with this interpretation is that, as Gudeman observes, "a genealogy in itself tells nothing about the recognition and quality of kinship relationships there enshrined" (1979, p. 62). The ramified relationships that can be reconstructed from such data were not necessarily recognized by the slaves themselves or by the masters, who recorded the simple facts of maternity and, sometimes, paternity. What are really needed, writes Gudeman, "are supporting data concerning actual slave kinship genealogies as well as the related interactions and behavior" (p. 62).

This is a high ideal, but how can the historian of British West Indian slave communities go about achieving it? One possible approach is to analyze slave naming patterns (Gutman 1976; Gudeman 1979). This is a difficult area in the understanding of slave life and will remain so until it can be determined how far slave names were chosen by the slaves themselves and how far they were imposed by the masters; further, it is uncertain how far the names listed by the masters in plantation ledgers had currency within the slave community, as will be revealed by the case studies considered below. Another approach, to be discussed in some detail in this essay, is to attempt to establish the relationship terminologies used by the slaves themselves within the slave community. The analysis and classification of relationship terminologies has, of course, been a major preoccupation of anthropology, and the limitations of the method have been much discussed (Needham 1974, pp. 50–61). Relationship terminologies have the obvious advantage of being expressed in categories understood by the people.

In order to resolve satisfactorily the question whether the slaves possessed a relationship terminology distinct from that applied to them by the masters, it would be necessary to locate and analyze a substantial corpus of slave testimony. But the British Caribbean produced relatively few slave narratives and relatively little recorded slave speech. Only one West Indian slave narrative (Pringle 1831) is known to the writer, and that pertains to the marginal area of the Bahamas and contains little material relevant to the study of relationship terminology. Oral evidence, obtained from slaves after emancipation, is also scant, though clearly this is an area that deserves much fuller investigation. European missionaries, concerned to change the spiritual and social lives of the slaves, recorded relevant slave speech in their letters and diaries. Other potential sources are the records of slave courts and the minutes of examinations before select committees concerned with slave rebellions.

In general, the verbatim recording of slave speech seems to have been rare in the British West Indies before the nineteenth century, and the context of conflict surrounding crime and rebellion may mean that the evidence provided is not representative of normal relationships in the slave community. Even in the nineteenth century many slave court records did not include slave testimony in any form, though of course the evidence often illuminates slave behavior. This is the case with most of the Jamaican slave court records (for example, Port Royal, Summary Slave Trials, 1819–34; Hanover, Slave Court, 1819–29; St. George, General Slave Court, 1822–31). The recorders of slave speech in court and committee rooms must all have been free, probably white men, so the opportunity for editing, emendation, and willful distortion always existed. Few inquiries, however, were explicitly concerned with questions of slave kinship, so the temptation to distort was lessened. More important, it needs to be asked whether relationship terms expressed in European and Creole languages and employed by both masters and slaves carried the same symbolic meaning for each group. Thus these data must be regarded, like all historical evidence, as potentially corrupt. But they do deserve study as relatively direct statements about slave kinship as seen by the slaves themselves.

Explicit statements by planter-historians provided the foundations for the most influential modern interpretations of slave kinship patterns. But few West Indian whites made any claims to an interest in slave culture. One who did, Augustus Hardin Beaumont of Jamaica, commented in 1836:

> As it is not, by any means, thought respectable to associate with negroes, or to know anything about their manners and habits, few planters know much about them. I know only one exception to the general rule, and that is, in the case of Bryan Edwards, the historian of Jamaica. I believe he is the only one who has ever taken the trouble of inquiring what were their opinions; there is also possibly another exception in Mr. Long, another historian of the island, but he looked upon negroes as a species of monkies. [PP 1836, p. 389]

But Beaumont claimed that because he had himself grown up among the slaves of Jamaica he "knew everything about them as respected their characters, opinions and civilization" and believed that other Creoles, "being brought up very much among the negroes, know their habits, their romances (for negroes who cannot even read, have, notwithstanding, a traditional literature, and some of their fables and tales are contrived with great ability), their superstitions and opinions" (PP 1836, pp. 352, 388). Some masters stated that they rarely visited the slaves' villages or entered their houses, and there is no doubt that West Indian slaves regarded their yards as private domains, the basis for a hidden community. Others among the master class claimed to have gone through hundreds of slave villages. However, one such, William Taylor, reflecting on the great 1831 slave rebellion in Jamaica, observed that "although living in the very centre of those people, yet I did not know what was passing amongst them, and I believe that to be a peculiar feature in Jamaica, in a slave community, that there may be living hundreds at your very door, and you do not know what they feel or what they are going to do" (PP 1832, p. 29).

Thus, whereas few West Indian whites cared to admit an interest in the internal culture of the slave community, even those who did claim such an interest lacked confidence in the nature of their knowledge and understanding. Further, a significant proportion of the West Indian slaveowners were themselves illiterate. As a result, slave speech was rarely recorded, and the oral "traditional literature" of the slaves referred to by Beaumont was largely ignored. It became important, to the literate masters, only in moments of conflict and crisis when the slave system itself was threatened—hence the importance of court records and select committee examinations.

A systematic study of slave perceptions of kinship based on recorded slave speech would need to comb thoroughly all the source materials referred to above and more, seeking out all examples of relationship terminology. The speaker, as well as the referent, would be identified and placed in context. Terminologies would be related to behavior, and a clear distinction made between terms of address and reference. It is to be hoped that this process would permit a detailed analysis of the terminologies (symbols, meanings) employed by West Indian slaves according to their roles and contexts in space and time, distinguishing males and females, Africans and Creoles, plantation and urban slaves, parents and children, young and old, plantation-fellows and outsiders, early arrivals and latecomers to the system, and so on. Such an analysis, of course, would require prolonged searching in the source materials. I do not pretend in the present essay to have carried through this task; I merely hint at some of the possibilities and potentials by looking at some selected cases, derived from court records.

Nicolas and Agathe

In January 1823 a slave belonging to Point Molenier Estate in Grenada was brought before the St. Georges Magistrates Court on the charge of willfully setting fire to a Negro house on the estate on Christmas Day, in which fire that house and two others were burned. Nicolas, in his defense, stated

> that Agathe had lived with him during three years and upwards. That she had two children by him. That for some time past her parents would not sanction their cohabitation, yet notwithstanding the said Agathe was in the habit of going to the house of the said Nicolas without the knowledge of her parents. That on the evening of the 25th ulto. he met Agathe at a dance on said Estate and asked her to go to his house, which she refused, on which a quarrel took place between them. That she afterwards went to the house of her mother and went to bed. That he the said Nicolas afterwards went to the said house and knocked at the door on which the mother of the said Agathe came out and abused him, pushing him down and declared that her daughter should never live with him again. [St. Georges, Magistrates Court, 1821–23, 18 January 1823]

Nicolas said that he then went to the house of Félicité and became jealous of a strange man he found there. When he left, Nicolas threw the fire from his pipe on the house. The fire then spread to Agathe's.

Agathe testified that she had lived with Nicolas for several years, "but that they had seperated [sic] for some time past on account of their not agreeing together." There were three children in her house when it was fired, she said. Polican, the estate's cooper, stated that he had found Nicolas quarreling in the house of Félicité, at about 8:00 P.M., and that Nicolas accused a Negro man of the Megrin quarter of trying to seduce his wife, Agathe. Pélagie, another slave, said that he heard Nicolas declare "that rather than Agathe should cohabit with another man he would burn her in her house."

Felix Preudhomme, a free man, told the court that Nicolas had confessed to him, saying that the act was done in a fit of passion. Nicolas begged that his garden be given not to Agathe but to his sister, and that his house be given to Agathe.

The court found Nicolas guilty, and he was hanged in the public parade, St. Georges, on 31 January 1823. His crime, of course, was one against property: actual destruction of three slave houses and jeopardizing the lives of slaves, the master's most valuable chattels. Thus the slave court (composed of two justices and three jurors) was concerned only with these property-related matters. The family and household concerns of the slaves, at the root of the case, were of no more than peripheral interest to the court. But the evidence provided by the direct testimony of the slaves does permit a fresh perspective on the role of kinship in the slave community.

In this particular case, it seems certain that the testimony recorded by the court was abbreviated and edited to suit legal standards. Such editing is not always so obvious, and later trial records sometimes appear to be much closer to verbatim reports. What is important in the present case is the question whether the terms used by the slaves to refer to kin were altered, self-consciously or otherwise, by the reporter. The following terms occur in the evidence: *sister, mother, daughter, wife, parents, children, cohabit, cohabitation, lived with*. Of these, *cohabit(ation)* may appear suspect, perhaps being used by the court reporter to vary the *lived with* also attributed to Nicolas, though Pélagie uses *cohabit* exclusively.

More important, it is difficult to know precisely what these terms meant to slaves and masters; they may have indicated joint occupation of particular physical premises, on a permanent basis, or something much more akin to a visiting relationship. It is of more interest, perhaps, that the word *family* is never used in the slaves' testimony, *cohabitation* being the term nearest to expressing a unity. And although Nicolas refers to Agathe's *parents*, it is striking that this and *cohabitation* are the only terms to imply a male role. Every one of the sex-specific kin terms used in the trial (*mother, daughter, sister, wife*) refers to females. It is also suggestive that, in the case of Nicolas and Agathe, it is females who seem to have the most powerful roles. Thus whereas Nicolas says that Agathe's "parents" withdrew their sanction of her "cohabitation" with him, he then specifies that Agathe went to "the house of her mother" and that it was her "mother" who came out and abused him. It is possible, of course, that Agathe's father lived on another plantation or was recently deceased, but there is no hint of this possibility in the evidence.

Nicolas asked that his house be given to Agathe, without specifying whether she should bring her parents with her. On the other hand, he made it clear that his sister, not Agathe, should have his garden. These wishes are suggestive of particular customary kin-related property controls among the slave community. Nicolas probably believed that Agathe and his children should be fed from her parents' provision ground, whereas his sister had no independent garden. In Jamaica the provision grounds of nuclear family households were worked by all members of the unit (PP 1832, pp. 351–470). Asked when children separated from the houses and grounds of their fathers, James Simpson of Jamaica replied: "When they form a connexion to have a family of their own and become domiciled, and sometimes so early as at fourteen or sixteen years of age, they claim a ground independent of their father; up to that period they work in their father's grounds" (PP 1832, p. 385). Conflict over gardens was not uncommon, though not always obviously related to conflict among kin. For example, Jim Duke of Springs Estate, Grenada, burned the house of Charlotte in 1823 because she refused to give him his share of the ripe provisions from the garden they had between them (St. Georges, Magistrates Court, 1821–23, 16 December 1823). The kin relationship of Jim Duke and Charlotte is uncertain: he had often come to her house for supper when he was young, and he still came now and then at the time of the act. Like Nicolas, Jim Duke was condemned to hang, but the court recommended mercy in view of his youth.

Willem and Madalon

The case of Nicolas and Agathe focused directly on conflict in family and household organization within the slave community, even though the crime that brought it before the masters' court was strictly a concern for property. Most of the cases that came before slave courts, however, were not explicitly involved with familial conflict, and the light they throw on relationship terminology as revealed by slave testimony is necessarily much more partial and refracted. Even in the case of Nicolas and Agathe, it is obvious that only a very partial cross section of family and household organization is given. The case of Willem and Madalon, to be discussed in this section, provides an example of the type of information that can be obtained from a court case not directly concerned with familial conflict.

In September 1821 Willem, "alias Sara, alias Cuffey," of Plantation Buses Lust, on the east bank of the Berbice River, was tried for "the crime of obeah and murder" (PP 1823). Willem was charged with having instigated the dancing of the Mackiesie or Minje Mama or Water Mama dance at plantation Op Hoop van Beter, on the west bank of the Berbice, and with having denounced the slave Madalon, who was then beaten to death by the slaves of that estate. Willem declared his innocence to the last. But he was convicted and sentenced to hang from the mango tree under which Madalon had been suspended and beaten, and to have his head severed and placed on a pole on the estate.

The Water Mama or River Mama was a common figure among West Indian spirit persons (Brathwaite 1971, p. 239; Beckwith 1929, p. 101; *Timehri* 1882, p. 298). In 1834 two slaves belonging to Lubertus van Rossum of Berbice, the owner of Willem of Buses Lust, were charged with dancing the "Makizie water or minji mama dance" at Plantation Waterloo, "and there pretending and feigning to have had an inspiration or revelation or intercourse with ghosts relative to poisoners or certain persons suspected of the crime of poisoning and . . . pretending to disclose and utter predictions or prophecies of or concerning the future . . ." (Prosecutions Book 1832–37, 5 April 1834).

In addition to the masters' concern about property (the murder of a slave) and about claims to supernatural powers (obeah) in the 1821 case, it is clear that they also felt threatened by Willem's collusion with Primo, Mey, and Kees, drivers on Op Hoop van Beter. The latter were charged with aiding and abetting Willem and "of disrespecting and setting at nought the subordination due and owing to their proprietors, and subjecting themselves, (the drivers,) in presence of the gang of negroes over which they were placed, to the implicit obedience of the orders and commands of the aforesaid Willem." Primo and Mey were sentenced to be suspended from the mango tree, to receive three hundred lashes each, and to be branded "and degraded as drivers, afterwards to be worked in chains on the said plantation Op Hoop van Beter, for and during the term of one year next following." The trial of Willem, then, involved questions regarding authority within the slave community as much as property.

Fourteen slaves were brought to testify in the case of Willem and Madalon. The court appointed one G. Schwartz as "interpreter in the English and Creole languages."

Willem testified that on the night he was arrested, a Wednesday, he had crossed the Berbice River in a small corial "to see my wife Johanna." William Sterk, the arresting militia officer, took "both him and his wife into custody." Here it is useful to note that the records of the trial can be supplemented by resort to the official slave registration returns, which provide detailed data on individual slaves. According to these registration returns Willem was about twenty-five years of age in 1821, a black Creole of Berbice employed in the field (T. 71/438, p. 655). His "wife" Johanna was sixteen years of age, a black Creole, the daughter of Elizabeth, aged forty-nine and also a Creole (T. 71/438, p. 119). As noted above, Willem denied all knowledge of the events surrounding the death of Madalon, so the only testimony of his was that concerning the visit to his wife. Johanna did not testify, nor was she charged with any offense.

Madalon was an African woman, "with African marks on the breast," aged forty, a field laborer (T. 71/438, p. 119). Munro, an African aged thirty-five, of plantation Vrouw Johanna (T. 71/438, p. 447), said of Madalon: "It was my wife" (PP 1823).

Madalon may also have been the mate of Quashee of Op Hoop van Beter. In giving his evidence, Frederic, a Creole field slave aged twenty-eight years, stated that on the day following her beating Madalon had been unable to complete her row but was helped by Quashee, a temporary driver "who also had her." The significance of the last phrase is somewhat ambiguous, but is made clearer in meaning by the evidence of Baron, an African, with regard to Willem: "When this man, Willem of Buses Lust, first came upon the estate, he inquired for the driver's house, where he remained till the evening, when he made acquaintance with the girl Johanna, whom he had afterwards for his wife." Thus the words "had her" probably refer to a union, whether temporary or long term. No slave named Quashee was listed for Op Hoop van Beter in 1819.

Whatever the complications of Madalon's conjugal status, Munro stated:

> On the Sunday I was there on Op Hoop van Beter the whole day, and slept there that night, she [Madalon] was then quite well. . . . I did not go to the estate to see my wife either on the Monday or Tuesday, but on the Wednesday a letter came to the Johanna, and the negroes informed [me my] wife was run away; went that evening to Op Hoop van Beter to inquire into the matter; found the negro Fortuyn on the bridge, as watchman, who told [me I] was not to go to the negro-houses.

However, Munro went, he said, to the house where Madalon had lodged and found there an old man, David (an African, aged forty, suffering from yaws), who told Munro he had no knowledge of Madalon's whereabouts, "as he was only a stockkeeper, and knew nothing of what took place in the field." The following Sunday, Munro obtained a pass from his master and returned to Op Hoop van Beter. On going to the slave village, he found "Monkesi Sara" of Buses Lust (Willem): "The Attetta Sara said to me, you know I am here; my father is here; and my mother; how did you dare to go first to the manager's house? To which I replied, I went only to show my pass. I asked the Attetta Sara if he thought I ought to have brought my pass first to him, or if he could read it?"

Here is evidence of a direct confrontation between Willem, the obeah-man, and the authority of the master, beyond that mediated through the master's representatives, the drivers. It is important, for present purposes, to observe that Willem connected his authority within the slave community to the presence of his father and of his mother, though the evidence of the slave registration returns suggests that these kinship references were strictly symbolic. Allegro, a Creole carpenter, said that Willem "called himself (Abdie Toboko) God Almighty's child," and Frederic, "God Almighty's toboko, or child." (In the slave registration returns, Willem was listed as the "child of Keef." No slave of this name was listed for Buses Lust in 1818. But "Keef" may have been an error for "Kees," a male African on the plantation who was aged forty-six to forty-eight years [T. 71/438, p. 655]. No "Keef" was listed for Op Hoop van Beter, and the Kees on that plantation was only twenty-six years old in 1819.)

Willem's authority and power within the slave community may have derived from his "parents" but it rested on his capacity to heal, and this capacity was challenged both by the master's hospital, with its European medicine, and by Madalon. Thus Kees, describing Willem as a "Confou man," who came to the plantation "in the house of the girl Johanna," stated: "I heard Willem tell Madalon she was the bad woman who caused so many strong healthy people on the estate to become sick." Isaac, calling Willem "a real Obiah man (Confou man)," said that Willem had been brought to Op Hoop van Beter by Fortuin, who "had one of his wives sick." Cornelia, an African, stated that Willem, Attetta Sara, "came on the estate and asked if we were sick, if so, he could cure us." He helped cure her: "he took three twigs of the cocoa-nut tree, and struck me on the head, and told me to go and wash myself." Adolff, another African, denied witnessing the beating of Madalon, "he being confined in the hospital; but the man Willem, who said he was sent by God Almighty, came to the hospital. His [Adolff's] child was sick, and his wife and another child were also in the hospital with him, Willem directed the children to be brought out, which they were by himself and his wife, and were washed by Willem, who took off two bits that were tied round the neck of one of them."

The kinship terms used by slave witnesses in Willem's trial were *father, mother, wife, wives, child,* and *children*. Although one of these terms has a specific male reference, it should be noted that it was used in Willem's probably symbolic salute to his father and mother. Of the fourteen slave witnesses called in the case, only two were females, and neither of them made any explicit kinship references. But the slave evidence made clear their recognition of the status of multiple wives and the close bonds and affection between family members (though, once again, the word *family* was not employed). It also showed up clearly the frequency of inter-plantation mating and the seriousness with which such relationships were regarded by the slaves.

The trial of Willem demonstrated clearly the conflict that existed between the power of the master and the authority of those slaves who had powerful roles in the internal social control of the slave community, the world of the "negro houses." What is relevant in the present context is that whereas the masters might be viewed by modern historians as patriarchal figures, they were rarely addressed by the slaves in kinship terms,[1] though the internal leaders of the slave community were commonly referred to in such symbolic terms. Several slaves testified that Willem was known also as "Attetta Sara," obviously a variation on *taata* or *tata*, a word common to many African languages that meant "father" or was used as a respectful form of address (Cassidy and Le Page 1980, p. 433). Similarly, the leader of the rebellion of August 1823 in Demerara, which led to the court-martial of Rev. John Smith, was well known to the slaves as "Daddy Quamina" or "father Quamina" (PP 1824, pp. 518–42), just as Samuel Sharpe, leader of the Jamaican slave rebellion of 1831, was commonly called "Daddy Sharpe" (Reckord 1968). In every case, it was the symbolic father who earned respect within the slave community, whether rebel or, as Willem, obeahman. This was the case in spite of the supposed devaluation of the father within slavery. More generally, it is clear that relationship terminology served as an important reference framework, both for genealogical and for other recognized kin.

Before leaving the case of Willem, it is of interest to note that it provides an early instance of the term *mati*. Baron, an African slave, stated that he had seen Willem at Op Hoop van Beter only on one Sunday: "He [Willem] was working at plantation Resolutie, and came over with several of his Mattees, and at sun-set they went away again. He was at the house of the woman Johanna. The negro Frederic also was in the same house, also Corydon" (PP 1823, p. 520). Exactly what relationship was implied by *mattee* is uncertain, because in modern Guyana and Surinam *mati* has a variety of meanings (Jayawardena 1963, p. 48; Price 1975, p. 165; Mintz and Price 1976, p. 37), bearing the same ambiguity as the English word *mate* from which it probably derives. In its widest definition, *mati* may mean only the members of a single plantation gang, and it is probable that this is what Baron intended to imply, as he referred to "several" and pluralized the word. It is unlikely he intended any genealogical connotations, but the sense of amity and ritualized friendship was no doubt implied. Willem's *mattees*, then, were seen as sharing a closely bonded friendship within the slave community, but beyond the bounds of recognized kinship.

The Masters' View of Slave Relationship Terminology

The slave masters of the British Caribbean frequently made up lists detailing particular characteristics of their slaves, but they were rarely concerned to record the slaves' relationships to one another. Slaves were seen, above all, as individual units of labor. In the early nineteenth century, however, the slave registration system required a far more systematic listing of the slave population than previously existed, and in some colonies this listing extended to a specification of family and kin relationships. To a limited extent, these data may not record faithfully the masters' *perceptions*, because some of the information was perhaps collected from the slaves themselves. Kin relationships were noted more often than family or household units, but in most colonies the data were confined to the names of mothers. In the slave registration returns this information was placed in a column headed, for Trinidad, "relations," and for St. Lucia, *parenté*; but in Berbice it came under "remarks tending further to identify," and in Belize under "remarks." The amount of detail varied considerably from colony to colony, and from master to master. In general, the purpose of the slave registration returns meant that the masters rarely noticed relationships beyond the bounds of their own holdings, even when they were aware of such networks.

Although a good proportion of the Berbice masters recorded the relationships of their slaves, it is unfortunate for the present study that there is not a coincidence between the testimony of the slaves in the trial of Willem and the existence of such data for plantation Op Hoop van Beter. In a few cases, however, Berbice masters provided quite detailed data on slave relationships as they understood them, and these are worthy of separate attention. One of the fullest returns was that for plantation Wellington Park, on the west coast of the Corentyne, which had a slave population of 169 in 1819 and was owned by Simon Fraser (T. 71/438, pp. 253–58). A separate comment was attached to each "family" group. For example:

> Sancho and Maria have been the property of the subscriber many years, always lived together, are extremely well behaved, and their fine family of five boys as promising as they can be, while any of them survive it may be easily ascertained what has become of the rest and whether others have been substituted.
>
> Quacco and Molly have been the property of the subscriber since first settlement on this coast [ca. 1804], always lived together and are very confidential slaves—never had children.

What is made particularly clear by the full set of comments is that the master recognized a significant number of unions as being stable over long periods of time and that he saw the family units as close-knit networks. Yet only a small number of relationship terms were employed: *husband* (implicit), *wife, son, daughter, children, brother, sister, orphan*. The word *family* was used strictly to refer to a group of children.

Fuller lists of relationship terms can be derived from the slave registration returns for Trinidad in 1813 and St. Lucia in 1815. The Trinidad masters were required by the Order in Council controlling the registration procedure to list as "relations" all slaves who had husbands or wives, "either by actual marriage, or by known and constant cohabitation, or who

Table 1. Relationship Terminologies Employed by Masters in the
Trinidad Slave Registration Returns, 1813

Males	Females
Husband	Wife
—	Mother
Son	Daughter
Grandson	Granddaughter
Brother	Sister
Nephew	Niece
Cousin	Cousin

Source: T.71/501–3.

had parents or children, brothers or sisters, among the slaves of the said
plantation" (Colonial Office 295/28). In practice, they employed a somewhat wider range of relationship terminology (Table 1). Most important,
they extended the range of reference to include collaterals and a third generation. In doing so, the masters introduced terms not noticed in the Grenada and Berbice slave testimony discussed in the previous section (Table 2).

Most of the St. Lucia slave registration returns were written in French,
but the relationship terms used have been translated into English in Table
3. Only the words *femme* and *homme* seem to possess any obvious ambiguity. The frequency of use of the relationship terms is known both for St.
Lucia and Trinidad but is not of particular concern here, as each individual could of course be attributed more than one label. It is worth pointing
out, however, that the more specific terms listed under *husband* and *wife*
for St. Lucia were rare. Only one slave was described as *mari actuel* and
only one as *mari de . . . , mais non pas le père de ses enfans*. A larger number
of husbands than wives were listed as *vivant avec . . .* , but this term was
more common than *cohabitant avec. . . .* Only two masters used the terms
reputed husband and *reputed wife*, and in each case they used these labels to
distinguish them from actual husband-and-wife unions.

The range of the relationship terminology employed by the masters in
St. Lucia was significantly broader than that found in Trinidad, taking
much more account of paternity and deceased individuals. This was the
case even though the Trinidad slave population exceeded twenty-five thousand, whereas that of St. Lucia was only sixteen thousand. In part, the
difference may be accounted for by the structure of the slave registration
procedure. But, overall, it seems clear that the masters of Trinidad and St.

Table 2. Relationship Terminologies Employed by Slaves in Grenada, Berbice, and Demerara (Selected Cases)

Grenada, 1822	Berbice, 1821	Demerara, 1823
	Genealogical terms	
Parents	—	—
Mother	Mother	Mother
—	Father	Father
Wife	Wife	Wife
—	Wives	—
Child	Child	—
Daughter	—	—
Sister	—	—
—	—	Brother-in-law
	Nongenealogical terms	
Cohabit	*Attetta*	Daddy
Live with	*Mattee*	Father
		Family

Source: St. Georges, Magistrates Court, 1821–23; Parliamentary Papers, Great Britain, 1823, 1824.

Lucia had rather different perceptions of the significance of particular relationships, recognizing variations within the slave population to differing degrees. A large proportion of the masters in Trinidad were of French descent, so the contrast cannot be explained simply as a matter of differing European conceptions of kinship.

It is more important, for present purposes, to ask whether the varying relationship terminologies of the masters in Trinidad and St. Lucia reflected any differences in the perceptions of the slaves. Paradoxically, an analysis of the family or household units suggests a higher proportion of mother-child units in St. Lucia than in Trinidad and a higher proportion of nuclear families in Trinidad. This difference stems, perhaps, from the structure of the returns. Many relationships (father-son, great-grandmother–great-grandchild, for example) can be inferred from the slave registration returns, using the simple genealogical links referred to earlier, but the terms listed in Tables 1 and 3 include only those stated explicitly.

The St. Lucia list of relationship terminologies employed by the mas-

Table 3. Relationship Terminologies Employed by Masters in the St. Lucia Slave Registration Returns, 1815

Males	Females
Husband (*mari/homme de* . . . ; *mari actuel*; *mari de* . . . , *mais non pas le père de ses enfans*; *ancien mari*; *vivant avec* . . . ; *cohabitant avec* . . . ; reputed husband)	Wife (*femme de* . . . ; *ancienne femme*; *vivant avec* . . . ; *cohabitant avec* . . . ; reputed wife)
—	1st wife
—	2d wife
—	Widow
Father	Mother
Grandfather	Grandmother
Son	Daughter
Grandson	Granddaughter
Brother	Sister
Half-brother	Half-sister
Uncle	Aunt
Nephew	Niece
Cousin	Cousin
Orphan	—
—	Daughter-in-law
Parenté	*Parenté*

Source: T.71/378–79

ters (Table 3) includes all the genealogical relationship terms recorded in the slave testimony from Grenada, Berbice, and Demerara (Table 2), with the exception of *parents*, *wives*, and *children* (because the St. Lucia list is concerned only with individuals) and *brother-in-law* (though *daughter-in-law* is included). Even the terms *live with* and *cohabit* are matched in the two lists. Nongenealogical relationship terms (such as *tata* and *mati*) are missing from the St. Lucia list because these were almost exclusively confined to use within the slave community. It is more difficult to be certain that any of the terms found in the St. Lucia list were never used by the slaves themselves, but it is very likely that *reputed husband* and *reputed wife* made sense only from the masters' perspective, and *half-brother* and *half-sister* also seem unlikely to have had currency among the slave community.

As is evident in the lists derived from direct slave testimony, the St. Lucian masters possessed more relationship terms for females than for males, but the difference was slight.

In terms of the value of the slave registration returns as data for the study of slave family and household structure, this comparison of perceptions of relationship terminology derived from the masters and the slaves suggests that the registration records do not provide a picture obviously at odds with the slaves' view of their relationships. It must be reemphasized, however, that the slave testimony analyzed here was always open to distortion, molding it to the masters' model, because it was written down (and translated and edited, in some cases) by whites. Again, it may be questioned whether the slaves and the masters always had the same meanings or symbolic relationships in mind when they used the same terms. For example, some modern Jamaican relationship terms have meanings other than, or in addition to, their meanings in standard English (see Table 4).

It seems certain that the masters had a much more restrictive, genealogical conception of the relationship terms than did the slaves. The slaves were sometimes accused by the masters of applying relationship terms

Table 4. Contrasted Meanings of Relationship Terms

Jamaican English	Standard English meaning
Aunt	Stepmother
Cousin	A relative outside the immediate line of descent (uncle, aunt, nephew, niece, cousin); a familiar title or term of address
Father-in-law	Stepfather
Granny	Grandfather, grandchild
Mother-in-law	Stepmother
Nana	Grandmother, or respectful form of address to any old woman
Papa	Father, grandfather
Sister	Polite term of address to a woman
Stepson	Son-in-law

Source: Cassidy and Le Page 1980.

quite arbitrarily. M. G. Lewis, for example, wrote that among the slaves of Jamaica it was "almost tantamount to an affront to address by the name without affixing some term of relationship such as 'grannie' or 'uncle' or 'cousin'" (1834, p. 288). But Lewis made it clear that the slaves used such terms only "for honour" (p. 288), not intending any true genealogical relationship. In the slave testimony considered here, however, such use of relationship terminology was rare and confined to the most powerful and respected members of the slave community (Attetta Sara and Daddy Quamina), a finding which suggests that the practice may have been informal, for use among slaves but not before the master's court. Alternatively, such honorifics may have been confined to address between generations and rarely used in referential contexts, as in modern Guyana (Smith 1956, p. 162). But, bearing these various qualifications in mind, the comparison of slave- and master-derived relationship terminology does appear partially to vindicate reliance on the slave registration returns, at least for their definitions of slave relationships.

The principal deficiency of the slave registration returns is that they confine slave kin networks within the arbitrary boundaries of particular slaveholdings, the possibilities for ramified relationships increasing with the size of the holding (Higman 1978). This confinement was a direct product of the purpose of registration and did not mean a failure among the masters to recognize the existence of networks extending beyond the slaves who were their particular property. The perception by the masters of ramified relationship networks appeared most clearly when they wished to trace runaway slaves. For example, in 1807 John Hawkesworth of Bridgetown, Barbados, advertised that one of his slaves, a girl aged twelve to thirteen years ("just breasting"), had run away (*Barbados Mercury*, 31 January 1807). Hawkesworth showed a considerable awareness of her network of relations: her mother, he stated, was Flora Chomley, living by the Old Church Yard. Her mulatto sister, Harriot, belonged to Mr. J. P. Clarke; a black sister, Betsy Ann, to Thomas Donovan; and another black sister, Judey Bab, to Miss Tull. Her father was a carpenter, living at Malloney's Estate in Christ Church. An aunt, Bynoe, belonged to Mrs. Backhouse, at the Gully. Another Barbadian master listed a runaway's mother, sister, aunt, uncle, and "connexions" (*Barbados Mercury*, 18 February 1809); and another listed mother, father, three brothers, two uncles, and uncle's wife, all at different locations (*Barbados Mercury*, 25 February 1812). Yet another Barbadian advertised that a runaway had failed to return home, "though invited to do so through his connections" (*Barbados Mercury*, 27 January 1816). All of this evidence suggests a considerable awareness of slave relationship networks among the masters, and a willingness to take advantage of them when it suited.

Conclusions

The purpose of this essay has been to investigate the data available for the study of British West Indian slave kinship patterns from the perspective of the slaves themselves, and to compare these data with those produced by the masters. I have approached this general aim through a comparative analysis of relationship terminology, because this analysis provides the most readily comparable data. My object will have been served if the essay has shown that a systematic investigation of recorded slave speech would repay the effort involved, by expanding the understanding of the inner life of the slave community.

A few questions and speculations may be permitted, in advance of this definitive study of slave relationship terminology. In the first place, the case studies discussed here suggest a fairly limited relationship terminology within the slave community. This is a situation which contrasts strongly with that of African and Afro-Maroon societies (Price 1975, p. 164; Taylor 1951, p. 75). But it is a pattern which resembles quite closely that observed in modern West Indian relationship terminology, with its heavy emphasis on lineal and sibling relations. As Mintz and Price comment, this resemblance is suggestive of "continuities between the limited growth of kinship institutions in these more heavily industrialized, mobile plantation forces of, say, the eighteenth-century Caribbean, and current forms of social organization in these same areas" (1976, p. 39). Again, the relative emphasis on terms specific to females in the slave testimony may be seen as a reflection of the centrality of the mother-child relationship. But it is important to notice that the slaves' terminology was undoubtedly bilateral and that nongenealogical terms of respect were directed only at males.

The evidence discussed here derives chiefly from terms of reference. Terms of address might be more valuable guides to the informal organization of kinship, but in modern West Indian communities at least, the range of relationship terms employed is not significantly enlarged by using that category (Rodman 1971, p. 154). For the slave community, terms of address can be established only indirectly from more self-conscious contexts. More important, it is necessary to distinguish between levels of recognized relationships. In modern West Indian societies, it is common for communities to regard a whole village or even island as "family" (Smith 1973, p. 135; Wilson 1973, p. 146). Such references (like *mati*) suggest only a generalized solidarity or equality, based on territorial as much as genealogical grounds. Other, more specific, terms (such as *father, uncle, shipmate*) were used in slave communities not to intend any true genealogical relationship but to imply either equality or deference. In some cases, such references were extended even to the masters. At another level, relationship terms were employed by the slaves with genealogical correctness. Each of these three levels of reference is of importance, but it is necessary to distinguish them carefully if a true picture of the slave community's perception of its kinship system is to be established and related to the structural organization of domestic groups.

Acknowledgments

I am particularly grateful to Stanley Engerman and Raymond Smith for their comments on a draft of this essay.

Note

1. There were exceptions. Cassidy and Le Page (1980, p. 433) quote M. G. Lewis (1834, p. 240) on the boisterous farewell Lewis received at his Jamaican plantation in 1818: "In particular, the women called me by every endearing name they could think of. 'My son! my love! my husband! my father!' 'You no my massa, you my tata!' said one old woman." On the same page Cassidy and Le Page quote Barclay (1826): "Little negro children running to meet their master . . . and vociferating the endearing expression *Tata come, tata come*."

References

Anderson, Michael
1980   *Approaches to the History of the Western Family, 1500–1914.*
            London: Macmillan and Co.
Barbados Mercury.
1807–16   Bridgetown.
Barclay, Alexander
1826   *A Practical View of the Present State of Slavery in the West Indies.* London: Smith, Elder.
Beckwith, Martha
1929   *Black Roadways: A Study of Jamaican Folk Life.* Chapel Hill: University of North Carolina Press.
Bolland, O. Nigel
1977   *The Formation of a Colonial Society: Belize, from Conquest to Crown Colony.* Baltimore: Johns Hopkins University Press.

Brathwaite, Edward.
1971   *The Development of Creole Society in Jamaica: 1770–1820.* Oxford: Oxford University Press, Clarendon Press.
Cassidy, Frederic G. and Le Page, Robert B.
1980   *Dictionary of Jamaican English.* Cambridge: Cambridge University Press.
Colonial Office, 295/28, fol. 250
1812   Order in Council, 26 March. Public Record Office, London.
Craton, Michael
1978   *Searching for the Invisible Man: Slaves and Plantation Life in Jamaica.* Cambridge: Harvard University Press.
1979   "Changing Patterns of Slave Families in the British West Indies." *Journal of Interdisciplinary History* 10:1–35.
Goveia, Elsa V.
1965   *Slave Society in the British Leeward Islands at the End of the Eighteenth Century.* New Haven: Yale University Press.
Gudeman, Stephen
1979   "Herbert Gutman's *The Black Family in Slavery and Freedom, 1750–1925*: An Anthropologist's View." *Social Science History* 3:56–65.
Gutman, Herbert
1976   *The Black Family in Slavery and Freedom, 1750–1925.* New York: Pantheon Books.
Hanover. Slave Court
1819–29 Jamaica Archives, 1C/1. Spanish Town.
Higman, B. W.
1973   "Household Structure and Fertility on Jamaican Slave Plantations: A Nineteenth-Century Example." *Population Studies* 27:527–50.
1975   "The Slave Family and Household in the British West Indies, 1800–1834." *Journal of Interdisciplinary History* 6:261–87.
1977   "Methodological Problems in the Study of the Slave Family." *Annals of the New York Academy of Science* 292:591–96.
1978   "African and Creole Slave Family Patterns in Trinidad." *Journal of Family History* 3:163–80.
Jayawardena, Chandra
1963   *Conflict and Solidarity in a Guianese Plantation.* London: University of London.
Lewis, Matthew Gregory
1834   *Journal of a West India Proprietor, Kept During a Residence in the Island of Jamaica.* London.

Miers, Suzanne, and Kopytoff, Igor, eds.
1977   *Slavery in Africa: Historical and Anthropological Perspectives.* Madison: University of Wisconsin Press.
Mintz, Sydney W., and Price, Richard
1976   *An Anthropological Approach to the Afro-American Past: A Caribbean Perspective.* Philadelphia: Institute for the Study of Human Issues.
Needham, Rodney
1974   *Remarks and Inventions: Skeptical Essays about Kinship.* London: Tavistock Publications.
Parliamentary Papers. Great Britain (PP)
1823   (348) *Trial of a Slave in Berbice, for the Crime of Obeah and Murder.*
1824   (333) *Further Papers, . . . Respecting Insurrection of Slaves, Demerara.* Vol. 23.
1832   (721) *Report from Select Committee on the Extinction of Slavery throughout the British Dominions.* Vol. 20.
1836   (560) *Report from the Select Committee on Negro Apprenticeship in the Colonies.* Vol. 18.
Patterson, Orlando
1967   *The Sociology of Slavery: An Analysis of the Origins, Development and Structure of Negro Slave Society in Jamaica.* London: MacGibbon and Kee.
Port Royal. Summary Slave Trials
1819–34 Jamaica Archives, 2/19, Vol. 3. Spanish Town.
Price, Richard
1975   *Saramaka Social Structure.* Rio Piedras: Institute of Caribbean Studies.
Pringle, Thomas, ed.
1831   *The History of Mary Prince, a West Indian Slave, Related by Herself.* London: F. Westley and A. H. Davis.
Prosecutions Book of the Court of Criminal Justice, Berbice, British Guiana
1832–37 National Archives of Guyana. Georgetown.
Reckord, Mary
1968   "The Jamaica Slave Rebellion of 1831." *Past and Present* 40: 108–25.
Rodman, Hyman
1971   *Lower-Class Families: The Culture of Poverty in Negro Trinidad.* New York: Oxford University Press.
St. George. General Slave Court
1822–31 Jamaica Archives, 2/18/6. Spanish Town.

St. Georges. Magistrates Court
1821–23   Supreme Court Registry. St. Georges, Grenada.
Smith, Raymond T.
1956   *The Negro Family in British Guiana: Family Structure and Social Statuses in the Villages.* London: Routledge and Kegan Paul.
1973   "The Matrifocal Family." In *The Character of Kinship*, edited by Jack Goody, pp. 121–44. Cambridge: Cambridge University Press.
T. 71/378–79
1815   Slave Registration Returns, St. Lucia. Public Record Office, London.
T. 71/438
1819   Slave Registration Returns, Berbice. Public Record Office, London.
T. 71/501–3
1813   Slave Registration Returns, Trinidad. Public Record Office, London.
Taylor, Douglas MacRae
1951   *The Black Carib of British Honduras.* New York: Wenner-Gren Foundation for Anthropological Research.
Timehri: Journal of the Royal Agricultural and Commercial Society of British Guiana.
1882   1:298. Georgetown, British Guiana.
Watson, James L., ed.
1980   *Asian and African Systems of Slavery.* Berkeley and Los Angeles: University of California Press.
Wilson, Peter J.
1973   *Crab Antics: The Social Anthropology of English-speaking Negro Societies of the Caribbean.* New Haven: Yale University Press.
Yanagisako, Sylvia Junko
1979   "Family and Household: The Analysis of Domestic Groups." *Annual Review of Anthropology* 8:161–205.

Establishing Colonial Hierarchies

A Tribute to the Household: Domestic Economy and the *Encomienda* in Colonial Peru

Enrique Mayer

Introduction

This essay will attempt an ethnographic reconstruction of a group of households in rural sixteenth-century Peru—the reverse of "model building." I have tried to use John V. Murra's superb work on Andean political and socioeconomic structures as a model for gaining an understanding of the daily events and concerns of those people who were the participants and routine practitioners from whose actions and behavior the model was abstracted originally.

In the first part of the essay the point of view of a common peasant, Don Agostín Luna Capcha (who did exist and whose testimony is known), is expressed as he thinks about the testimony he is about to give during a *visita*. The administration and organization of his and his wife's time and efforts and the resources that he will need in order to produce or acquire the many items he is forced to give in tribute concern him. His domain is his home, and in order to administer it, he thinks about work. Because the economy is embedded in society and household matters, his thoughts about work lead him to consider domestic affairs and family and kinship matters, as well as village and regional concerns that affect him.

With the "substantive" (Polanyi's term) and meaningful insight gained about the operation of one such household, the essay moves on to analyze variations in types of households at this time and place, differences in household composition, and the processes that account for the differentiation. I rely on ethnographic analogy, because I conducted an ethnographical study of the village of Tangor (spelled "Tancor" at that time) in the Chaupiwaranga region, headwaters of the Huallaga River in the Huánuco region, the residence of Agostín Luna Capcha (Mayer 1974). I have tried to flesh out and fill in where the historical data are skimpy. My purpose is to illustrate, to give meaning to, and to make the reader understand a group of people who were struggling to survive in a remote period of time and in a distant land.

There is a second purpose to the essay. The events related here took place in 1562, only thirty years after the European invasion. It was a period of flux and change. By reversing the process of generalization—that is, by particularizing situations—we can focus on social change and the meaning of that change to these people. The Spanish institution of the *encomienda* (a royal grant of a group of Indians given to a Spaniard) provides the essay's context. The *encomienda* is that of Juan Sánchez Falcón, in the area of Huánuco, who was given the privilege of collecting tribute from the Indians granted to him. His *encomienda* included about four hundred households of Yacha (a small ethnic group) and *mitimae* (a group of Cuzco people brought by the Inca to man fortresses in conquered territory).

In order to collect the tribute, Sánchez Falcón was bound to the application of the old Andean institutionalized processes and mechanisms that the Inca and the local ethnic lords had been using to extract revenues from the agricultural peasant population. Despite the total crisis that the European presence wrought among these people, conditions existed for continuing past economic institutions. At the same time, the old procedures—when applied to benefit the new masters, whose purposes were very different—meant that these institutions were transformed in the way they functioned and were perceived. This essay tries to show these transformations and their implications for the peasant household. Because the institutions changed, their meaning altered; because the legitimacy of their operation was questioned, the whole system was challenged. The *curacas* (see Glossary, page 328) of the area commissioned Hernando Malquiriqui of Chacapampa to travel to Lima and appeal to the viceroy to have the tribute level lowered. And so the legal proceedings were initiated.

The judicial instrument the Spaniards used for these situations was the so-called *visita*. It was a house-to-house and village-by-village inspection made to determine the validity of claim and counterclaim and to make recommendations to the viceroy, who then would rule on the matter. John Murra republished this *visita*, with other pertinent documents and essays, in 1972 as volume 2 of the *Visita de la Provincia de León de Huánuco en 1562 (Ortiz de Zúñiga, 1967–72)*. The rich source material contained in this and other such bureaucratic documents published in the last decade has played an important role in shedding new light on precolonial society. Volume 2 of this *visita* constitutes my main data source and analytical focus.

The study of the *encomienda* is one instance in which we can look at the articulation of different but linked economic systems. The *encomendero* used ancient Andean institutions to obtain goods that he then sold through the extensive commercial networks that began to develop to support the mining and urban economy of the Spaniards. With respect to his subjects the *encomendero* was manipulating the strings of a peasant-based, precapitalist economy, whereas in his dealings with other Spaniards, he behaved as a capitalist merchant trying to sell his goods at the best going price in order to gain the highest monetary return. Historian Rolando Mellafe expresses this duality in this way:

> These documents are the result of three completely different currents; one derived from the forms and ways in which in pre-Hispanic times the Indians worked and complied with their tribute obligations; another current derived from the needs and exactions of their *encomenderos* and *caciques*; and the third current has to do with the exclusive relationship of the crown with the political economy of its territories and its protectionist efforts toward its Indian populations, expressed primarily in the crown's intervention in matters like fixing the tribute rate that the *encomenderos* were allowed to garner. [1967, p. 338; my translation]

The historical period that produced the *visita*, about midway between its inception and its deemphasis and eventual liquidation, is also the period in which the crown began more and more to interfere with and direct the fate of *encomiendas*. The Toledan reforms that began in 1570 radically altered Andean social institutions, changed tribute to a head tax to be paid to the crown (though this does not imply that for a long time the Indians were not paying tribute to both crown and *encomendero*), and through *reducciones*, drastically reordered the relations of the villagers. After the Toledan reforms many of the institutional continuities that had originated in Inca society were drastically cut off.

Saturday, 14 February 1562

After an all-night rain, the dawn was cloudy. The residents of Tancor went about their usual tasks, even though they were conscious of new and strange masters who spoke a different tongue, rode horses, and wore armor. War had come, and they had been defeated. The new Spanish city, León de Huánuco, was located in the big valley below. Indeed, many economic, social, and political relationships were now oriented toward the lowlands, whereas only thirty years before, their former masters had dominated them from the highlands.

As the sun began heating the valley, the mists drifted upward past the settlements of Wangrin and Wakan, and the lower parts of the narrow ravine of the Colpas River became visible from Tancor. Then they saw them: a party of horsemen followed by carriers on foot was slowly climbing the hill. It was the feared inspection party of the Spaniards and their own headmen, the *curacas*. By noon they would arrive in the village.

From the moment the inspection party was sighted, all normal activities in the village stopped. After a moment of panic, the rhythm of activities changed drastically. Many youths grabbed warm clothing, food, and coca and fled the village to hide in the mountains and in caves as far from pathways and settlements as possible. Women secreted food and possessions. While lighting the fires to cook the welcome meals, they nervously rehearsed the prayers and gestures that the new priests required them to adopt. Children were distributed among different households and instructed not to give their parents away. The old *quipucamayoc* limped into his hut to get his colored knotted strings and started fingering them, remembering, as each knot passed through his fingers, what had been committed to memory for each. At the last moment the Tancor headman, who had carefully noted the hurried rearrangements of normal family life into these newly constituted households, and who remembered to forget the existence of the youths who had vanished into thin air, noticed that no fodder had been prepared for the horses of the Spaniards. He also had omitted to warn the next village that it would be inspected after Tancor. Later he would regret this omission, for his kinsman, Don Antonio Pumachagua, headman of Guacor, was caught unprepared for the unexpected inspection. He bumbled his oral account and was publically whipped and punished because "he had lied in his testimony."[1] Once, long ago, the Tancor headman had also been tied and beaten with a stone on the back, that time by the Inca inspectors, when they caught him covering for youths who were evading the levy of able-bodied men for the *mit'a* tribute (p. 54).

By the time the visiting party—Iñigo Ortiz de Zúñiga, the *visitador*; Juan Sánchez Falcón, the *encomendero*; their legal representatives; the scribe; the Greek translator, Gaspar de Rodas; and their own *curaca*, Don Juan Chuchuyaure; as well as soldiers, priests, and carriers—had arrived, a false appearance of normalcy had been restored to the village (pp. 10–23). While the ceremonial greetings were taking place and the party was settling down, the *encomendero* looked around suspiciously. He was convinced that many of the people he owned by a grant from the king were hiding to escape being counted: their absence would diminish the tribute he would be able to collect. He would keep his eyes open to catch these shifty Indians, particularly that man he had seen before, the potter Agostín, whom he remembered as a potential troublemaker. Today's inspection would be thorough indeed.

Each additional able-bodied man counted would bolster the *encomen-*

dero's argument that these Indians could pay the original tribute level that he had been authorized to collect thirteen years ago and that the Indians were appealing as too heavy a burden. He needed to win the suit brought against him, as the tribute these Indians were giving him was necessary to enlarge his already-thriving business. It was, after all, worth the discomfort of traveling so far into the interior to ensure success.

The Testimony

Dijo llamarse Agostín Luna Capcha de treinta y cinco años (p. 82). (He says that he is called Agostín Luna Capcha, thirty-five years old.)

I was born in the time of the Inca, though, since my youth, I have heard and seen aspects of Christian and Spanish ways. Occasionally I have been taught the catechism, I have seen the use of money, escaped being shot when I participated in the big rebellion of Inca Illa Thupa twenty years ago that forced the Spaniards to withdraw from the fortress of Huánuco Pampa (Varallanos 1959, pp. 119–23; Murra 1975, p. 186), and watched how, with depressing regularity, their armies have looted the storehouses of the Inca, of the sacred *Huacas* (p. 57), and of the villages. There have been years of famine.

Y su mujer se llama Inés Quispe de treinta y cinco años (p. 82). (And his wife is called Inés Quispe, thirty-five years old.)

My wife was born and raised in Tancor. So was I, but because my forefathers were placed here in the time of the Inca as potters, I am a Caurino (p. 81). Even though I am not one of them, Inés's parents agreed to the marriage because her older and younger brothers had died, so that they had a shortage of hands to work the lands. Now we have children.

Tiene dos hijas y un hijo que se llama Catalina Chacara de cinco años, otro que se llama Felipe Guaya de cuatro años, otra que se llama Bárbora Vica de dos años (p. 82). (He has two daughters and one son called Catalina Chacara, five years old, Felipe Guaya, four years old, and Bárbora Vica, two years old.)

Dan marido y mujer una pieza de ropa de algodón y para ello les da su encomendero el algodón (p. 82). (Husband and wife give one piece of cotton cloth, and for this the encomendero supplies the cotton.)

Oh, this horrible business of weaving! It never ends. My wife's hands keep turning the spindle to make all the thread. The cotton that the *encomendero*'s henchmen give us is lousy quality—wild cotton, hard to take the pips out, difficult to spin and never enough. I am sure that he cheats us. Were it not for our neighbor, the tile maker, who has to go to town to pay his tribute in labor at the *encomendero*'s house (p. 80), and who barters chickens and *chuño* for extra cotton, we could never fulfill our quota (p. 58). Sometimes I am so tired that I fall asleep at the backstrap loom. But I have to keep weaving, for it is necessary to have enough clothing for myself and my family, quite apart from the beautiful piece that we burn as part of our sacrifice at the annual ceremony. I hope that the inspector does not find out that I actually weave more than I said, one for my own quota, the other for my father-in-law (p. 120), and the third for the *curaca*. Weaving never ends. What does the *encomendero* do with so much cloth? My ancestor once came back from serving the Inca in the army wearing a beautiful woven piece given him by the Inca (Murra 1975, p. 158). Now

Table 1. Hierarchy of Headmen from Agostín Luna Capcha's Point of View

Level	Headmen	
All Yacha (dual headmanship)	Don Antonio Guaynacapcha (second *curaca* of Yacha, with residence in Caure)	Don Juan Chuchuyaure (first *curaca* of Yacha, with residence in Paucar)
Pachaca (unit of 100 tributaries)	Don Antonio Guaynacapcha (several villages)	Don Gonzalo Tapia (several villages)
Chacapampa	Don Pablo Almerco (headman of a section of people in Caure, Natin, and Chacapampa)	Don Hernando Malquiriqui (headman of a section of people in Tunan, Quisicalla, and Chacapampa)
Tancor		Headman unknown
	Agostín Luna Capcha was part of a contingent of three families from Chacapampa.	Other Tancor residents were not recorded in this *visita*, for they were not *encomendado* to Juan Sánchez Falcón.

we all dress in rags and still keep weaving. The Spaniards must eat the cloth that we all weave.

Dijo que da seis tomines al año (p. 82). (He says that he gives six tomines per year.)
Six *tomines* in cash I am to give! Sometimes I give it and at others I don't. When I go to León to work as a water carrier or take things to sell I have money (p. 63); and when there is no other debt, I give it to Don Pablo Almerco, my headman (see Table 1), on account of my obligation of the six *tomines* (p. 129). Six *tomines*, almost one peso—so hard to gather the coins. When I cannot complete it, I have to make it up to him in other ways. When he asks me, I work for him, and when there is a feast, I bring food, and we help in cooking and serving; but of these and other things we do not keep account (p. 161). I hear it said that Don Pablo has many dealings and much money. He always says how he pays all our obligations in silver, so it must be that way. Who knows? I could go to the mines to earn more *tomines* (p. 120), but the work is too hard, so I will not go. This silver is an amazing thing. If I could only find out how to get more of it.

Y dijo que da una gallina al año (p. 82). (And he says that he gives one chicken per year.)
Chicken for the *encomendero*; chicken for getting cotton; chicken for food; chickens got killed today to feed the soldiers; chickens get into the maize; chickens make noise in the morning; chickens lay big eggs; chickens don't fly; chickens live in the house instead of in the wild; chickens eat leftovers; chickens shit all over my weavings; chickens scratch in the yard. Damned chickens!

Dijo este indio [que es] con los de Chacapampa (p. 82). (This Indian says that he is with those from Chacapampa.)
I am from the section of Caure people who live in Chacapampa, and that is where my labor tribute, my communal *mit'a*, is accounted for, and it is for my headman, Don Pablo, that I work, not for the one over here. Not that there is no land in Chacapampa (p. 81); with so many people dying off there is plenty of land around all over, but the maize in Tancor tastes so much better and produces more and is less risky. People here make fun of me and call me a *marka masha* (a brother-in-law of the village), because of my marriage, and make me do all the menial things in the ceremonies to drive home the point that I am an outsider. But, then, they trust me, too, because I am a little removed from them. They come individually and ask me favors and entrust to me important missions. By liv-

ing here, I avoid all those obligations from my own kinsmen, who would have to come here to ask me. I can also avoid the obligations of the Tancorinos, if I find this convenient, because they are not my kin, but my wife's. Still, I have to do so much weaving and work for my father-in-law that I often wonder if things would have been easier if I were living with my own people.

Y que con los de Chacapampa hace para el tributo chacaras de maíz y papas en las tierras de Chacapampa (p. 82). (And with those from Chacapampa he makes for tribute potato and maize fields in Chacapampa lands.)

Chacapampa is northwest of here, and they get the rains earlier than we do; so they are always a few weeks ahead of Tancor in producing these foods. I have to find out when the headman and the community decide to start the *chacmeo*, the breaking of the ground with our footplows, and when I know the day, I go one or two days in advance to stay with my kinsmen. I bring the food gifts from here, since they like the squashes and *numia* beans that grow so well in this area.

When I arrive in Chacapampa, I visit my *curaca*, who comes down from Caure for the ceremony, and it is for it that I usually have my piece of fine cloth ready for him so that he can use it for the *chacra jitay* ceremony (see Mayer 1972, pp. 360–61, for a contemporary version of the ceremony, and Mayer 1979 and Mayer and Fonseca 1979 for a description of how the sectorial fallow system works today). He wears his new cloth during the ceremony, and he looks so dignified when he sits with the village elders chewing coca and deliberating which sector of land should be assigned for this year's potato crop. Each year a new sector as big as half a hillside is opened and left to begin its fallow for several years. Once they decide on which sector to work, Don Pablo and the elders of the community set aside land for the *encomendero*'s tribute, for the church tithes, for themselves, and for the people too old to work it themselves. After that he assigns land to all the families in the community for their food. Although I am present, they do not give me land to work, because I have enough in Tancor. Then we make up the teams that will work and, praying and dancing, we begin to work the lands for tribute, for the church, and for the *curaca*, as well as for the elderly. There is music and drink and food.

The teams of plowmen race each other to see who can finish their assigned task of breaking the ground of a whole field with their footplows first. The women encourage us with songs and drink. When we have finished our section, we get another one assigned. At the end of the day the teams that have worked the most sections are honored and the others taunted. Chacapampa's way of working is different from how they do it in

Tancor, because there, once you finish your assigned section, you have completed your task for the day and can rest. It takes more days to get the work done in Tancor. That is why my own kinsmen say that Tancor people are lazy. Usually we complete all the plowing of the higher-lying (*jalka*) and lower-lying (*kichwa*) fields in two days (see Fonseca 1972, pp. 315–38, for a description of the ethnoecology of the area and its significance in agricultural activities). Starting high, we finish working near the village settlements.

After that I return to Tancor while the people of Chacapampa continue helping each other break the ground of their individually allotted fields. This is, of course, the time I use to work on my wife's assigned fields in Tancor, after the Tancor people have had their own land-distribution ceremony.

When the rainy season stops and the dry season has passed and the new rainy season is about to begin again, it is time for me to go back to Chacapampa to plow the furrows and plant the tubers. And when the people in Chacapampa have finished planting their own fields, I go back, because it is time to start to plant maize for tribute. That feast is even nicer than the *chacra jitay* for potatoes. We eat corn foods, and there is so much *chicha* distributed that we all get drunk. When that is finished, I have to come back to Tancor to plow and sow my father-in-law's field and carry him home after the day's work, because he is so happy that he has had his corn planted (Juan Ossio [personal communication] observed this carrying of a father-in-law in contemporary Andamarca).

When I was a young man and unmarried, I had to spend a lot of time keeping the fields clear of birds. All of us still have obligations to fulfill beyond the actual plowing and planting (p. 78). But now that I live in Tancor, so far, I have been exempt from these time-consuming tasks. At least, Don Pablo has not yet approached me for any of these tasks, which I'd have to do for a whole year in Chacapampa, and I do not think that he will. In Tancor perhaps I will have to accept one of these tasks, since this is where I live.

So I return to Chacapampa quite often, after planting maize, to hill the potatoes and after that to weed and cultivate the corn, and then comes the second hilling of the potatoes, of the *ocas* and *mashuas* and *ollucos* (*oca* is *Oxalis tuberosa*; *mashua* is *Trapeolum tuberosum*; and *olluco* is *Ullucu tuberosum*, the three complementary and important Andean tubers), and so on until harvest time. Chacapampa is where I pay my tribute obligations together with my Chacapampa people.

De [estas tierras de maíz y papas] pagan lo que les cabe de tributo (p. 82). (From these lands they pay what they have to for tribute.)

There are two different groups (*parcialidades*) of people living in Chacapampa: those who pay their tribute to Gonzalo Tapia (pp. 123–28), and we, who belong to Pablo Almerco, who lives in Caure. We give seven *fanegas* of maize (though four of them he commuted for extra pieces of cloth) and we give two *fanegas* of potatoes, all out of our communal work (p. 128). What is left over we take to sell at the mines of Corco and the *tambo* of Chuquiguamisca and other places. Some of the surplus also goes for *camarico* ("something done in favor of he who is absent in *mit'a* obligation, contribution of food for those who could not cultivate, gifts" [Murra and Adorno 1980, p. 1083]) of the *encomendero*'s servants (p. 128).

The tribute has to be delivered in Huánuco at the *encomendero*'s house (p. 129). Because our llamas have been killed in all the wars, every year we have to carry more and more of the loads on our backs. This is the hardest part of our tribute work. Carrying our own food makes the task twice as hard. My parents tell me that when they carried loads for the Inca, along the way to Quito and Cuzco (p. 55) they were fed by him. It takes four to five days to get the caravan bearers from here to Huánuco. When we get there we are very tired.

Dijo que se ocupa con los de Chacapampa dos semanas en las chacaras de Pitomama de su encomendero (p. 82). (He says that he occupies himself with the Chacapampa people two weeks in the fields of Pitomama that are his encomendero's.)

These maize fields of the *encomendero* are one league from Huánuco, and all of Don Pablo Almerco's people from Caure and Chacapampa as well as Gonzalo Tapia's people from Chacapampa are responsible for the production of six *fanegas* of maize (a *fanega* here is a unit of land and not a measured volume of products, as above). I have to go and plant and harvest with the married adult men and spend two weeks and four days at it (p. 129), and the old men who can still walk, women, and boys and girls from Chacapampa and Caure go to weed and cultivate the fields, and that takes two weeks (p. 129). The poor people of Gonzalo hate going there because it takes so much time, and they have to weave even more than we do (p. 124)! That man Juan Sánchez Falcón not only gets maize and potatoes from our own communal fields, but also from his lands that we have to work.

Dijo que le cabe dos meses al año de servir con los de Chacapampa a su encomendero en Huánuco en traer leña y yerba y aderezar la cequia del molino y algunas paredes cuando se lo manda (p. 82). (He says that he is obligated to serve for two months with the people of Chacapampa at the encomendero's in Huánuco, bringing firewood and fodder and clean-

ing the canal of the water mill and repairing some walls when he is ordered to do so.)

For two months I have to be his servant in his house! As long as I can plan ahead when it is that I have to go, it is all right. But when I am ordered to go without warning, then problems arise. My fields get neglected, I fall behind in my weaving, and I do not find the time to work as a water carrier. For me it is most convenient to go after the harvests here in Tancor and Chacapampa, but so far I have had to go at all other times and at short notice. When we are in Huánuco we are treated like prisoners. They lock us up at night and feed us little, so that actually we have to bring some of our own food. At least lately, the *encomendero's mayordomo* has started giving us a little bit of coca. His horses, mules, and cows eat so much grass, and we have to carry it on our backs from far away.

Y que no se lo paga el encomendero y que no sabe si es obligado a ello o no (p. 82). (And that his encomendero *does not pay him and he does not know whether he is obligated to do so according to the tribute assessment or not.)*

It is not fair! When I work in Huánuco as a water carrier I get paid, and when I work in his mansion carrying grass I do not get paid! . . . I do as I am told.[2]

Y dijo que se ocupa cinco meses en todo lo que trabaja y hace para el tributo no entendiendo otra cosa (p. 82). (And he says that it takes him five months to do all that he works and makes for tribute without seeing to other things.)

Sure! I spend almost half a year working for the *encomendero*, although it seems to me that it is all the time. Take spinning. My wife and I spin all the time, whenever our hands are free. In this way it takes two months to spin the raw cotton into yarn and another ten days to respin it after it has been dyed. Two days to dye it, if you do not count all the time spent in collecting the firewood necessary to boil the dye. Then one day to make the warp. Ten days to weave, if I have time to do it continuously. Usually I have to do it on three or four separate occasions, because I have to do this and that in the village, or in Chacapampa, or in Huánuco, before finishing it. Time spent on actually weaving and preparing the materials is one thing; the time elapsed from the beginning of the process to the end is another.

Working in Chacapampa, counting the days coming and going, comes to another month to get the tribute crops produced (two days *chacmeo*, two days hilling and likewise for second hilling, two for harvest, and two for carrying the crops from the fields to the village makes about ten days).

Calculate the same time for the maize crop, and that makes twenty days. Then there are eight days of carrying the crops to the *encomendero*'s house and coming back. Two months of *mit'a* at the *encomendero*'s, two weeks at the Pitomama fields. Who calculates the time it takes to earn the *tomines*? Even without this, it comes to more than five months!

But this is really a stupid way to ask the question! I spend about half of my waking time working for the *encomendero*, and he gets much more out of all the work than I myself get when I work the other half for my own things. He can use our different kinds of labor power in different ways. He can disperse us and make us work at home during part of the day at spinning or weaving while we are technically "off duty" to look after our own crops and affairs. He even benefits from our leftover food by making us give him chicken. On the other hand, he can pool all our separate household labor capabilities to work one large field in Chacapampa per year for potatoes and one corn field. He gains even more from us by rotating all of Pablo Almerco's and Gonzalo Tapia's people in Pitomama to get a constant supply of workers for his fields. Though I go to his house only for two months, he has servants all year round. The cotton that his other Indians grow in Huánuco (p. 228) he gives back to us to spin and weave into cloth, and because he gives us the cotton, we have to give more cloth (p. 159). We work the fields of his tile makers, herders, and so on, when they are too busy to do so for themselves. Throughout the year we work in combination on our own subsistence and on the tribute tasks. This way, any task that would take us half the time, because we need less, now fills our days and weeks and tires us out. Every task we do gets intensified through tribute.

Y que lo hace descansadamente cuando no le dan prisa para la ropa, y cuando se la dan, aún no puede hacer su vestido ni el de su mujer ni de sus hijos (p. 82). (And that he does it at his own restful pace when they do not press him for the cloth, and when they do, he does not have the time to make his own clothing nor that of his wife or his children.)

It really is a question of timing and how I can distribute my time. If the *encomendero* wants his cloth and wants me to serve in his house in Huánuco during the rainy season, when I am supposed to look after my fields, then it is much harder to comply. On the other hand, if he lets me assign my own work in such a way that all the tasks get evenly distributed throughout the year, then the tax burden is more manageable for me and my wife.

For instance, when we work our fields, she has to cook for all the people coming to the work party. That means that all the ingredients have to be prepared well in advance, the firewood and the helpers she needs; and if there is going to be *chicha*, one really has to calculate weeks ahead. I have to go and collect the firewood; it has to dry; and then the preparations take a week in order for the corn to germinate and the *chicha* to ferment properly. So even if the actual plowing only takes a day or two, if I am not able to be busy those days before my field gets plowed, it is a disaster. To calculate only two days to plow is wrong, anyway, even if one would disregard the extra days of preparation. For every helper who comes to work in my field, I have to return the working day in full. And until they ask me, I have to be living in the village during the whole plowing season waiting, even though I am not actually working the whole extent of the season.

When outsiders begin organizing our lives, it costs us much more to provide the same amount of tribute. This *encomendero* is so demanding that we have to comply, and, out of fear of punishment, we tend to think that his work is more important. What should be more important—our own subsistence—becomes relegated to second priority until we have completed our obligations. By the time we have done so, we are tired, our resources are exhausted, and so we tend to cut down and skimp in the work implied in the satisfaction of our needs. The drudgery of working for our own needs is thus increased.

Since the coming of the *encomendero*, our resources have changed, but the *tasa* (the level and specifications of our obligations) has remained the same. The fact that the people are fewer than before and more diseased (p. 86) means that fewer households have to work harder to maintain the same production levels. But it is not only that; other kinds of resources have also changed. For instance, in Caure there is no cotton; it is too cold for it to grow. Before the Spaniards came, the Caure people had cotton lands in the lowlands, which they have now lost, so now the *encomendero* supplies the cotton, and because of that, the levy of woven cloth doubles (p. 123). The *mitimaes* of Ananpillao have their own cotton fields, so they give fewer pieces of cloth (these transplanted populations, called *mitma* under the Incas, came from Canta, Cajatambo, Urcos de Atapillao, and Checras in the present-day Department of Lima, put there by the Inca "to guard a house where he used to sleep when he came to conquer these lands" [p. 239]). If you calculate the work in producing the cotton, it still comes to less than the extra weaving that we have to do (p. 239).

Because our resources are changing, and the *encomendero*'s tastes are different, matters get more complicated. We Caure people have so much pasture; therefore we are supposed to give six sheep per year to the *encomendero* for each of the important Catholic festivals that they celebrate. But we have not had too much luck in raising the Castilian sheep, and there are too few of them in the pastures. So instead, Caure people now give eighteen and one-half pieces of cloth, with the *encomendero* supplying the cotton (p. 159). Just imagine the increase of work that all that extra weaving implies for us.

Substitutions in the items of our *tasa* can work in our favor, too. For example, in Quiu, the village on the other side of the valley, there is a famous rebellious old man who still is not a Christian, Alonso Acachagua, who spins five extra balls of *cabuya* string in lieu of the two pesos he is supposed to pay (p. 76). Don Juan Chuchuyaure, the head *curaca* of all of us Yachas, is asking the *encomendero* to substitute a cash payment for the heavy burden of supplying maize (p. 57). There is internal substitution, too. When I get sick and cannot work for a long time, I talk to my *curaca*, and he may excuse me, but then he has to shift my obligation to other families, since it is clear that the *encomendero* will have no mercy on me or on the *curaca* who is responsible for the delivery of the whole amount (p. 56), and he does not care how the items are collected among ourselves.

There is inequality in the distribution of work, too. My neighbor, the tile maker, is an *indio oficial*, a full-time specialist. He has to make tiles for the *encomendero* all year round, because in the time of the Inca, we were the potters placed here because of the clay. Now the old man has finished working for the *encomendero* and is in Tancor, but he has left his son, who has learned the trade, as his replacement. The old man used to come to Tancor two months in the year to plant his own fields (p. 81). At times he was too busy even to spare time for that, and Don Pablo had fields worked for him in Chacapampa by all of us. Although the old man has less independence, he has narrower and more specialized tasks to fulfill at which he spends more time than we do. Juan Perico Quispecoro is completely exempt from tribute. He is the *yanacona* of Antonio Guaynacapcha, the headman of the Yachas (p. 131), yet he too weaves, but the cloth is for his headman and not for tribute.

Don Juan and his wife in Chacapampa are both ancient and they have finished with their tribute obligations; they are too old. Nevertheless, their sick daughter spins enough thread for one *anaco*, which other people then weave (p. 130). For me, even if the *tasa* remains the same, the difficulty of producing my share will change over time. In a few years my children will be bigger, and they can then work and help in the fields and house. For my wife the burden will be easier, since she will have more free time once the children stop needing her, although for me it will mean bigger *chacaras* to feed their increased appetites. This extra help, however, has to be counterbalanced with the increased obligations that I will have to meet. My parents-in-law are getting older, and I will have to increase my contributions to them, and there is no guarantee that Pablo Almerco, aware of how my children are growing, will not slap additional contributions on me.

Although our share of the burden is more or less equitably distributed, adjusted by Don Pablo according to our ability to produce, the actual burden of how much it costs us to produce the tribute depends very much on how our own needs vary throughout the year and throughout our lives, and according to our ages and needs and our obligations to our kinsmen. Since the tribute is fixed, it is our own needs that do not get satisfied when the burden of work gets too much.[3]

Dijo que no sabe cuanto le cabe al dicho pueblo de Chacapampa en lo del tributo, mas de que hace lo que su principal le reparte y no le da cuenta del repartimiento que entre ellos se hace de lo que le cabe al dicho pueblo (p. 82). (He says that he does not know what Chacapampa's share in the tribute is, that he only does what he is assigned by his headman, who does not tell him of the distribution of work that is done by them or what is due for that village.)

All I hear from Don Pablo and Don Juan is that we have to give more and more. They never cease haranguing us to keep weaving; they nag us for *tomines* and exhort us to work all the time. Whenever I deliver the tribute to Don Pablo, he starts worrying out loud about the many items he has to collect and how slow and unwilling the people are in giving the tribute. He dislikes doing such an unpopular thing. He mumbles to me in confidence that often, when people have not complied and he is pressed by Don Juan, he makes up the difference from his very own stores and supplies. But then the headman and the *curacas* have more and can count on all the help from us. Since the *encomendero* came, there have been so many substitutions, changes, arrangements, and secret agreements between the *curacas* and the *encomenderos* that nobody knows anymore if what the *curacas* collect from us is equal to what they are supposed to. My neighbor here, he says that the *curacas* are enriching themselves at our expense. This may be so, but on the other hand, Don Pablo has never refused to help me when I needed him. I know nothing.

Y dijo que tiene ciertos andenes en que hace sus chacaras para sus sementeras que le bastan para él y sus hijos (p. 82). (And he says that he has certain terraces on which he makes his own fields, which are enough for him and his children.)

There is land everywhere, because our people are diminishing very quickly, and also because the Inca is gone and does not force us to produce food here in the villages for his *tambos* and storehouses. All those beautiful terraces built by our ancestors are beginning to decay, and nobody makes an effort to maintain them the way they used to. People have lost respect for the land. Who has the time!

Y tiene algunas por sembrar (p. 82). (And he still has some that have to be planted.)
Since I am an outsider in Tancor, my wife's father and his brothers tend to ask me first to help them plow their fields. They will return the work when I plow mine. Thus it is my fields that usually get worked last, for it is not seemly that I initiate the exchange and get them to work for me first. But once I have worked on their fields, they will come and return the work to me. That is why I have not finished yet. I have to calculate the day that it will be convenient to all of them to plow my field and then go and ask them to return the help they owe me. I hope that the rains hold up for a few more weeks so that my allotted fields will be nice and soft for the day of plowing.

Y que no tiene chacaras en Chacapampa (p. 82). (And that he does not have fields in Chacapampa.)
How can I? As it is, I have to split myself into too many parts and tend to the fields there and here at the same time. If I could, there would be advantages to that, though, since that reduces the risks of crop failure, and as they harvest earlier than we do here, I would be able to get fresh food earlier. But it can't be done.

Y que allí hay muchas donde si se pasase tendrá las que el cacique le diere (p. 82). (And that there are many there, and were he to move there, he would have those his headman would allot to him.)
Every year they distribute potato land, and they give maize land for longer periods, because one can repeat that crop for many years without rotation. Should I want it, all I have to do is ask for it, because my *ayllu* is there and it is *ayllu* land, and my *curaca* guarantees that as a member I have the right to it. I also have a right to land in Chacapampa, because I go and work on my tribute quota in their communal fields and I go to Pitomama with all my *allumasi* (*ayllu* mates) to work on the *mit'a*. So, should I ask for land in Chacapampa, they would have to allot me my share.

Y dijo que no tiene ganado alguno (pp. 82–83). (And he says that he has no kinds of domestic animals.)
The land here is too steep and too rough to keep animals. Moreover, I do not have the extra family members at the right age to spend the time

herding them. Nor do I have animals because I am not sure the Tancorinos would give me grazing rights, seeing that I am but an outsider.

Ni se quejó ninguna cosa de todas las que les fueron preguntadas como a los demás (p. 83). (Nor does he complain about anything that he was asked about.)
Bah!

Household Types

Agostín Luna Capcha's house was number 33 on the *visitador*'s list. Thanks to the work of archaeologist Ramiro Matos (1972, pp. 367–82), we can picture a house similar to his in 1562. Matos surveyed the village of Wakan, within the *visita* territory and half an hour's walk from contemporary Tangor. Entrance to a house was gained through a narrow path that crossed the flat roofs of several higher-lying neighboring houses, onto a frontal patio where crops were sorted and dried in the sun. These crops were ultimately stored in an underground dug-out place that was carefully lined with stones and covered and kept clean by one of the flagstones that made up the patio floor. The patio was where many hours were spent spinning and weaving, as well as completing most of the other daily household tasks, because it was sunny and warm. The structure was shaped like an irregular square on the outside and built of thick, flat, fieldstones interspersed with mud; inside, the two or four rooms were small and confined, serving as storage places for food, implements, clothing, and raw materials, as well as sleeping quarters. One of them was the smoke-filled kitchen, where the women cooked squatting near the stove. They fed the stove with twigs and used clay cooking pots and jars to boil and toast. Guinea pigs scuttled about feeding on potato peel and other food scraps and nesting in the cracks of the walls. All cooking utensils and ingredients were within easy reach from the sitting position. On the walls of other rooms were niches—some square, others irregularly shaped—filled with small things like coca bundles and the skulls and bones of Agostín's wife's ancestors, removed long ago from the central burial place to serve as a kind of protective shrine.

The majority of Yacha households consisted of a husband-wife team (who headed the household) and their children. There were a few households with three generations, a situation that would result when either spouse's widowed father or mother joined the new group after being left quite alone at the death of the partner. Other such extended units could include spouses' unmarried brothers or sisters, or even a sister with children of her own. There were rare instances of unrelated children being reared in some households (p. 130). In some cases the head of the household was absent on *mit'a* duty, herding, trading for cotton in Huánuco, or working in the mines (pp. 112, 126, 122, 119).

In contemporary village ideology the marriage bond forms the basis of a new and independent household (Mayer 1977), and we can assume that this was the case in *visita* times and before (Murra 1956, p. 169) and that it was an ideal worth striving for but not very easily achieved. The high number of incomplete nuclear families (in a few cases, even of orphans) is a clear indication of the difficult times the Yacha were having in reaching or sustaining this ideal. The prevalence of incomplete nuclear families must also imply that many of these people from broken homes found it hard to seek refuge with kinsmen and incorporate themselves as part of these other households and thus had to struggle alone.

Finally, I must mention the infrequent situations (e.g., pp. 92, 140, 203, 204) in which the *visitador* separated joint households into two distinct tribute units. In these cases an elderly couple lived with their growing children, one of whom (usually the son) was married and bringing up his own children in the same household. Yet tribute was assessed separately, counting the new couple as another unit with its own cloth, money, and *mit'a* obligations. One such example (p. 219) was an uxorilocal marriage in which an outsider settled in with a local family and married the daughter.

The natural cycle of marriage-based domestic groups can account for these variations in household composition, where the process of becoming independent households is plainly under way but not complete, and where the cycle has run its course and the remnants of the original, older households attach themselves to those of their offspring (Goody 1966; Lambert 1977).

We can also gain some insight into marriage patterns by examining the records of the *visita*. Many women in these houses are listed variously as *mancebas* (mistresses or concubines), *mujeres de servicio* (servant women), *viudas* (widows), and *solteras* (single women). Murra (1972, pp. 389–90), Hadden (1967), and Mayer (1972, p. 49) suggest that for at least some of the *mancebas* and *mujeres de servicio*, the existence of polygynous households is indicated.

There are two persistent concerns in the use of these terms in the *visita* that need clarification. If the couple has not had the Christian marriage sacrament, even the sole wife is called the man's *manceba*. When there is more than one "wife," neither relationship sanctified by the sacrament, both are *mancebas*. If there is more than one wife, and one is "properly" married, the others are relegated to the *de servicio* or *manceba* categories. Little is known about the marriage rites of the Yacha at that time, yet one old man insisted loudly enough for the scribe to record that one such *amancebado* marriage was *a su ley* (according to his laws) (p. 88).

The *visitador* was instructed to find out about marriage customs from the *caciques*, but they answered evasively and stressed only the point of Inca legitimation of marriage, rather than describing the local customs connected to the kinship system, as Don Francisco Coñapariguana explains: "The Inca governor they had would come once a year and in the plaza of each village the young men and women would gather. Then the Inca official would give each man the woman he wanted for a wife. He would tell him to treat her well, and serve her well. To her he would say the same and that she should serve her husband. And so they became husband and wife. And all those born out of that union were held to be legitimate and could inherit. And that this could only be done by the aforementioned Inca and not by the *caciques* nor anyone else" (p. 31).

Yet the answer is evasive in part, because it is unlikely that the local kinsmen, parents of bride and groom, and such considerations as status, wealth, and prescriptive or proscriptive marriage rules did not play an important part in the marriage process, as they are known to do in other societies. What Don Francisco's answer implied is that upon marriage a man became a full *tributario*, that the ceremony of giving official blessing to the marriage was probably also part of the census-taking procedure (Mayer 1972) duly recorded in the *quipu*, and that at this time the newly established tribute unit would get its duties assigned: perhaps the man would be required to join the army or become a member of a carrier team, or perhaps the man's *mit'a* duties—tasks in which he was accompanied by his wife—would be assigned (Murra 1956, p. 172). The Inca were interested not so much in legitimating marriages as in using such normal social processes to regulate and administer their revenue-gathering system (Murra 1956, p. 170). Insofar as Inca interests were served by regulating marriages, we can say that the tribute system had a hand in the regulation of household composition and formation.

Many of these procedures remained in force legally in the *visita*, for it was the married Indian who counted as the true *tributario* on whom the *tasa* was assessed (p. 265). Even today, it is customary in Andean marriage processes for the couple to go through several ceremonies spread out over a number of years, each succeeding ceremony being more binding and definitive concerning the rights and obligations of the spouses and their respective kin than the preceding one. One of these steps, usually late in the marriage, is the civil and religious wedding, in which state and church legitimize the union long after the community and the kinsmen have done so (Carter 1977; Isbell 1977).

The new Christian restrictions on polygamy caused the *curacas* many headaches in 1562. Out of the nineteen village headmen and *cacique principal* households, seven were able to appear monogamous at the time of the *visita*. Don Andrés Auquilliqui declared in his household, in addition to his wife, one *india de servicio* who "is single. And if this woman would want to marry, he would not object. He was given this girl by his *cacique* Don Francisco Coñapariguana and he has no *concierto* [intercourse?] with her" (p. 39). Three other headmen declared that they were *amancebados* with only one wife.

The cases of plural marriages are more complex yet. There were three headmen with two wives, three with three, one with four, and one with five wives. In addition, one was an accidental case of monogamy, because one of two wives had died (p. 149). *Mitimae* headman of Xigual, Juan Condor Guaya, was under pressure from both Andean and Spanish systems. He said that he had "two *indias de servicio* and that he [was] not married [by church] with either"; one of them was given to him by his *cacique* (Coñapariguana) and the other by the *cacique* Canagua for a wife (*por mujer*) (Canagua was the *curaca* in charge of the *mitimaes* at the time of the conquest and was succeeded by Coñapariguana because Canagua's son was too young to rule [p. 27]). He had not married the second yet because of the steadfast implacability of the priest (p. 45)! We can surmise that priestly rancor was due to Condor Guaya's refusal to get rid of the other. We can only guess whether the last part of his statement—"that he will marry her when the priest comes" (p. 45)—indicated that he was capitulating.

The process of getting rid of what for the Indians were very legitimate wives has a legal dimension revealed in the document and a practical aspect that remains more obscure. Juan Chuchuyaure had children by his four wives (aged fifty, twenty-five, twenty-four, and thirty-five). In the house-to-house survey, the first woman is listed as *su mujer*, the second as *india de servicio*, and the third and fourth as *mancebas*. Who decided to list them this way? Were the *curaca*'s words arbitrarily translated? In his previous testimony under oath in Huánuco, Chuchuyaure had said that he "had three *indias de servicio* available for marriage" (p. 61).

Antonio Guaynacapcha was also under pressure. In his house list there appeared one wife, one *manceba*, and one *india de servicio* (p. 168). In Huánuco he had at first listed two *indias de servicio*. Then he was questioned about having children by them, and he modified his testimony to say that, in addition to his wife, there were three *indias*, and that one of the *de servicio* had borne his children (p. 65). Clearly, European distinctions do not fit the Andean situation.

That some of these women were in fact of a kind of servant status can be gleaned from Cristóbal Contochi's case. Under priestly pressure he wanted to marry one woman (p. 180). Another *manceba* had borne him two daughters. A third was listed twice, once as his *manceba* and once as the wife of his servant (a young man reared in his household). If this is another example of headman "generosity," by which the headman could "give" wives to people of lower status than himself (as seen in Coñapariguana's case), this document has revealed an interesting new feature of such giving (Murra 1975, pp. 29–30, 175–76).

The person most clearly in a position fully to utilize these marriage customs to his advantage was Don Francisco Coñapariguana himself. He listed one wife and three *indias de servicio*, about whom he said that one was an invalid, that the others were living in his *chacaras* (fields), and that he supplied them with salt, *ají* (spicy peppers), and a house (p. 32). When his house got inspected, it turned out that he had children by two of the *indias de servicio*, as well as a son by one whom he had once had but who had since "fled." He had nine children with whom to forge future marriage alliances. In addition, he was an active recruiter of *yanaconas*, some of whom may have been part of his actual household, while the rest were separate but attached to households in the locality; the *yanaconas* exploited products in distant, ecologically favorable zones (Murra 1975, pp. 62–74). All of this activity made his residence and his productive activities the largest economic unit, with thirty-two people declared, of whom eighteen were adult men and women (pp. 199–200). It was no small achievement!

It seems that in a few cases male servants were reared from childhood on in the headman's household. In these situations, the *visita* recorded the name and age and such statements as "This young man is not from here" (p. 33), or noted that they were orphans or reared for the "love of God" (pp. 180, 173). Unattached relatives who could be entrusted with managerial affairs, such as nephews, aunts, and foster mothers, swelled the productive and administrative capacity of these headman households also. That such a household required a greater physical space and greater storage capacity is amply demonstrated by Craig Morris's (1967, 1972) archaeological excavations of one such house, in which large *chicha*-making pottery vessels seemed to form the greatest quantity of ceramic remains.

Curaca households, larger and better endowed, had a greater productive capacity and the ability to provide a greater variety of goods for themselves. This capacity allowed headmen to play a crucial role in the local politico-economic structure, as classic "big men." In exchange for "generous" gifts—the distribution of luxuries, feasting, open hospitality and aid for needy people—a *curaca* household could count on services such as having houses built and roofs thatched or fields worked and harvested when these services were "requested" (pp. 28, 35, 36). The capacity to mobilize resources and to distribute benefactions accounts for differences in leadership and power between such high-ranking *curacas* as Juan Chuchuyaure, lord over two hundred households, and Pablo Almerco, village headman of sections of three villages. That many *curacas* used the position to enrich themselves was a common accusation, given the shifts in the economy under the Spaniards (Spalding 1974).

In contrast, commoner houses were smaller, in number of members as well as in structure. Only 26 of the 436 commoner households—that is, about 5 percent—were polygynous, and the *visita* consistently recorded the women in them as *mancebas*. Missionary pressure produced strange responses, such as the case of the man who discarded his older wife, "who used to be his *manceba* but now is only in his house," in order to keep in official marriage the second, much younger woman (p. 145). As Murra points out, in enough cases to merit further looking into, these are *yanacona* families attached to some *principal* (1975, p. 238), able to evade tribute, Christianization, and other pressures caused by *curaca* protection, protection that worked to the advantage of both parties (Murra 1967, p. 390). The other households reported the children of their secondary wives without problem.

The Burden of Tribute

In Inca times, says Don Juan Chuchuyaure to the *visitador*, the burden of tribute was easier on his people because there were more people than now, because each tribute-paying family was responsible for a fixed amount to be delivered yearly, and because the very old did not work (p. 56). Moreover, the assessment then was made "according to the houses they had, not as it is now, when we have to deliver a fixed quantity per year, divided (*repartido*) amongst those people available" (p. 56). The change from a sliding scale of tribute according to the number of extant households to a fixed quantity that was divided among a diminishing tax base implied an increased burden of tribute on every household.

This increased burden fell unequally on the existing households. One-third of the households did not pay tribute, and thus the burden was shifted onto the remaining two-thirds, of which approximately another third were in some way or another incapacitated or diminished in their ability to contribute fully. There were three categories of exceptions from tribute: status reasons (10 percent of all households), permanent retainership to *curacas* or *encomenderos* (14 percent), and physical incapacity (22 percent).

Within the category of status exemptions, the headmen obviously came first. If we go over their testimony carefully, however, it becomes clear that there were gradations and hierarchies (see p. 34). Don Juan Chuchuyaure (p. 109) and Antonio Guaynacapcha (p. 168), the two "dual" *caciques principales* of the Yacha, and their colleagues of the *mitimae* groups (pp. 189, 199), were clearly exempt, despite having the largest and best-endowed households. Lower-ranking subdivisional headmen, such as Pablo Almerco (p. 160), said that they contributed a full quota of textiles and money and that they organized the production of the *menudencias* (little items of the list), such as cinches and tablecloths. In addition, they accompanied their people to the *mit'a* fields nearby and to Huánuco in order to "command them" (p. 211).

The second group of exempt households was the *forasteros* (members of other ethnic groups). In the Inca system, the exemption of an outsider from the *quipu* list of one group would make sense, because that person would be fully accounted for, together with the reason for his being placed where he was and the kind of contribution that he made, in the *quipu* of his own group; otherwise, such people would be counted twice. In many cases this system was still functioning, as when *forastero* units were on record as contributing with their own group (p. 174). In one house in Quiu the tribute obligations were split between two *encomenderos* (p. 79). But by 1562 many *forasteros* became displaced and, until the *visita*, were able to slip through unnoticed. When caught, however, they were enumerated and made to contribute as the rest from then on (p. 96).

We can add to this second group the *huidos* and *no visitados*, that is, those who fled or otherwise avoided the impositions of the *encomienda* system. These cases, too, are proof of the desperation of many households. Take as an example the *encomendero*'s shepherd, who fled in panic when thirty-two sheep entrusted to his care died and who never came back to his wife and children (p. 207).

Sixty-seven households made up the group of full-time specialists and retainers: forty-seven worked for the *encomendero*, and twenty were attached to various *curacas* and headmen. Those who worked for the *encomendero* break down as follows: five house servants, seven field and agricultural workers, nineteen caretakers of animals (cows, sheep, goats, pigs, and horses), eight craftsmen (potters/tile makers, carpenters/lumbermen, millers, and fishermen) and, finally, five unspecified *yanaconas*.

Permanent exemption from tribute obligations, however, was a mixed blessing. Despite the liberation from weaving and attending *mit'a* obligations, many complained that they were not given enough time to work on their own subsistence activities (p. 220), or that they were overworked (pp. 101, 125), or, most frequently, that they did not get paid. To these claims the *encomendero* replied that the value of their salaries was discounted to the *curacas* by exchanging salary value for specific items in the *tasa* (p. 254). One carpenter, even though he said that his work burden was not too hard, would nevertheless have preferred to pay tribute like all the others (p. 117).

The situation of the *yanaconas* attached to *curacas* was radically different from that of those who worked for the *encomendero*. The twenty households listed as such were unevenly distributed among the *principales*: Juan Chuchuyaure had four; Gonzalo Tapia, two; Francisco Coñapariguana, nine; and others, one each. Coñapariguana explained that these people were mostly outsiders from Caxatambo and Condesuyo obtained by him through his own *industria* [effort?] (p. 200). Perhaps his position as headman of Quechua *mitimaes* placed by the Inca to man fortresses (p. 199) explained his success in obtaining *yanaconas*; but on the other hand, he may also have been in a better position to protect postconquest refugees. Of the lower-ranking headmen, only Pablo Almerco had one attached *yanacona* household (p. 168), a fact that shows the limits of the institution of *yanaconaje* within such a small ethnic group as the Yacha.

Murra has cautioned against equating the *yanaconaje* with such European categories as slave, servant, or liegeman. Furthermore, he stresses the ambiguous and complex nature of the *yanaconas*' status, how they were recruited, and their functions (1967, pp. 390–91; 1975). In 1562 many of these families were still free from tribute obligations, though increasingly they "helped" (p. 146) by giving chickens, working with others in communal fields, and weaving or spinning a little (p. 168). Their activities in the service of their *curaca* were varied: some were full-time specialized herders (p. 108); others cultivated fields at some distance from their *curaca*'s residence (pp. 79, 127); and all stated that they wove for the *curaca* (e.g., p. 127). Chuchuyaure's trusted Riquira wove and traded for him and presumably helped him administer people and resources (p. 102). These families constituted separate households, cultivated land for their own sustenance, and received reciprocal gifts of clothing, meat, coca, salt, and spices from their *curacas* (pp. 61–65). In addition, in some independent households there were unmarried women who were in the *curaca*'s service to help make *chicha* (p. 103).

The transition from specialized worker or from *yanacona* of the *curaca* to specialized worker or servant of the *encomendero* was a radical break from the past, despite the obvious continuities and willful forcing of this Andean institution into a European mold. It was against this change that the people affected complained most, for the quantity of work was no longer constrained by tacit mutual consent, nor did the *encomendero* have any respect for reciprocal norms (as is demonstrated by the fact that the people all complained of not being paid).

Physical impediment, old age, or widowhood were not automatic reasons for exemption. Only 34 percent of the 107 households with these handicaps could be considered in some way exempt. Even so, for practically all of them some sort of minimal contribution of spinning, if not the weaving of a minor piece, was listed. There was also a sizable number (42 percent) who contributed less than their full-paying neighbors. The remaining 24 percent seemed to be able to comply with the full assessment, despite widowhood, old age, or some other impediment listed for the head of household. Sixty-six percent (74) of the households claiming exemption were not even complete nuclear families: their median composition was between one and two persons per household, whereas the rest of the population had a median between three and four. The average composition of exempt households was barely 2.5 persons per family, compared to 4.23 for all households taken together. When more than three persons were listed in the household, the number of households actually exempt began to drop dramatically in relation to those that paid tribute—complaints of old age, widowhood, and the like notwithstanding. Nor should it surprise us that 33 percent of the people in this category complained that delivering whatever tribute they were assessed was very burdensome; only three households did not protest, partly because their contributions were reduced in comparison to what other families in the same village gave. Six widows in one village were in such straits that the *visitador* ordered their assessments abolished immediately (p. 193).

In Inca times a clear distinction had been made between a certain social age at which a man was freed from the more onerous and energetic tribute requirements (army and *mit'a*)—though he still performed many lighter communal tasks and an occasional administrative or supervisory but honored task—and physically incapacitating old age (called in the *visita*, *viejos muy viejos para el trabajo*) (Rowe 1958; Murra 1956, p. 172; Murra and Adorno, 1980, pp. 196–98; Mayer 1972, p. 345). We find in the *encomienda* a willful distortion of this distinction. Old age was there defined literally rather than socially, as a stage in life at which the most onerous tribute exactions were to cease. The fine gradations of diminishing obligation and increased responsibility and honor were simply abolished.

The brunt of the tribute base fell on 251 households (52 percent of the total), of which one-third complained about the burden of tribute and another third said that they got by; for the remaining third, unfortunately, no answer is recorded. The reasons people gave for finding the tribute burdensome provide an insight into the workings of the "domestic economy" (Sahlins 1972). I dealt above with the issue of physical incapacity and cases of widower- or widowhood. What is interesting here is how this factor combines with other features of the domestic unit. If death, incapacity, or having one's spouse taken away by force (p. 157) struck the household in combination with too many children (p. 221), sick children (pp. 162, 165, 166), or too many members to support (e.g., pp. 162, 165, 182, 191), then it was very difficult to sustain the household, let alone pay tribute. Such difficulties applied equally to incapacitated parents without children (p. 191), children who had left their parents (p. 120), or old people who were alone and without help (p. 125). For all of these people we can add the European term *poor*, a term that to Andean people most frequently meant a person without kinsmen to help out (*waccha*, the contemporary Quechua term for "orphan," is synonymous with *poor*) (Mayer 1972, p. 358). In short, these were households that had problems maintaining viability owing to accidental lack of skilled labor power (Sahlins 1972, pp. 69–74). There was one case of near blindness that prompted the couple to have their weaving quota done by others, whom they paid by working on the other people's agricultural tasks (p. 120).

The other kind of complaint concerned the nature of the tribute itself: "too much tribute" and "too much work" were the most straightforward replies (seven cases); the more accurate reply, "it takes too much time" (twelve cases); was explained more fully as "too many occupations in which to expend effort and to hire oneself out" (pp. 242, 121).

The fluctuating nature of the tribute burden comes out in the observation that "sometimes there is too much work and at others not" (p. 211). And, finally, the interrelationship between subsistence tasks and tribute was explained as "too much work on tribute and his own"; "there is no time left to make his *chacaras* nor to clothe himself and his wife and children" (pp. 150, 162).

Specific complaints about tribute ran the whole range: full-time specialists complained about the distance and time it took to cut wood in the jungle (pp. 230, 231); the sandal maker complained that he had to make all the sandals normally assessed to one *pachaca* (a unit of one hundred tributaries) (p. 119; Hadden 1967 studied one such); all complained about spinning, the onerous services to the *encomendero* (such as carrying food and fodder), the farm work, the making of *adobes* and walls, and the *mit'a* in general.

My suspicion that this "loaded" question concerning the burdensome nature of the tribute provoked—as it should have—a political reply is confirmed by the fact that in some places, such as Coquin and Chuchuco (pp. 133–58), strings of like-minded answers to the effect that tribute was burdensome were recorded after a while as *igual que los demás* (the same as the others) until the suspicious *visitador* demanded a reason. Then followed entries to the effect that "he did not give a reason" (e.g., p. 151), and toward the end of the *visita*, the record of the answers was omitted altogether.

I tried to determine whether there was any difference in terms of household composition between those who said that the tribute was burdensome and those who did not. No differences emerged when the number of household members, the type of family (nuclear, extended, couple, or less than nuclear), or even consumer/worker ratios (Chayanov 1966, p. 59) were compared in the two groups. Rather, I think that the Yacha peasants answered the question by comparing the new system to that of their Inca masters: the new system was found wanting.

Conclusion

What was a household in Yacha territory in 1562? It was a residential unit, with a house, crop storage, and cooking facilities. It was inhabited by a married couple and their children and occasionally augmented by the attachment of relatives of either spouse or of children's spouses. Households considered to be poor were composed of the remnants of a previously existing marriage; wealthier households had more wives and *yanaconas*.

The household was a consumption unit that provided for most of the basic subsistence needs of its members on a regular basis and took care of infants and aged or infirm residents. In addition, it was a pool of labor capabilities, a source of physical energy and available skills that were deployed in a diversified manner in agriculture, herding, handicrafts, construction, and transportation, and it provided itself and the society in which it lived with basic goods and services. Because this productive power peaked during a portion of its developmental cycle, at certain stages the household was capable of generating a surplus. At other times its diminished productive skills and power may have required subsidies from the community in which it was embedded. The transition to *encomienda* in colonial times implied that many of the institutional mechanisms that ensured help with work, goods in kind, exemption from tribute, and so on were breaking down and leaving many destitute. Finally, like households everywhere, it was the place where manpower for armies and unskilled work could be recruited.

The household was also a node and center of a complex web of reciprocal exchange flowing into and out of it (Alberti and Mayer 1974). Labor services, goods, gifts, ceremonial exchanges, and so on were the expression of a complex network of kinship and social and political obligations that linked the household to others, to the rest of the community, and to the larger social world. It is quite likely that this web of links to other households, despite the heavy burden of work, was richer, denser, and more complex than it is today, even though the *visita* did not tap this dimension very well (Mayer 1974).

Despite its autonomy as a consumption unit, the household was only a component of the productive system in general, though it was the key element and the pattern setter as well. It was thoroughly embedded within a hierarchy of larger social units, each one partially intervening in the productive process. The household had access rights to land, yet it had to follow the restrictions that bound it to the community. Moreover, given the collective nature of Andean agriculture (Murra 1975, chap. 2; Mayer 1979; Mayer and Fonseca 1979; Guillet 1979, chap. 3), it is erroneous to emphasize the household exclusively when we consider it as a unit of production. Yet the rhythms and cycles of the household affected other productive parts of the system. Allowance had to be made for subsistence production of the household, which, in itself, was diversified in its activities. If labor had to be taken away from subsistence activities, then it had to be diverted at times when these activities slackened in the activity calendar, or else the time off had to be short enough not to interfere with subsistence production. The full-time specialists and the *yanaconas* had to be supported by other households, or they, too, had to stop their specialist activities to feed themselves from their own crops. When the labor of the household was intensified, it was usually allowed to intensify along all the lines of production that it was undertaking already. When the opposite strategy was taken, of allowing the household to specialize, even if it had to be sustained by the others, the specialized households found the tribute burden heavier than did the rest. Thus there were limits to the number of specialists that could be sustained by the nonspecialists. Under the Inca system, such households, though permanently removed from the community, were fed either by the state or by their masters, or else they were given enough land to feed themselves.

And last but not least, the household was a unit of account in the tribute system. The basic accounting unit was the married man. Murra translates the chronicler Cobo as follows: "No one paid tribute who lacked a wife or land"; "it is only from the marriage day on that men became tax payers and took part in public works" (1956, p. 169). Although, technically, several levels of accounting existed in the *encomienda*, starting with the global amount that the Yacha population was to deliver (the *tasa*) and passing through the several *curacas* and headmen who were responsible for assigning and collecting portions of the *tasa* at lower levels, the assignments stopped at the level of the household. Indirectly, and in a very real sense, this individual assignment implied the economic backing of the household's organizational capacity to produce the tribute. All the spinning and weaving and the other handmade objects, the chickens, and the money assessed could be delivered only if behind every *tributario* there was a viable and functioning household. The great majority of complaints about the difficulties in giving tribute arose precisely when the person in question did not have the support of a viable household. Even communal tasks in the local or the *encomendero*'s fields, where the household was a supplier of labor but not the direct producer, could be accomplished effectively only if the tribute payer had his own production to sustain him. The relations not only of production but of reproduction came to rest within the *tributario*'s household. Thus, beyond the problems of accounting, it was the Yacha household that was the crucial node where the extraction of surplus began.

The tribute obligations and household composition fed into each other, magnifying the problems of those households already in trouble and easing the burden of those better able to produce. Despite attempts at reducing and adjusting the burden of tribute according to composition, the subjective evaluation of basic unfairness came to the fore. Moreover, the changes that the *encomendero* introduced into the system (quite apart from the quantitative increase in tribute the *encomenderos* demanded) had an ultimately deleterious effect on the level of household welfare. Diminished subsistence production and increased levels of disease and mortality can be shown to be directly linked to the *encomienda* system. There is also ample evidence of household disruption owing to runaways, work avoidance, and physical punishment. The Yacha were very aware that, despite the apparent institutional continuity from the past, the times had radically changed for the worse.

Acknowledgments

I am grateful to the faculty and staff of the Department of Anthropology and the Institute of Latin American Studies of the University of Texas at Austin, for it was while I was a visiting professor and scholar there that I wrote this essay. Efraín Trelles, Richard Schaedel, Helaine Silverman, and all the participants in the Social Science Research Council seminars in New York and Ixtapan de la Sal provided very helpful comments.

Notes

1. Ortiz de Zúñiga 1972, p. 116. Subsequent references to this source are given in the text in parentheses; all translations are mine.

2. Excerpt from Pablo Almerco's testimony: "He says that he sends people for five months, four Indians in the first four months of the year, and in the fifth month three Indians, and that the *encomendero* pays for this, but he does not know how much, nor how, and he only does what his *cacique*, Don Antonio Guaynacapcha, orders him to do" (p. 160).

3. Excerpt from Ana Guacho's testimony in Chacapampa: "Her *amancebado* (non-Catholic married) husband is gone to trade for cotton, because they are naked, and indeed it was evident to the *visitadores*" (p. 127).
Excerpt from Teresa Capia's testimony in Chacapampa: "She says she is sixty years old, widowed, three children. That in giving all that they are required, it is too much work because she is old and poor and they cannot work that much" (p. 131).

References

Alberti, Giorgio, and Mayer, Enrique
1974   *Reciprocidad e intercambio en los Andes Peruanos.* Lima: Instituto de Estudios Peruanos.
Carter, William E.
1977   "Trial Marriage in the Andes." In *Andean Kinship and Marriage*, edited by Ralph Bolton and Enrique Mayer, pp. 177–216. American Anthropological Association Special Publication, no. 7. Washington, D.C.: The Association.
Chayanov, Alexander V.
1966   *The Theory of Peasant Economy*, edited by Daniel Thorner, Basil Kerblay and R. E. F. Smith. Homewood, Ill.: American Economic Association.
Fonseca, M. César
1972   "La economía vertical y la economía de mercado en las comu-

nidades alteñas del Perú." In *Visita de la Provincia de León de Huánuco en 1562 (Iñigo Ortiz de Zúñiga, visitador)*, 2:315–338. Huánuco, Peru: Universidad Nacional Hermilio Valdizán.

Goody, Jack
1966   *The Developmental Cycle in Domestic Groups.* Cambridge Papers in Social Anthropology. Cambridge: Cambridge University Press.

Guillet, David
1979   *Agrarian Reform and Peasant Economy in Southern Peru.* Columbia: University of Missouri Press.

Hadden, Gordon
1967   "Un ensayo de demografía histórica y etnológica en Huánuco." In *Visita de la Provincia de León de Huánuco en 1562 (Iñigo Ortiz de Zúñiga, visitador)*, 1:369–380. Huánuco, Peru: Universidad Nacional Hermilio Valdizán.

Isbell, Billie Jean
1977   "Kuyaq: Those Who Love Me: An Analysis of Andean Kinship and Reciprocity in a Ritual Context." In *Andean Kinship and Marriage*, edited by Ralph Bolton and Enrique Mayer, pp. 81–105. American Anthropological Association Special Publication, no. 7. Washington, D.C.: The Association.

Lambert, Berndt
1977   "Bilaterality in the Andes." In *Andean Kinship and Marriage*, edited by Ralph Bolton and Enrique Mayer, pp. 1–27. American Anthropological Association Special Publication, no. 7. Washington, D.C.: The Association.

Matos, Ramiro M.
1972   "Wakan y Wamalli: Estudio arqueológico de dos aldeas rurales." In *Visita de la Provincia de León de Huánuco en 1562 (Iñigo Ortiz de Zúñiga, visitador)*, 2:367–382. Húanuco, Peru: Universidad Nacional Hermilio Valdizán.

Mayer, Enrique
1972   "Censos insensatos: Evaluación de los censos campesinos en la historia de Tangor." In *Visita de la Provincia de León de Huánuco en 1562 (Iñigo Ortiz de Zúñiga, visitador)*, 2:339–366. Huánuco, Peru: Universidad Nacional Hermilio Valdizán.

1974   *Reciprocity, Self-Sufficiency and Market Relations in a Contemporary Community in the Central Andes of Peru.* Latin American Studies Program Dissertation Series, no. 72. Ithaca, N.Y.: Cornell University.

1977   "Beyond the Nuclear Family." In *Andean Kinship and Marriage*, edited by Ralph Bolton and Enrique Mayer, pp. 60–80.

American Anthropological Association Special Publication, no. 7. Washington, D.C.: The Association.

1979   *Land Use in the Andes: Ecology and Agriculture in the Mantaro Valley of Peru with Special Reference to Potatoes.* Social Science Unit Publication. Lima: International Potato Center.

Mayer, Enrique, and Fonseca, M. César

1979   *Sistemas agrarios en la Cuenca del Río Cañete.* Lima: Oficina Nacional de Evaluación de Recursos Naturales (ONERN).

Mellafe, Rolando

1967   "Consideraciones históricas sobre la Visita." In *Visita de la Provincia de León de Huánuco en 1562 (Iñigo Ortiz de Zúñiga, visitador),* 1:323–344. Huánuco, Peru: Universidad Nacional Hermilio Valdizán.

Morris, Craig

1967   "Storage in Tawantinsuyu." Ph.D. diss., University of Chicago.

1972   "El almacenaje en dos aldeas de los Chupaychu." In *Visita de la Provincia de León de Huánuco en 1562 (Iñigo Ortiz de Zúñiga, visitador),* 2:383–404. Huánuco, Peru: Universidad Nacional Hermilio Valdizán.

Murra, John V.

1956   "The Economic Organization of the Inca State." Ph.D. diss., University of Chicago.

1967   "La Visita de los Chupachu como fuente etnológica." In *Visita de la Provincia de León de Huánuco en 1562 (Iñigo Ortiz de Zúñiga, visitador),* 1:427–476. Huánuco, Peru: Universidad Nacional Hermilio Valdizán.

1975   *Formaciones económicas y políticas del mundo andino.* Lima: Instituto de Estudios Peruanos.

Murra, John V., and Adorno, Rolena, eds.

1980   *El primer nueva corónica y buen gobierno por Felipe Guaman Poma de Ayala* (Waman Puma). Serie América Nuestra, no. 31. Mexico City: Editorial Siglo XXI.

Ortiz de Zúñiga, Iñigo

1967–72   *Visita de la Provincia de León de Huánuco en 1562.* 2 vols., edited by John V. Murra. Huánuco, Peru: Universidad Nacional Hermilio Valdizán.

Rowe, John H.

1958   "The Age Grades of the Inca Census." In *Miscellanea Paul Rivet Octogenario Dicata,* 2:500–522. 31 Congreso Internacional de Americanistas. Mexico City: UNAM.

Sahlins, Marshall
1972   *Stone Age Economics*. Chicago, Ill.: Aldine, Atherton.
Spalding, Karen
1974   *De indio a campesino: Cambios en la estructura social del Perú colonial*. Lima: Instituto de Estudios Peruanos.
Varallanos, José
1959   *Historia de Huánuco*. Buenos Aires: Imprenta López.

Cultural Continuity, Structure, and Context: Some Peculiarities of the Andean *Compadrazgo*

Juan M. Ossio

In this essay I try to understand one of the most significant social relationships of Andean rural society by analyzing both its cultural manifestations and its actualization in the behavior of the actors. This social relationship is *compadrazgo* or, more specifically, spiritual *compadrazgo*, generally associated with the sacrament of baptism and with *padrinazgo*. A central argument is that the contemporary institution of *compadrazgo* embodies structural continuities from pre-Hispanic Andean culture, a fact that can be demonstrated through a careful analysis of present-day rituals.

As in many other parts of the world, in Andean society three kinds of social relationships are, according to Gudeman (1972), the constituent parts of the *compadrazgo* set wherever it occurs:

1. *Compadrazgo* proper, which links, in a supposedly permanent union, the parents of a child to its baptismal sponsors. Those who are united by this kind of link are generally of the same generation and use the self-reciprocal term *compadre*. In some parts of the Andes an asymmetrical usage is preferred.

2. *Padrinazgo*, which links the baptismal sponsor to the baptized. This relationship includes people of different generations who generally use the nonreciprocal terms *padrino* and *ahijado*. The behavior of the actors in this social relationship is always asymmetrical; the *ahijado* is always subordinated to the *padrino*.

3. Parenthood, which is the relationship between parents and children. In this case there is no strong ritual content in behavior.

In Andean society we can identify a fourth element in the *compadrazgo* set, as the children of both parents and sponsors formalize links expressed in the use of a particular set of terms.

Compadrazgo as an institution has been discussed in several ethnographic monographs and in comparative studies based on functionalist and, more recently, structuralist theoretical premises. Various descriptions have been offered:

1. It is a mechanism that furthers social solidarity (Redfield 1930; Gillin 1945; Foster 1953; Mintz and Wolf 1950).
2. It is a substitute for a disrupted kinship system (Foster 1953).
3. It is a dyadic contract in societies with disrupted kinship systems (Foster 1953) or with bilateral kinship systems (Gudeman 1972).
4. It is a social relationship that, wherever it occurs, is constrained by the dogma of the Catholic church, its distinctive feature being to entrust the spiritual and natural domains to two different sets of persons—the spiritual and the natural parents (Gudeman 1972).
5. It is a form of social exchange with either a symmetrical or an asymmetrical shape, but not both at the same time (implicit in Hammel 1968 and Gudeman 1975).

In contrast to these views I offer several arguments:

1. Andean *compadrazgo* cannot be explained simply as a mechanism that furthers social solidarity because this can be said of any institution, such as the religious cargo system, the multiple types of ceremonial kinship, and so on, all of which coexist with *compadrazgo*.
2. Rather than being a substitute for a kinship system, Andean *compadrazgo* requires kinship as its foundation.
3. *Compadrazgo* can be seen as a dyadic contract at an individual level, although this is not the only level from which it can be viewed. There is a collective level at which it appears as a link between groups that rest on bilateral kinship, but whose stability depends on certain endogamous tendencies.
4. *Compadrazgo* does not seem to be constrained by Catholic dogma. On the contrary, there is some evidence that a form of ceremonial kinship resembling spiritual *compadrazgo* existed in the Andean area before the arrival of the Spaniards. Also, evidence from some Amazonian groups, as well as from the Andean pre-Hispanic period, suggests that the allocation of natural and spiritual domains to two different sets of parents is not completely absent in other cultural traditions. Moreover, there is evidence that the constituent parts of the dogma of baptism have not been completely understood by the indigenous populations.
5. Insofar as it includes two levels, *compadrazgo* may give the appearance of symmetrical exchange at a collective level, but at an individual level it is an asymmetrical exchange.

This case not only deviates from current assumptions about *compadrazgo*; it also shows the importance of the contexts in which an institution is made manifest, as each of them may convey a different impression of its nature. Because this finding has generally been ignored by anthropologists, mechanistic and reductionist views have resulted.

The data on which this analysis is based were collected in Comunidad de Andamarca, an Andean community located in the Provincia de Lucanas, Departamento de Ayacucho, Peru. The main village lies about 3,550 meters above sea level, and its population (although very mobile) can be estimated at about 3,000. The size of its territory, according to the same Andamarquinos, is 89,000 hectares. Of these, 2,000 hectares are said to be for cultivation; the remaining 87,000 are described as pasture lands. The native language is Quechua, but most of the men are bilingual. The community is linked to the provincial capital and to Lima through several roads that are used by different bus companies.

The main economic activities of the Andamarquinos are agriculture and herding. Agriculture is dominant and demands most care. Crops include maize, potatoes, *ocas*, *ollucos*, *mashuas*, barley, broad beans, and peas. The herding of llamas, alpaca, sheep, and cattle, unlike agriculture, brings cash into the community. Almost all the shop owners declare that they got started with money derived from herding. There are more than sixty shopkeepers, a number which suggests that Andamarca participates intensively in the market economy. Thanks to this participation, and to the wealth of the community, five people own lorries. In addition, the Andamarquinos as a whole have developed a transport cooperative that owns one lorry and two buses and is in the process of purchasing three other buses.

Links to the Peruvian national society are also evident from the three primary schools located in the main village, the technological center, the status of Andamarca as a community and district at the same time, and the large number of migrants that live in Lima and other parts of the coast. However, these links have not affected the maintenance of many traditions and a strong religious system that includes the worship of saints, mountains, and other natural manifestations and the celebration of costly fiestas. Nor has it destroyed a technology based mostly on human or animal energy, or the strong sense of solidarity that rests in great part on social relationships in which kinship is highly prominent.

Types of Ceremonial Kinship

A salient feature of Andean ceremonial kinship is the large number of types that coexist even in small communities. Gillin (1945) recognized fourteen types of ceremonial kinship for Moche, a community on the northern coast of Peru; in Andamarca we recorded ten types; and a similar profusion has been reported from other communities, such as Sacsá in the

Mantaro Valley. In Huaylas, Doughty (1968) recorded about seventeen types.

Not all ceremonial kinship falls into the category of *compadrazgo*, nor is *compadrazgo* always associated with ritual that involves the sponsorship of a human being or of a material object. The occasions that generally give rise to the formalization of a *compadrazgo* and a *padrinazgo* link owing to the sponsorship of a human being are

1. Birth, when the midwife who delivers a child may stand in a relation of *comadre* to the parents of a child.
2. Baptism, which in the Catholic church is the main ritual of social initiation of the individual.
3. Preventive baptism, an early baptism, without the participation of a Catholic priest, that is performed to prevent the soul of a child from going to a dark place or harming the living if the child should die.
4. Nail cutting, when the child's nails are first cut.
5. Hair cutting, when the child's hair is first cut.
6. Ear piercing, when the daughter has her ears pierced for earrings.
7. *Misa de salud*, three successive masses performed to prevent a child from being trapped by the earth when it is beginning to walk.
8. Confirmation, a ceremony associated with the First Communion in the church and administered by a bishop, who generally visits the main districts at intervals of several years; it is not a very important stage.
9. Marriage, the Catholic ceremony, which may not give rise to a bond of *compadrazgo*, just to *padrinazgo*. In some communities there is more than one *padrino*.

Other types involve the sponsorship of material objects, but these are not so important and do not create very firm bonds.

On the basis of my experience in Andamarca, and of Gillin's (1945) evidence on Moche, I have concluded that the ceremonial kinship network of a middle-aged person includes an average of eight types, not necessarily embodied in different sponsors. The extension of the ceremonial kinship network of an individual depends not only on the types of ceremonial kinship but also upon such factors as stage of the life cycle, wealth and prestige, and the fact that under almost any type of ceremonial kinship there are sponsors for oneself or for one's own children; or one may act as sponsor of the children of others. This breakdown gives rise to an important distinction producing two relationships belonging to a common ceremonial kinship type: the receiving *compadre* and the giving *compadre*.

In Andamarca, as in many other parts of Latin America, the *compadre-*

compadre relationship is more important than the *padrino-ahijado* relationship, both in the degree of interaction and in the norms that regulate behavior. It is so important that the meaning of the terms has been extended to include an apparently contractual relationship without any kind of sponsorship, as in the case of *compadres de respeto*. This relationship may be contracted merely to maintain friendly relations, or to unite groups of siblings, co–parents-in-law, and the other relatives of a married couple. The term *compadre* has even been incorporated into the kinship terminology to designate the co–parents-in-law of a married couple; and the siblings of the intermarrying couple also treat each other as such in their mutual interaction (see Figure 1, p. 133). *Padrinazgo*, on the other hand, is always associated with a form of ritual sponsorship and is never extended without it. If people of different generations or statuses intend to contract a permanent and peaceful relationship they choose to become oath father and oath child to each other.

In Andean society, *compadrazgo* is a relationship generally conceived in terms that resemble those of affinity, and it is relatively independent from *padrinazgo*. In Andamarca and in other communities of Ayacucho and Apurímac, even *compadrazgo de bautismo*, the most important of all types, may be settled not at the moment of baptism but at the moment of marriage. Furthermore, it often happens that at baptism, others than those who actually sponsor the ritual become *compadres* to the child being baptized.

Spiritual *Compadrazgo*

In Andamarca and in most of Ayacucho and Apurímac, as just stated, *compadrazgo de bautismo* or *compadrazgo espiritual* is the most prominent type of ceremonial kinship. Its importance can be demonstrated by the precedence that is granted to the people who fulfill this role in relation to ceremonial kin and by the elaborate nature of the ritual and the symbols associated with it. I focus attention upon spiritual *compadrazgo* for these reasons. Spiritual *compadrazgo* is also representative of the other types of ceremonial kinship in Andamarca, and it contrasts with the *compadrazgo espiritual* of other parts of the world. Though it is not equally important in all Andean communities, it is an Andean interpretation of a Western institution, not simply at an institutional level but at a structural level. The principles that underlie the Andean kinship system are also behind *compadrazgo espiritual*, an institution associated with affinity both at the symbolic level and within the system of kinship relations. At this stage of the research it is difficult to go further, but the analysis suggests that the relative importance of *compadrazgo*, as opposed to *padrinazgo*, derives from its being an alliance mechanism complementary to marriage. In this regard, there is evidence indicating that a sister may be exchanged for a *compadre*.

I first present a description of the institution and then discuss its association with affinity, before laying out its underlying principles and comparing them with those of kinship and with a type of pre-Hispanic *compadrazgo* described by the sixteenth- and seventeenth-century chronicler Felipe Guaman Poma de Ayala. Finally, I compare spiritual *compadrazgo* with marriage.

General Description of *Compadrazgo*

As we have seen, *compadrazgo de bautismo* is not always created at the time of a child's baptism but is, in many communities, established at the Catholic marriage of the parents. This fact is evidence of the parallelism that exists among kinship, affinity, and *compadrazgo*.

Another peculiarity is that sponsors for the baptism of future children offer themselves, instead of being selected by the married couple. Their willingness to become future baptismal godparents is expressed at the wedding. At the church door there is a *quille*, an arch made of branches of a tree, the curved part of which is wrapped in a white fabric tied firmly to the branch by a couple of ribbons and twisted at intervals from one end of the fabric to the other. Below the two extremes of the curved part a thread is tied, and from it hang several silver coins. Two people (generally a conjugal couple, for reasons that will appear later) hold the ends of the arch and wait for the married couple to come out.

The couple emerges carrying flowers collected from all the attendants at the wedding and accompanied by their marriage godparents (*padrinos de matrimonio*), who again are a couple. The godfather is positioned to the right of the groom and the godmother to the left of the bride. All of them pass under the arch and walk, covered by it, to the groom's house to continue the wedding celebration. Once they are in the house the bunch of flowers is wrapped up in baby clothes, as if it were a newly born child, and is handed to those who held the *quille*. They jokingly pretend to baptize the bunch of flowers, and a name is given to it. It is then handed around to the relatives of both bride and groom, who eventually return it to those who carried the arch. Finally, they deliver the bunch of flowers to the groom and bride, who will store it away.

The bunch of flowers is known as *wayta ahijado* (godson of flowers), and it symbolizes the children who will be born from that marriage and become the godchildren of those who held the *quille*. From this moment the *compadrazgo de bautismo* relationship between them and the bride and groom is settled, and it is assumed that all the children born of this marriage will be sponsored at baptism by them.

Later, when the children are born, the sacrament of baptism is administered to them, first in the form of "preventive baptism" (*agua de socorro*) and later as baptism proper. The first ritual generally takes place during the first week after birth. At this time a Christian name, borrowed from the saint celebrated on the day of birth, is assigned by the *padrino* or *madrina espiritual*. No elaborate celebrations mark this occasion, and no Roman Catholic priest participates. According to the informants, the purpose of the ritual is to allow the soul of the child to go to heaven in case the child dies. The souls of children who die without this ritual are believed to go to a dark place (*tutaya ucuman*) or to remain in this world "suckling on stones because they never suckled from their mothers."

The second ritual is like a confirmation of the first but is performed in the church by a Catholic priest and is followed by a great celebration in the parents' house, a celebration that demands heavy expenditures by both parents and *padrinos*. Because of the need to accumulate savings, this ritual is generally delayed until the child is one or two years old. The celebration in the parents' house often lasts for three days, and the expenses are high because relatives of both parents and *padrinos* have to be supplied with food and drink for the whole period. It is important to ensure a large attendance because money (known as *qelpuy*) is collected for the child, just as money is collected at a wedding ceremony.

The behavior between *compadres* is surrounded by an elaborate etiquette that emphasizes the idea of respect and rests on religious and social values. This etiquette enables the *compadres* to act as intermediaries not only in the conflicts that may arise between their godchildren but also in those between the godchildren's parents and their siblings. For this reason they are generally appointed as executors of wills.

The value of respect is so highly prized that conflicts rarely occur between *compadres*. Their behavior is extremely formalized and dominated by rules of reciprocity. Apart from the working contexts in which they help each other, these rules are expressed in the excess of generosity manifested in the exchange of gifts. It is regarded as an offense not to receive a gift, and if it is not reciprocated proportionately the receiver is considered to be selfish. This implicit competition causes tensions, especially because the relationship between *compadres* must be preserved from conflict. A gift is always accompanied by words that emphasize the effort required to obtain it; this practice invests the material object with the affection of the giver and increases its value. The receiver reciprocates with alcoholic drinks. To refuse these mutual offerings would be an offense or contempt.

It is not surprising that in the celebrations such as roofing a house, where the *compadres* fulfill a central role, they end up completely drunk.

The ceremonialism that surrounds *compadrazgo* is enhanced by the fact that it is the only social relationship that is celebrated in fixed feasts of the annual calendar. These feasts are the Jueves de Compadres and Jueves de Comadres, which fall on the two Thursdays preceding carnivals; the Día de Todos los Santos on November 1, when *guaguas* (cakes in the shape of babies or animals) are given to godchildren; and Good Friday, when the spiritual godparents whip their godchildren as a penance for their sins and to lead them to righteousness.

Periphery and Social Introduction in the Role of the Spiritual *Compadre*

From these rituals and from other evidence, it appears that *compadrazgo espiritual* is associated with a peripheral realm, or marginality, and with the role of "social introducer," or sponsor. It is also linked to a system of parallel transmission that is deeply rooted in the Andes.

To start with the latter, I have noted already that the *quille* has two ends and is held by a couple or, even better, by a married couple, signifying that they are the spiritual *compadres* of the bride and groom. It is believed that all rituals that engender *compadrazgo* and *padrinazgo* relationships have to be sponsored by persons of the same sex as those being sponsored. It is said, for example, that if at the moment of baptism a godparent carries in his or her arms a child of the opposite sex, the child will probably suffer or become ill. Given that the *compadrazgo espiritual* link is settled, ideally, at the moment of a marriage, when children are not yet born, sponsorship by a married couple is preferable because the couple can sponsor all children of the marriage.

The association of the *compadres de bautismo* with the *quille* in this ritual context is remarkably similar to their association (and that of other types of *compadres*) with the roof of a house in the *huasichacuy* (house-roofing ritual). In this context the *compadres* of the owner of a new house attend the final stage of construction, carrying a tin cross and a pair of ribbons of different colors as presents. The cross is placed on the outside and the ribbons on the inside of the roof. These ribbons are tied to the *mayu* (river) or central roof beam by the sons-in-law of the householders, and throughout the night the guests, in pairs of couples, plait and unplait the ribbons to the rhythm of music appropriate for this occasion. This plaiting and unplaiting, as well as the pattern that is formed after tying the two ribbons in the roof (or in the *quille*, as mentioned above) is called *puytu*.

Together with *gengo*, which is a zigzag pattern, the *puytu* is a Pan-Andean motif associated with the flowing of liquids, fertility, the union of contraries, and, in general, socialization. The variety of contexts in which the *puytu* appears leads us to consider it a fundamental symbol in Andean society. In old Quechua vocabularies it has the sense of "dome" or of "roof" (Santo Tomás 1951, p. 342).

These data suggest that the *compadres de bautismo* or spiritual *compadres* are associated with marginality and with the role of introducing to society those who are getting married. They escort the newly married couple, under the *quille*, through the socialized space of the village until they arrive at the groom's house. If this ceremony takes place in a church outside the community, then the procession under the *quille* is from the community boundary to the groom's house. Once in the groom's house the couple will be accepted socially by their respective *ayllus* (cognatic descent groups) through the ceremony of *perdonanakuy*. The *quille* is dismantled after the wedding ceremony, and the bridal pair are recognized as adults, or full social beings.

Another symbolic activity involving social initiation is that of *covering*. The gifts given by godparents to godchildren at the time of baptism consist of clothes and the *pampana*, a robe, sometimes of silk, with motifs representing the sun, leaves, animals, and so on, used to cover a baby in the cradle. Another context in which gifts involve the covering role of *compadres* is the kin group feast at the time of maize sowing. Here the *compadres* of the owner of the land to be sown, and also his affines, give to the owner and his wife real or paper flowers that they place in their hats. As we shall see later, this idea of covering is also congruent with the ideal that the *compadrazgo* relationship is a structural position that should be superimposed upon affinity, but is not suitable for consanguines.

The Andamarquinos' conception of the *compadres* as social introducers is confirmed by their interpretation of baptism and by the similarity between baptismal *compadres* and various kinds of sponsors performing analogous roles in rites of passage in the pre-Hispanic period. This evidence confirms the Andean nature of *compadrazgo* in Andamarca, as well as in other parts of Peru.

According to Stephen Gudeman:

> Behind all the observed compadrazgo variants lies the historical Christian theological distinction made between man as a spiritual and natural, or cultural and biological, being. Through baptism the passage from the state of original sin to the state of grace is achieved: man is thought to be conceived with the sin of Adam; he is regenerated when this sin is "washed away" during baptism and he is re-

born to Christ and a second set of parents, the minister and sponsor. A belief in man's dual nature is found, of course, in many cultures. What is distinctive about Christian spiritual sponsorship is that these two aspects of the human personality must be entrusted to different sets of persons: the natural and spiritual parents. [1972, p. 47]

In other words, the essential elements that constitute the dogma surrounding baptism are a dichotomous conception of human beings as composed of matter and spirit, or body and soul; the notion of original sin inherited from Adam and Eve, because they disobeyed God; the idea of Christ as son of God, redeemer of men, and founder of the Christian community; the notion of the priest as vicar of Christ; and finally, a conception of salvation in heaven as opposed to condemnation in hell, and the beliefs that derive from this one, such as acceptance of the concepts of purgatory and limbo.

In Andamarca all the elements that constitute the dogma of baptism are present, but with distinctive connotations, sometimes not precisely defined. The dichotomous conception of human beings as body and soul is certainly accepted, but not the belief that human beings have only one soul. One generally hears that men have three souls and women seven and that these are not static entities; rather, their presence in the body varies with the life cycle. Matters are similar with other elements of the dogma. For example, Adam and Eve are sometimes believed to be the names of a single male individual who becomes a mythical hero. Because time is conceived in cyclical terms, and sin is never thought capable of being inherited, the idea of original sin has not been understood. Christ is thought of as an ambivalent personage. He is seen sometimes as an anticultural hero and sometimes as the main God, but the idea of "redeemer" is not deeply rooted.

Nearest to Catholic dogma is the idea that children must be baptized in order to go to heaven and avoid going to *tutaya ucuman* or suckling stones. However, a comparative analysis of the beliefs and funeral rituals appropriate to children and adults reveals that heaven and its opposite, hell, are not conceived as places of reward and punishment since they are not thought to be eternal residences. Damnation is a threat more to the society of the living than to the deceased. The deceased may obtain eventual salvation, but so long as he or she is damned, living persons may be endangered. Also, the idea of heaven is appropriate to baptized children who die before having sexual experiences, and therefore without having committed incest. Incest is regarded as a major sin and as the most important reason for damnation. Heaven is linked to immaturity, to the inability of children to commit incest, and not to the idea of reward for earthly behavior. Just as adult funeral practices seek to keep the soul of the deceased away from the living, because they are potentially incestuous and therefore damned, so children should be buried as adults as soon as their sexual capacities are developed.

On the other hand, the beliefs about, and funeral rituals of, unbaptized children emphasize the idea of an absolute nonsocial status that endangers the living society. For instance, it is said that they should never be buried in a cemetery, because such burial would risk the outbreak of dangerous storms and hail and the destruction of crops by frost. In order to protect against these consequences, unbaptized children are generally buried at night beneath the crosses that surround the valley of the community and that have the purpose of protecting the crops from frost. The people who bury these children are usually consanguineal kin of the parents, and they are called *contrapadrinos* (countergodparents).

The funeral rituals and beliefs relating to baptized but not yet fully mature children indicate a status that is still in the process of maturation. As in the case of the unbaptized, they are buried by night, but a godparent carries the body to the grave. Like adults they are buried in the cemetery (a socialized space), but on a different side: adults are buried on the west, baptized children on the east, which is associated with the idea of origin or beginning. Moreover, bells are tolled when a child dies, but whereas three tolls signal the death of an adult man and seven that of a woman, the bells for children of both sexes are tolled intermittently. The differences in the beliefs and funeral rituals for these three stages may be summarized as in Table 1.

From the foregoing analysis it may be suggested that the main contrast between Andean baptism and that derived from the Christian tradition is that the former incorporates the individual not into a society different from that of humans, but rather into a particular stage of social development. Christian baptism implies a distinction between a realm of humans and a realm of God and incorporates the individual into the latter. The Andean version of baptism casts the *compadres*, in their role as godparents or sponsors of children, as social initiators, and as such they do not differ significantly from the ritual sponsors found among some Brazilian groups, such as the Gê.

To entrust the natural and the cultural side of the human personality to different sets of persons is not peculiar to the Christian tradition. Evidence may be found, for both Quechua and Aymara culture, in rituals such as the *rutuy chicuy* or *chucchu rutuy* (hair cutting), the *huarachicuy* (putting on of first loin cloth), or the *quicuchicuy* (first menstruation) (Gonzales and Galdo 1976; Duviols 1976; Avila 1966), or in the Aymara

Table 1. Beliefs and Funeral Rituals Associated with Various Stages of the Life Cycle

	Prebaptismal child	Postbaptismal child	Adult
Name of the soul	*Malpa*	*Angelito*	Possible *condenado*
Destiny of the soul	*tutaya ucuman/* periphery of community	Heaven	Joropuna/ periphery of community or Punas
Relation with the society of the living	Destruction of crops by hail, frost, and other meteorological phenomena	?	*Condenados* devour 3 humans to achieve salvation
Burial site	Beneath calvaries or crosses dispersed in the hills around the valley	Left or east side of cemetery	Right or west side of cemetery
Social category of person(s) carrying corpse to cemetery	*Contrapadrino* (consanguine of deceased)	Spiritual *padrino*	Real or classificatory son-in-law
Time of day of burial	Night	Night	Day
Number of bells tolled to announce death	None	Intermittent	3 for men, 7 for women
Wake	None	Festive	Solemn
Mourning	None	None	Black clothing

ritual of *sucullu*, which consisted of taking children less than one year old out into the plaza during Corpus Christi (Bertonio 1879, 2:332). The sponsorship roles were assumed by the maternal uncle and his wife or the paternal aunt, people who in the Andean kinship system were classed as affines (Zuidema 1977). The most remarkable evidence is provided by the Indian chronicler Guaman Poma de Ayala, who lived in the Province of Lucanas during part of the sixteenth and seventeenth centuries and who describes rituals in the preconquest period as follows:

> There existed baptism by word and people were baptized and they gave the names of their parents. The women received those from their mothers. Fiestas were made for these occasions. Kinship and *compadre* and *comadre* relationships were established with the person who gave the name by word. These are called father brother, mother sister (male speaking) or brother and sister (female speaking). This is how children became baptized during this time: "yaya uauqui mama nana o tura o pana. . . ." [1968, p. 67; my translation]

Later, speaking of the Indians of his own time, Guaman Poma says:

> [Regarding] the good order and laws of marriage, the brother-in-law was called *maza* and the brother-in-law called him *caca* [*sic*] since antiquity without committing idolatry. They were married and became *compadres*. Those *compadres* from the marriage were called *socna* and those from baptism were called *uayno*. The men who were relatives were called *uauquicona* and the women *panicona*. And they never sinned or married because they said that they had become *compadres socna* or *comadres uayno uauqui pani*. These *compadres* gave their help at work and in other needs, or when they were ill or when eating and drinking, or at a fiesta, at sowing time, at death or crying after death and at all times while they lived. Later their children and descendants, grandchildren and great-grandchildren would continue serving each other and would keep the law of God.
> [p. 848; my translation]

Unfortunately, I have not been able to determine the significance of the Quechua terms by which these *compadres* were designated. Nevertheless, the fact that the *terms* existed and that Guaman Poma translated them as *compadres* is impressive evidence that the European institution had its Andean equivalent. This description also refers to certain structural relationships that are very much alive in contemporary Andean *compadrazgo*. For instance, ties were at Guaman Poma's time inherited from parent to child, as far as great-grandchildren—an indication that, as in the present, there was a collective aspect to *compadrazgo*.

The link to name giving is also noteworthy, since this practice was central to certain pre-Hispanic rites of passage that required a ritual sponsor. The allusion to name transmission suggests, as Zuidema has pointed out (1977, p. 245), a kind of parallel transmission in which males inherit the name or surname of their father and females that of their mother. This suggestion is consistent with the data in the baptismal records from the area of Lucanas Andamarcas, dating from the end of the seventeenth century, in which feminine and masculine names may be distinguished. It is also consistent with Avila's description of the hair-cutting ritual for children born with a *parca* (two crowns) in their hair. According to this early seventeenth-century extirpator of idolatry, if the child born with a *parca* was male, the maternal uncle cut his hair, whereas if it was female, the cutting would be done by the *ipa* or paternal aunt (Avila 1966, pp. 196–97). Finally, we have already seen that these parallel ties still exist in that *padrino* and *madrina* are forbidden to give names to their opposite-sex godchildren and to carry them in their arms for baptism or to the cemetery when they die.

The Collective Dimension of *Compadrazgo*

So far, we have discussed *compadrazgo* as it relates to the social induction of individuals. However, this is not its only dimension; through Guaman Poma we have begun to see that *compadrazgo espiritual* also has a collective dimension, corresponding to the structure of extended kinship groups and marriage exchanges.

The ceremonial context in which spiritual *compadrazgo* is forged is the moment of marriage, and consequently the relation between the godparents and the future godchildren is not solely dyadic. The link is established between an individual, or pair of individuals, and all the descendants of a matrimonial union. Accordingly, it is common to find that full siblings—sometimes even half-siblings—have the same person or couple as baptismal sponsors. Thus the number of children does not increase the number of spiritual *compadres*. Other mechanisms are used to achieve this increase, and once more they involve relations between groups.

Just as the baptismal sponsor is linked with all the children of a couple, so the *compadre* tends to be linked with all the real or classificatory siblings of the couple to whose children he was baptismal sponsor. In turn, all these are linked with his own real or classificatory siblings. In practice, age and demographic factors limit the extent to which this is the case. Nevertheless, owing to the extension of the kinship system, the model is largely realized in practice even though the *compadrazgo* relationships are not all of the spiritual type. Ties of *compadrazgo* that follow collateral kinship lines are not necessarily sponsorship roles; they may be like those created around the *compadrazgo de respecto*. As in the case described by Guaman Poma, these extensions may be made between relatives of *compadres* who belong to different generations. In Andamarca one finds extended families who have been linked by ceremonial kinship ties of different types for three generations.

Another expression of these collective tendencies is the fact that the term *compadre* has been incorporated into the kinship terminology, referring to a position superimposed on the affinal domain. This kinship position is that of co–parents-in-law, siblings of co–brothers- or sisters-in-law, or the corresponding relatives of a conjugal couple.

An examination of Figure I reveals that the position of the brothers of a married couple is similar to the position maintained between co–parents-in-law. In other words, it might be said that the link joining the former is an extension of the affinal relationship that exists between their parents. This is confirmed by the fact that the elder brother of a son-in-law usually addresses his brother's father-in-law by the self-reciprocal term *laysi*, or *compadre*.

The symmetrical relationship of co–parents-in-law and their respective descendants, and also of their ascendants, which is expressed in their use of the term *compadre*, recalls the description by Billie Jean Isbell of the use of the term *aura* in the community of Chuschi: "*Aura* indicates a symmetric relationship between two consanguineal groups joined by marriage. The term is used when the speaker is referring to the members of the group who stand in a reciprocal relationship to his consanguineal group, the *ayllu*. *Aura* is therefore a symmetric concept relating to collectivities" (1978, p. 113). It is important to note, moreover, that in Chuschi the individuals who constitute this category of *aura* also see themselves as *compadres*. In this respect Isbell tells us: "When asked to gloss the term in Spanish, informants responded that *aura* are like compadres or spiritual relatives" (p. 113).

In order to understand the nature of this kind of collectivity, which incorporates the *compadres* within a kinship structure, we must bear in mind the characteristics of another group upon which this collectivity is based. This social group is the *ayllu*, a term that can mean a group based upon locality, or symbolic criteria, but that also means, as it does here, a kindred or cognatic group (Ossio 1981).

As a kindred, the *ayllu* is an unbounded group that appears as such only in particular contexts, of which the most important is the prohibition of marriage. The *ayllu* is generally defined as a group of relatives with whom, in order to avoid incest, a person should not marry. This prohibi-

Figure 1. *Compadrazgo*, Affinal and Consanguineal Links

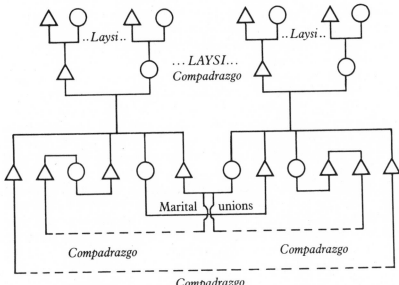

tion is frequently extended up to the fourth degree of consanguinity, which includes common ancestors up to four generations removed. Of course, in practice there is much room for flexibility, especially because the male lines are stronger than the female ones, owing to the influence of certain patrilineal principles.

The *aura*, or the *compadrazgo* social realm, insofar as it is the wider group that emerges from the interaction of the respective *ayllu* of a conjugal couple, finds expression on those ritual occasions when the couple occupies a central place: a wedding ceremony, roofing a house, or sowing a maize field.

This overlapping of *compadrazgo* links with those of affinity is also expressed in a number of symbols and attributes that are common to both. For example, just as the baptismal godparents give clothes and the *pampana* to cover their godchildren, so the mother-in-law gives to her son-in-law and daughter-in-law such objects as a shawl (*lliclla*), a poncho, a decorated sash (*chumpi*), and other kinds of clothing.

In the kin group celebrations at the September sowing of maize, as previously noted, both affines and *compadres* of those who are performing this task in their *chacras* (land plots) come bearing paper or real flowers that are placed in the hats of the married couple who owns the *chacra*. In these contexts it is also customary for the sons-in-law or, alternatively, the *compadres* of the *chacra* owners to carry the latter on their shoulders from the site of the sowing to their house in the pueblo, because of their drunken state. Another feature connecting affines and *compadres* in the sowing context is that they are the only categories of kinsmen who sow on the borders of the land or on the path.

In funerary contexts the obligation incumbent upon baptismal sponsors to carry the corpse of a godchild and place it in the grave is analogous to the obligation incumbent on sons-in-law to carry the body of a parent-in-law or of a child of the latter who has died in adulthood. Another analogy can be seen in the obligation of godchildren and sons-in-law to carry wood for the funerals of their *padrinos* and parents-in-law, respectively.

This parallelism between affines and *compadres* is also evident in the *huasichacuy* (roof-of-the-house ritual), though with certain differences. We have already seen that the *compadres* are the ones who give the tin crosses that decorate the outside of the roof and the ribbons with which the *puytu* will be made. The sons-in-law of the house owner, for their part, fasten the ribbons to the central beam, or *mayu*, and form the *puytu* by crossing the ribbons on part of the wood adjacent to the central beam. They also conclude the ceremony by installing on the roof the crosses brought by the *compadres*.

The association of affines with the roof of the house has a long history in the Andean world. In a 1614 document discussed by the French historian Pierre Duviols we read that

> when they built new houses, the first beams they put in were called *macssas*, which means brothers-in-law or sons-in-law. These beams were painted with figures of snakes, lions, and bears. . . . The sons-in-law or brothers-in-law of the person building the house brought these beams; hence the name given to the beams. These sons-in-law or brothers-in-law were the first to compete to put the rest of the wood in place. . . . They completed as far as the roof, leaving only a little work, the *concho* or place for *chicha*, to be built the next day . . . and what was left of the house to cover was done by the *macssas* and other relatives. [Duviols 1976, p. 284; my translation]

Nearly 360 years later, Enrique Mayer described a similar ceremony that takes place in the community of Tangor (Cerro de Pasco), in which these same categories of affines, with their female counterparts (*lumtshuys*, or daughters-in-law), perform similar roles and give similar gifts: *palos lumtshuys* and other A-shaped beams (Mayer 1977).

Other examples from the departments of Amazonas, Junín, and

Ayacucho are described by Morote Best (1956). Here the evidence for the association of *compadres* with affines is outstanding. Speaking of the town of Jauja (Department of Junín), Morote tells us that in "the zafa-casa (*wasi qatay*) covering of the house or '*wasispiy*,' finishing of the house, the ceremony begins when the roof has been completed. The owner nominates *padrino* (*masha*) beforehand: and the *padrino* has an iron cross forged for the opening of the roof, and hires an orchestra. The *madrina* (*lumtchuy*), also nominated beforehand, undertakes for her part to have a hut made of *uksha*, a kind of straw from Puna" (p. 15; my translation).

Finally, Morote's reference to the ceremony of the rooftop in the town of San Javier de Alpabamba (Parinacochas-Ayacucho) is also interesting:

After eating, the compadres who are guests undertake to close the opening left for this purpose in the "eye of the house" (*ñahuin*). When the *ñahuin* has been covered, they collect some pieces of rope and make the *atocc* (fox); that is, they make the image of a fox, as accurately as possible, out of the pieces of rope left over from the roofing. Then they hang the *atocc* from a string fastened to one of the beams of the house and one of the men makes it dance by giving little pulls on the string. The comadres dance with the fox, singing to the sound of the bass drum. [p. 18, quoting from the "Monografía de la Provincia de Parinacochas"; my translation]

Our attention is drawn in the first case to the affinal terminology assigned to the *padrinos* and in the second case to the association of the fox with spiritual kinsmen, because in several regions of the Andes this animal is called *compadre* and is described as a character who is marginal to society and whose excess of vanity, avarice, and envy always leads him to a sad end.

The close similarity between spiritual and affinal kinsmen and their linkage with symbols such as the fox, with sowing on the border of the land or on the path, and with the ornamentation of the roof of the house suggest that the idea of covering, previously mentioned in relation to *compadres*, apart from conveying the idea of social induction, is linked to a structural position that could be defined as peripheral to the group of consanguineal kinsmen or *ayllu*.

Structural Implications of *Compadrazgo*

Gudeman considers

that at least two patterns of godparent selection characterize the *compadrazgo* in contemporary cultures; one is an inflexible rule; the other is a series of variations that seem to be correlated with, though not entirely caused by, the broader social context in which they are found. These two patterns are:

1. Parents universally are prohibited from choosing themselves as godparents.
2. Within a culture parents are constrained by one of three selection forms: choice reversal may be prescribed, permitted or prohibited. The first rule provides for a symmetrical relationship between parent and godparent while the latter can lead to an asymmetric bond. [1975, pp. 221–22]

Pursuing his thesis that the Catholic dogma of baptism, with its distinction between the natural and the spiritual person, constrains the variations of *compadrazgo* in different societies, Gudeman suggests that the first pattern of selection has its origin in a social value that has been recognized as such from Mauss to Malinowski and Tylor to Lévi-Strauss, by means of which "parents can establish links with others from outside their immediate families" (p. 229). On the other hand, this value is also complementary to and reinforced by the dogmatic postulate that assigns the spiritual and the natural aspects to different persons.

The Andean material, especially that from Andamarca, is in agreement on this point, but in conflict when explaining the predominance of nonreciprocal or asymmetric selection in different systems of *compadrazgo*. Gudeman says:

One possible argument is the following. The godparenthood complex is found primarily in the context of bilateral kinship systems. In such systems continuing and discrete groups are never formed on the basis of kinship principles alone. Another element, deriving from locality, the polity or elsewhere must intervene for perpetual groups to be established. In such situations where corporate groups are not based on kinship the reciprocal form would have to be established between conjugal pairs alone; it would not be a continuing structural relation between groups over generations. Conversely, the prohibition upon choice reversal would force parents to engage in more spiritual relationships than the reciprocal form, and this might seem to fit better the fluid structure. [1975, p. 233]

Not fully satisfied with this explanation, because it contains elements of functionalism that he recognizes as unverifiable, Gudeman returns to the soul-body opposition in the dogma of baptism and suggests that the predominance of the asymmetric or nonreciprocal relationship of *compadrazgo* may be explained thus:

First, since the godparent is conceptually higher than the parent, the bond has an inherent or incipient asymmetry which may or may not be socially recognized. . . . Second, since the spiritual is greater than the natural, the reversal of choice could result in a structurally difficult situation in that two persons would be both natural and spiritual co-parent to one another and each would have a higher and lower position with respect to the other. The prohibition upon choice reversal preserves the distinction between the natural and spiritual parent, and avoids an ideologically confusing situation. [1975, p. 234]

This is an extremely suggestive argument, and Gudeman's assumption develops new possibilities for the study of social systems; I do not believe, however, that the Andean material supports his explanation in either social or ideological terms.

Gudeman's explanation of the predominance of asymmetrical selection in social terms has been influenced by Hammel's 1968 study of *compadrazgo* in Yugoslavia, in which for the first time this institution was studied in collective terms and in terms of the categories of restricted and generalized exchange suggested by Lévi-Strauss (1969). Hammel was able to use these categories because the rural zones of Yugoslavia where he worked are characterized by kinship groups (*zadruga*) organized according to patrilineal principles. Consequently, these groups are discrete and have clearly defined boundaries.

Having identified the groups, Hammel notes that "the same group which is corporate in respect of material property, name, and the *slava* is also corporate in respect of *kumstvo* (*compadrazgo*) statuses and the rights and obligations incumbent on them," and also that "*kumstvo* was by its very nature an intergroup exchange and contributed to the structure of the larger society" (pp. 44, 73). On this issue he points out that where asymmetric exchange of *padrinos* predominates, as "in the south and east, the tendency is for continuity, stability and simple unilateral linkages between named patrilines"; in the zones where symmetrical exchange predominates, as "in the west, the tendency is towards frequent changes of relationship, complexity of ties, and direct reciprocity" (p. 77). According to Hammel, this material "supports Lévi-Strauss' hypothesis (1949) that systems of direct exchange show less solidarity than those of unilateral prestation" (p. 77).

These two studies of *compadrazgo* reflect not only the present state of investigation of this theme but also the advances in the understanding of social systems in anthropological theory. The material from Andean society supplements them and has the advantage of showing clearly that a bilateral kinship system may also serve as a basis for the organization of *compadrazgo* in collective terms and for the simultaneous existence of principles of asymmetric and symmetric exchange. This demonstration is made possible by the introduction into the analysis of a double dialectic involving the interplay of relations between groups and between individuals and groups.

In this society the system of *compadrazgo*, or rather the system of ceremonial kinship in general, has the merit of showing clearly that we are not dealing with an institution that makes up for a possible deterioration in the kinship system, as Foster (1953) suggests, or that acts as an agent to maintain the solidarity of the group. The extended family actually retains great importance, and acts as a platform in the shaping of the ceremonial kinship system. At the same time there is a parallel system—complex yet highly structured—of religious cargos, by which the community is articulated as a whole. Thus, functionalist explanations are inadequate to account for the ceremonial kinship system in the Andean society.

The kinship system of this region, being bilateral, does not give rise to the formation of continuing and discrete groups based exclusively on kinship, such as occur in societies with unilineal kinship systems. But this does not mean that it is not possible for any form of kinship organization to emerge. Kindreds, cognatic groups, and incipient unilineal, patronymic groups are possible. Indeed, in many parts of the Andes we find the concepts of *ayllu* and *casta*, which refer to just such collective entities. Moreover, the people have a bifurcate merging kinship terminology that is collaterally extended up to our equivalent of third cousin, and in the ascending and descending lines to great-grandparents and great-grandchildren, respectively. The limits of these cognatic groups correspond to the extension of the kinship terminology, as can be seen in the context of affinity, because marriage may be contracted only between persons who are considered to be consanguineally unrelated. Deriving from this rule, marriage in Chuschi gives rise to two symmetrical groups, which are defined in opposition to one another and which refer to one another as *aura*. As I have said, these are none other than the respective *ayllus* of a man and a woman who marry; in their relations with one another the members of these collectivities adopt the name *aura*.

As already stated, *compadrazgo* has the same characteristics as *aura* and thus acquires a collective value. Just as the *auras* are two symmetrical collective entities, so *compadrazgo* has this attribute, because the term *compadre* is used reciprocally in the same way as the term *laysi*, which refers to co–parents-in-law and to the parents of co–parents-in-law (who also regard one another as *compadres*). Thus there may be three (or more) generations of *compadres*, as these ties, besides being extended to the siblings of a married couple and their lineal ascendants, may also be extended to the descendants of their collateral kinsmen. It would seem that this pattern of *compadrazgo* ties corresponds to the reiterative nature of marriage ties between kindreds, and that both these systems of exchange influence each other and tend to give a certain demarcation to ego-centered groups that are by nature impermanent and with imprecise boundaries.

Given that *compadrazgo* implies a relationship of group to group, and also one of individual to group, which is apparent in the activity of sponsoring a ritual, and given that there is more than one type of *compadrazgo* tie, the selection of *padrinos* reveals a form of exchange that is simultaneously symmetrical and asymmetrical. The clearest cases of symmetrical exchange are those in which couple A acts as *padrinos de bautismo* to the children of couple B, and one of B's siblings or children in turn acts as *padrino de bautismo* to the children of A or to some of that couple's siblings. Another case is where couple A act as *padrinos de bautismo* to the children of couple B, while couple B (or siblings of couple B) act as *padrinos de misa de salud* to A's children. Rarely do we find cases of two couples being both giving and receiving *compadres* in the same type of *compadrazgo* relationship, and this rarity demonstrates the asymmetry of the exchanges.

In the case of *padrinos de bautismo*, it should be remembered that the ties are made at the time of marriage, before there are any children, and the sponsors should be a married couple so that there may be no discrepancy between the sex of the sponsor and that of the child. Asymmetry in this case thus emerges from the need to have previously married couples acting as *padrinos*; as a result, giving *compadres* are almost always older than receiving *compadres*. This asymmetry is expressed in the form of preferential treatment of giving *compadres*. In the area of Ayacucho and Apurímac, however, this preferential position is normally obscured by the terminological and ideological emphasis on symmetry, whereas in Cuzco, in Puno, and in the Aymara region certain asymmetrical tendencies are seen, in that terminologically the parents of an *ahijado* are treated as if they were *ahijados* themselves, and the term *padrino* is extended even to the children of the actual *padrinos*. By contrast, in Andamarca parents and godparents treat themselves as *compadres* and emphasize the idea of equality, although in practice giving and receiving *compadres* are differentiated, and their children use the term *huauje* (brother) to address each other.

Marriage Exchange

It is at the level of marriage exchange and affinal terminology that the structural aspects of *compadrazgo* are most evident in modern communities and are best documented for the pre-Hispanic period, as has been shown by Zuidema (1977).

Though the marriage system cannot be described as either "prescriptive" or "preferential," the pattern is similar to that which we observe at the level of *compadrazgo*. There is a tendency to reiterate the marriage ties between two kindreds or to combine marriage with *compadrazgo* exchanges, in a way that makes possible the development of a pattern of direct exchange at different levels. There are many cases where group *A* gives a woman or a man to group *B* and in return receives another woman or a man or a giving *compadre*. In order to include as many people as possible in a direct exchange system between two or more bilateral groups that combine marriage and *compadrazgo*, people of the opposite sex marry and those of the same sex become *compadres*. From the point of view of marriage, these exchanges cannot take place in a subsequent generation because the two groups merge in the children; from the point of view of *compadrazgo* this merging does not happen. We have already seen that the *compadrazgo* relationship is reproduced in a subsequent generation when the children of godparents and parents call themselves "brother."

Both *compadrazgo* and marriage show a pronounced endogamous tendency at the level of the community and other sublocalities, a tendency counterbalanced by the explicit prohibition on setting up these links between relatives or members of the same *ayllu*. The proscriptive regulations are extended up to fourth-degree relatives in both cases; the reiterative pattern of both institutions, and the collective image that it projects, can be partly explained as a mechanism to avoid the danger of committing incest.

In order to understand this endogamy, we should remember that Andamarca has a population of less than three thousand, and about 85 percent of marriages are endogamic. Apart from the large number of consanguineal categories within which one is forbidden to marry, the incest prohibition is extended to affines and to the numerous ceremonial kin, who have to be recruited beyond the consanguineal realm. Given these conditions, we may well imagine what would happen if for each child (generally numerous, because ideally one should have twelve children) there was a sponsor from a different family for each of the types of *compadrazgo*. The result would be that the endogamous ideal of the community would be untenable, and the community itself would become exogamous. Thus the extension of ceremonial kin ties through the kindreds or *ayllu* is essential in order to maintain the integrity of the community, and at the same time to allow it to reproduce itself and to give a certain permanency to social groups that are rather weak from a descent point of view.

Affinal Terminology

The collective and individual dimensions of this system are reproduced almost exactly in the terminology for affines, assuming a symmetric or asymmetric aspect depending upon whether it is seen as the interaction of two collectivities or of an individual and a collectivity. The first type of relationship is similar to that of *compadres*, which can itself be seen as an affinal relationship, because a reciprocal term such as *laysi* is used. The asymmetrical aspect, on the other hand, is seen in the relation of individual to group: the son- and daughter-in-law address their parents- and brothers- or sisters-in-law by nonreciprocal terms. The mother- and father-in-law and their parents and children call the son-in-law *masa* and the daughter-in-law *lumtshuy*. These latter call their father-in-law *soguero* and mother-in-law *soguera*, while addressing their parents as *machuy* and *aulay* and their children as *tiuy* and *tiay*.

These three generations of affines were called, according to ancient Quechua vocabularies and other sources, *caca* (men) and *aque* (women). *Caca* was also the term that was applied to the maternal uncle and that from an early date was translated as *tío* (uncle). It is interesting to note that this term now applies to the wife's brother and thus reveals the continuity of the asymmetrical sense of the use of the term *caca*. It also confirms the point, upon which Zuidema (1977) has been so insistent, that the mother's brother is an affinal relative and that given the unity of the lineage of the sister's son, this latter inherits the relationship of affinity that his father maintained with his mother's brother, who was the father's wife's father (see Figure 2).

Figure 2. Affinal Terminology

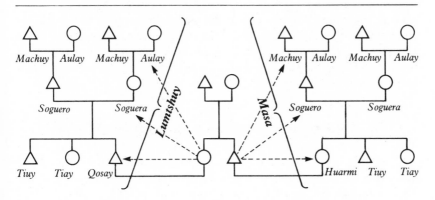

Ceremonial Kinship and Marriage

Marriage and the ceremonial kinship system influence each other, and there are many parallels between them. They differ, however, in that the ceremonial kinship system *presupposes* marriage, particularly in the case of those types which derive from the sponsorship of a ritual and which take the form of *compadrazgo*. *Compadrazgo* involving sponsorship establishes a link between two couples, and not between two individuals, as is the case with marriage. In collective terms, the kindreds of four individuals may serve as channels for the extension of *compadrazgo* ties. In marriage, the interaction is between the kindreds of two individuals, which from then on will develop further ties of affinity, ties of *compadrazgo*, and new marriage ties with one another. A less pronounced difference between the two institutions is that the descendants of the two pairs of *compadres* can renew the ceremonial kin tie, even though they will become *hermanos* (brothers), whereas the descendants of a married couple cannot renew the marriage tie until approximately four generations have passed. Thus ceremonial kinship only generates other ties of ceremonial kinship, whereas marriage creates ties of consanguinity, affinity, and, potentially, *compadrazgo*.

Another important difference between marriage and *compadrazgo* is the monogamous nature of the first and the plural nature of the second. In marriage an individual may have only one spouse at a time; in *compadrazgo* there is no restriction on the number of links that an individual or couple may forge. In this respect the ceremonial kinship system is analogous to the religious cargo system: both are accumulative, and this accumulation occurs during the life cycle. Thanks to this dynamic attribute of *compadrazgo* and of ceremonial kinship in general, a person's social networks may be expanded to the point where the person receives the necessary support for sponsoring the highest religious cargos, which involve the whole community. It is not surprising to find that those who sponsor the patron saint of the community, who is at the top of the religious hierarchy, are generally people who have reached their peak in the accumulation of property and ceremonial kin and whose children are about to reach the age of marrying. When the children start to marry, there begins the dismemberment of their parents' property.

The Optional Nature of *Compadrazgo*

Although *compadrazgo* tends to follow structural lines deriving from marriage and from kindred solidarity, it is also intrinsically optional. Thus, although the *laysi* or co–parents-in-law are potential *compadres*, because they belong to the respective kindreds of a married couple, they actually become *compadres* only when they seal this bond before the image of a saint. This restriction also applies to those who become only *compadres de respeto*, as well as to *compadrazgo* that involves sponsorship. This optional aspect shows the individual dimension of the institution, expressed in the fact that no two individuals or couples have the same ceremonial kinsmen. From a social point of view this individual dimension corresponds to the bilateral nature of the kinship system, in which, with the exception of full siblings, every person has a different stock of consanguineal relatives, and also to the proscriptive rather than prescriptive nature of the ideology of the marriage system.

Conclusion

Compadrazgo in Andean society stands as an indicative case of the vitality of a sociocultural system that incorporates foreign institutions, yet permits them to remain mere forms with a content completely different from that which they had originally. We have been able to recognize this distinction between form and content because our use of certain structural premises has enabled us to identify the constituent parts of this institution, the meaning that the social actors attach to them, and their similarity to the constituent parts of other institutions, such as kinship and marriage, whose Andean nature has been more explicit. The material upon which we have based our analysis derives principally from Andamarca, but we have compared it with data from several other communities distributed over Peru and Bolivia. The resemblances allow us to extend our findings to the Andes as a whole, at least as a plausible hypothesis. The contexts we have selected include various kinds of rites, kinship terminology, and social networks that involve the interaction of groups and individuals. Finally, it can be said that all these contexts coincide in suggesting that the basic meaning of *compadrazgo* in Andean society is that of a mediating institution between individuals and between groups and that its legitimacy derives from its collective dimension, which in Andamarca proclaims the symmetrical or equilibrated value of this relationship.

Acknowledgments

Most of the ideas and evidence in these pages derive from a study carried out in the Comunidad de Andamarca between 1970 and 1978, financed by the Wenner-Gren Foundation for Anthropological Research, the Ford Foundation, and the Pontíficia Universidad Católica del Perú, to all of whom grateful acknowledgment is given. Additional evidence derives from other ethnographic monographs based on material from various parts of the Andes (see the References) and from an investigation being developed in the Mantaro Valley and Huancavelica in collaboration with Dr. Norman Long of the University of Durham and with the support of the Social Science Research Council of Great Britain.

References

Avila, Francisco de
1966   *Dioses y hombres de Huarochirí*, translated by J. M. Arguedas.
[1598?]   Lima: Museo Nacional Historia and Instituto de Estudio Peruanos.
Bertonio, Ludovico
1879   *Vocabulario de la lengua Aymara*. La Paz: Edition Facsimilar.
Doughty, Paul L.
1968   *Huaylas: An Andean District in Search of Progress*. New York: Cornell University Press.
Duviols, Pierre
1976   "Une petite chronique retrouvée." In *Errores, ritos, supersticiones y ceremonias de los indios de la provincia de Chinchaycocha y otras del Perú*, edited and commentary by Pierre Duviols. *Journal de la Societé des Américanistes* 63:275–97.
Foster, George
1953   "Cofradía and Compadrazgo in Spain and Spanish America." *Southwestern Journal of Anthropology* 9:1–28.
Gillin, John
1945   *Moche: A Peruvian Coastal Community*. Institute of Social Anthropology Publication no. 3. Washington, D.C.: Smithsonian Institution.
Gonzáles Carré, Enrique, and Galdo Gutierrez, Virgilio
1976   *Introducción al proceso de socializatión Andina*. Serie Tricentario. Ayacucho: UNSCH.
Guaman Poma de Ayala, F.
1968   *El primer nueva coronica y buen gobierno*. Paris: Institut d'Ethnologie.
Gudeman, Stephen
1972   "The *Compadrazgo* as a Reflection of the Natural and Spiritual Person." *Proceedings of the Royal Anthropological Institute of Great Britain and Ireland for 1971*, pp. 45–71.

1975   "Spiritual Relationships and Selecting a Godparent." *Man*,
            n.s. 10:221-37.
Hammel, Eugene
1968   *Alternative Social Structures and Ritual Relations in the Balkans.*
            Englewood Cliffs, N.J.: Prentice-Hall.
Isbell, Billie Jean
1978   *To Defend Ourselves: Ecology and Ritual in an Andean Village.*
            Latin American Monographs no. 7. Austin: University of
            Texas, Institute of Latin American Studies.
Lévi-Strauss, Claude
1969   *The Elementary Structures of Kinship.* Translated by J. H. Belle
[1949]   and J. R. von Sturmer. London: Eyre and Spottiswoode. [Orig-
            inally published in French as *Les structures élémentaires de la
            parenté.* Paris: Presses Universitaires de France.]
Mayer, Enrique
1977   "Beyond the Nuclear Family," in *Andean Kinship and Mar-
            riage*, edited by Ralph Bolton and Enrique Mayer, pp. 60-80.
            American Anthropological Association Special Publication no.
            7. Washington, D.C.: The Association.
Mintz, Sydney W., and Wolf, Eric R.
1950   "An Analysis of Ritual Co-parenthood (Compadrazgo)." *South-
            western Journal of Anthropology* 6:341-68.
Morote Best, E.
1956   "La Zafa-Casa." *Cultura* 1:13-30.
Ossio, Juan M.
1978   "Locality, Kinship and Ceremonial Kinship: A Study of Social
            Organization of the Communidad de Andamarca, Ayacucho—
            Peru." D.Phil. thesis, Oxford University.
1981   "Expresiones simbólicas y sociales de los ayllus andínos." *Et-
            nohistoria Anthropologica Andena, Segunda Jornada de Historia*,
            edited by Amalia Castelli, Marsha Kotch de Paredes and Mari-
            anne Mould de Pease, pp. 189-216.
Redfield, Robert
1930   *Tepotzlan: A Mexican Village.* Chicago: University of Chicago
            Press.
Santo Tomás, Domingo de
1951   *Gramatika o arte de la lengua general de los indios de los Reynos*
[1560]   *del Peru*, vol. 1. *Lexicon o vocabulario de la lengua general de los
            indios de los Reynos del Peru*, vol. 2. Lima: Instituto de Histo-
            ria, Universidad Nacional Mayor de San Marcos.

Zuidema, R. Tom
1977   "The Inca Kinship System: A New Theoretical View," in *Andean Kinship and Marriage*, edited by Ralph Bolton and Enrique Mayer, pp. 240–281. American Anthropological Association Special Publication no. 7. Washington, D.C.: The Association.

Love, Race, Slavery, and Sexuality in Jamaican Images of the Family

Jack Alexander

Introduction

Lady Maria Nugent, daughter of an American colonist and wife of the British governor of Jamaica, kept a diary during her stay in Jamaica from 1801 to 1805. In her diary she recounts a visit to one of the "better" sugar plantations in the island:

> As you enter the gates, there is a long range of negro houses, like thatched cottages, and a row of cocoa-nut trees and clumps of cotton trees. The sugar-house, and all the buildings, are thought to be more than usually good, and well taken care of. The overseer, a civil, vulgar, Scotch officer, on half-pay, did the honours to us; but, when we got to the door of the distillery, the smell of the rum was so intolerable, that . . . I left the gentlemen, and went to the overseer's house, about a hundred yards off. I talked to the black women, who told me all their histories. The overseer's *chère amie*, and no man here is without one, is a tall black woman, well made, with a very flat nose, thick lips, and a skin of ebony, highly polished and shining. She shewed me her three yellow children, and said, with some ostentation she should soon have another. The marked attention of the other women, plainly proved her to be the favourite Sultana of this vulgar, ugly, Scotch Sultan, who is about fifty, clumsy, ill made, and dirty. He had a dingy, sallow-brown complexion, and only two yellow discoloured tusks, by way of teeth. However, they say he is a good overseer. [Wright 1966, p. 29]

In this essay we will find the image of the overseer, his *chère amie* of polished ebony, and their yellow children hidden in and structuring the everyday perceptions of family life experienced by middle-class Jamaicans.

Our informants will eventually lead us to their understanding of their place in Jamaican society, for that understanding permeates their family lives. We will find that the power of their image of the family lies in its ability to resolve the paradox of legitimacy in a colonial society. What characterizes the "colonial situation" is a racial, social, and cultural split between the dominators and the dominated, whereas on the other hand legitimacy—"the means by which ideology is blended with power" (Fried 1967, p. 26)—is a cultural phenomenon consisting of beliefs that justify the exercise of power. How can there be legitimacy, which requires a common culture, when the essence of the colonial situation is a total split between the dominators and the dominated? It is the image of the family that formulates legitimacy in the Jamaican colonial situation. Thus this essay heeds the contention of Smith "that more attention should be paid to the particularity of the historically generated cultural forms characteristic of the area and to the social practices through which those forms operate in the specific conditions of contemporary Latin American societies" ("Introduction" above).

The collection and analysis of the data in this essay have been based on the method and theory of David M. Schneider and Raymond T. Smith (Schneider 1972, [1968] 1980; Schneider and Smith, [1973] 1978). The data consist of a set of interviews with eleven middle-class Jamaican informants collected between 1967 and 1969. Interviews were approximately weekly and lasted between one and two hours. The shortest set was seven interviews over two months; the longest set was thirty-one interviews over fourteen months. All interviews were taped and transcribed, a process that provided a set of texts to analyze.

The analysis assumes that culture consists of a pure level of domains, such as kinship and age, which consist of a set of collective representations that cohere, and that pure domains combine on a conglomerate level to create domains—such as the family—that are guides for action (Schneider 1972, pp. 40–41). Therefore the analysis begins with a description of pure domains, proceeds to describe how these combine into the domain of the family, and finally shows how the cultural domain of the family is related to action in the society.

Kinship

The first interview with each informant began with the request "Please tell me all your relatives." Requests for clarification of the question were turned back on the informant, who was encouraged to clarify the question for him- or herself. The aim of the technique is to set a framework in which informants choose how to present their relatives so that their presentations represent their own conception of relatives and can be analyzed as such.

Informants asked for two types of clarification. With one kind of question the anthropologist was asked, on the basis of his presumed superior knowledge, to define for the informant exactly what a relative is, the informants believing themselves to have an imperfect concept of this term. Thus, these informants' collective representation of kinship may be said to reside in an ideal or objective realm. The informant fills this collective representation with personal meaning, listing not "Father" but "my father" and listing relatives by personal name. The intimate tie and analytic distinction between the informant's collective representation and the personal meaning given to it is illustrated by the fact that, if we construct this collective representation, we can see how the informant manipulates it and thus reveals personal meanings. For instance, kin listed and the order of kin are highly consistent among informants, yet one informant did not mention her father at all in the first interview. Our suspicion that this absence tells us something about her is amply confirmed at the beginning of the second interview. "I left out a most important person. . . . In the days when my mother was a girl, to have an illegitimate child in a small district was a great disgrace. . . . I was illegitimate, an unfortunate thing. So after I came to the age of discretion, I personally felt a great remorse. And I still do."

Examples of the second kind of question are "Do you want the dead ones?" "Do you want more than the close ones?" Having defined *relatives* for themselves, the informants still need further clarification in order to determine which persons are relatives. The collective representation *relatives* is ambiguous when put to use.

These two kinds of original questions express from the outset two related themes that run through the interviews—a collective representation of kinship conceived by the informant to exist in an ideal, objective realm and an ambiguity in the use of this collective representation.

When also asked to define *relatives*, informants have difficulty producing a definition they find adequate, and if they come up with a definition they find adequate, it is easy to push them into a position where they become uncertain. Informants offer two reasons for this difficulty. One is that kinship concerns feelings that are illogical and difficult to conceptualize. The second is that having referred to their feelings as an essential part of the meaning of *relative*, they find that their feelings do not consistently distinguish between relatives and nonrelatives, because one component of the meaning of *relative* is independent of their feelings: "I was interpreting family in one conversation as consanguinity, as blood relationship, and another time I was interpreting it as a sort of emotional, inclusive group, and I think people vary between the two posts, at least I do, according to circumstances."

If we examine more closely informants' feeling of kinship and their idea of blood relationship, we can discover why the conceptual vagueness and inconsistency do not normally disturb them.

The most common feeling informants associate with kinship is the feeling of belonging.

> A: So the relationship isn't distinguished by the fact that you help those people more than others?
> I: No.
> A: Or that you feel closer to them.
> I: No. There is a—how can I find the right word?—there is a feeling of belonging. That's all there is.
> A: A feeling of belonging.
> I: A feeling of belonging. That's the best way I think I can describe it. But it does not obligate you at all.

The objective fact of blood relation is the possession of a common physical substance. Though informants regard blood relationship as an objective fact of nature, it has a further meaning to them: "I would very much like to know, which I will never know, where the various families I'm comprised of come from. . . . My parents accentuated the white side. Well, we all know it's a healthy mixture. The fact that we know we're so mixed up . . . there's nothing we can do about it. We must just accept ourselves as we are."

Thus, I am, in some way and to some extent, the physical substance I consist of, and insofar as I share some of that substance with others, we are the same. For informants a blood relation means that they share the same substance and to that extent share a common identity. It is this sense of common identity that the biological fact of blood relationship conveys to them.

The feeling of belonging and the meaning of a common substance fit together and reinforce each other. The impact of the collective representation, consisting of these two apparently disparate elements, is revealed in the following observation by a male informant:

> I: Now, I feel a person outside could not have the same love for a child that a mother would have.
> A: How about a father?
> I: A father too. I don't know, Jack, but I never thought about it. I tell you something. When I got married, my wife went to the hospital; I said, "Now, there's one thing, I ain't touching that child. Do you hear me? No, sir, I ain't looking after no pickney, you know." And it just never, well, I just, and I wondered what I would do. I never had any feeling. I don't know how to ex-

plain. And yet, the evening when I came home from work and stopped off at the hospital and the nurse showed me, well, that is your, when I go and looked on it, a feeling passed through me that changed my entire, something inward took place, a transformation, instantly I felt it, and I knew that I was no longer a single person, and I had a responsibility, and I had something, my child, and it has never left me since. I don't know if it has happened to you?

Here we see the power of symbols. The stimulus of a newborn child is endowed with a meaning that produces a powerful feeling that manifests itself in the world of ideas as a sense of common identity ("I knew I was no longer a single person") and a sense of belonging.

We can state the collective representation of *blood relatives* as follows: blood relatives share a common substance that is a part of nature, and thereby and to that extent, they share a common identity, which gives them a feeling of belonging. Thus, the symbol of blood relations, of substantial unity, creates meaning in certain physical objects in the world, persons defined as relatives, and this meaning arouses feelings in the actor.

What has from the beginning of the section appeared to be an inconsistency and even contradiction between two elements of the collective representation of relatives turns out to be highly consistent and mutually reinforcing.

Having revealed the collective representation of relatives that lies behind and gives shape to the accounts of individual informants, let me show that the meaning this representation gives to experience can best be understood as the resolution of a problem of meaning arising from action.

The collective representation of relatives asserts the fact of a permanent fundamental mutuality of interest between persons defined as relatives in the sense that the welfare of one is the welfare of the other; it asserts what Schneider terms "enduring diffuse solidarity" ([1968] 1980, p. 50) or what Fortes terms the "axiom of amity" (1969, p. 219). This cultural assertion of a permanent mutuality of interests between persons focuses on part of the inherent characteristics of social experience and proclaims this part to be the whole. Insofar as persons are social beings they are interdependent. Therefore, they are means to one anothers' ends, and this interdependence creates a mutuality of interests. This same interdependence also creates the possibility of a conflict of interests, because by withholding him- or herself a person can thwart the achievement of the ends of someone else with whom he or she has a social relation. Therefore, the collective representation of relatives, which asserts a total and permanent identity of interests, operates as an ideology that marks off a category of relations for which it asserts the reality of one aspect of social experience, mutuality, at the expense of another aspect, conflict.

The ideology of relatives asserts the permanent mutuality of interests in a particular symbolic form. A physical identity is asserted, the meaning of which is a feeling that is formulated as a feeling of belonging. This physical identity is asserted to be a natural, given, permanent condition.

Thus, perceptual experience—for instance, a newborn child—is given thinkable form by the symbol of shared physical substance, the meaning of which is a feeling that takes thinkable form as a feeling of "belonging." Now the thinkable form, the symbol of shared substance and belonging, can make most sense, for an anthropologist, if we assume that people think in order to act. Anthropologists will most fully explain the collective representation *relative* if we suppose that humans give meaning to experience in order to formulate choices and in order to live with the consequences of choices, for they must choose; the choice can be formulated only by humanly attributed meanings. Can we say anything about why (1) the symbol for "enduring, diffuse solidarity" is shared physical substance and a feeling of belonging, and why (2) the symbol splits into what is formulated by the culture as an objective and a subjective aspect?

The answer to the first question is that in order to assert the existence of a category of social relations in which mutuality is inherent and conflict is not, the mutuality is expressed as a natural phenomenon, that is, one over which humans have no control. Mutuality is formulated not as a possibility, opportunity, or obligation, all of which imply human choice, but as a fact outside the realm of human choice. How is this formulation a solution to a problem of meaning arising from action? If we impute to humans the experience of choice, then the definition of an unchangeable mutuality of interests will make sense only if it is defined as outside the realm of human choice.

Let us turn now to the second question—the split of the collective representation *relative* into objective and subjective aspects. The formulation of *relative* as a given natural fact in a sense lifts *relative* out of the realm of human choice. However, it is a characteristic of Jamaican culture that phenomena defined as outside the realm of human choice are conceived of as outside the realm of human responsibility. An American example is the effort currently being expended to choose the fate of one's ascribed sex role. A Jamaican example is the fact that in Jamaica race is an ambivalent phenomenon; on the one hand, it is conceived as a very deep, given component of the person, and on the other hand, precisely because it is a characteristic over which a person has no control, informants treat it as an extraneous fact for which they take no responsibility. Within kinship itself its ascribed character can be and often is taken as grounds for denying its relevance for action: "you can choose your friends, but not your relatives."

In short, on the level of meaning, what is defined as an objective fact of nature cannot be in itself a meaningful ground for a motive of action. Because action involves choice, any reason that denies the realm of choice is senseless as a reason for choice; it does not, so to speak, give a reason for effort. It is only what is formulated as a subjective state—for example, calculating the benefits to be gained from alternative actions or a feeling of belonging—that can make sense as a basis for action.

In fact, the area marked off as *relatives* is experienced as an area of action; whether informants' behavior is in accord with the norm of enduring, diffuse solidarity or not, it is experienced as an action, not a reflex. It is this experience of action that demands, so to speak, a subjective aspect in the collective representation of relative. It is the permanent, given aspect that demands an objective aspect in this collective representation.

In everyday life the collective representation *relative* works smoothly, for after all, that is what it is designed to do. It is only in marginal situations that its nature as a solution to an intractable problem of meaning in action appears.

In addition to a spontaneous kin list, a genealogy was collected from each informant. In the genealogy each link was explored for further links, so that the genealogies were much larger than the spontaneous kin lists. One feature of these genealogies is especially relevant for our present purposes. In eight cases the genealogies trace back to an ancestral couple; in three cases they do not. The eight informants with ancestral couples are all of middle-class origin; the three informants who do not have an ancestral couple are all of lower-class origin. The significance of the ancestral couple can be understood by examining one case more closely. The following are an informant's descriptions first of her ancestral couple and then of another ascendant couple.

> I: From what I was always told, my great-grandmother who married McManus, she was supposed to be the daughter of a slave.
> A: And a planter, did you tell me?
> I: Well it's always these people that came out on the plantations, some of them may have been overseers, I don't know which, but he would have been a, probably would be English.

> I: My mother's mother's mother had eleven or twelve children, but my mother's mother was the only one that lived to have children. . . . And she didn't live very long either, because she married first at eighteen, and then she married at twenty-one, and then she died when my mother was seven, so she must have been

about twenty-eight or thirty when she died. . . . The first husband was an old man named Dixon. She wanted to marry somebody rich, and he died and didn't leave her a farthing. He left it to her if she didn't marry again. . . . When she was twenty-one, she married Mr. d'Estaing. She died seven years after.

For the ancestral couple, the color and legal status of the woman are crucial; for the mother's mother legal status and color are not mentioned, whereas the facts that she was the only one of many siblings to survive long enough to have children, that she died very young, and that she married twice in that short time are crucial. The fact that she died young is mentioned twice and is connected with the fact that it is the mother's mother's mother who raised the informant's mother. For the male member of the ancestral couple, place of origin, color, and occupation are crucial; on the other hand, what is crucial for the mother's father is a series of facts (not given in the quotation) such as his place of origin and the fact that he died shortly after his wife. Family experiences do not enter into descriptions of ancestral couples as they do in the descriptions of other ascendants. Ancestral couples are presented exclusively in terms of impersonal characteristics that define social position in the society—color, nationality, and occupation. Relatives who are ascendants are defined by characteristics that are of significance only to the informant and those close to him or her; these characteristics are meaningless to outsiders. Ancestral couples are defined by characteristics that are of common significance, such as class, status, power, and race. Later we will see how informants link these contexts.

Affinity

The collective representation of marriage formulates the experience of diffuse, enduring solidarity as created, in contrast to the given solidarity of consanguinity. The collective representation of marriage is approached here through an analysis of an account of courtship. In this account the contrast between love and friendship reveals the nature of the collective representation of affinity:

1 She was in one dorm and I was in another and she used to pass through my dorm and I saw her and I thought she was nice-looking and all that, but just remained there, you know. [A friend introduced her, and our informant invited her to a Christian Conference.]

5 So I went, and when we were there we chatted at times. I realized that I was getting too interested in her, because I understood that she had another boy-friend. . . . So I didn't go back. For a while.

But we both were involved in this Christian group and through this we saw each other. . . . We developed a deeper interest in each
10 other and we went on. . . . I suppose for her there was this conflict. There wasn't such a conflict for me, because although I liked her, I saw her when I wanted, and I went out with her when I wanted, and we had good times, and it didn't really affect me that there was somebody else; at any rate I didn't sort of consider her being my
15 girl-friend. Well, she always felt that she liked this fellow. . . . We were just friends. I mean we went out together and had a good time. [Then one weekend the group took a mountain-climbing trip.] We traveled together. The whole trip sort of made us realize that we were in love with each other. So it wasn't just a matter of friend-
20 ship. We really found that we loved each other. But there is this other fellow.
[Summer came; they separated to follow their independent plans.] We both wrote each other. And I suppose in writing a lot of things are sort of set down . . . and when we came back we realized that
25 we can't sort of fool ourselves. Because we used to deny it. We used to tell our friends we were friends, but it was nothing. . . . As this new year went on we developed in our friendship, and I don't think any real significant things happened except that we got closer, got more friendly. [She was now in her final year at the university, and
30 he was one year behind her.]
But I realized the big question was there. Was I to sort of make up my mind now as to whether I wanted her or not? I made up my mind that we would do something. So we got engaged. That summer she went home. This was sort of a test to see . . . whether we
35 would wake up in absence, and for her to think away from me and the whole artificial situation on campus. . . . We wrote a lot, and during this time we really realized that we wanted each other.
One night after she returned I just said "Let's get married," and she said "yes." . . . I had remembered that she always dreamed of wak
40 ing up on Christmas a new bride. . . . So I said "Let's get married Christmas Eve." And we did.

There are seven elements that structure the contrast between love and friendship. Some of these contrasts may appear obvious, but it is important to make the analysis systematic.

1. Love and friendship are distinguished by intensity, love being a more intense form of personal relationship. "The whole trip sort of made us realize that we were in love with each other. So it wasn't just a matter of friendship" (lines 18–20).

2. The difference in degree of intensity amounts to a qualitative difference, because one can have several friends, but only one lover. "We really found that we loved each other. But there is this other fellow" (lines 20–21). These two facts are incompatible and demand some resolution. Thus love is an exclusive relation.

3. It is striking that, though love follows on friendship, after the couple are described as in love our informant reverts to describing the relationship as a friendship (lines 25–27). Why this apparent contradiction? Because the word *friendship* can apply to the development of a relationship, but the word *love* cannot. Therefore, when our informant wishes to describe the development of the relationship, even if it has already advanced to the state of love, he must revert to the word *friendship*. For our informant two persons "realize" they are in love (lines 18, 24, 37) or "find out" that they are in love (line 20), but love does not develop. In contrast, the two "develop" their friendship (line 27) or get "more friendly" (lines 28–29); they do not "realize" or "find out" that they are friends. Thus love either does or does not exist, whereas friendship can become greater. Where friendship admits of degrees, love is absolute.

4. From this same contrast between "realizing" the existence of love and "developing" a friendship we can also conclude that love is involuntary and friendship is voluntary. A person does not decide to be in love; the person finds out whether he or she is in fact in love. In contrast, friendship develops by choice: "we developed in our friendship" (line 27).

5. Love is constant; friendship need not be so. As friends "I saw her when I wanted, and I went out with her when I wanted, and we had good times" (lines 11–13). In contrast, the best proof of love is constancy through separation: "That summer she went home. This was sort of a test" (lines 33–34).

6. Love arouses a sense that there are two aspects to the personality. For our informant to say that "we realized we loved each other," and "we found we loved each other," he must assume that love was part of each of them and they were unaware of it. It follows that the existence of love is not dependent on one's awareness of it. Nor is it simply a question of being aware or unaware of love; it is possible to have a false awareness. It is possible to think one is in love when one really is not. Thus their separation was an occasion to see if they were dreaming or "really" in love. In contrast, because the informant does not "discover" that he has been a friend, there is no assumption in friendship of two aspects of the person in imperfect communication.

7. What difference does it make whether the person is aware of love? Awareness provokes the necessity of a decision. Given the awareness of love it becomes necessary to decide whether to make a commitment. "Was I to

sort of make up my mind now as to whether I wanted her?" (lines 31–32). Why the necessity to make up one's mind? For it might be thought that if two persons love each other, they will, of love's accord, stay together, and if they do not love each other, what could be the point of making up one's mind on the matter? What assumptions could underlie our informant's perspective? A possible explanation is that love remains incomplete without conscious assent. The informant's account assumes not only that two aspects of the person—unconscious and conscious—exist but also that these two aspects embody contrasting principles. One aspect is associated with the awareness of choices and with decisions; choices and decisions do not exist when the person is unaware. It is as though the impelling force of love has a source outside awareness and that integration of the person requires assent of the conscious aspect of the person, which is given by the faculty of decision, which is a faculty of consciousness.

Thus there are seven elements that structure the contrast between love and friendship. (1) Love is an intenser, friendship a milder, relation. (2) Love is an exclusive, friendship a nonexclusive, relation. (3) Love is an absolute, friendship a graded, feeling. (4) Love is involuntary; friendship, voluntary. (5) Love is a constant, friendship a fluctuating, feeling. (6) Love provokes an awareness of a conscious and unconscious aspect of the person; friendship does not. (7) Love provokes an integration of the conscious and unconscious aspects; friendship does not. The components of the contrast between love and friendship provide a structure of collective representations in terms of which the informant can relate his unique experience of courtship.

There are two conclusions to draw from this analysis. In contrast to friendship, love is linked to a collective representation of the personality that consists of two elements: an unconscious, involuntary element and a conscious, voluntary element. Furthermore, love orients persons to the problem of integrating these two elements of the personality.

Conjugal love and marriage involve two elements, an unconscious, involuntary element of the personality as well as the voluntary element discussed above. Although marriage is a voluntary decision, the decision is made with reference to what is experienced as an integration of the voluntary and involuntary aspects of the personality.

The cultural structures of cognatic and conjugal love have similarities. In both cases there is a voluntary and an involuntary element. Still, it is true that in cognatic love there is an element of substance—blood—and in conjugal love this element is absent. This difference between the structures of cognatic and conjugal love arises from the fact that diffuse, enduring solidarity is conceived as coeval with existence for blood relatives and as created for spouses. Appropriately, cognatic love is symbolized by bodily substance, which is coeval with a person's existence, and conjugal love is symbolized by a sudden emanation of love.

Once again we see that diffuse, enduring solidarity asserts a permanent mutuality of interests between persons, when in fact social relations inherently contain the possibility of conflict as well as mutuality. The fact of alternatives is covered by the assertion that diffuse, enduring solidarity arises from a realm where there are no choices—the unconscious, involuntary realm. Because in fact there are alternatives (conflict or mutuality), there must be an experience of choice in action, and this choice is represented in the voluntary, conscious aspect of the person. The power of the collective representations lies in their capacity to express and, most important, to integrate these two aspects of experience. It is the power of the collective representations of kinship and affinity in integrating two aspects of the experience of action that makes them effective means of talking about other aspects of social life.

Illegitimacy

Such other aspects of social life have already entered into our informants' speculations. Early in the section entitled "Kinship," our informant referred to her illegitimate birth, a notion that has nothing to do with the solidarity of kinship and affinity. Illegitimacy is a feature of every informant's discussion of family life, and its relation to kinship and affinity is well illustrated by these two quotations:

> I: I know a rather respectable middle-class man who has had a string of outside children, and his viewpoint is it doesn't say a man must not have bastard children, but he must take care of them. He has given them all his name, he has educated them very well, and he still occupies his position of respect in the community, but if his sister or his daughter did produce a bastard, I think she would have to pay her penalty in terms of loss of regard in the community.
> A: In a case like this people would know?
> I: Yes.
> A: Nobody would go around and fuss about it?
> I: No.
> A: Does it make a difference how he treats these outside children?
> I: No.
> A: Is there any concern with how the women are treated?
> I: No.

A: How do the wives take all this?

I: It would differ with the personality of the wife. Some would be very angry and repudiate any knowledge or association; some would take them into the homes.

A: You mentioned to me the first time we were talking that one of your brothers has an illegitimate son.

I: Yes.

A: Was he in the home at all?

I: No. Illegitimacy is sort of frowned on by the family and by many people, so the mother not being the type that we had expected, he grew away from us. Occasionally he calls on one of the family. Whenever he meets one member of the family he introduces himself.

A: Is this something that your brother and the rest of the members of the family keep very quiet?

I: Yes, he was born when my brother was teaching, and many teachers have lost their posts because of that.

A: Was this something that caused upset in the family?

I: The mother might have been somebody like that one you see coming up here [informant points out the window to a poor, black woman walking up the street]; that type of person. He had to keep it away from the family.

A: Is it something that would ever be discussed in the family?

I: My sister would mention it to me that "Imagine this chap came and tried to introduce himself."

A: Has he ever got in touch with you?

I: Yes, he came introducing himself as my nephew. I found I wasn't going to take any responsibility for him. . . . I avoided him. He has the tendency to embarrass the father. The mother was that type; the grandmother. You see illegitimacy can turn out to be something that some people can make capital out of, or try to. Which is normal to a certain extent, and abnormal in one way. In that the normal affections that a child would expect from whoever is supposed to be his father are not met in the home. Therefore they have to be abnormal in their approaches. Well, I personally can't accept any responsibility for him. . . . Interesting enough my nephew said this chap came and introduced himself. He had never known of him. And he said he was at some friend's place and this chap was there and introduced himself as my cousin. He felt rather funny about it. . . . When he introduced himself as a cousin my nephew wasn't sure which side of the family, from his mother's side or from his father's side. So he had to ask him all these things to get the story. When it did get around, he shunned him.

These quotations show us first that illegitimacy is an improper yet expected feature of middle-class Jamaican life. It provokes shame and silence, yet there are no structurally generated sanctions against it; indeed, it is a structural feature of middle-class family life. The pervasive presence of illegitimacy means that there is a contrast between legitimacy and illegitimacy and that this contrast overlays the cultural structure of kinship and affinity. The contrast between legitimacy and illegitimacy is a contrast between responsibility and irresponsibility. Legitimacy brings with it the "normal" expectation of affection and responsibility. Illegitimacy brings with it irresponsibility in the sense that the terms of the kinship relationship are subject to personal preference. Whether a man supports his "outside" children and whether his wife takes them in are matters of personal preference. The contrast between responsibility and irresponsibility shows itself in many ways in our interviews. For instance, the responsibility of legitimacy can be experienced as an onerous obligation in contrast to the spontaneous genuineness of illegitimacy, or it can be experienced as a fuller expression of kinship than the passing, lustful relation of illegitimacy. Yet no matter how the contrast plays itself out, it always has the effect of driving a wedge between the unconscious and the conscious elements of kinship and affinity. Insofar as legitimacy enters into the definition of a kinship relation—and it always does to some degree—it shifts the content of conscious choice in kinship and affinity from an element that flows from the unconscious given to an element that flows from imposed responsibilities.

The contrast between legitimacy and illegitimacy invariably brings with it, in our informants' accounts, other domains of culture. Illegitimate relations, our accounts show, are acceptable for middle-class men, but not middle-class women, so that illegitimacy automatically brings with it notions of the sexes and of class. Illegitimacy also always entails notions of race. Therefore we follow our informants to their notions of sex roles, race, and class.

The Male in the Family

This section focuses on the collective representation of men in the family. The marginality of males in the Caribbean lower-class family is a standard focus of Caribbean scholarship. Our middle-class informants are as interested in the marginality of lower-class males as are scholars, though with a more explicitly moral evaluation: "The Jamaican man has a great responsibility to see to it that motherhood and childhood do not deteriorate into becoming casualty listings from some wild game he sets out to play in the field of sexual indulgence, but rather that these be developments growing out of a serious covenant into which he enters with loving care and sober commitment. If he is slow in acknowledging this responsibility, the state must have ways of reminding him."

Here the marginality of men is formulated in the moral contrast between "sexual indulgence" and a "serious covenant" undertaken with "responsibility." Interestingly, here the reference is to Jamaican men in general, not just lower-class men. The image of the male as marginal to family life appears as a major focus in the middle class as well as the lower class.

In the middle class there is much argument between men and women over their proper roles in the family. Much of this argument can be understood as a symptom of changing sex roles in the society; but the issue is formulated by the participants in moral terms—the greater commitment of the woman than the man to the family. The woman does more of the work in the family, say informants, because the man is not sufficiently committed to it:

> I: I have met so many men who have had to be a burden of the
> family responsibility.
> A: I'm not talking of the lower class.
> I: No, no. Middle class. In fact, I believe sometimes they are worse
> off than the lower class. Because people tend to believe that they
> belong to the middle class and they are reasonable. I know too
> many women, especially teachers with families, and they have to
> just shoulder the responsibilities. A large number. The men ei-
> ther gamble it out or have other women, that sort of thing.

The belief in male lack of commitment—irresponsibility—might be a weapon wielded by women against men, but men hold the same conviction. The depth of this belief in male irresponsibility is revealed in the image of the father held by middle-class male informants. "My father was an unusual man. In my young days I thought of him as a very happy-go-lucky person who valued a good time, valued 'the boys.' I thought him in those days somewhat irresponsible, and it was my mother who kept the family together."

The image of the marginality and irresponsibility of the male in the family must be understood against the background of the counterexpectation of the man as the dominant authority figure in the family. One informant, who was a teacher, worked briefly as a domestic in the United

States: "Family life in the United States is really shocking. Here men are kings; there women are queens. Here, if there is a limited amount of food the man gets a proper share, and then the rest is divided up. I realize my husband works hard and has many responsibilities; though I work hard at school, not as hard as he, and I don't expect him to do housework. . . . In America, a woman would shout her husband down; here you just couldn't do it." The assumption that male dominance is the suitable state of affairs is clear. Therefore, insofar as the male is perceived as lacking, it is in comparison to the dominant authority figure he is expected to be.

The indicator par excellence for middle-class Jamaicans of the male's irresponsibility and weakness is his sexual unfaithfulness. An example comes from one of my earliest and most frequently repeated field experiences. When middle-class persons asked me what I was doing in Jamaica, and I told them I was studying family life, they usually laughed and told me that there is no family life in Jamaica. Often they then launched into a discussion of illegitimacy and promiscuous mating in the lower class in order to demonstrate their point. However, permitted to run on in this way, they invariably came to the point of saying that the middle class was not really so different. The evidence they presented for this assertion was always the same: that men in the middle class "run around" just as much as in the lower class, but are careful to maintain proper appearances with a public home, middle-class wife, and legal offspring and private "outside" relations with a lower-class mistress and illegal offspring. It is important to note for the purpose of our analysis that the marginality of the middle-class male is formulated in the same sexual and moral terms as the marginality of lower-class males: sexual indulgence versus the responsibilities of a "serious covenant."

So the irresponsibility that, informants assert, distinguishes the lower class from the middle class turns out to be, informants also assert, a characteristic of the middle-class male as well. What does distinguish the middle-class from the lower-class male is that the middle-class male operates on two tracks at the same time. In her study of sex roles in a Jamaican town, de Veer (1979) shows that in the lower class, men are considered to be irresponsible in comparison to women. For a male to become a responsible family member he must undergo a religious transformation that will control his general, irresponsible inclinations (p. 96). In contrast, the middle-class male has both a "responsible" legal family and an "irresponsible," illegitimate, "outside" relationship. (This fact has been discussed in the literature; see Braithwaite 1953; Jayawardena 1962.)

There is one final feature in the image of the male, because his irresponsibility is also defined as an assertion of status: "The moment they are rich, men now earning a good salary, or what we call, going back to our middle-income group, going up in more salary, he must have one or two girlfriends, outside you know. He has to share his time between his home and things like that."

Summarizing this description of the collective representation of the male in the family, we find that he is stereotyped as marginal to family life, and this marginality is evaluated morally as irresponsible and is so by contrast to a counterexpectation in which the male is dominant and the authority in the family. The flaws in the male are most powerfully expressed in his sexual indulgence, which is contrasted to a "serious covenant." Finally, the very sexual indulgence that is the mark of inadequacy is also judged to be a mark of status. In my analysis I will show that the representation of the male is a bridge between the domestic and the public domains and that the image of the male in the family is a reflection of and an expression of his image in the public domain.

Race

I begin the analysis of the collective representation of race by considering very briefly the use of racial terms by informants. The vast majority of racial descriptions are of physical appearance. However, these elements of physical appearance are significant because they are taken to be outward signs of race. Race is conceived to be a component of the inner bodily substance, which is passed down from generation to generation. At the same time, physical appearance is considered a somewhat unreliable indicator of race. For instance, it is freely acknowledged that siblings who have the same racial composition can have very different physical appearances.

The relation of appearance to race is further indicated by the fact that informants have a restricted and general meaning for racial color terms. The restricted meaning refers specifically to skin color; the general meaning refers to a number of features—skin color, hair, eye color, and facial features. One must have both meanings in mind to make sense of this remark: "His wife is quite dark, but beautiful black hair. Dark in complexion, but beautiful black hair . . . down to her shoulder." To say that a woman was dark but had long hair would be unnecessary unless *dark* in itself implied some other kind of hair. At the same time, if *dark* had only the general meaning, then the fact that the person has long black hair would require the informant to change her term rather than restrict its meaning. The general meaning encompasses a number of physical features in addition to skin color, because in theory color and these features are related. Thus white skin goes with straight hair, blue eyes, and fine features—all Caucasian racial features. Similarly, a black man, by virtue of his African descent, is assumed in the absence of contrary evidence to have curly black hair, brown eyes, and heavy features. Yet, just as informants recognize that appearance is an unreliable indicator of blood, so do they realize that color and other physical features may in fact not vary together.

What sense can we make of the fact that informants use terms that apply to appearance when they are interested in appearance as a sign of race and yet know that appearance is an unreliable indicator? Originally, color terms were accompanied by a set of terms that referred directly to racial composition: *sambo, mulatto,* and so on. These terms, however, have almost entirely dropped out of use in favor of color terms. Even the term *mulatto* to indicate any degree of Negro "blood" has been largely replaced. One informant answered the question as follows: "I suppose I describe more from the point of color, because most of us are sort of mixed up." Thus the use of color terms for racial description makes possible the continued identification of persons in terms of their racial mixture, when the exact mixture is unknown. For color to act as a sign of racial mixture, informants assume a continuum from pure Caucasian, or pure white, to pure African, or pure black. This continuum expresses the principle that despite the generations and centuries of racial mixture, racial identity consists not of a homogeneous type but of varying mixtures of two distinct racial types—"white" and "black."

When we analyze informants' talk about race (as distinct from their use of racial terms) several themes appear: (1) the significance of race as both a deep and a superficial phenomenon, (2) the relation of race to identity, (3) the relation of race to a hierarchy of social honor, (4) the justification of this hierarchy, and (5) the relation of race to solidarity.

1. Informants are intensely ambivalent about the importance of race: "As far as my sister Mary, you wouldn't imagine that she had colored blood at all. . . . I don't think it means anything much to Jamaicans. Do you think so? I mean, in talking to different Jamaicans? What matters to them is when a person is in a different class. People are terribly conscious of hair. I'll try to label these persons [racially], but this is something that we probably haven't thought of, or it just rolls off the tongue without your having given it much thought."

Ambivalence over the significance of race has two sources. One source is the impropriety of caring about race; because it makes invidious distinctions between persons, race is something that ought not be important. The other source is the ambivalence over the relative importance of achieved and ascribed characteristics. On the one hand, informants believe that people are what they make themselves; because they have no control over their race it is irrelevant. On the other hand informants believe that within rational people who choose their destinies there are also forces that are part of them, but over which they have no control. During the research a large riot erupted in Kingston, and many people feared that civil order was threatened. One informant, who had previously described the decline of racial consciousness in Jamaica, told me that the Kingston Gun Club had enlisted as special marshals and were patrolling with loaded rifles. "And," he concluded, "you know what color they are" (Gun Club members tended to be at the white end of the color continuum). The informant assumed that race is the ultimate basis of solidarity.

Thus the subject of race immediately raises a conflict for informants over its relative importance as an ascribed characteristic. The conflict is not resolved. The assertion that race is or is not important rarely remains uncontradicted for long, and consequently it is expressed above all in ambivalence.

2. Insofar as it is conceived to be important, race is thought of as having a specific ascribed significance, which is illustrated in the following notes of an interview:

> Color played a very great part in his life. When he asked about his ancestry and his father told him it went back to a slave woman that was very important to him. Made him realize where he really belonged. Which had troubled him. He could say he was a Jamaican, but that was not really satisfactory. Would ask himself where do I really fit in. Is there such a thing as a Negro quality? The writing of Aimé Cèsaire and others helped him. Made him realize there was such a quality. . . . It was not an artificial development, but a question of discovering what was there. Black was identified with poverty and one tended to identify with whites and colored. Now he has a feeling of kinship, having discovered himself as a Negro.

In constructing their own identities persons find it sensible to refer to their race, and in considering race they find it sensible to consider their identities. In what way is race an attribute of identity for informants? A comparison can be helpful. Erikson suggests that the definition of American identity is that of the person who has a wide range of options and chooses among them on his or her own (1963, pp. 285–87). The identity established for our informants more commonly focuses on group membership: "I'm considered Chinese. . . . I am really in a sense three-quarter Chinese. Am I? Yes, three-quarter, I am . . . of course, our physical features stamp us Chinese." In contrast to American identity, Jamaican identity focuses less on a typical mode of action and more on a community of action. Erikson has pointed out that identity includes an image of a person's place in the community (1968, pp. 45–53). This aspect of identity is what the cultural definition of race formulates. However, the effect of the cultural definition of race is to fragment and make problematical this identity, because it defines, as we have just seen, the community as composed of two distinct elements (white and black) and their mixture, a mixture that does not amalgamate. For some, this racial identity leads very far into the experience of mixture and fragmentation. One informant presented the fact that his family does not suffer from sickle-cell anemia, albinism, or rope scars at healing (all believed to be inherited black characteristics) to demonstrate that "from my immediate bloodstream I don't know of any that are really colored."

3. Informants frequently deny that race is hierarchically evaluated; therefore it is important to note that, consistently, when they feel they have received less than the respect due an equal, they suspect that race is the cause. One informant recalled an incident when he was twelve years old: "He was standing around at a gas station eating mangoes. A car came in for gas, and the station attendant gave him the gas cap to hold while he filled the tank. The driver grabbed the cap away and cursed him fiercely. He felt he was being treated as a menial. It might have happened even if he had been white, after all his hands were dirty with mango juice; still it was the way the man spoke to him."

4. Less evident than the hierarchical evaluation of race is the ambivalence with which this hierarchy is conceived. This ambivalence is expressed in the touchiness with which the subject is discussed. Informants all framed the matter the same way: race is a subject people do not discuss freely and openly; it remains understood.

The reasons for this ambivalence are revealed by informants' discussion of color prejudice. Informants can easily expand on the wickedness of color prejudice; to claim superiority on the grounds of race is wrong. Yet they cannot discuss racial differences without implying superiority and inferiority; hence the ambivalence.

Ambivalence over racial status exists because there is no cultural justification for distinctions based on race. In India, for example, status is justified by the ideology of purity, but there is little evidence for such an ideology among our informants. Indeed, if racism is to be strictly defined—"the doctrine that a man's behavior is determined by stable inherited characters deriving from separate racial stocks having distinctive attributes and usually considered to stand to one another in relations of superiority and inferiority" (Banton 1967, p. 8)—then it might be argued that there is little evidence of racism as part of the culture of our informants. Though informants do see race as associated with superiority and inferiority, the association is not biological. For informants racial hierarchy is the result of a historical association of race with both social dominance and style of life. They define being white as superior to being black because whiteness has brought with it advantages in the society. Secondly, white is superior to black because it is associated with a superior style of life; white is civilized, black is uncivilized.

What is crucial to see is that the association between race on the one hand and superior life-style and dominance on the other hand is, from the point of view of informants, a matter of historical fact, not biological necessity. (This type of ideology is more common than might be supposed. See Arendt's 1951 discussion of race thinking before racism.) For informants, whites did dominate, speak English, practice certain conjugal customs, eat certain foods, and so on.

Thus the culturally defined superiority of white over black follows from the culturally asserted historical association of white with superior social position and superior style of life. The earlier analysis of the use of racial terms revealed that appearances are interpreted as signs of an inner physical condition; the analysis of the significance of race to informants reveals that it is significant for its association with a superior style of life and dominance. Whereas the link between appearance and race is conceived to be biological, the link between race and superior style of life and social position is conceived to be historical. It remains to be shown that though the association of race with superior or inferior power and style of life is conceived to be the result of historical events, the association of races with distinctive power and styles of life is conceived to be the consequence of an intrinsic property of race.

5. Racial differences imply hierarchical and invidious distinctions between persons; conversely, racial similarity implies equality and solidarity. The idea that people of the same color are equal and belong together is most clearly expressed in the discussion of marriage. Much has been made by scholars of a white bias, especially as expressed in the desire to marry up in color. What is as true, but much less noted, is the bias toward marrying someone of the same color: "If a man is a doctor or lawyer . . . if he earns money he could marry a girl from that class, he could. Because they have the feeling that it will upgrade their children. But the funny thing about it is that by and large the colored people resent this kind of action in a colored person. Because they feel that he would be turning against his group. And women in particular felt there were girls out here of educational standing good enough that he could have found a wife. This desire on his part to marry out of his color they didn't accept."

Furthermore, the notion of union between persons of different races has an air of illegitimacy around it: "You hear people talking, just describing other people and say 'She's a mulatto; her father was a Scotsman.' It's a good word, but it is also used as a curse word. 'She was the product of a promiscuous relationship.'"

Finally, informants formulate the illegitimacy of unions between races in their beliefs about the origin of Jamaican society. For informants the origin of contemporary society is in the illegal union of a white male master and a black female slave and their illegal mulatto offspring.

In the cultural definition, the solidarity that arises out of racial sameness is an intrinsic property of that racial sameness. People stick together because they have the same blood, and there is no more explanation necessary. At the same time the definition of race as a continuum consisting of an unamalgamated mixture ensures that racial solidarity will be a fragile condition easily dissolvable by the racial differences that the culture always formulates. Let us now return to the problem of the cultural definition of race and hierarchy.

Although solidarity is defined as an intrinsic property of racial sameness, the hierarchy of racial difference is defined as an accidental property resulting from historical events. As we have already noted, there is little evidence of a belief in intrinsic racial superiority (that is, little evidence of racism); the superiority of white arises from its association with superior social position and life-style, and not vice versa. We can make most sense of this complex of beliefs by inferring that for informants common life-style and common social position are results of racial solidarity; because persons of the same blood stick together they develop the same life-style and function as a group to maintain or improve their position in society. Consequently, although the superior social position and style of life of whites are not biological consequences of race, they are still essentially and not accidentally white. That is why a colored person who lives according to the superior life-style or who marries a white person is pursuing a life-style that is not "really" his own and is marrying outside his group; just as a colored person, no matter how white he may look, is never "really" white. Thus, although life-style and social dominance are in one sense achieved characteristics—persons can acquire proper speech and wealth—in another sense they are defined as intrinsically white and therefore as ascribed characteristics.

The relationship between race and hierarchy as defined by informants leads to the relation between the collective representations of race and those of class and status.

Class and Status

Scholars have often asserted that race is a language for talking about class interest or the subjective form that objective class interest takes. My own observation is that informants have no difficulty talking about class interests when that is what they want to talk about, and in general they are keenly aware of class interests. Furthermore, informants can talk about race without referring to class. Nevertheless, there is a relation and a tension between race and class, because from one perspective they are conceived to be distinct and from another perspective they are conceived to be related.

From one perspective there is, for informants, a fundamental distinction betwen race on the one hand and class and status on the other: "Mark you, this woman is of good station; I mean socially. Physically-wise she is considered black, but her attributes are definitely of his social status." From the other perspective class and race are related, because they are conceived to be aspects of a single hierarchy. A person who is middle class is expected to be also midway in the racial hierarchy. In order to understand the tension between race and class let us proceed to an analysis of the culture of class, particularly the impact of the pure domain of class on the conglomerate level of family life.

Though informants find it difficult to define classes, the same criteria appear consistently in their discussions: income, education, standard of living, occupation, group membership, and attitude. "Those cousins are able to earn as much money as those of us who were able to pass our exams. It's only that because of their limited education and their whole social outlook their life is at a very low ebb. The question of having a nice home, nicely furnished, with books, possibly getting married, and having a settled home, that is not the sort of thing you would find them doing. They would prefer to have drinking parties, to play the horses, to just live and let live." Here one can observe how rapidly education, standard of living, attitude, and group membership can be interchanged, and how they are contrasted to income. Education, standard of living, attitude, and group membership should be considered different aspects of the same basic feature, in contrast to income.

One can understand the contrast between income and the other features by first grasping the meaning of education for informants. Education can refer to skills acquired through formal schooling, and informants are keenly aware that education provides skills that influence occupational possibilities and thereby income. But it is in another sense that education is contrasted to income. Historically, in Jamaica education has been defined as a Christianizing, civilizing force. Thus a prominent minister wrote in 1853:

Unallured by the enjoyment of civilized society and by whatever is sublime and beautiful in natural scenery;—the dwarfs of the rational world, their intellect rising only to a confused notion and imperfect idea of the general objects of human knowledge; their whole thoughts, indeed, confined within the range of their daily employments and the wants of savage life. By some writers they have been described as an inferior species of the human family. . . .

Acquiring a taste for knowledge and a love of virtue, they will receive into their midst the term of all vitality and the secret of all strength. . . . When gently led forward by the humane of every nation they shall, under the *egis* of an overshadowing Providence, run a career of honourable progression in all that adorns and elevates the species, with the boasting inhabitants of more privileged climes.

To realize these anticipations nothing is required but the introduction of a liberal and enlarged scheme of sound education among the more respectable classes of the coloured and black population. [Phillippo 1843, pp. 191, 211–12]

Thus, in Jamaica education came to mean a training in civilization, particularly manners. Our informants continue to accept this historical meaning of education. For them, to be educated means to know how to behave properly, in a civilized manner. "The middle class is defined by education, not money. The education they have had, which gives them the responsibility of setting standards, the tone, the pattern of behavior."

Standard of living has two meanings also for informants: it can refer to material possessions or to decency and propriety. In the second meaning the significance of material possessions arises out of their role in maintaining a decent and proper way of life. Having such possessions as a house and a car is part of decent living, as are speaking English and being well mannered. It is the second meaning that is contrasted to income as a defining characteristic of the middle class:

> You will find some of the loveliest homes. Yet, as far as I know you would never think of classifying those people as middle class. Because the standard of living is altogether on a lower plane. . . . So I think we would have a more proper gauge if we were to take it on an educational basis. . . . The general feeling there is I haven't got an education and I can find the money I want to spend just the same. So standard doesn't matter to him at all. You have that basic middle class where money is not the sole object, but they believe in living a decent life, having a good family life, educating their children as best as possible, and living a clean, decent life.

To understand the complex of features that are contrasted to income, it is necessary to consider the meaning of income for informants. In the face of the consistent assertion that it is education, style of life, and so on that define the middle class, one wonders why income is introduced at all. Income stands for the ability to appropriate valued goods and resources: "In the past teachers told children there was no point trying to achieve a bank job on account of their color. If your people had money you were going to do medicine or something like that, well that's different. . . . But I mean if you were just a mediocre middle-class family."

Informants feel the need to justify their income. They all introduce the theme of working hard and struggling to establish and maintain a position in society. Yet the middle-class sense of dignity rests more on the ends for which income is utilized than on the means by which it is gained. Informants deserve their income by virtue of the morally superior uses to which they put it. These uses are the educated standard of living on which so much emphasis is placed in the discussion of class.

We can clarify the meaning of the middle-class self-definition by contrasting it to the middle-class definition of lower and upper classes. Although informants realize the competition from below, there is little attention to classes as conflicting groups or quasi-groups. Rather, informants conceive of a moral hierarchy and focus on the moral superiority of the middle class:

> I: For example, if you go to St. Elizabeth you'll find the squatters on the estate. They never own an inch of land for themselves. They work on the sugar cane estate and they are just like coolies. . . . They generally live on the outskirts and they build up a big community like that. But those are not holdings. They just pitch a house here, pitch a house there and they live in that sort of fashion. And the standards of living are very low. It's just a question of living on the little that they earn on the estate from week to week. . . . We've had families that are poor people, but they are on their own farm and you couldn't classify them as lower class; you'd have to classify them as middle class. Their outlook is different altogether. There is a greater ambition standard there, that type does everything for his child's education. . . . Whereas the other is just a hit-or-miss livelihood.
>
> A: What makes people upper class?
>
> I: Well, because of money. And inheritance. . . . A man couldn't just get himself up there unless he was born of wealthy parents. . . . There isn't the urge, that deep necessity for striving as the middle-class man would have. So you find that the upper-class boy might eventually just come with a little basic training back home and continues on his daddy's property.

Thus informants characterize the upper and lower classes in the same way. The lower class is basically "careless," though there is a segment that does care but is simply too poor to be middle class. The upper class has money without having to work for it and tends not to concern itself with leading a moral life. The assertion that the middle class works for its money and, most important, uses it in a moral and civilized fashion expresses the sense of dignity of the class.

Now we can understand the relations among our informants' conceptions of race, class, and status. Race and class are conceived of as distinct in that race is a "physical thing" and class is the money one has; race and status are similar in that both connote a hierarchy, and that hierarchy is expressed in a civilized style of life. It is the civilized style of life that links race and status to a single hierarchy and creates the presumption of consistency among race, class, and status and the strain that arises when they are inconsistent. Precisely how the links among race, class, and status are forged will be described in the following section. A crucial part of the civilized style of life, the sense of dignity, is family life, to which we now turn.

For the middle class marriage is a prerequisite to living together and having children, whereas for the lower class it is not. Therefore the contrast between marriage and nonlegal union has class meaning. Illegitimacy and nonlegal unions, as we have shown earlier, are framed in the light of a contrast between seeking immediate pleasure without consideration of its consequences and responsibility or acting with consideration for the consequences of one's actions—"sexual indulgence" in contrast to "loving care, sober commitment, and more than token responsibility." Because illegitimacy and nonlegal unions are signs of putting immediate pleasure above responsibility, it follows that legal marriage is a sign of placing responsibility equal with or above immediate pleasure, accepting obligations regardless of their impact on the immediate satisfaction of needs. It also follows that the middle-class commitment to legal marriage is a commitment to responsiblity over immediate pleasure. Yet this commitment is flawed, for in the middle class's own view of itself men participate in nonlegal unions with lower-class women as well as in legal unions with middle-class women. Middle-class men are distinguished from lower-class men not by their capacity to rise above immediate pleasure, but by their split orientation toward pleasure and responsibility. (It is important to keep in mind that we are describing middle-class beliefs, not practices.) Finally, the very behavior that is a sign of flawed honor—male nonlegal unions—is also an assertion of middle-class male power, as was noted in the section entitled "The Male in the Family."

Why is there this cultural focus on the two faces of men's family behavior? Studies of family life in many societies show that outside relations are common for men without being the subject of cultural focus. The answer to the question requires us to integrate our analyses of the domains of kinship, marriage, sex roles, race, class, and status.

The Myth of Origin

The situation we are analyzing appears to be a curious one. Weber observed that "even pariah people . . . are usually apt to continue cultivating . . . the belief in their own specific 'honor'" (1968, p. 934). In the Jamaican middle class we appear to have a group that harbors a belief in its own dishonor. Why the flawed self-image of family life presented by our informants?

In order to understand the self-image of the family we must understand the origin myth that is the charter of the middle class, and perhaps of the society.

Informants believe that the middle class originated in the nonlegal union of a white male master and a black female slave, which produced an illegitimate brown offspring of status midway between slave and master. This belief is clearly expressed in the genealogies of those informants who see themselves as of middle-class origin; as mentioned earlier they all trace their genealogies back to a white male master, black female slave, and illegitimate mulatto or brown offspring. It is at this point of origin alone that class, status, and race correlate directly. It is here that the link connecting race, class, and status is forged, that class terms have direct implications for race terms and vice versa. There are two class terms that have an automatic race significance, *slave* and *master*. *Slave* automatically implies *black*; *master* automatically implies *white*.

How is the story of the origin of the middle class to be taken as a myth? It operates to anchor current practices in their origins and does so by a distinctive sense of time. This mythical time has been analyzed clearly by Lévi-Strauss: "On the one hand, a myth always refers to events alleged to have taken place long ago. But what gives the myth an operational value is that the specific pattern described is timeless; it explains the present and the past as well as the future" (1963, p. 209).

The myth of middle-class origin operates in just this way. It relates events that have taken place in the past and that are yet still in the present, not simply as past causes of present conditions, but actually present. The origin myth formulates in the minds of informants the underlying, fundamental principles of the society against which all variations are measured.

The distinctive mythical time is expressed by race: white blood and black blood have been passed down from the beginning of society, from generation to generation, endlessly mixed and still distinct, into the present. Race thus establishes the historical rootedness of the society and its members' place in it, and does so in a way that locates that historical rootedness directly in the experience of persons' bodies, thus to a certain extent fusing the continuity of the person with the continuity of the society. The tension between race and class expresses change; it is an experience of the present as a contrast to the past. Every time people experience inconsistency among race, physical appearance, status, and class, they are referring the present to a past in which in the beginning there were two groups—one English, white, civilized, master, and solidary; the other African, black, uncivilized, slave, and solidary—who mixed without amalgamating. Every time people perceive themselves or others in terms of race they commit themselves to a view that sees the present as the result of a long process of mixture in which the two elements are always kept track of—because they have never really joined.

In the myth of origin the family plays a central part, and thereby the myth links the domains of kinship and affinity with the domains of race, class, and status. The myth distinguishes the parts of society and integrates them in terms of male irresponsibility and the distinction between legal and nonlegal union. These are of course precisely the features of family life that draw the attention of scholars and natives alike. It is puzzling that middle-class males are perceived as marginal by our middle-class informants, for they are in reality more commonly a part of the family than are lower-class males. For instance, a male is far more likely to be the head of a middle-class than of a lower-class household. Furthermore, the features of male behavior that are pointed to as evidence of male marginality are commonly found in many societies with sharp sex-role differentiation.

The answer to this puzzle lies in the relation of man's place outside the family to his place inside the family. Here I wish to study the interaction between the evaluation of the male outside the family and the evaluation of him inside the family. I wish to show that the evaluation of the male in the family can be influenced by the evaluation of the male in the public domain, and that this influence can operate independently of what the male actually does in the family. The phenomenon to which I refer has been described well for another group:

> The Eastern European Jewish . . . type of family is in many respects mother-centered and mother-dominated. . . . Mother exercises control over the daily run of affairs and over her children's behavior, as well as over most of the practical aspects of her husband's life. The father's authority tends to be so remote that it does not impinge much upon the details of the children's daily lives. Fa-

ther may be, according to modern psychiatric concepts, a "dependent personality," . . . ; but—and this is the decisive point—there is no stigma attached to his so-called dependency. He has well-defined privileges and rights, many of which are denied to the mother. His prestige is largely based on the religious value system. . . .

The mother acts mainly as the manager of the household and . . . the father acts as a representative of the family in the community and of the community in the family. . . . The community may be a religious collectivity sustained by a common value system. In such a social setting, whether or not father dominates family life, the respect he commands among its members is sustained by the values of the community. [Coser 1974, pp. 365, 367]

Thus in the Eastern European Jewish community the values of the society bestow prestige on the male in the public domain, and this prestige penetrates the domestic domain irrespective of what the male does there. In colonial Jamaica the values of the society demean rather than support the nonwhite male, as is reflected and expressed in a double definition of the middle-class male within family life.

In the dominant ideology, non-English men are in a subordinate position in the public domain because they do not possess enough "civilization," which is a prerequisite to gaining responsibility; and this lack of public responsibility and civilization is symbolized by the definition of the male in the family. The essence of this definition is that the male is both responsible and irresponsible and that he follows his natural uncivilized inclinations, as well as channeling his inclinations in a civilized way. Thus the ideology that links race, class, and status to the family through the male is a way of talking about his middle-class position in the public domain. It is to the position of the middle class in Jamaican society that we now turn.

The Middle-Class Field of Social Action

The origin of the middle class lies in the freedmen of Jamaican slave society. The freedmen were an utterly distinctive product of Jamaican slave society and in time became a dynamic force in their own right in that society. Freed slaves and the descendants of freed slaves, they were frequently the offspring of white free masters and black female slaves. They occupied a position midway between slaves and free men, no longer slaves but lacking the full civil rights of free men. Though whites and blacks had their origins in Europe and Africa, Jamaican plantation slave society required substantial adaptations that gave the Jamaican slave society its own distinctive character. Whites, surrounded by a sea of black slaves, developed a cohesiveness and spirit of equality, despite their economic differentiation, that was unparalleled in Europe. Africans, though they came from diverse tribes and though they were internally differentiated economically, were united by their common lot as slaves and plantation laborers.

Several social principles characterized this society. The plantation combined European capital with a large supply of unskilled African labor and tropical land to produce crops (primarily sugar in the Jamaican case) for export to the European market. This economic activity was the central but not the only principle that determined social relationships. Certainly the threat and use of force were essential to the maintenance of social relationships, as is evidenced in the frequent incidence of individual and group slave rebellion and the violence with which it was repressed. Certainly the ideology of racism flowered from its seed in England into a central principle of the society. The assertion of the superiority of "civilized" whites over "uncivilized" blacks was common among whites. There is no way of knowing how widely or deeply racism was accepted by blacks, but it established for blacks an inescapable frame of reference. Finally, in complex relation to the use of force, which divided white and black, and to racism, which defined the division, was a private world of personal relations and common customs that crosscut the social groups. The Scottish overseer, his ebony woman, and their yellow offspring illustrate the web of personal relations and common custom created in Jamaican society:

> Every unmarried white man, and of every class, has his black or brown mistress, with whom he lives openly: and of so little consequence is this thought that his white female friends and relations think it no breach of decorum to visit his house, partake of his hospitality, fondle his children and converse with his housekeeper. . . . The man who keeps his black or brown mistress in the very face of his wife and family and of the community has generally as much outward respect shown him, and is as much countenanced, visited, and received into company especially if he be a man of some weight and influence in the community, as if he had been guilty of no breach of decency. [Stewart, quoted in Dunker 1960, p. 60]

Though demographic data are sketchy, it is estimated that 9 percent of the population were freedmen by 1820 (calculated from Brathwaite 1971, p. 169). Freedmen filled interstitial occupations in the economy, primarily as artisans, tradesmen, and clerks; by 1823 they provided half the militia (Dunker 1960, pp. 76–83, 199).

By the end of the eighteenth century freedmen were exerting pressure for increased rights; though on the whole in a conservative way. They argued their rights by virtue of their white fathers, their loyalty to whites, their possession of English education and manners, the property interests they held in common with whites, and finally their status as the only true natives of Jamaica (Dunker 1960, pp. 153–74). On the other hand, their claim to full rights, however conservatively stated, challenged a social order legitimized by a racial ideology, and furthermore, they were willing to use the support of the Abolitionists in the British Parliament.

In 1832 freedmen were granted full rights, and in 1838 slavery was abolished. White, "civilized" owners and black, "uncivilized" slaves were no longer owners and slaves, and so the racial and status ("civilized") components defining these two groups came to the fore. The colonial government substantially expanded church and school, both of which were to inculcate white, English, civilized values that would turn black Africans into good citizens without eliminating the ultimate superiority of whites (Smith 1966, 1982, first developed this notion of postemancipation society, which he labeled "creole society").

By the end of the nineteenth century the middle class that was developing and expanding was diverse in character and changing in personnel, yet showed itself to be a development of the freedmen of slave society. By means of education this group came to fill positions in the expanding civil service, teaching, religious, legal, and clerical occupations. A prosperous group of farmers and produce traders also developed, who, though they did not owe their position to education, tended to provide the rural support for the "civilizing" educational and religious systems.

The middle class articulated its interests in a way that clearly built on that of its predecessors, the freedmen. It came to assert its achieved English civility as a justification for its position and as a status line separating it from the lower class. Because English civility was ultimately a white characteristic, the same argument that justified the middle-class superiority over the lower class also justified its subordination to the white upper class. The continuity between the middle class and the freedmen of slave society is also revealed in the fact that this class, like the freedmen before it, was disproportionately colored, rather than white or black.

In the twentieth century some members of the middle class began to achieve economic power and demand more political power. Middle-class leaders articulated a democratic nationalist ideology in justification of their claims. The roots of nationalism lay in the eighteenth-century freedmen's claim for the rights of natives. What was new in the ideology was its democratic and antiracist character. But there it was deeply ambiguous. It could be said that the new elite was trained in schools with English models and that its nationalistic demands were in large part claims that it had mastered the English lesson and could function as effectively as the English. Its anti-racist character was a claim that persons should be judged by their ability to act like civilized Englishmen, regardless of their race. The racism that had supported authority remained as a strong tendency of the elite to separate itself from, while it led, the lower class: "Leaders are what the labourers want. Good leaders, Temperate Speeches, work within the bounds of British Principles and Policies, with grim determination you must win" (quoted in Post 1969, p. 382).

The ideology of democratic nationalism embedded in racism, fashioned by the middle class in the pursuit of its interests, clearly developed from the original freedman interests and ideology. It is this ideology that we finally reached in the analysis of our informants' beliefs about their family lives. Thus the middle class of Jamaica symbolizes, acts out, and makes real for itself its conception of its legitimate place in a colonial society through the definition of the male role in the family.

Acknowledgments

The ethnographic present is 1967–69, when most of the fieldwork on which this essay is based was done. That fieldwork was supported by the National Science Foundation through a grant (NSF-GS-1709) to a project directed by Professor Raymond T. Smith, and by NIH Training Grant No. 1-FI-MH-34477-01A2 (CUAN). The fieldwork and its analysis benefited greatly from the advice of Raymond T. Smith. Sections of this essay have previously appeared in Alexander 1976, 1977a, 1977b, and 1978. I am grateful to the editors of the *American Ethnologist* and the *Journal of Comparative Family Studies* for permission to reproduce them here.

References

Alexander, Jack
1976   "A Study of the Cultural Domain of 'Relatives.'" *American Ethnologist* 3 : 17–38.
1977a   "The Culture of Race in Middle-Class Kingston, Jamaica." *American Ethnologist* 4 : 413–35.
1977b   "The Role of the Male in the Urban Middle-Class Jamaican Family: A Comparative Study." *Journal of Comparative Family Studies* 8 (no. 3): 369–89.

1978   "The Cultural Domain of Marriage." *American Ethnologist*
        5:5–14.
Arendt, Hannah
1951   *The Origins of Totalitarianism.* New York: Harcourt, Brace.
Banton, Michael
1967   *Race Relations.* New York: Basic Books.
Braithwaite, Lloyd
1953   "Social Stratification in Trinidad." *Social and Economic Studies*
        2:5–175.
Brathwaite, Edward
1971   *The Development of Creole Society in Jamaica: 1770–1820.* Ox-
        ford: Oxford University Press, Clarendon Press.
Coser, Rose Laub
1974   "Authority and Structural Ambivalence in the Middle-Class
        Family." In *The Family: Its Structures and Functions,* edited by
        Rose Laub Coser, pp. 362–73. New York: St. Martin's Press.
de Veer, Henrietta
1979   "Sex Roles and Social Stratification in a Rapidly Growing Ur-
        ban Area—May Pen, Jamaica." Ph.D. diss., University of
        Chicago.
Dunker, Sheila
1960   "The Free Coloured and Their Fight for Civil Rights in Ja-
        maica: 1800–1830." M.A. thesis, University of London.
Erikson, Erik
1963   *Childhood and Society.* 2d ed. New York: W. W. Norton and Co.
1968   *Identity: Youth and Crisis.* New York: W. W. Norton and Co.
Fortes, Meyer
1969   *Kinship and the Social Order: The Legacy of Lewis Henry Mor-
        gan.* Chicago: Aldine Publishing Co.
Fried, Morton
1967   *The Evolution of Political Society: An Essay in Political An-
        thropology.* New York: Random House.
Jayawardena, Chandra
1962   "Family Organisation in Plantations in British Guiana." *Inter-
        national Journal of Comparative Sociology* 3:43–64.
Lévi-Strauss, Claude
1963   *Structural Anthropology.* Translated by Claire Jacobson and
        Brooke Grundfest Schoepf. New York: Basic Books.
Phillippo, James M.
1843   *Jamaica: Its Past and Present State.* Philadelphia.

Post, Ken
1969   "The Politics of Protest in Jamaica, 1938: Some Problems of
            Analysis and Conceptualisation." *Social and Economic Studies*
            18:374–90.
Schneider, David M.
1972   "What Is Kinship All About?" In *Kinship Studies in the Morgan
            Centennial Year*, edited by Priscilla Reining, pp. 32–63. Wash-
            ington, D.C.: Washington Anthropological Society.
1980   *American Kinship: A Cultural Account.* Chicago: University of
            Chicago Press. Original publication Englewood Cliffs, N.J.:
            Prentice-Hall, 1968.
Schneider, David M., and Smith, Raymond T.
1978   *Class Differences in American Kinship.* Ann Arbor: University
            of Michigan Press. Original publication, *Class Differences and
            Sex Roles in American Kinship and Family Structure*, Englewood
            Cliffs, N.J.: Prentice-Hall, 1973.
Smith, Raymond T.
1966   "People and Change." In *New World: Guyana Independence Is-
            sue*, edited by George Lamming, pp. 49–54. Georgetown,
            Guyana: New World.
1982   "Race and Class in the Post-Emancipation Caribbean." In
            Racism and Colonialism: Essays on Ideology and Social Structure,
            edited by Robert Ross, pp. 93–119. The Hague: Martinus
            Nijhoff.
Weber, Max.
1968   *Economy and Society: An Outline of Interpretive Sociology.* 3
            vols. Edited by Guenther Roth and Claus Wittich. New York:
            Bedminster Press.
Wright, Philip, ed.
1966   *Lady Nugent's Diary of Her Residence in Jamaica from 1801 to
            1805.* Rev. ed. Kingston: Institute of Jamaica.

Hierarchies and Enterprise:
The Use of Kinship in
Adversity and Prosperity

Dynastic Growth and Survival Strategies: The Solidarity of Mexican Grand-Families

Larissa A. Lomnitz
Marisol Pérez-Lizaur

In this essay we argue that the basic unit of family solidarity in Mexico is a three-generation descent group we shall call the grand-family. Our research on shantytown (Lomnitz 1977) and upper-class (Lomnitz and Pérez-Lizaur 1978, in preparation) households in Mexico City suggests that the grand-family is a cultural structure that tends to reproduce itself and remain constant over time.

The material aspects of life, such as items exchanged in reciprocity—the "speech" of social relations—change in response to specific historical situations, economic factors, and technological innovations. In contrast, culture, the basic code (or "grammar") that makes society intelligible to its members, changes very slowly. In this essay we use *family* as a *cultural* category that implies a set of norms governing expected behavior between kin and, as part of the grammar of behavior, reinforces the economic, social, and ritual aspects of solidarity. Such behavior is grounded in repeated acts of exchange and is reflected in an ideology shaped by the values and beliefs of the kin group and its members.

A grand-family is composed of a couple, their children, and their grandchildren, so that a person's "meaningful others" include parents and siblings as well as spouse and children. There is no drastic change in parent-child relations when children marry and form homes of their own; solidarity and mutual assistance continue. Each person adjusts to the expectations of the members of the grand-family and expects their support in return. Basic family obligations include economic support, participation in family rituals, and social recognition. The latter involves the impact of individual status changes on the entire grand-family and, perhaps more important, the corporate sharing of social networks. That is, the social relations of all members form a resource pool to be tapped when the need arises.

The physical and social expressions of solidarity vary by class, household arrangements, and stages of growth within the same family unit. Among peasant households the patrilinear grand-family often dwells in a family compound, with a separate home for each nuclear family, all built on the same property. Usually, at marriage, female offspring move into the husband's family compound and sons move away, leaving only the youngest son at home, together with unmarried children and daughters whose husbands do not own land. Each grand-family is an agricultural work unit based on any of a variety of economic cooperation schemes. For example, men may support the household by regular cash contributions, while women share cooking and child-rearing duties; at other times, each nuclear family manages its own affairs.

When a grand-family migrates to the city (usually in stages over several years), it is forced to reorganize residence patterns and redefine its internal forms of solidarity. The first migrant is often a bachelor, who lives among strangers. If he marries, he may move in with his wife's parents until he and his wife can set up an independent household. Should two or more brothers migrate with their respective nuclear families, they may establish an extended household, sharing cooking and expenses. (Such variations among shantytown residents in Mexico and other Latin American countries have been reported by Lomnitz 1977; Balan and Jelin n.d.; Browning 1971; Arizpe 1978; and Butterworth 1962.) Although the family's basic structure as a solidary unit remains the same, changes in residential arrangements lead to revised expectations of exchange and interaction between kin. To demonstrate how those arrangements vary according to the prestige and economic prominence of a grand-family, we describe the forms of interaction in grand-families from two socioeconomic strata of Mexico City: the shantytown and upper-class households.

The Shantytown

The shantytown in question contains about 180 households; some 70 percent of the heads of households and their spouses have migrated from rural areas since 1940 (Lomnitz 1977). Virtually all residents are of a marginal (or "informal") socioeconomic status, a stratum of the working class not integrated into the modern economic sector or into the state apparatus, and plagued by chronic job insecurity—a group that includes 50 percent of the working population of Mexico City (Secretaría de Programación y Presupuesto 1979). Typically, they are not entitled to social security or other welfare benefits, they earn incomes below the legal minimum, and they work intermittently as manual laborers in the construction industry or hold similar nonunion jobs as street vendors, house servants, waiters, janitors, craftsmen, repairmen, and proprietors of informal home enterprises.

Household formation in shantytown is a dynamic process of random factors (housing vacancies or the availability of kin ready to move in when a vacancy occurs) interacting with three variables:

1. Kinship: a household is either nuclear or extended.
2. Residence: the house is under a single roof, on a single plot, or jointed. A single-roof household shares one residental unit. In a single-plot household a series of dwellings share one plot of land. In a jointed type, the household occupies two or more adjoining residential units not originally built for one household.
3. Domestic function: the household members do or do not share expenses.

Single nuclear family households are in the minority, and about half of those are waiting for a vacancy near relatives elsewhere in shantytown. Only 15 percent of the households are nuclear households with no relatives in shantytown.

Thirty-five percent of the households are of the jointed type: members of the grand-family share neither cooking duties nor household expenses; each nuclear family apparently leads a separate economic life. There is, however, an intense reciprocal exchange system that includes a variety of domestic functions: the grand-family shares a common outdoor area used as a laundry, kitchen, and children's playground. The jointed household provides the security of cooperation between close kin while allowing its component nuclear families a certain amount of autonomy and privacy.

The major portion (50 percent) of shantytown households are single-roof or single-plot extended households, usually containing three generations: husband and wife, their children, and some of the children's nuclear families. Single-roof grand-family members frequently share household and cooking expenses, whereas among single-plot households, only a minority share such expenses.

In studying the residence changes of married couples from the time of their migration or marriage, we found that 16.7 percent began as neolocal households, 22.8 percent settled initially with the wife's kin, and 37.6 percent lived first with the husband's kin. Nearly one-third of the neolocal households were older couples who had taken up residence with children already established in shantytown. Thus, only 11.7 percent of all couples had actually founded independent households upon marriage or arrival in the city.

Instances of patrilocality are not substantially greater than those of matrilocality. Furthermore, in 8 percent of the cases the marriage partners met in shantytown and, belonging to neighboring households, settled with the kin of both husband and wife. These statistics support both the expected impact of bilaterality and the conclusion that preservation of the grand-family structure is the basic consideration in determining residence. Few nuclear families remain in their initial residences for long. The trend is instead one of frequent residence changes, depending on economic and social circumstances, stages in the family life cycle, housing vacancies, personal relationships among kin, and so on. The initial choice of residence is often a primarily economic consideration, despite the potential problems of crowded living conditions or conflict between affines. Anticipating such problems, couples who can afford to do so establish neolocal households. However, maintaining such a residence becomes increasingly difficult: succeeding childbirths, economic problems, job losses, or the defection of a husband press many nuclear families to seek the shelter and protection of the grand-family. This factor helps explain the increase in jointed households, both matrilocal and patrilocal, from 27.4 percent (upon marriage) to 35.4 percent (at the time of the survey).

The typical shantytown couple begins married life in an extended household formed by the parents of the husband or wife. A husband's other relatives may also shelter the couple, or if the husband lacks relatives in the city or has relatives who cannot offer shelter, the wife's relatives may do so. Occasionally the wife's relatives offer land or other inducements to keep the couple nearby; indeed, matrilocality seems to sustain greater family harmony, especially among the women interviewed.

The Upper and Middle Class: The Gómez Family

To investigate the opposite end of the economic spectrum, we studied 143 upper- and middle-class nuclear families in Mexico City, interrelated by a network of some 350 consanguineal kin descended from Don Carlo Gómez (1820–71). Leopoldo Gómez, the family's first major entrepreneur, settled in Mexico City as a bachelor in 1883. He later brought his mother and siblings to join him and set up a three-generation network in Santa María la Rivera, an upper-middle-class neighborhood in Mexico City. After Leopoldo died, his sons (with their wives and children) moved and began separate grand-families.

Leopoldo, Jr., bought a large section of property in the Anzures development; Pablo did the same in Las Lomas. They subdivided their properties and gave lots to their sons and daughters as they married. The

result was a number of three-generation family compounds in close proximity, with close communication and sharing of rituals. First cousins grew
up together, almost as siblings, and the bonds between them had important consequences for the subsequent generation.

Since the family began migrating to Mexico City, each nuclear family
has maintained a separate residence and household economy. However,
the homes are not randomly located but tend to cluster. In fact, in 80 percent of the cases, three-generation extended families live on the same
block or street or in the same neighborhood. Grand-families (or family
"branches") are named for the neighborhood where they live, or lived
originally—for example, the Popotla Gómez, the Anzures Gómez, and
so on.

The ideal, once a man becomes the head of a grand-family, is for him
to move away from his siblings and form a family compound—and eventually a family branch—of his own. Thus, neolocality is (as in shantytown)
a measure of economic self-sufficiency, although the grand-family remains
the unit of kin solidarity. However, because kinship is bilateral, there is
intense competition over the choice of grand-family ties. In this competition, residence is of paramount importance; it affords intimate interaction
and closer ties between offspring and to a particular lineage. The tug-of-
war involves many factors: urban (availability of residence); economic
(relative economic power of the grand-families); social (prestige, bonded-
ness, and ideological aggressiveness); and personal (harmony or conflict
between affines). The competition may be settled at marriage; more often,
it lasts until the couple establishes a neolocal residence and heads its own
grand-family.

Table I provides numerical data on residence patterns of the Gómez
family. Of 177 new couples, only 25 chose neolocal residence, often because of job requirements; all others settled near one or the other set of
parents. Usually the Gómez parents proved more attractive to the new
couple. Overall, 86 of the 177 known choices of initial residence were either ambilocal or located near a Gómez parent. This is not surprising if the
male partner was a Gómez: virilocality is the cultural ideal (Foster 1965;
Nutini 1968). However, uxorilocality among Gómez women is even more
prominent than is virilocality for Gómez men. The strength of the Gómez
family is demonstrated by its ability to draw women affines into its sphere
as well as to retain most of its own women (cf. Lomnitz-Adler 1982; Olivera 1976, pp. 65–96).

Upper-class residence patterns are reinforced by economic considerations: entrepreneurs regard it as a sound investment to purchase block-
sized chunks of real estate—particularly in elegant new residential devel-

Table 1. Residential Pattern of the Gómez Family: Tendency to Live near the Family

	Initial residence[a]	Initial only[b]	Final residence[c]
Neolocal	25	7	26
Virilocal	36	5	27
Uxorilocal	51	12	37
Ambilocal	20	7	15
Unknown	45	10	31
Total	177	41	136
Gómez men			
Neolocal	10		13
Virilocal	29		19
Uxorilocal	14		9
Ambilocal	16		11
Unknown	18		21
Total	87		73
Gómez women			
Neolocal	15		11
Virilocal	8		8
Uxorilocal	37		29
Ambilocal	4		4
Unknown	26		11
Total	90		63

Source: Data from lists of residence.

Notes: *Residence* means that the couple lives near the parents' home, not in the same residential unit. When the residence of one of the spouses was unknown, it was so annotated.

a. Initial residence is the first after marriage.
b. Just-married couples were asked only for their first residence.
c. Final residence is the most recent known.

opments—to ensure a prestigious location for the grand-family. A lot in such a development is considered the ideal wedding present, especially for a daughter. It has, in fact, become customary for women to inherit real estate, although productive enterprises are transmitted only to male offspring. Thus, even when a Gómez woman marries into a more powerful family, there is still a chance she will live near her consanguineal kin, whereas if she does move to her husband's compound, at least no vital Gómez business interest will fall into his hands.

Among the middle class, patrilocality is culturally prescribed. Yet a Gómez woman often establishes a matrilocal home, either because her husband's family is less strongly bonded or because he is from out of town. Finally, although the Gómez are all, strictly speaking, neolocal, the definite tendency among the middle class is for grand-families to live as close together as possible and to spend most of their time together. Only after both parents are deceased and the couple heads its own grand-family will the couple move into a new neighborhood (even the powerful entrepreneur Leopoldo Gómez remained in his parents' household until their deaths). Since 1960, however, greater residential dispersion has occurred among the middle class, owing to an increase in middle-class housing developments marketed competitively (that is, on the installment plan).

Residence patterns are similar for lower-, middle-, and upper-class families: a couple strives to have its offspring establish households nearby. Success in establishing a strong three-generation family compound enhances the prestige and social power of the grand-family, and of its formal head.

Different residential patterns among different social classes reflect unequal economic opportunities. Upper- and middle-class nuclear families can afford homes of their own. In the shantytown they usually cannot; thus, most people there live in extended households with a variety of economic arrangements and frequently shifting residences.

The jointed family household is, in all cases, the preferred solution. It combines the practical advantages of the nuclear household with the cultural ideal of the grand-family. Among the poor, a jointed family household may consist of a set of dwellings with shared outside space and facilities. The dwellings are huddled together because the family cannot depend on telephones or automobiles for interaction. Among the upper class, homes are large and seemingly self-contained; yet physical closeness is such that first cousins are constant playmates and grown-ups visit daily.

Solidarity in the Shantytown

Solidarity requires physical proximity. In the shantytown, in spite of the dismemberment of the grand-family structure caused by migration, we find a tendency to reconstruct extended family groups with available kin: fraternal extended families, cousins' extended families, and so on. Each immigrant moves in with relatives and has members of his grand-family join him as soon as practicable.

Whenever a settler is asked about his relatives, he tends to name first the members of his nuclear families of procreation and orientation—that is, his grand-family. Next, he mentions relatives who live close by. If his parents live with relatives elsewhere in Mexico City, those relatives may be included in the close kin group, although after the parents' death, relationships with such persons tend to fade. Ties with relatives in the rural area of origin depend on the degree of kinship. With members of the immigrant's grand-family, regardless of marriage or location, an important relationship is maintained. The significant unit of solidarity always includes the parents and siblings.

Solidarity in shantytown is a function of social, residential, and economic distance and of *confianza*—a psychosocial measure of the readiness of two actors to maintain a reciprocal exchange relationship—and is expressed by the intensity, frequency, and generalization of exchange within networks of reciprocal assistance. On the basis of these criteria, shantytown household solidarity can be grouped into three major divisions (from strongest to weakest): (1) households of extended families living together, sharing expenses and domestic functions, in which a parent (usually a mother) heads a three-generation family; (2) a jointed household formed by the extended family in the absence of an elder parent, in which exchange is intense but each nuclear family has a separate household economy; (3) mixed networks that include non-kin neighbors. Thus, the grand-family ranks highest in solidarity (Lomnitz 1977, pp. 133–35).

Expected solidary behavior among grand-family members persists through the lifetime of the grand-family—that is, the lifetime of both parents. After both their deaths, each married child heads a grand-family of his or her own. Although the sibling bond persists beyond the parents' death, the descent group has primary allegiance. Newly married couples—neolocal, patrilocal, or matrilocal—continue patterns of solidarity with the grand-family as before, patterns that include (1) economic assistance during and after migration (housing, food and clothing, loans, tools, services such as personal connections for jobs, training in a skill, caring for the children of working mothers, and so on) and (2) moral support (caring for the sick and the aged and participation in rituals).

All grand-family members are expected to attend rites of passage for any other member. To a lesser extent, cooperation is also expected of more distant relatives. Between non-kin neighbors, such behavior may be ritualized through fictive kinship, a mechanism for instituting behavior characteristic of consanguinity.

In sum, social solidarity is the expected behavior of consanguinity and is strongest in the consanguineal descent group—the three-generation grand-family.

Solidarity Within the Upper Class

The history of the Gómez family reflects a process of kin-directed social cohesion analogous to that in shantytown. The grand-family was reconstituted, and the core of a solidary kinship group formed, as soon as possible after immigration. This group established norms of cooperation and developed intense social, ritual, and economic exchange.

The family was soon marked by economic inequality. Leopoldo became a wealthy entrepreneur; his siblings remained members of the middle class. Their relationship eventually changed from one of reciprocity to that of patron and client. However, Leopoldo's example demonstrates that patron-client relations within the grand-family structure can maintain expectations of solidarity as intense and enduring as those of reciprocity. That he became a wealthy man and expended great effort to legitimize his social prominence never diminished Leopoldo's allegiance to his grand-family. His widowed mother was honored as head of the family and remained the center of family life until her death. Leopoldo never stopped providing assistance to his sisters, never missed a family ritual, and became godfather to many of his nieces and nephews.

After the death of Mamá Inés (Leopoldo's mother), each son became the head of his own grand-family and eventually of a separate branch of the Gómez family. Each branch developed its own traditions, but each gathers once a week for dinner in the parental home. Considerable information is exchanged, and children are imbued with the ideology of expected kin behavior. Information is also exchanged regularly via the telephone, visits, and frequent rites of passage that require the attendance of most of the Gómez family. Grand-family members are expected to attend all rituals; selected members of other branches may be invited to various ritual occasions.

Parents' responsibility to their children and children's obligations to their parents do not end when the children marry. Among the entrepreneurial branches a son usually works for his father until the father dies. Indeed, adult sons are often their father's (sometimes reluctant) subordinates well into maturity—a mark of filial piety and loyalty to the enterprise. The grand-family's head sees himself as the proprietor of a legacy to be built up for his grandchildren. Even if a son has little inclination for business, it is the father's duty to find him a niche in the enterprise and, if necessary, to support him financially.

An entrepreneur's daughters are also well provided for. Upon their marriage, the father will attempt to provide them a home and to find an attractive position in the firm for the son-in-law. The daughter's children will eventually also receive such care, either from the father or from brothers, who are frequently reminded of their duty to care for their sisters and sisters' children throughout life. After the father dies, the enterprise is divided up among the heirs, although the mother retains spiritual and emotional authority and continues to host the weekly dinner until her death.

One of the most important aspects of grand-family solidarity is the sharing of social networks and social resources. Social contacts are an important feature of life in all social classes in Latin America: through friends and relatives one obtains economic support, jobs, loans, bureaucratic favors (in the middle class), and support for survival (in urban lower classes). Grand-family members share social contacts in a type of generalized reciprocal exchange. This is, in fact, perhaps the only corporate possession of the grand-family, but it has profound economic, political, and social implications for the individual. For example, economic cooperation includes business deals between brothers that usually continue despite the economic rivalry that tends to ensue upon the father's death. Lifelong loyalty is the rule, and generalized exchange the expected behavior, among brothers and sisters and their respective offspring.

Siblings of the grand-family head who have shared the grand-family's solidarity often transmit these bonds to first and second cousins. In general, the level of solidarity tends to decrease as the degree of consanguinity becomes more remote. However, affines are incorporated, as far as possible, into the Gómez family structure. That is, marriage bonds are strengthened through consanguineal ties: a Gómez's wife becomes a blood relative only if she has his children.

In conclusion, solidarity in the Gómez family resembles that in the shantytown: in both cases it is based on consanguinity; both levels define the grand-family as the basic unit of cooperation; and both participate in economic, social, and ritual exchange, although the items of exchange vary greatly by class. Whereas shantytown settlers expect food, shelter, and clothing, members of the entrepreneurial class expect a dowry, home, job, or legacy. For both, the consanguineal kin group forms a close-knit social and economic unit.

Conclusion

There are indications that the notion of grand-family presented here extends to other areas of Latin America and perhaps to the Mediterranean (Lisón-Tolosana 1970; Campbell 1976; Ianni and Reuss-Ianni 1973), although we are not yet prepared to argue this point. However, our findings do suggest that, in Mexico, the grand-family is the basic unit of solidarity in all social classes, and that variations in structure are, in part, socioeconomic adaptations to the same cultural riddle. The system implies that an individual belongs initially to two grand-families, that marriage involves an implicit rivalry between the parents of husband and wife for the allegiance of their offspring, and that this rivalry is resolved when the couple heads its own grand-family. The dialectic of cooperation and conflict within the grand-family helps explain residential trends in the shantytown and among the urban upper class. It also clarifies the reciprocal exchange network in shantytown and patron-client relations among the urban bourgeoisie. Finally, it illuminates the pervasive use of ritual and intense social interaction among kin.

We suspect that the wealth of kinship studies on the United States and Britain (e.g., Schneider and Smith 1973; Firth, Hubert, and Forge 1970; Macfarlane 1979), heavily weighted toward the study of nuclear families as social and productive units, has helped obscure the importance of the grand-family in Latin America. That is, the dominance of Anglo-Saxon "common-sense categories—including those which have been incorporated into social science" (Smith 1978, p. 338)—often makes it difficult to establish new analytic models. We offer this study as a first step toward such a goal.

Acknowledgments

The editorial assistance of Michael Sullivan is gratefully acknowledged. Translation of the first version of this paper was made by Cinna Lomnitz. The research was supported partially by a Guggenheim Fellowship awarded to L. Lomnitz.

References

Arizpe, Lourdes
1978   *Migración, etnicismo y cambio económico.* Mexico City: El Colegio de México.

Balan, Jorge, and Jelin, E.
n.d.   "Migración a la ciudad y movilidad social: un caso mexicano."
          Mimeo.
Browning, Harley H.
1971   "Propositions about Migration to Large Cities in Developed
          Countries." In *Rapid Population Growth*, edited by Harley
          Browning, pp. 273–314. Baltimore: Johns Hopkins Press.
Butterworth, Douglas
1962   "Study of the Urbanization Process of Mixtec Migrants of Ti-
          laltongo in Mexico City." *América Indígena* 22 : 257–74.
Campbell, J. K.
1976   *Honor, Family and Patronage*. Oxford: Oxford University Press.
Firth, Raymond; Hubert, Jane; and Forge, Anthony
1970   *Families and Their Relatives: Kinship in a Middle Class Sector of
          London*. London: Routledge and Kegan Paul.
Foster, George
1961   "The Dyadic Contract: A Model for the Social Structure
          of a Mexican Peasant Village." *American Anthropologist* 63 :
          1137–92.
Ianni, Francis A. J., and Reuss-Ianni, Elizabeth R.
1973   *A Family Business*. New York: Mouton Books.
Lisón-Tolosana, Carmelo
1970   "The Family in a Spanish Town." In *Readings in Kinship in
          Urban Society*, edited by C. C. Harris, pp. 163–78. Oxford:
          Pergamon Press.
Lomnitz, Larissa
1977   *Networks and Marginality: Life in a Mexican Shantytown*. New
          York: Academic Press.
Lomnitz, Larissa, and Pérez-Lizaur, Marisol
1978   "The History of a Mexican Urban Family." *Journal of Family
          History* 3 : 392–409.
In prepa- "Family and Enterprise: The History of a Mexican Kinship
ration   Group."
Lomnitz-Adler, Claudio
1982   *La evolución de una sociedad rural: Historia del poder en Tepoz-
          tlán*. Mexico City: SEP/FCE.
Macfarlane, Alan
1979   *The Origins of English Individualism*. Cambridge: Cambridge
          University Press.
Nutini, Hugo
1968   *San Bernardino Contla*. Pittsburgh: University of Pittsburgh
          Press.

Olivera, Mercedes
1976   "The Barrios of San Andrés Cholula." In *Essays on Mexican Kinship*, edited by Hugo G. Nutini, Pedro Carrasco, and James M. Taggart, pp. 65–96. Pittsburgh: University of Pittsburgh Press.
Schneider, David, and Smith, Raymond T.
1973   *Class Differences and Sex Roles in American Kinship and Family Structure*. Englewood Cliffs, N.J.: Prentice-Hall.
Secretaría de Programación y Presupuesto
1979   *Características de los marginados en las áreas urbanas de México*. Mexico City: Coordinación del Sistema Nacional de Información.
Smith, Raymond T.
1978   "The Family and the Modern World System: Some Observations from the Caribbean." *Journal of Family History* 3: 337–60.

Creating Kinship:
The Fostering of Children
In *Favela* Families in Brazil

Ruth C. L. Cardoso
(Translated by Elizabeth Hansen)

Adoption has always posed an interpretative problem for kinship analysis, because it is generally assumed that kinship is nothing but socially recognized consanguinity and affinity. Adoption, therefore, comes to be seen as compensatory kinship, a means of providing pseudoconsanguineal status for those who—whether parents or children—would otherwise be lacking. Yet in some societies adoption or the fostering of nonconsanguineal kin is so extensive as to throw doubt on this theory of compensation (see Schildkrout [1973] for a discussion of the material on urban Africa). In Latin America and the Caribbean, as well as many parts of Africa, informal adoption is extremely widespread. This is particularly the case among low-income populations, including those who live in the densely populated slum areas on the fringes of major cities. Social scientists who have studied such populations have generally insisted on discussing kinship as though it were an instrumental device for solving the problem of making a living, or surviving. If families are found to be extensive, then it is supposed that more workers permit an increase in family income, and therefore the pattern of extended kinship is a means of maximizing mutual aid. If families are small, or nuclear, economic strategy is again invoked as an explanation.

The contradictory nature of such explanations is not immediately apparent because they are all based upon the same utilitarian premises. The life projects of families who have migrated from the rural areas are seen as the search for higher levels of income. The varied forms of domestic organization are explained away as the result of "modernization," as if urban life produced changes by contagion. Alternatively, there is an appeal to the inherent conservatism of recent migrants, but neither explanation accounts for the variety of behavior, diverse strategies, and complex subterfuges used by migrants to organize their lives in the cities of the New World.

In this essay attention is focused upon relations between parents and children within families as a means of getting at the deeper levels of meaning that inform kinship behavior. I show that although kinship is defined by consanguinity, this is only a part of the definition, and not an essential part at that. *Socialization* or *training*, in the broadest sense of that term, can also be the basis of real kinship ties. The term *filhos de criação*, which might be translated as "children by socialization," expresses this fact.

Brazilians of all classes believe that kinship is created through the transmission of blood from parents to children, but they believe also that the training of children in manners, morals, obedience, respect, and similar social graces is intrinsic to the transmission of kinship identity. These two dimensions are always present, regardless of social context, but they receive different emphasis depending upon the class situation in which people find themselves. Adoption is a particularly interesting phenomenon because it appears to be class-linked, in that it occurs most frequently among poor migrants to the cities and has generally been interpreted as an instrumental means of maximizing kinship connections.

The data presented here were collected as part of a study of the strategies by which a group of ten families living in the *favelas* of São Paulo, Brazil, manage to exist under conditions of extreme economic hardship. The field research was directed by Lucio Kowarick and the author.

General Concepts of Kinship, Marriage, and the Family

We were led to an interest in adoption through our discovery that one of our informants, a black woman who was caring for a white infant and lavishing upon it all the care and attention one would expect of a model mother, had two biological children of her own, aged six and four years, which she had never cared for herself. They had been raised by a sister and a friend, respectively. The apparent ease with which women in general, and this woman in particular, directed their maternal "instincts" to children with whom they had no consanguineal tie led us to investigate the meaning and significance attached to consanguinity itself.

The concept of family operative among our informants cannot be reduced to a simple list of compatible features; it contains contradictory elements, the whole ensemble of which constitutes the concept of family. We assume that everyone in Brazilian society shares a certain representation of family, but this general notion has to be used with care in understanding various concrete situations. The representation itself has to be constructed by the analyst out of the partial expressions contained in our interview materials, the relations between the parts being used to explain the whole.

We began our interviews by asking couples what they thought about marriage. The answers were unanimous in pointing to married life as a desirable state of affairs, although legal marriage was occasionally criticized. "I got married but it didn't work out. It's better to live together without getting married" (J, *m*).*

Although being single seemed attractive to many, it was thought to be transitional; constituting a family was fundamental for everyone. The women were more emphatic in their defense of marriage, but the men, while recognizing the greater freedom of being single, admitted that family life was more economical and provided opportunities for saving. Marriage is considered to be a good strategy for diminishing leisure expenses; owing to the complementarity of male work (outside the household) and female work (inside the domestic sphere), it becomes possible to achieve greater comfort. However, it would be an impoverished interpretation to see in these statements an explanation of marriage as just a matter of economic advantage. In the context of the *favelas*, the *peões* (single men, separated from their families of origin) were always living in a transitional situation, dependent upon help from women, whether that help was paid for or not. A house full of men is neither comfortable nor practicable; it is just not normal.

If marriage is desirable, it is because it leads to a family, and by that is meant procreation. Our informants made statements about the desirability of having children or not, some remarking that without children one could perhaps live well and have fewer worries. But no one thought that a couple without children formed a family in the true sense of that term. Children are an integral and necessary part of the family, because they bring greater pleasure (L, *f*), or because they will care for the parents in their old age (N, *f*), or even because they will impose a welcome and ennobling degree of suffering. For all informants, children are at one and the same time a source of pleasure, suffering, and help, because all these things are encompassed by the notion of family.

When we formulated the question in a yet more personal way, "If you could, would you marry and not have children?" the value placed upon children appeared with even greater force: "Of course not. I'd want at least one child" (A, *f*). "Sometimes a person can think that way, but when

---

*Informants are identified in the text by an initial followed by a lowercase *m* or *f* to indicate sex. See list on pages 202–3 for brief description of each informant.

their faith comes back, they have children . . . Unless the woman can't have children" (N, *f*). Only occasionally did one find a statement such as "Life would be carefree. We wouldn't be finished before our time" (F, *m*).

Again then, children are seen to be a source of worry as much as of happiness, but they are inevitable. It is unthinkable to form a family without the desire to have children. Involuntary infertility, an expression of the divine will, is accepted and might even be seen as an advantage, because worries and preoccupations can be avoided, but the initial desire to have children must be there. The continuity made possible by offspring is integral to the notion of family, which implies group continuity. This is a dynamic notion that presupposes distinct cycles in which assumed roles undergo transformations as they are undertaken by new individuals.

The importance of children in defining and constituting a family can be illustrated by the case of P, a young man married for the first time and still without children, and his wife, who had four children by a previous marriage. When asked whom he considered to be members of his family, he answered, "My father, my mother, and brothers and sisters. But in a few days there'll be a family here too." His wife answered the same question by saying, "My children." Only when the new baby was born would the man be a father and a husband in the full sense, and only then would the new family be properly constituted. It is interesting to note that among the popular classes an expression is used that makes the word *family* synonymous with *children*. When a woman is pregnant it is said that she is "expecting a family" (*esperando família*).

Consanguinity, Socialization, and Adoption

The full constitution of a new family through the birth of children would seem to place a great deal of stress upon consanguinity as the basis of family life, and indeed this interpretation is borne out by the extent to which women are reluctant to accept a man's children from a previous union. However, this point raises the issue of the importance of socialization and training in the constitution of kinship ties.

The kinship system is clearly bilateral, with consanguinity on the father's side being as important as that on the mother's. However, the relation between ascendants and descendants is conceptualized as a matter of the educational process* within the family, rather than as depending on

---

*Translator's note: In Brazilian Portuguese, *educação* (education) refers to the socializing of children in manners, morals, obedience, respect, etc. *Instrução* (also translated as "education") refers to the acquisition of skills and learning, as in school.

continuity of blood lines alone. The function of the mother is valued especially because she is the prime socializer; her role is to "care for and give advice." As one woman put it, "The mother stays with the child all day; she has to tame it and to teach it" (A, *f*). This woman was abandoned by her husband and goes out to work, so that she does not spend the whole day with her son. The idea that parents must discipline their children and point them in the right direction by teaching them moral norms and occupational responsibility is extremely generalized in Brazilian society. The intimate connection between mothers and children, rooted in the mother's primary role in socialization, makes women indispensable in the organization of domestic units. An adult male without a wife is an incomplete and incapable being; a mother with her children is an accepted form of family in spite of the difficulties involved in that situation.

The recognition of descent as bilateral reinforces the paternal link through the continuity of names, whereas the maternal side is strengthened by the mother's constant care for the child. These two kinds of relations initiate a system of obligations that continually link the older and younger generations. The obligation to educate the young is inscribed in this system of permanent exchanges, and for this task, women are seen to be essential. The consanguineal and educational aspects of intergenerational linkage are profoundly interrelated. For example, it is thought to be much easier to educate consanguines than nonconsanguines, and this is one reason why women oppose the idea of raising children from their husband's previous marriages. It is assumed that unless these children are very young, they will not accept a foster mother's authority. However, all interviewees, whether male or female, were unanimous in affirming that they made, or would make, no distinction between *filhos de criação*—their adopted children—and their own children.

Adoption is so frequent among the lower classes that almost all our informants had at least one case in their family. It is tempting to assume that adoption arises because of the conditions experienced by *favela* dwellers, conditions that range from predominantly male migration to the terrible problems of nutrition and health that increase this group's morbidity and create instability in domestic units. Reasons for adoption are almost always stated in terms of the moral obligation to help an abandoned child, and especially the child of a relative. Whatever the reason for the incidence of adoption, the fact is that it is an intrinsic part of the kinship system, and the expression *filhos de criação* synthesizes very neatly the two dimensions of intergenerational relations and shows that parents can produce sons and daughters by means other than procreation.

It would be wrong to think that the process of creating kinship through socialization operates in isolation from the belief that kinship is rooted in consanguinity. The two ideas work together, but without either being wholly determined by the other. The deeply felt obligation to help anyone who is in need is reinforced if that person happens to be a relative. Apart from anything else, there is always the possibility that if one adopts the child of a nonrelative the parents may claim it back sometime in the future. As already noted, it is also believed that it is much more difficult to socialize a child who is not related, or at any rate that the socialization must be more sustained, thorough, and reinforced. *É de pequeniño que se torce o pepino* (You have to train them while they are young) is a popular proverb that summarizes accurately the feelings and ideas of people in general. If there is no consanguinity in the relation between adoptive parents and child, then the socialization process alone must constitute the basis of reciprocity between the generations. The mechanism is discussed by Zonabend (1980) in his biography of an orphan who was raised in Burgundy by maternal relatives toward whom she was forced to maintain a constant debt imposing varied and interminable obligations. This is "diffuse, enduring solidarity" with a vengeance (Schneider 1980).

For the lower class at least, the raising of children is seen as a sacrifice that children must reciprocate by accepting parental discipline and guidance. That acceptance should be expressed in obedience. It follows therefore that correct and well-oriented socialization guarantees gratitude. Though consanguinity provides some contribution to this sense of gratitude, it is much less important than training. Almost everyone told us that children are a great deal of trouble because they are disobedient, and parental concern is focused upon the difficulty of "domesticating" their children—whether consanguines or adopted. The family system works and reproduces itself through a system of reciprocity that unites different generations, and for this purpose it uses the language of consanguinity. The term *filhos de criação* states clearly that by virtue of their socialization within a kinship group, these children are incorporated into the system of consanguinity.

Conclusion

Our research has established the profound importance of adoption among the Brazilian urban lower class, while at the same time confirming that the belief in blood as the defining feature of kinship is just as viable as among middle- and upper-class people. It is clear that for the middle and upper classes the existence of property and processes of inheritance introduce complications into the practice of adoption and invest consanguinity with a somewhat different meaning—or at least a different emphasis of meaning. However, there are also differences in kinship ideology between classes, differences that would be illuminated by a careful study of reactions to adoption.

In popular novels or television soap operas one finds that kinship relations are always described in terms of conflicts between parents and children or between siblings (Alves 1981). *Fotonovela* magazines* of wide distribution contain stories in which consanguinity is fundamental in explaining the continuity of family virtues and defects. In these stories socialization plays a secondary role, because it is never efficacious in transforming a dubious character into a virtuous one, and it is even less so in canceling the virtues inherited from older generations (Eid 1980). Although these magazines, like the soap operas, are widely followed by people who are not middle class, it is clear that their reference group is the upwardly mobile aspirants to middle class status, and they reflect the values and cultural presuppositions of those higher classes.

It would seem therefore that the middle classes lay primary stress upon the family as a biological unit, and in these classes there is a correspondingly less frequent incidence of adoption. The question with which we must end is, are these differences produced only by material factors? Our answer is that it is precisely the cultural elaborations upon central themes that contribute to, and even constitute, the differences between groups. A purely economistic explanation will not suffice, for there are too many possibilities of manipulating such hypotheses. Adoption among the lower class is not a ready means of economic success. On the contrary it can be quite onerous, but the practice is rooted in the emphasis given to socialization in the constitution of kinship ties—an emphasis that cannot be explained away by the impulse to maximize economic advantage. For the Brazilian lower class, adoption and fostering are culturally acceptable means of creating *real* kinship ties. Though this finding is not unrelated to the life situation of urban migrants, it also throws light upon the power of cultural creativity, rather than reflecting a blind response to economic hardship.

List of Informants

(J, *m*) A man who has lived with R for about a year, is an adoptive father, and works as a bricklayer.

(R, *f*) An adoptive mother and ex-domestic servant.

---

*Translator's note: *Fotonovelas* are romances conveyed by means of photographs and captions printed in a comic book format.

(L, *f*) A woman who began to live with her third husband during the research period; she has two children from previous marriages and has never been employed in São Paulo.

(F, *m*) A father of nine sons and a janitor; he is legally married to N.

(N, *f*) A mother of nine children and a housewife; she is legally married to F.

(A, *f*) A mother of one child, who has been abandoned by her husband and is working as a domestic servant.

(P, *m*) A man in his first marriage who lives with C and her two children and who works as a bricklayer; they are expecting the birth of their first child.

References

Alves, Yvonne Maggie
1981   "A quem devemos servir: Impressoes sobre a novela das oito." Mimeo.
Eid, Arthur
1980   "Os caminhos da felicidade na foto-novela." *Revista Plural* No. 6, Julho–agosto.
Schildkraut, Enid
1973   "The Fostering of Children in Ghana." *Urban Anthropology* 2: 48–73.
Schneider, David M.
[1968] *American Kinship: A Cultural Account.* Chicago: University of
1980   Chicago Press.
Zonabend, F.
1980   *La mémoire longue.* Paris: PUF.

Ideology and Practice in Southern Jalisco: Peasants, Rancheros, and Urban Entrepreneurs

Guillermo de la Peña

Preliminary Assumptions

The argument of this chapter presupposes a distinction between two concepts: kinship ideology and kinship organization. By kinship ideology I understand a set of shared propositions on how people culturally defined as kin should behave toward one another, including behavioral prescriptions—both vague and specific—for the incumbents of particular statuses. Such propositions are in turn justified by explicit or implicit metaphysical conceptions of human nature and/or beliefs in divine laws. By kinship organization I mean a set of specific norms that coordinate the activities of an enduring, goal-oriented group, whose membership is defined in terms of a kinship idiom (see Parsons 1956; March and Simon 1958; Firth 1961, p. 40). The relationship between ideology and organization is a very complex one; since Evans-Pritchard's classic study of Azande witchcraft (1937), anthropologists have shown that contradictory norms and beliefs often coexist within a single society. Although such contradictions are frequently sources of open conflict and change, I suggest that those ideological prescriptions which support and complement organizational norms are likely to persist over time as relevant criteria for evaluating everyday activity.

Here I use this distinction between kinship ideology and kinship organization to examine data from southern Jalisco, a region in Mexico (1) where there are a variety of classes, segments, and social categories; (2) where the members of the society share a cultural tradition including classificatory kinship terms and certain crucial kinship values and ideal norms; but (3) where one finds kin groups organized differently in different social classes and/or social categories.* In addition, (4) kin groups tend to change

* There are at least three possible relationships between kinship ideology and kin group formation. In the first, ideology includes clearcut organizational principles and predictable kin

as regional economic structures transform and develop, and (5) kinship values transform as well, although (6) these transformations are not the same for all social categories and classes.

Why Kinship?

Southern Jalisco provides an example of change, in a Third World (or "peripheral") country, from "mercantile-agrarian" to "agro-industrial" capitalism (Wessman 1981, p. 245). In both phases, the existence and reproduction of noncapitalist forms (e.g., of subsistence production) are important to system maintenance. One implication is that access to resources and goods is mediated, not simply through the market, but through multiplex social relationships as well (cf. Gluckman 1962, p. 26). In turn, this multiplexity implies that the position of actors in relation to the means of production is not the sole governing principle for either interclass or intraclass relations. Rather, in many circumstances, other specific alliances are more relevant than class interest (cf. Johnson 1972; Robertson 1980). The political process—the distribution of power, the upholding of order—is not carried out exclusively by impersonal state apparatuses. Instead, the state resorts to personal links to manifest itself. Thus kinship becomes overwhelmingly important: property and citizenship rights are transmitted by kinship, and families are the relevant organizing units for specific tasks such as the socialization of small children (kinship functions often found in societies where market relationships are universally present).

Moreover, kinship becomes an object of manipulation in all social spheres: it has a "tactical use" (Bloch 1971) in economic and political matters. Therefore the reproduction of kin groups and kinship alliances is vital, not only for generating people (the labor force), but for reproducing the very fabric of society. In this sense kinship is an aspect both of the infrastructure (as a means of access to material resources and production) and of the superstructure (as a means of expressing and justifying the act of appropriation) (Godelier 1975, p. 10).

However, even if in tribal societies kinship is *the* social structure, this is not the case in southern Jalisco's dynamic society. Other groups and alliances emerge, market transactions occur, the state tends to overshadow social life, and people choose among a variety of institutional norms and

---

groups do emerge, as in the lineage systems described by Evans-Pritchard (1940) and Fortes (1945). In the second, the principles exist but groups do not necessarily form; such is the case of Balinese *dadias* (Geertz and Geertz 1975). I am concerned with a third possibility: there are kin groups, but no general rules for group formation derived from the kinship ideology.

ideologies to justify their actions. The question is, under what conditions do people have recourse to kinship norms rather than, or in addition to, available universalistic legal codes?

A general answer lies in the weakness of the institutional order; in many situations "public law cannot guarantee adequate protection against breaches of non-kin contracts" (Wolf 1966, p. 10). Moreover, certain people—a group including smugglers and Mafiosi as well as many entrepreneurs, politicians, and lumpenproletarians—need an alternative moral code because their activities are not considered legal or "normal." On the other hand, situations of high risk and uncertainty (for instance, some entrepreneurial activities) require trust relationships, which are easily expressed in kinship terms (Long 1977; de la Peña 1982, pp. 142–46). In all these situations, the more flexible the meaning of the term *kin*, the more easily "the private relation of trust may be . . . translated into cooperation in the public realm" (Wolf 1966, p. 9). (See the uses of the terms *tío* and *compadre* among middle-class Chileans as illustrations of this type of categorical relation [Lomnitz 1971].)

Kinship content cannot, however, be reduced to a manipulative rationale for economic advantage and personal security; manipulators must reckon with the altruistic, suprasituational content of kinship. Obvious transgressions result in generalized mistrust toward the transgressor and drastically diminish the transgressor's possibilities for manipulation. Yet no situation is entirely defined by kinship norms, and the possible usages of kinship are never coterminous with kinship institutions. In terms of action (with due respect to Meyer Fortes), there is no such thing as an exclusive "kinship domain"; it is instead necessary to examine the uses of kinship within the varied contexts of people's practical concerns (cf. Geertz and Geertz 1975, p. 169).

Strategies and Class

In this essay I analyze kin groups involved in practical tasks: production, consumption, and reproduction (both biological and social), and argue that their organizational structure (the allocation of roles to members) is a function of the strategies through which such tasks are carried out. Because definitions of production, consumption, and reproduction vary in different classes, kin group strategies reflect class strategies.

Production must be examined in the context of regional, national, and international patterns of the division of labor; thus "class strategy" is not to be divorced from its historically specific configuration. Consumption, on the other hand, is not static and given but dynamic, shaped by historical processes. Consumption is conditioned, not merely by the objective possibility of appropriating goods of a certain type, but also by cultural definitions of need. Consumption is also determined by concrete mediations between the act of appropriation and the act of consumption. For example, the peasant cannot eat the maize he has harvested (or replace the energy needed to keep cultivating) unless a woman cooks the grain for him in a certain manner. In turn, biological reproduction must be seen in the context of social reproduction: children brought into a system of production and consumption inherit not abstract rights but a concrete way of life. Thus, the incorporation of children is mediated through social relationships that permit and encourage activities crucial for production and consumption.

The Regional Context

By 1867, when the Mexican Federal Republic was restored, southern Jalisco had a degree of unity, a rich folklore, and even a regional identity (Roberts 1980). Ecological heterogeneity (de la Peña 1977) and the relative abundance of natural resources accounted for the variety in primary production. Two sizable towns—Sayula and Ciudad Guzmán (previously called Zapotlán el Grande)—competed for the title of regional capital (Olveda 1980) and exercised effective influence over the overlapping hinterlands of lesser towns, villages, hamlets, and ranches, and over a handful of impressive haciendas.

Guadalajara, the state capital of Jalisco, had little active presence in the life of the southern region. Although Guadalajara was only 100 kilometers from Sayula and 140 from Ciudad Guzmán, communication was limited to horses, the mule trade, and infrequent stagecoaches. Federal power from Mexico City was, at most, a hovering menace that could bring trouble but never stayed long. Such circumstances encouraged the growth and consolidation of a regional elite who considered themselves the spiritual descendants of the old colonial *encomenderos*. These lords of land and wealth monopolized economic, political, and even military power in the realm. Even the church, severely wounded by disentailment laws, derived its power largely from links with the landowners. The elite, in their fortlike haciendas or in seigneurial houses in the larger towns, were linked by kinship and business alliances that, from their perspective, defined the unity of the region. In turn, their alliances with landowners in Colima, Guadalajara, and Mexico City linked the region with other segments of Mexican society and economy.

The success and viability of the elite depended on the functioning of the hacienda and the regional market (on the history of the region, see de la Peña 1979, 1980; de la Peña and Díaz de la Serna 1981; González de la Rocha and Escobar 1979; Veerkamp 1981). During the nineteenth century liberal legislation helped the haciendas expand and consolidate—at the expense of Indian village lands (Arreola 1963; Lameiras 1981). As economic institutions, haciendas reached a high degree of complexity, based on control over different types of land, capital resources, and labor.

A selected part of the hacienda land—usually an irrigated tract—was planted in commercial crops (sugar cane, wheat, rice, tobacco, and so on) and was tilled by both permanent and seasonal paid labor. The permanent labor force frequently lived within the *cascos* (nucleus) or in nearby hamlets. Most rain-fed land was given to sharecroppers (landless people from peasant villages) who cultivated maize. These sharecroppers, together with free landholding peasants, worked seasonally for the haciendas on the commercial crops and in the building and maintenance of roads and irrigation works. Many haciendas also possessed forests, pasture land (used for cattle raising or let to independent rancheros), fruit and agave plantations, and even iron mines. The haciendas had operated sugar and timber mills and mescal distilleries since colonial times. After 1840, they imported British machinery and launched more sophisticated enterprises: a paper mill and smelting plant in the Tapalpa sierra, sugar refineries and alcohol factories in Sayula and Tamazula.

Most products were sold and consumed in southern Jalisco, although some cattle and part of the sugar, tobacco, alcohol, and rice were sent to Guadalajara, to Colima, and to Mexico City. *Hacendados* controlled a substantial part of the regional market through hacienda credit stores and specialized (sugar and alcohol) retail shops. Additionally, they sometimes owned general stores in towns and villages. However, in most settlements there was room for the emergence of medium- and small-scale merchants and for the street markets that operated at religious fiestas and periodic fairs. These markets stimulated the cottage industries that proliferated in the second half of the nineteenth century.

Regional integration depended on the power of the elite to subordinate other social classes, a subordination not achieved without conflict and violence. A second precondition for regional dynamism was a lack of both political and economic integration. During the regime of Porfirio Díaz (1877–1910), however, local *caciques* were increasingly subordinated to centralized authority, free trade was fostered throughout the nation, international investment was encouraged, professional bureaucrats and policemen entered the scene, interstate taxes were abolished, and the railway between Guadalajara and Colima was inaugurated. As a result, the haciendas had to reorient production toward the national and international market, and then suffered the world economic crisis of the 1920s and 1930s. The revolution (1910–20) and the *cristero* religious rebellion (1926–30) created a climate of conflict and insecurity. And as their crafts were displaced by the avalanche of mass-produced goods brought by the railway and the expanding road network, small-scale manufacturers and artisans fled to Guadalajara, which became a center of small industry (Arias 1980).

The oligarchy was largely replaced by the new state apparatuses; in addition, market crises and agrarian reform in Jalisco during the 1930s caused the final ruin of the haciendas. The elite moved to Guadalajara and Mexico City and became businessmen, middle-class professionals, or white-collar workers. Agrarian reform did not, however, create new alternatives for most peasants and workers in southern Jalisco. The population of the area grew from 100,000 in 1800 to 200,000 in 1885. Since then it has stagnated, in spite of a high fertility rate and a declining mortality rate. Two interrelated phenomena—dislocation of the local employment structure and massive emigration—occurred as sharecropping and peasant farming were displaced by sugar cane, sorghum, and other commercial crops. A new type of enterprise, the corporate agroindustrial and industrial enclave, emerged to control vast amounts of regional resources and raw materials and orient production to the national and international market, yet provided relatively few local jobs. Such enterprises were under the control, not of the local elite, but of the government agencies and of national and international capital.

How did these sweeping changes affect different groups and social categories in Jalisco? To answer, it is necessary to consider social categories as interdependent. Peasants, for example, must be analyzed in the context of the hacienda organization that ordered much of their behavior. As the region changed, peasants, *hacendados*, rancheros, artisans, and merchants also changed, though not always passively. Some local *hacendados* helped bring the railway into the region and thereby contributed to the crisis. Many peasants and rancheros were active in the revolution, the *cristiada*, and the agrarian reform movement. Indeed, all social categories developed strategies to survive the economic crisis. Thus the processes of change were the outcome of a complex interplay between external forces and local actors (Smith 1978, p. 330). The study of kinship provides a privileged field for investigating this interplay.

The Traditional Kinship Ideology

Fieldwork indicates that in southern Jalisco virtually all men and women over fifty years of age, whether rich or poor, rural or urban, share and articulate a common stock of kinship values, even if their behavior deviates from ideal norms. This ideology has been described in novels about southern Jalisco (Refugio Barragán de Toscano's *La hija del bandido*; José López-Portillo y Rojas's *La parcela*; Juan José Arreola's *La feria*) and was originally a result of successful Spanish colonization practices, including severe punishment of moral deviants and the imposition of patterns of prestige (see the section entitled "Latin America and Kinship Studies" in the Introduction to this book). Its maintenance depends on continuing actions of the church and government agencies and on the ways individuals and groups accept, uphold, and manipulate cultural values. Yesterday's *hacendados* did not trust a laborer who was not a "good family man" and a good Christian; today's employers often voice the same concerns. Saint Paul is read and commented on at every religious wedding, and Melchor Ocampo at every civil marriage ceremony (both explicitly proclaim the authority of a man over his wife and children and the inferiority of women in economic and political matters); and "family morals" is a frequent subject of Sunday sermons. In villages and towns, children attend catechism classes on Saturday afternoon as devout spinsters advocate sexual abstinence and obedience to parents. Moralistic folk tales reinforce religious preaching, and there are numerous customary ways to brand deviants; for example, in Sierra del Tigre villages women suspected of having sexual relations outside marriage are accused of witchcraft (see Plunket-Nagoda 1981). Finally, people often invoke kinship principles to justify their conduct.

Virtually all ideological prescriptions are either logically derived from, or justified in terms of, four central principles: (1) parents represent God on earth vis-à-vis their children; (2) commonality of blood demands similitude and love; (3) all siblings are equal before their parents; and (4) males are superior to females. This fourth principle is obviously incompatible with the third, and potentially conflicts with the first two.

The first principle implies that the only justification for sexual intercourse is the procreation and raising of children. A further extrapolation is that a monogamous, indissoluble, religiously contracted marriage is the only legitimate institution for the transmission of life and the socialization of respectable human beings. Parents are responsible before God for the qualities and deficiencies (physical and moral) of their child, because God has entrusted them with the continuation of his endless creative task. (Abhorrence of birth control is probably related to this belief.) In turn, children are to show total obedience and respect to their parents. The importance of *compadrazgo* stems from the fact that godparents share the parents' divine mission (Gudeman 1972). Similar co-responsibility gives meaning and importance to the roles of uncles, aunts, and grandparents, who are expected to protect and correct the children of their siblings and offspring and, in turn, to receive respect and obedience.

Bilateral consanguineal ties are derived from the second principle, commonality of blood. In practice, only members of the elite are able to trace their lineage beyond three generations, and as is common with upper classes, they are especially precise about links to important persons (cf. Strickon 1965, p. 335). Even so, the number of consanguineal kin for any one individual is large, frequently more than 150. *Ser de la misma sangre* (to be of the same blood) is an explanation of physical or psychological resemblance. The greater the amount of blood shared, the greater the expectations of mutual benevolence (cf. Lomnitz and Pérez-Lizaur 1978; Schneider 1968). By extension, affinal kin should also be loved because they share the spouse's blood.

The principle of sibling equality implies partible inheritance. That a woman has rights equal to her brother's is reflected in the use of the mother's as well as the father's name; nor do women lose their maiden name upon marriage. Whether single or married, young or old, offspring are entitled to affection and help from their parents and are obliged to reciprocate, especially in their parents' old age. Illegitimate children have lower status, but the father is expected to acknowledge paternity, provide for their raising, and, if he is well off, include them in his will.

The principle of male superiority is deeply rooted in Catholic belief, as well as in Spanish and colonial law—a matter illustrated by the *patria potestas* of King Alfonso X (Willems 1975, p. 55), the frequent exclusion of women from inheritance in entailed estates, and the allocation of communal land plots in Indian villages (de la Peña 1982). During the nineteenth century, liberal legislation abolished both entailed estates and communal property, and explicitly recognized female rights to equitable inheritance. Although such rights are unquestioned in southern Jalisco today (as well as a hundred years ago), belief in male superiority persists. A man is thought to be more intelligent and judicious, as well as morally and physically stronger. A man is expected to be ugly, strong, and morally consistent (the three *f*s: *feo, fuerte, y formal*); a woman is expected to be beautiful, weak, and inconsistent, and must be watched and shielded by men, who are "naturally" entitled to female obedience. Female sexual misbehavior (premarital sex or adultery) represents blatant disobedience to male authority and dishonors the family, because the father, the brother, or the husband failed to exercise his authority. (Although extramarital sex is not explicitly condoned for men, it is shameful only if a man deserts his wife and children for the other woman.) Similarly, active participation of women in economic management is a severe blow to the prestige of males in the household: *les faltan pantalones* (they don't have enough pants; i.e., they lack manhood).

To understand how people conform to the image of a "good family man" (by definition also a good citizen [López-Portillo y Rojas 1870, pp. 22–23]), in spite of explicit and implicit contradictions among these four principles, I refer again to Evans-Pritchard (1937). The Azande selected beliefs and values without regard to their compatibility with beliefs and values upheld in other situations. I suggest that this "situational selection" is best understood by examining how people interpret and manipulate the same ideological principles in the context of different kin group organizations. Therefore, I examine the emergence and operation of kin groups among three social categories: peasants in the village of Amacueca, cattle-raising rancheros in the Sierra del Tigre, and urban entrepreneurs in Ciudad Guzmán. In addition to their historical and ethnographic context, I focus on the conditions under which different structural features of kinship groups are viable.

In southern Jalisco, people use the word *family* to refer both to a specific kin group and to close kin (distant kin are usually *mis parientes*, not *mi familia*), and I use *family* to gloss the kin groups I analyze. Some authors suggest that *family* is a meaningful concept only when understood in relation to household and class: "The entities in which people live are not families, but households" (Rapp 1978, p. 280). But households do not have an inherent organizational structure (Smith 1978); "households vary systematically as to resource base, and their ability to tap wealth, wages and welfare" (Rapp 1978, p. 299). To understand the logic of household organization one must look at its operation diachronically, discovering the ways in which people are recruited into the household, the resources to which they have access, the goals toward which resources are pooled, how and when members are expected to leave the household, and how new households are generated. The family (as I use the term in this essay) is the actual unit of cooperation that makes household cycles viable (Smith 1956; Yanagisako 1979).

Case 1: Peasants of Amacueca

The Setting

Situated on the lower eastern slopes of the Sierra Tapalpa, at 1,842 meters above sea level, the village of Amacueca has for centuries been renowned for its fruit, vegetable, and cereal production. Each house stands in the center of an orchard, and the entire village is an immense garden, crisscrossed by steep, cobbled, winding streets, and channels running from orchard to orchard. Several water springs, nourished by mountain drainage and underground currents, provide the basis for small-scale irrigation and a relatively high population density (Palerm and Wolf 1972, p. 37). Villagers also cultivate rain-fed land, both in the sierra slopes and in the neighboring Sayula Valley (Ciudad Real 1976, 2:85–87; Tello 1945; Munguía 1976; de la Peña 1980).

By the end of the nineteenth century, Amacueca had become the municipal seat of a territory of 131.8 square kilometers. It boasted a tiny elite of landowners, merchants, and moneylenders who controlled local government and maintained a local primary school. Eighty percent (2,332 hectares) of the *municipio*'s best (plains) land was occupied by nine ranchos (smallish haciendas) of 150 to 550 hectares. Most ranchers also owned cattle, pastures, and forests in the lower sierra, and lived in Sayula. The remaining land on the plain was distributed among some fifty farms of two to four *yuntas* (8 to 16 hectares) each. (A *yunta*—literally, "a yoke of oxen"—refers to the amount of land that could be cultivated by a peasant household using oxen and plow: between 4 and 5 hectares.) Among these farmers several also made money from commerce, cattle, soap workshops, tanneries, and usury. Arable land in the hills and slopes was owned by approximately two hundred families, each with no more than 8 or 9 hectares and occasionally as little as half a hectare. Almost without exception, these families also possessed fruit orchards within the village perimeter. Finally, a number of families had only a small orchard and no land outside the village (de Alba 1978–80, pp. 21–24).

Even if outsiders thought of Amacueca as an Indian village, ethnic labels had become irrelevant as criteria for social differentiation. What counted were class differences, expressed in terms of access to land and commercial wealth. However, the difference between smallholders and landless peasants was no longer crucial, because partible inheritance and population increases had reduced smallholdings drastically. Between 1800 and 1900 this land atomization made sharecropping common practice for the sons of smallholders, as it had been for the landless. In 1909, 220 sharecroppers cultivated the rain-fed land of the nine large holdings in the *municipio*, and many others worked for rich Amacueca farmers. Thus, my references to peasants do not distinguish smallholders and sharecroppers.

Family Organization

For the Amacueca peasant, production, consumption, and social reproduction were based in the extended patrilocal family, with the household as pivot. Depending upon the stage of the developmental cycle, this extended family could span three generations living in the same household; at other times nuclear families lived separately but in close proximity (González Chávez 1981, in preparation).

Residence and inheritance arrangements for adult offspring were as follows: women frequently married before the age of twenty, received a small marriage settlement (clothes and domestic animals), and moved to the husband's lodging; spinsters remained in the parental household. Men seldom married before age twenty-three, and it was not uncommon for a forty-year-old bachelor to live with his parents. Marriage partners were seldom chosen from outside the village. Youths had some say in the choice of a spouse, and there was a period of courting before marriage, but it was unthinkable to marry without parental supervision and approval. At marriage a man initially took his wife to his father's household: older sons tended to establish independent households with their father's help, whereas younger sons remained in the paternal house one or two years after they had married. Usually the youngest son lived in the paternal household until the father died, and then inherited his father's house and orchard and had the responsibility of lodging and caring for spinster siblings and his father's sisters in their old age.

A married son who left his parents' household was helped by his father to obtain a house and an orchard. If the father's orchard was large enough, it could be subdivided among sons, who built houses on their shares. But it was more common to buy part of an orchard from a widow, a childless couple, or a fellow peasant in urgent need of cash. Orchards were not always available, a difficulty that sometimes caused extreme atomization of orchard land.

The son also needed land to grow food for his new household. If the father had enough land of his own, the son received part of it. However, in many cases the son gained access to land by sharecropping. Because a landowner usually gave land to trusted people, it was an important peasant strategy to invite one or two landowners to be godfathers so that the sons could obtain land.

In principle, sharecropping implied that land and seed were provided by the landowner, and work and implements by the sharecropper, with the harvest divided equally. However, when a youth started independent farming, he often had to borrow oxen, plows, and even machetes and hoes from the landowner—charged against his share of the harvest. If paid laborers were needed, half of their cost was the sharecropper's expense. Thus, to save labor costs, ongoing cooperation of the extended family was necessary.

One rain-fed *yunta* in the plain yielded sixty to seventy hectoliters of maize in a good year, more than double the amount required by the average household. But hilly land was less productive, and not all years were equally good. In practice, a sharecropper often had to borrow maize from the landowner. To avoid perpetual indebtedness, peasants might share-crop an extra *yunta* or a *coamil*. (The *coamil*, a smallish plot in the steeper hills or bush, was worked by hoe and required long fallow periods between plantings. The owner normally received only one-tenth of the harvest; his major benefit was having the land cleared for grazing cattle.) In any case, the help of sons was needed to ensure financial solvency. As the number of households increased, more food was required, but there was also more labor available

Peasants also needed money—to buy food, oxen and agricultural tools, clothes, and houses and orchards for their sons—which came from two sources: the domestic orchard and the sale of labor. An orchard is a highly complex system of production that requires continuous care and labor investment. At the turn of this century, each orchard usually had between twenty-five and thirty varieties in production (Bárcena 1895, pp. 543–44). Terraces and irrigation channels had to be maintained, and each species had its own time of seedbed preparation, planting, weeding, pruning, and harvesting. All family members were involved, but men performed the more skilled or risky tasks. Orchard produce had a very secure market, and a well-kept orchard provided money throughout the year. The wholesalers of certain products (e.g., walnuts and coffee beans) exported to Guadalajara were often important farmers or landowners. Thus a sharecropper protected his contract, not only through *compadrazgo*, but also by selling the orchard products to his patron.

In selling their labor, peasants had several alternatives: they could work in the orchards of the rich, who often needed temporary workers at harvest; poor peasants could also work in the orchards and maize fields of more prosperous peasants, or of peasants whose households and/or extended families were not numerous enough to work their land. Laborers were also needed for commercial crops grown within the *municipio*. Finally, a man could work at various tasks in the large estates of the Sayula haciendas, and women could find permanent or occasional jobs as domestic servants.

The Impact of Regional Transformation

Changes in the system began when the railway tempted landowners to use larger tracts of land for cattle raising, displacing some sharecroppers. But the railway also increased demand for orchard crops, and because orchard production is labor intensive, this change increased the possibilities for local employment. Later, from 1911 to 1920, revolutionary violence frightened landowners, rich farmers, and merchants, many of whom sold their land and fled to Guadalajara. In 1921 a group of sharecroppers and smallholders submitted a petition for land to the Agrarian Reform Commission in Guadalajara. The commission was slow and inefficient, and new waves of violence—the *cristero* rebellion lasted from 1925 until nearly 1935—prevented peaceful land distribution. Finally, in 1935, an *ejido* was constituted in Amacueca, but only twenty-five peasants in the village received land, eight hectares each. Two years later other settlements in the *municipio* received *ejido* holdings, but most of the best land was still in the hands of private owners (de Alba 1978–80, pp. 49–52).

In 1940 the situation of the Amacueca peasant was very similar to that of his grandfather. Even if he had an *ejido* holding, it was small and could not be legally subdivided. The sons of the *ejidatarios* still depended on sharecropping, on landowners for *habilitación* (equipment) and implements, and on wage labor to make ends meet. However, after 1940, more drastic changes began.

First, landowners, and some *ejidatarios*, used land on the plain to grow commercial crops. The drilling of wells expanded available irrigated land, which was used for cane until the sugar mill in the Amatitlán hacienda went bankrupt and alfalfa replaced sugar cane. Rain-fed land was gradually occupied by commercial crops, too, especially after the introduction of sorghum, which is more resistant than maize to drought and fungi and has a higher market value. As a result, all the land on the plain is now in the hands of prosperous farmers (including some *ejidatarios*) who grow alfalfa and sorghum with the help of machinery and hired casual labor. Since 1965 sharecropping has been totally confined to the hills.

A second change since 1940 has been the deterioration of the orchards. Not only has the amount of water available for irrigation decreased, but the amount of family labor invested in the orchards has decreased owing to emigration. Since 1930 more than three thousand people have left, partly because of the lack of land available for sharecropping. During the last decade, many trees in the orchards have suffered disease and death. Particularly serious has been the plague that attacked the walnut trees, the product with the highest market value. Members of the traditional elite who previously made most of their money from the fruit commerce went bankrupt and left. The present-day local rich are people who hold land, lend money, and monopolize the sorghum crops sold to multinational corporations.

These phenomena have had several consequences for peasant family structure: adult sons find it difficult to establish themselves independently; little land is left for sharecropping; *coamiles* are more plentiful, but their productivity is very low. Thus the sons lack money to buy houses or land. Sometimes sons stay permanently in the father's household after marriage, and there are some cases of uxorilocality. But it is more common for males to emigrate before marrying. Some return to Amacueca after saving money, but many remain in California, Arizona, or Guadalajara, and a father often finds himself without the help of adult sons. Moreover, absent sons frequently fail to send money home.

The labor of women and children has therefore become much more important in central productive tasks. It is common for a little boy to spend practically all his time in the fields, cultivating maize in a *coamil* or working for a wage in the alfalfa plantations. He begins when he is five or six years old, is capable of taking charge of many chores by age ten, and becomes a trained farmer at fourteen. Women and girls, who were previously in charge of many orchard activities but who worked in the fields only at harvest time, now work in maize cultivation and sometimes in the alfalfa fields. In addition, in the many households where all the adult men are frequently absent owing to labor migration, the household is run by the mother with the help of the eldest boy or girl. As a result, household consumption has become dependent more on items purchased at the store than on what can be produced by the family.

Child labor and labor migration have therefore become two important strategies for the peasant family (see González Chávez 1981, pp. 149–74). Migration brings money into the household; in this sense it differs little from the search for temporary wage employment fifty years ago. However, migratory labor patterns also contribute to the decline in population. People are acutely aware of the lack of viability of traditional activities, and the lack of local alternatives. This awareness has led the peasants to increased interest in formal education for their children. Little schooling is needed to find work as agricultural workers in the United States, but crossing the border has become expensive and difficult. Formal education is necessary to obtain a stable job in Guadalajara, or even in Ciudad Guzmán. Since 1970 children have been able to attend secondary school in Amacueca.

School attendance, however, conflicts with the household's need for child labor. This conflict is solved by a family strategy: the older boys and all the girls may "sacrifice" themselves and work while the younger boys study. Or the father may organize family labor so that children have time to attend school and do their homework. For example, a man may start working in the fields at five o'clock in the morning, rather than seven, so the children can go to school at nine; he might also extend the workday until darkness makes it impossible to carry on. Yet another strategy is for the eldest son to find work in Guadalajara or Ciudad Guzmán and have one or two brothers live with him and attend school there; he often brings a sister as well to cook and do the housework, forming a sort of household branch in the city. For these young migrants, as for the Amacueca migrants in general, the patrilateral extended family has ceased to be the significant unit of cooperation; the relevant unit is now a flexible network that may include patrilateral and matrilateral kin, affines, and even neighbors and close friends.

Case 2: Rancheros of Sierra del Tigre

Except for two small Indian villages, the vast Sierra del Tigre was virtually unpopulated until the second half of the eighteenth century (González 1979). Before 1750 only a handful of shepherds and cowboys worked for absentee landowners, who, in turn, neglected their enormous, unkempt *latifundio*. But by 1800 the sierra had witnessed the birth of ranchero society: there were some one hundred dispersed ranchos, all founded by descendants of old shepherds or migrants from neighboring Michoacán. Local tradition holds that the tenants were descended from a mythical Sephardic lineage. Whatever the case, many rancheros had a striking physical appearance: tall, strong, and fair, with dense, long beards. To this day their great-grandchildren scorn the "Indians"* and the "servile" valley agriculturalists (*gente corriente*, "vulgar people").

The Patriarchal Family

The core of the rancho was the household of the bearded patriarch. The hut (*jacal*) was built of mud and wood and had a large common bedroom, a kitchen, and a sort of portico that functioned as a working and living room. The household was surrounded by a corral inhabited by poultry, pigs, donkeys, horses, and mules. Not far from the corral was an *ecuaro*, a small plot of land where the family grew maize, squash, beans, and chilies for domestic consumption. The rancheros also cultivated fruit orchards and magueys and kept beehives. But most of the land—200 to 500 hectares—was utilized for cattle grazing.

After marriage, sons remained in the paternal rancho, whereas a daughter left the territory to settle in her husband's rancho or village. Each married son (having obtained the patriarchal license to set up an independent household) built a *jacal* and prepared an *ecuaro* near his father. A rancho could have as many as thirty *jacales* (a total of 250–300 people)

---

* "Indians" are people of certain villages: Mazamitla and Quitupan in the sierra, and San Sebastián and San Andrés in the Zapotlán Valley, Amacueca in the Sayula Valley, and so on. The term does not necessarily have racial connotations: some dark-skinned rancheros descended from mulattoes in Sahuayo or Sayula, for example, were not discriminated against.

housing the patriarch's sons and grandsons and their respective nuclear families, and together forming a single social and economic organization. The organization's primary task was to provide food for its members. The *ecuaro* could be as large as one *yunta* and, on good land, could yield a yearly maize harvest of 1.5 metric tons, along with enough beans, squash, and chilies for a nuclear family of up to six people. However, if the *ecuaro* was smaller or built on hilly land and worked by hoe, labor had to be invested and/or the *ecuaro* expanded to produce enough maize. Expansion was also necessary when the nuclear family reached a size of eight or more.

Adult males were expected to spend most of their time taking care of the cattle; thus female and child labor were crucial for agriculture. Women were also in charge of raising the children, cooking, manufacturing garments, taking care of animals, and keeping beehives. If the children were too small to work, or the mother was unable to devote much time to agricultural chores because of pregnancy or child care, a young *jacal* owner had to depend on help from his father and siblings to feed his family. It was common practice for children to move to their grandfather's or father's brother's *jacal* if help was needed.

The rancho organization also needed money. The rent due the landowner was perhaps one hundred pesos per year (estimated from Brading 1978, p. 102)—the equivalent of twenty to twenty-five well-developed heifers. To cover that amount and to ensure against drought and illness, a patriarch had to have at least forty or fifty healthy cows and five to ten healthy breeding bulls. Such a herd required a minimum of 100 hectares of pasture—in practice, control of up to 250 hectares—just to pay the rent. Money was also needed for rites of passage; tithes; household items; hats and clothing (though these were sewn by rancho women, cloth had to be purchased); bread and salt; and machetes, poles, lances, guns, plows, hoes, and ropes.

Many of these items were supplied by roving muleteers in exchange for honey, cheese, wax, mescal spirit, and *cecina* (dried beef). The patriarch and his sons also made periodic trips to Michoacán and Jalisco to sell cattle and hides (see Serrera 1977), and returned with household goods, work implements, and sometimes a small trunk of gold coins.

Under what conditions was this rancho organization viable? It had a fixed territorial base and, because the land belonged to the landlord, could not be divided by inheritance. The territory was not densely populated and could absorb new families. In fact, some rancheros sublet part of their land or hired newcomers as paid laborers because they had too few kin to work the land. A masculine labor force was highly valued; even though cattle did not demand continuous care, male guards were needed to protect the ranch against marauders, thieves, and fugitives from an endless civil war (Olveda 1980). Commercial trips required men armed with lances, machetes, and guns. Women were also indispensable: high fertility was valued; young women were jealously guarded and outside suitors fiercely rebuked by rancho males, not only because of family honor, but also because of the value of female labor. Thus patrilateral parallel cousin marriage became an accepted (though not prescriptive or exclusive) practice, and kept women at the rancho.

The organization of work and distribution of products required strong hierarchical authority. The lack of rigidly enforced discipline was thought to weaken territorial control and cause failure in commercial ventures. Within the rancho the patriarch was second only to God. His was the last word concerning marriage (both of men and women), cooperation among *jacales*, and the settlement of disputes. In addition, he controlled the money obtained from the sale of cattle.

Children and young people were to obey not only their parents but also their parents' generation—particularly their fathers' brothers. Indeed, children often had meals at or even lived in the *jacales* of their paternal uncles. A young man was expected to work for his father, his grandfather, and his father's brother. A girl kept close to her mother, but was occasionally sent to help her father's mother and her father's and brother's wives. A widowed mother was to heed her grown sons, especially in matters concerning rancho organization.

The Breakdown of the Patriarchy

Some rancheros saved considerable amounts of money. Then around 1850 a few of the rich rancheros migrated to towns and villages to begin new, more secure, and more civilized lives. Other rancheros bought land in the outskirts of the sierra, and between 1860 and 1870, the owners of the five biggest *latifundio* in the Sierra del Tigre sold their land to tenants (Moreno García 1980, pp. 110–11; Moreno Ochoa 1975, pp. 93–99). Once a rancho became the private property of a patriarch, he could divide it among his children; in fact, the death of founding patriarchs brought land divisions in most ranchos, and land sales became more frequent. Even people who had previously worked as hired laborers or who had sublet land became landowners.

For example, José Guadalupe González Toscano, the son of a subtenant of the rancho Llano de la Cruz, was born in 1821. He married the daughter of the main tenant in 1846 and with her help, after fifteen years of hard work, saved 750 pesos; he bought 350 hectares in 1861. When he died in 1872, Guadalupe owned more land and 200 cattle. His four sons and three daughters inherited equal shares; later, the sons bought more land and developed independent enterprises, though they continued to live in the same compound of huts (cf. González 1979, pp. 65–66, 78–81). Other rancheros were not as lucky, or as clever. They often inherited little land and sometimes sold that to pay debts. The poor rancheros, together with new immigrants, constituted a distinct class who had to hire themselves out as workers and cultivate land as sharecroppers. After 1860 it was difficult to lease a tract of sierra and start an independent rancho.

The lives of the rancheros were radically transformed when they joined forces to found villages. Village life became a symbol of civilization and progress, with churches, schools, free and abundant commerce, and security against marauders. The first new village, El Valle, was started in 1865, Concepción de Buenos Aires in 1869, La Manzanilla in 1872, Unión de Guadalupe in 1883, and San José de Gracia in 1888. The old patrigroups (descendants of the founding patriarchs) again became relevant organizational units as they recruited village builders and settlers. Each village became identified with a handful of surnames, although many landless families with no ties to the patrigroups also came to live in the villages.

The urban structure of the villages—a perfect grid—reflected the division of the classes that existed at this point in the sierra. The rich lived near the central square (and the church) in vast houses of adobe, red brick, and tile. Tight unity of the patriarchal corporation became a thing of the past; father, sons, and grandsons worked independently and organized consumption separately. The increasing dependence of households on manufactured goods, and their constant need for money, separated their domestic economies. However, a married man would visit his father's house every evening to drink chocolate, chat and exchange information with siblings, and receive his parents' blessing. Cooperation (e.g., reciprocal labor) among siblings and patrilateral cousins was still frequent, although village residence made it possible to cooperate also with matrilateral cousins, affines, and *compadres*.

The poor lived in mud, reed, and timber huts along the village outskirts. Married sons built huts near their fathers'. When a man worked permanently as a cowboy or sharecropper for a ranchero, he took his family to live on the rancho. Differences in life-style between landowners and the landless became sharp; class intermarriage had been common during the 1850s and 1860s but was extremely rare by 1900—although it was not uncommon for poor women to bear illegitimate children by wealthy males.

Few of the landowners were really wealthy, because partible inheritance had reduced the size of the ranchos over time. For example: in 1862 the hacienda Cojumatlán sold its land to 36 tenants; fifty years later their number had increased to 167 landowners. Revolutionary violence later prevented the commercial trips essential to rancho economy; some rancheros sold their land and moved to the cities. The revolution found few followers in Sierra del Tigre, but the *cristero* rebellion involved important local leaders and many men. The solidarity of the patrigroup provided a useful idiom for the cohesion of rebel squads (see Fábregas, Díaz, and Rodríguez 1979 on the *cristero* rebellion in Los Altos).

The Contemporary Crisis

In the 1930s the villagers were deeply divided by the Agrarian Reform program. The priest in San José de Gracia persuaded some rancheros to divide the land before government bureaucrats arrived in the locality (González 1979, pp. 217–25). Even so, many rancheros fired their sharecroppers and put cattle on the land. The sharecroppers, often relatives and/or *compadres*, were forced to leave. Nonetheless, the government divided large holdings among the landless. The poor quality of the land, however, and the lack of technical assistance compelled the *ejidatarios* to look for supplementary work, which was hard to find in the region. Haciendas in the Sayula Valley, formerly a source of seasonal employment for the landless and petty rancheros, had disappeared. The remaining prosperous ranchos' herds were ravaged in the 1940s and 1950s. For many people emigration was the only solution. The Sierra del Tigre is now the most radically depopulated area in southern Jalisco; for example, Unión de Guadalupe's population of 2,200 in 1890 has declined to less than 900 today.

Since 1960 the opening of roads through the sierra has supported the emergence of small-scale entrepreneurs. Two activities are especially profitable: the import of manufactured goods to villages in Sierra del Tigre and the production and export of dairy products. But the entrepreneur's success depends on his ability to diversify and combine many activities. Moreover, diversification requires the entrepreneur to create new positions and channels of action (Leeds 1965), and to recruit trusted persons in order to minimize uncertainty. These trusted persons are, of course, kin.

A relevant case is that of Juan Chávez, who lives in Unión de Guadalupe. His father, a descendant of one of the founding ranchero families, inherited a very small tract of hilly land and made his living as a roving merchant. Juan, born in 1921, learned to read and write at the school in Unión de Guadalupe and then accompanied his father on trading ventures. As an adolescent Juan spent long periods in Atoyac and Ciudad Guzmán, where he learned the trades of barber and carpenter. He returned to Unión de Guadalupe and combined these trades with itinerant commerce. In 1948 he married the daughter of a local shopkeeper and, with the help of his wife and in-laws, opened a shop, which was kept well stocked with supplies conveyed by his father's mules. When a dirt road was opened, Juan bought a truck and became a major transporter of cattle and dairy products. As his daughters grew up they became more active in the shop. His sons worked in the transport business and later in a small cheese and cream factory that Juan opened in 1975. Juan bought machinery and dairy cattle, thanks to financial help from two sons who had emigrated to the United States and returned with money (see de la Peña and Díaz de la Serna 1981).

Juan Chávez is an exceptional case. There is no room for many entrepreneurs, and few migrants return to invest their earnings. Families are scattered throughout Ciudad Guzmán, Guadalajara, and the U.S. border, as members struggle to establish themselves without the benefit of the old patriarchal system.

Case 3: Urban Entrepreneurs in Ciudad Guzmán

When José Albino and Tomás de Mendoza, two young brothers from Cotija, arrived in Zapotlán el Grande (Ciudad Guzmán) in 1830, the town had eight thousand inhabitants, who made a living from agriculture, commerce, and pig raising (de la Peña 1979). Tomás soon left for Guadalajara and lost contact with José Albino, who settled permanently in Zapotlán. José's saddlebag full of gold coins—the inheritance from his father, who made his small fortune breeding mules—paid for a large house on the outskirts of town.

José also bought land, which he let to sharecroppers, and opened a store. He traveled to Colima in search of overseas goods for the store and there met Antonia Ochoa, the daughter of a rich import-export merchant and member of a prominent Colima family. They were married in 1832 and had three children: Josefa María, Martín, and Rafael. The business prospered; José bought more land and manufactured copper caldrons, which were in demand for soap production. He also bought shares in a regional paper factory and later resold them at a profit. When he died in 1860 his store operated as a sort of bank: credit documents signed by José could be exchanged for goods in his own store, as well as in other commercial enterprises and haciendas.

José's life-style was modest. His wife rose at dawn to cook, do the housework, and run the store. The two boys and the girl started working as soon as they learned to read and write. Martín and Josefa married and left the household. Rafael, the youngest, stayed in the house after his father's death and, in later years, reunited his father's estate, which had been divided by inheritance. Martín died of malignant fever, leaving a wife and three small children. His half interest in the store was worth about twelve thousand pesos. Rafael persuaded his sister-in-law, who did not work in the store, to allow him to run the business and pay her a yearly interest of 6 percent on Martín's share. In 1867 Rafael's brother-in-law also died. Rafael gained control over the whole of his father's land in exchange for paying Josefa María a yearly interest of 5 percent on an estimated value of eleven thousand pesos. Rafael's sister and his sister-in-law later resented these arrangements, but he refused to renegotiate the terms and finally bought them out. As a result, relations were extremely strained among the family in Zapotlán, although Rafael and his children maintained friendly contacts with their Colima cousins.

Rafael had had at least one mistress, a lower-class woman who gave birth to a son, recognized by Rafael in his will. Rafael did not marry, however, until 1871, a year after his mother's death. He wanted a hardworking woman—not a "useless doll" like his sister-in-law. He despised the elegant women of some *hacendados* who dressed in silk and demanded that their husbands build palaces for them. Rafael finally went to Colima to look for and marry his cousin Isabel Rosa Ochoa y Ochoa, whose dowry was fifteen thousand pesos. Isabel gave birth to four girls and two boys and ran the store until her death in 1910.

Rafael's businesses prospered. The population of Zapotlán increased to fifteen thousand in 1878, to twenty thousand in 1888, and to nearly thirty thousand in 1900 (Muriá 1976, p. 35). Rafael took land from peasants and indebted Indians, bought two sugar cane haciendas in the southern valleys, raised cattle, developed a brick factory after an earthquake destroyed half the town, and exploited small-scale mines. As soon as his sons, Salvador and Albino, could ride, they traveled with their father, rising at four or five in the morning and remaining busy for up to twelve hours every day. They also had to learn to read and write and handle numbers.

Rafael's daughters were educated as ladies at an elegant boarding school in Guadalajara. One of them became a Sacre-Coeur nun, and the eldest married another Ochoa. Rafael's trips to Guadalajara became more frequent after 1890 as the railway opened new opportunities. He befriended the aristocracy, and his life-style changed; he bought expensive furniture and made his house more comfortable.

Rafael died in 1902. In earlier generations the Mendoza siblings quarreled and even separated after the father's death. But Salvador and Albino remained single and lived together for another twenty years in the old family house with their mother and youngest sister (who never married). When Isabel Rosa died in 1910, the brothers stayed on in the house, although they closed the store (partially because the revolution brought chaos to commerce and communication). The brothers worked together managing their three hundred sharecroppers, real estate properties, sugar cane plantations, and sugar mills. In the early 1920s they responded to agrarian reform by building a sugar refinery that held no land and processed cane for both private landowners and *ejidatarios*. The refinery was a great success and has outlived all other sugar mills in the region.

It did not, however, remain a family business. Continuous expansion demanded capital, which came from Mexico City and Guadalajara. And Salvador and Albino finally married (both to members of the Guadalajara elite) and grew apart. Salvador died childless in Mexico City; Albino retired to Guadalajara and left one son and three daughters. None of the children worked for their father, nor did they join efforts to form any family enterprise.

Summary and Conclusions

Because bilateral kinship systems are unbounded, they require people to select a limited number of kin for frequent and meaningful interaction (Lomnitz and Pérez-Lizaur 1978, p. 393). It is pertinent to ask what principles govern this selection process. Norman Long has argued that because "the kinship universe [in the Peruvian highlands] is open-ended and characterized by a lack of clarity concerning behavioural norms," people face "the necessity of introducing into an existing kin relationship certain non-kinship criteria in order that the relationship may be more precisely specified in terms of the types of benefits, obligations and patterns of exchange that can be expected" (1977, p. 158). I believe Long is talking, not about "kinship," but about kinship ideology. Following his argument, I contend that in southern Jalisco kinship ideology does not provide clear-cut patterns of cooperation and/or specific interaction with kin of different types. Furthermore, I hold that ideological principles of kinship do not constitute a logically coherent system; rather, open and latent contradictions are part and parcel of the ideology. Thus, people have to manipulate moral values and ideal norms to prevent cognitive dissonance and social conflict.

In this essay, I have focused on the patterns of cooperation that emerge in goal-oriented kin groups. Although these patterns are ultimately justified by kinship ideology, they are specified by the position of a given social category within a regional structure of class relations. In turn, relations among class, family organization, and kinship ideology are articulated by the viable strategies through which the goals of production, consumption, and social reproduction are attained. The breakdown and/or transformation of family organization is conditioned both by its lack of viability at a given historical period and by the actors' perception of existing alternative strategies.

The organization of the peasant family in prerevolutionary Amacueca occurred in the context of relations between the peasantry and a dominant class of local landowners and merchants. For this dominant class the contract of sharecropping provided an efficient means of controlling rain-fed maize production with virtually no risk or investment in the production process. The extended peasant family, defined as a unit of productive cooperation, ensured that one sharecropping contract would mobilize the labor force of several individuals. Peasant families also assumed the costs of reproducing a seasonal labor force for harvesting sugar cane and other commercial crops, as well as the costs of producing the fruits and vegetables that wholesalers bought cheaply and sold profitably in markets within and outside the region.

For the peasants themselves, the family was a context in which labor resources were pooled to generate the food, money, and services necessary to survive and be minimally happy. This context implied (1) the consolidation of a residential unit (the household), either neolocal or patrilocal, composed of a man, his wife, and their offspring; (2) the emergence of patterns of cooperation, within and among households united by patrilateral ties, over a span of three generations; (3) the recognition of a hierarchy of authority whereby the senior married male (usually the father) could demand absolute compliance from other household members (in the three-generation patrilateral extended family, the senior male—usually the grandfather—demanded allegiance as coordinator of cooperative tasks among households); and (4) the segregation of roles by sex and age. Men worked in the fields, did the strenuous orchard tasks, and undertook casual and seasonal wage labor; women and children were in charge of all other tasks within the orchard, cared for household animals, and performed domestic chores.

Outside the family framework, the Amacueca individual found few alternative life-styles. Some people did leave the village: women usually found work as servants, and men sought their fortunes in distant towns. But these were not considered enviable choices. It is both an index and a consequence of contemporary change in family organization that a large number of people now wish to leave Amacueca to seek alternatives to the perceived lack of viability in traditional family life.

Changes in peasant family organization are determined by changes in the relationship between the peasantry and the dominant class. Wage laborers substitute for peasant sharecroppers as people are displaced from fields and orchards. Lack of access to productive land and massive emigration have resulted in the emergence of households of varied composition. Wage labor and the absence of men have decreased the importance of cooperation among households and of male authority. Role segregation is less rigid as children and even women work in the fields, and cooperation is largely determined by consumption strategy. Nevertheless, men seldom cook or perform domestic chores; they expect wives, mothers, sisters, or daughters to provide food and a homey atmosphere. Migrants seldom settle permanently without taking a female (preferably a wife) along; even students take a sister with them to the city. Cooperation among household members and kin is still important in child rearing (reproducing the labor force), but does not continue to show preference to patrilateral ties. Rather, people select relatives of all sorts, or even nonrelatives, depending largely on the opportunities for interaction.

The traditional ranchero family was also organized as a cluster of patrilaterally interconnected households, and role segregation by sex and age was at least as rigid as among the peasantry. Ranchero cooperation in productive activities was much more extensive than among peasants: the patriarch's authority reached almost every aspect of individual lives, and everyday intermingling among households was intense. Again, the local setting provided no productive resources, food, or desirable shelter outside the family organization. One striking difference between peasants and tenant rancheros was that the latter could (before 1900) accumulate capital, become landowners, and change their residences or their occupations.

When tenant rancheros became landowners, the tight unity of the patriarchal family was severely undermined by land divisions, and the authority of the patriarch was no longer needed to coordinate the activities of a large number of people. Resettlement from ranchos to villages allowed cooperation among other than patrilateral kin; consumption became more dependent on the market and increasingly independent of the extended family. On the other hand, some rancheros never managed to buy land, and instead became wage laborers and sharecroppers. For them, the patriarchal bond was also lost; if wage laborers were available, rancheros who could afford to pay them did not need recurrent help from kinsmen.

Later, as migration became a vital strategy for both landowners and the landless, cooperation among siblings and other kin helped provide minimal predictability and security in an uncertain venture. Also, the help of household women in the migration process became essential for the satisfactory organization of consumption. No one would accept as normal "the idea of an individual living in a 'room,' eating at another house with the person who is 'boarding' him, visiting a lover for sexual relations and sending clothes to be washed somewhere else by 'a washer'" (Smith 1978, p. 353)—conditions common for the Caribbean lower classes.

The Mendozas provide an example of a very different family organization. I do not present their case as typical, but neither were they unusual among the urban entrepreneurial class. The productive activities in which they engaged were viable without recourse to cyclical help from a large number of unpaid laborers; that is, there was no need for systematic labor exchange among households, and they did not form the bounded extended family of the peasants or rancheros. The help of many trusted persons was nevertheless convenient and necessary for the smooth functioning of the Mendoza business, and cultivating friendly ties with numerous, flexibly defined kindred was a strategy for opening and maintaining channels of information and access. Of particular importance was the creation of affinal links with elite families in Colima and Guadalajara.

Household members were, however, active in management of the family enterprises. The roles of the Mendoza women changed over time: Rafael's mother and wife ran the family store and raised the children, but his daughters and granddaughters received refined education and set up life-styles similar to that of the Guadalajara elite. Cooperation among brothers was conditioned by the fact that they long remained single and under their parents' roof. Rafael's marriage at age thirty-six, one year after his mother died, may have been motivated by his need to have someone organize consumption for the household. His sons married in their forties, under similar conditions.

Finally, a word must be said about the ways in which people manipulate and change ideological principles. In peasant and ranchero traditional families, we find a marked preference for patrilateral ties. Patrilateral solidarity emerged from labor exchange patterns, which were in turn reinforced by the sexual division of labor and residence patterns. Such incongruity with bilaterality is a contradiction that has never been totally resolved, but the notion of bilaterality persists. This persistence may be related to the fact that land rights were never corporately held by a patrilateral kin group (see Murdock 1960) and to the continuing importance of even unsystematic transactions with the matrilateral kin.

The contradictions between sibling equality and male superiority (as manifested in differential rules of inheritance) are more difficult to explain. By and large, men inherited crucial productive resources—tillable and pasture land, industrial and commercial property—because women were considered unable to manage them properly. Women often inherited, or were given as dowry, houses, money, furniture, and cattle. In fact, the sexual division of labor in the traditional family organization meant that a woman seldom had the chance to prove herself a proficient farmer, merchant, or cattle rancher. In many cases women had bitter quarrels with their brothers, brothers-in-law, and even husbands over the inheritance and management of property. An example is Rafael Mendoza's successful but divisive attempt to control both his sister's and his brother's wife's inheritance. Safa (1979) has recorded a similar case in which the question whether a woman's property was to be managed by her husband or her brother was never resolved.

The ideology is slowly changing. It is no longer universally held that parents are absolutely responsible for, and have absolute authority over, their offspring. This belief is especially weak among persons who can perceive viable careers outside the family organization. Similarly, hierarchical and authoritarian relationships between kinsmen of different generations tend to be downplayed, whereas solidarity and mutual help are emphasized. Recognition of and emotional attachment to bilateral ties persist, providing a useful idiom with which to consolidate a wide network of potential allies for business and migration purposes. Finally, the belief in women's inferiority in nondomestic matters is receding, particularly among the emerging urban middle class of migrants from ranchero and peasant backgrounds. This group hires servants to handle domestic arrangements, so that women can aid the family's upward mobility by developing their careers. This practice not only increases income but also expands the network of possible alliances. In contrast, upper-class women are often denied permission to attend college or seek employment; they are still considered the guardian angels of domestic values and of a prestigious life-style that must be carefully maintained and reproduced.

Acknowledgments

Earlier versions of this essay were presented at the conference on Theoretical Aspects of Kinship in Latin America and the Caribbean (New York, 1980; Ixtapan de la Sal, 1981), organized by Raymond T. Smith and Larissa A. Lomnitz under the auspices of the Social Science Research Council and the American Council of Learned Societies. I am grateful to all the participants in this conference for their comments and criticisms. I also received encouragement and helpful suggestions from the participants in departmental seminars at El Colegio de Michoacán (Zamora) and the University of California (Santa Barbara), where I presented synopses of this essay, and from Pastora Rodríguez Aviñoá, Bryan Roberts, Humberto González Chávez, Mary I. O'Connor, James Wessman, and Jean Meyer, who took the trouble of reading it carefully. I am also grateful to Margarita Martínez, Jeanette Woodward, and Rose Mucci for their efficient typing.

Since 1976 I have directed a field station for research and student training in southern Jalisco, which has contributed to the writing of several articles and theses. Thus, the data presented here are the result of a collective fieldwork effort. I refer specifically to some colleagues and students who have written on the areas and villages I deal with; yet the general feeling of the region comes from discussions with many others to whom I am equally grateful. Of course, they do not necessarily agree with my ideas and interpretations. I also acknowledge the help of several institutions that have financed the field station: Centro de Investigaciones Superiores del INAH (now Centro de Investigaciones y Estudios Superiores en Antropología Social), Universidad Autónoma Metropolitana (Iztapalapa), El Colegio de Michoacán, and Consejo Nacional de Ciencia y Tecnología.

References

Arias, Patricia
1980   "El proceso de industrialización en Guadalajara, Jalisco: Siglo XX." *Relaciones: Estudios de Historia y Sociedad* 1 (no. 3): 9–47.
Arreola, Juan José
1963   *La feria*. Mexico City: Joaquín Mortiz.
Bárcena, Mariano
1895   *Estadística de Jalisco*. Guadalajara: Imprenta del Gobierno.
Bloch, Maurice
1971   "The Moral and Tactical Meaning of Kinship Terms." *Man*, n.s. 6:79–87.
Brading, David A.
1978   *Haciendas and Ranchos in the Mexican Bajío: León, 1700–1860*. Cambridge: Cambridge University Press.
Ciudad Real, Antonio
1976   *Tratado curioso y docto de las grandezas de la Nueva España*. Mexico City: UNAM.
De Alba, Manuel C.
1978–80 "Actividad política en un municipio del sur de Jalisco." Licenciatura thesis, Universidad Iberoamericana.
De la Peña, Guillermo
1977   "Industrias y empresarios en el sur de Jalisco: Notas para un estudio diacrónico." In *Ensayos sobre el sur de Jalisco*, pp. 1–36. Cuadernos de la Casa Chata, 4. Mexico City: CIS-INAH.
1979   "Empresarios del sur de Jalisco: Un estudio de caso en Zapotlán el Grande." In *Simposio sobre empresarios en México*, 2:

47–81. Cuadernos de la Casa Chata, 22. Mexico City: CIS-INAH.

1980 "Evolución agrícola y poder regional en el sur de Jalisco." *Revista Jalisco* 1 (no. 1): 38–55.

1982 *A Legacy of Promises: Agriculture, Politics and Ritual in the Morelos Highlands.* Manchester: Manchester University Press.

De la Peña, Guillermo, and Díaz de la Serna, Cristina

1981 "Migración circular, redes sociales y cambio socioeconómico." Paper presented at the Primer Encuentro de Investigación Jalisciense: Economía y Sociedad, Guadalajara, Mexico.

Evans-Pritchard, Edward E.

1937 *Witchcraft, Oracles and Magic among the Azande.* Oxford: Oxford University Press, Clarendon Press.

1940 *The Nuer.* Oxford: Oxford University Press, Clarendon Press.

Fábregas, Andrés; Díaz, José; and Rodríguez, Román

1979 *El movimiento cristero: Sociedad y conflicto en los Altos de Jalisco.* Mexico City: CIS-INAH/Nueva Imágen.

Firth, Raymond

1961 *Elements of Social Organization.* Boston: Beacon Press.

Fortes, Meyer

1945 *The Dynamics of Clanship among the Tallensi.* London: Oxford University Press.

Geertz, Hildred, and Geertz, Clifford

1975 *Kinship in Bali.* Chicago: University of Chicago Press.

Gluckman, Max

1962 "Les rites de passage." In *Essays on the Rituals of Social Relations*, edited by Max Gluckman, pp. 1–52. Manchester: Manchester University Press.

Godelier, Maurice

1975 "Modes of Production, Kinship and Demographic Structures." In *Marxist Analysis and Social Anthropology*, edited by Maurice Bloch, pp. 3–27. London: Malaby Press.

González, Luis

1979 *Pueblo en vilo: Microhistoria de San José de Gracia.* 3d ed. Mexico City: El Colegio de México.

González Chávez, Humberto

1981 "Terratenientes, campesinos y empresarios capitalistas: Un estudio socioeconómico local: Amacueca." Licenciatura thesis, Universidad Iberoamericana.

In preparation "Educación y cambio social en el sur de Jalisco." Master's thesis, El Colegio de Michoacán.

González de la Rocha, Mercedes, and Escobar Latapí, Agustín
1979   "Centralización e intermediación: Las agroindustrias del sur de Jalisco." Licenciatura thesis, Universidad Iberoamericana.

Gudeman, Stephen
1972   "The *Compadrazgo* as a Reflection of the Natural and the Spiritual Power." *Proceedings of the Royal Anthropological Institute of Great Britain and Ireland for 1971*, pp. 45–71.

Johnson, Allen W.
1972   "Landlords, Patrons, and Proletarian Consciousness in Rural Latin America." Columbia University. Manuscript.

Lameiras, José
1981   "El Estado que parte y reparte . . . : El caso de los ejidatarios indígenas de Tuxpan, Jalisco." Tercer Coloquio de Antropología e Historia Regionales, El Colegio de Michoacán, Zamora.

Leeds, Anthony
1965   "Brazilian Careers and Social Structure: A Case History and Model." In *Contemporary Cultures and Societies of Latin America*, edited by D. B. Heath and R. N. Adams, pp. 379–404. New York: Random House.

Lomnitz, Larissa
1971   "Reciprocity of Favors in the Urban Middle Class of Chile." In *Studies in Economic Anthropology*, edited by George Dalton, pp. 93–106. American Anthropological Studies, no. 7. Washington, D.C.: American Anthropological Association.

Lomnitz, Larissa, and Pérez-Lizaur, Marisol
1978   "The History of a Mexican Urban Family." *Journal of Family History* 3:392–409.

Long, Norman
1977   "Commerce and Kinship in the Peruvian Highlands." In *Andean Kinship and Marriage*, edited by Ralph Bolton and Enrique Mayer, pp. 153–176. American Anthropological Association Special Publication, no. 7. Washington, D.C.: The Association.

López-Portillo y Rojas, José
1870   *Discurso pronunciado en el salón de sesiones de la sociedad católica de Guadalajara*. Guadalajara: Tipografía de Dionisio Rodríguez.

March, James G., and Simon, Herbert A.
1958   *Organization*. New York: John Wiley and Sons.

Moreno García, Heriberto
1980   *Guaracha: Tiempos viejos, tiempos nuevos*. Morelia and Mexico City: FONAPAS Michoacán, El Colegio de Michoacán.

Moreno Ochoa, Angel
1975   La sierra del Tigre: Ensayos históricos. Guadalajara: Author.
Munguía, Federico
1976   Panorama histórico de Sayula, capital de la antigua provincia de Avalos. Guadalajara: Departamento de Bellas Artes del Gobierno de Jalisco.
Murdock, George P.
1960   "Cognatic Forms of Social Organization." Viking Fund Publications in Anthropology 29:1–14.
Muriá, José María
1976   "La jurisdicción de Zapotlán el Grande del siglo XVI al XIX." Anales del Instituto Nacional de Antropología e Historia 6 (época 7a): Issue 54:23–42.
Olveda, Jaime
1980   Gordiano Guzmán: Un cacique del siglo XIX. Mexico City: SEPINAH.
Palerm, Angel, and Wolf, Eric
1972   Agricultura y civilización en Mesoamérica. Mexico City: Sepsetentas.
Parsons, Talcott
1956   "Suggestions for a Sociological Approach to the Theory of Organizations." Administrative Science Quarterly 1 (nos. 1 and 2):63–85; 225–239.
Plunket-Nagoda, Patricia
1981   "La dinámica de la desintegración sociocultural: El caso de La Manzanilla de la Paz, Jalisco." Publicaciones Antropológicas de Occidente 1 (no. 1):3–15.
Rapp, Rayna
1978   "Family and Class in Contemporary America: Notes toward an Understanding of Ideology." Science and Society 42 (no. 3): 278–300.
Roberts, Bryan
1980   "Estado y región en América Latina." Relaciones: Estudios de Historia y Sociedad 1 (no. 4):9–40.
Robertson, A. F.
1980   "On Sharecropping." Man, n.s. 15:411–29.
Safa, Patricia
1979   "Empresarios agrícola-ganaderos en Zapotlán el Grande." Licenciatura thesis, Universidad Iberoamericana.
Schneider, David
1968   American Kinship: A Cultural Account. Englewood Cliffs, N.J.: Prentice-Hall.

Serrera, Ramón M.
1977   *Guadalajara ganadera: Estudio regional novohispano.* Sevilla: Escuela de Estudios Hispanoamericanos.
Smith, Raymond T.
1956   *The Negro Family in British Guiana: Family Structure and Social Status in the Villages.* London: Routledge and Kegan Paul.
1978   "The Family and the Modern World System: Some Observations from the Caribbean." *Journal of Family History* 3: 337–60.
Strickon, Arnold
1965   "Class and Kinship in Argentina." In *Contemporary Cultures and Societies of Latin America*, edited by D. B. Heath and R. N. Adams, pp. 324–341. New York: Random House.
Tello, Fray Antonio
1945   *Crónica miscelánea de la santa provincia de Xalisco.* Guadalajara: Librería Font.
Veerkamp, Verónica
1981   "La comercialización y distribución de productos agrícolas a partir de un mercado semanario: El tianguis de Ciudad Guzmán." Licenciatura thesis, Universidad Iberoamericana.
Wessman, James W.
1981   *Anthropology and Marxism.* Cambridge, Mass.: Schenkman Publishing Company.
Willems, Emilio
1975   *Latin American Culture: An Anthropological Synthesis.* New York: Harper and Row.
Wolf, Eric
1966   "Kinship, Friendship and Patron-Client Relations in Complex Societies." In *The Social Anthropology of Complex Societies*, edited by Michael Banton, pp. 1–22. ASA Monographs, no. 4. London: Tavistock Publications.
Yanagisako, Sylvia Junko
1979   "Family and Household: The Analysis of Domestic Groups." *Annual Review of Anthropology* 8: 161–205.

Sex Roles and Economic Change

From Honor to Love: Transformations of the Meaning of Sexuality in Colonial New Mexico

Ramón A. Gutiérrez

This essay is a history of values surrounding marriage formation in colonial New Mexico. My specific concern is to explain the growth of individualism as manifested in a marked preference for spouse selection based on romantic love over arranged marriages. The analysis begins with a discussion of the honor ideology brought to New Mexico by Spanish colonists in 1598, focusing on the ways personal subordination to familial concerns was maintained. Next, I examine the sources of conflict and points of convergence among honor, Christian theology, and rituals of communal solidarity, showing how values stressing individualism were embedded in these ideologies. There follows a discussion of the economic changes that occurred in New Mexico in the 1770s—market growth and the burgeoning of a capitalist mode of production. Finally, romantic love is compared with familial honor values concerning spouse selection.

Colonial Settlement and the Honor System

In 1598, 130 Spanish conquistadores and their dependents ventured north from the Valley of Mexico to colonize the Kingdom of New Mexico, carrying with them seeds, tools, livestock, and a royal charter granting them far-reaching honors, lands, and the right to extract Indian tribute. The kingdom stretched geographically along the Rio Grande Valley from what is today El Paso, Texas, to Taos Indian Pueblo. The area had been inhabited since the twelfth century by the sedentary Pueblo Indians and the nomadic Apache and Navajo. From its initial colonization to the 1770s, New Mexico was peripheral to the empire, isolated, engaged in subsistence agriculture, and totally dependent on the yearly mule trains from central Mexico for provisions that could not be produced locally. Aside from a major readjustment in the level of Indian exploitation after the

Pueblo Revolt (1680–92), the pace and tenor of existence changed slowly (Scholes 1935, 1942; Simmons 1968).

The Spanish cultural idiom, through which differential access to and control over the means of production was maintained in colonial New Mexico, was honor. Honor divided society along both a vertical and a horizontal axis. The vertical dimension, or honor-status, provided a single continuum of precedence rights to which all persons were impelled to submit. The particular honor-status hierarchy that existed in New Mexico had been established in Reconquest Spain as a way of rewarding persons active in the expansion of the realm. Because honor was an awarded and ascribed status, its maintenance and perpetuation over time depended on the honor--virtue continuum. Honor-virtue divided society horizontally along recognized class boundaries, and on the basis of reputation, or the reproduction of ideal values of social conduct, established the order of precedence to which peers would submit. Because precedence at the upper levels of the social order guaranteed control over more resources, it was usually among the aristocracy and elites that the most intense conflicts over virtuous conduct ensued (for studies of the honor system in Spain see Caro Baroja 1965; Pitt-Rivers 1965; García Valdecasas 1948; and Castro 1972).

In matrimonial negotiations, honor required the strict exercise of parental authority to assure that misalliances, born of love or lust, did not occur. The status and future of a family could be seriously threatened if an inappropriate marriage or sexual relationship introduced a person of unacceptable ancestry into the group. The labor force was reproduced through the female's childbearing capacity, and maternity was undeniable, whereas paternity was not. Therefore male supervision of female sexuality was strict, involving the seclusion of women and the placing of high symbolic value on virginity.

The Concept and Practice of "Love"

The egalitarian and subversive notions of natural love were in sharp contradistinction to the hierarchical motivations of stern parental supervision of matrimonial choice. Love stemming from concupiscence was antithetical to honor because it undermined established authority relationships. Such love glorified personal autonomy and recognized that the human agent was an integration of body and soul, of the animal and the spiritual. Sexual passion was an intrinsic desire of the species, natural and free. The egalitarianism of love and sex arose from its obliviousness to class and kinship considerations. Love pangs welled up within the individual and were true only to the person's conscience (Gluckman 1955, pp.

54–80; see also Oostendorp 1962; Goode 1959, pp. 34–47; Shorter 1977, pp. 120–67).

The admission of love in a kinship-based society such as that in colonial New Mexico could have dire consequences. It had to be prevented through strict supervision of youthful social interaction by family elders. The nature and extent of control varied by social class. The wealth and power of the aristocrats could be seriously threatened by a misalliance, and therefore in the socialization of their children they took care to deter transgressions against parental authority. They had the most to lose—their bloodlines, their honor, their patrimonies—if a son or a daughter placed personal desire over family considerations. The difference between the aristocracy and popular classes in spouse selection was one of degree rather than kind. Marriage transactions involving actual or symbolic patrimony were usually minimal among the lower class, but the stability of the husband-wife relationship was essential to familial reproduction and the creation of support networks; therefore, children often enjoyed greater freedom of expression and participation in the selection of a mate.

The best way to assure that familial considerations would be paramount and to inhibit action based on personal desire was to preclude the expression of love. The easiest way to do this was to arrange infant marriages or betrothals. By the time the child reached adolescence he or she would be faced with a fait accompli. There would be little choice but to accept parental wishes, and the issue of love was unlikely to arise. One New Mexican folk poet described the mechanics of this practice.

On the day of my birth
They christened me
They found me a wife
And they married me.   [Espinosa 1926, p. 149]

An equally common strategy to minimize individualistic behavior among children was to segregate the sexes and confine women to limited social spaces. Because women were judged the weaker sex, frail to the pleasures of the flesh and the desires of men, they had to be isolated. Governor Bernardo López de Mendizábal in 1663 said that he guarded the purity of his female servants by keeping them in a bedroom adjacent to his, with access only through his room. In 1702 Francisca de Salazar of Santa Fe advised a friend that the only way to protect a daughter's virginity was to keep her always behind locked doors (AGN, Inquisición, 1663, vol. 594, fol. 244; AASF, DM 1702, no. 5, reel 60, p. 272).

Female seclusion and premarital sexual segregation meant that when children finally did marry, they frequently lacked the most rudimentary knowledge of their mates. The 1703 statement of María Archuleta was typical of others made by New Mexicans at the time. María knew her proposed husband, Miguel Martín, "only by sight." Residence in the same village assured men some familiarity with the eligible women, but if the nuptial candidates were from different towns, the chances of their having met before their engagement or marriage were slight. María Michaela Tafoya of El Paso said in 1802 that she had journeyed with her uncle José García to Bernalillo on the pretext of attending the St. Peter's Day festivities. Instead of partaking of the celebrations, they called at the home of Juan Domingo Archiveque, where she met a son, Juan Pablo. María later discovered that the purpose of the trip was "no other . . . than to meet me so that they could ask for my hand in matrimony." The next time she saw Juan Pablo, his parents proposed the marriage. She had thus laid eyes on Juan Pablo only twice before they were joined in wedlock (AASF, DM 1703, no. 6, reel 60, pp. 302–3; AASF, DM 1802, no. 25, reel 66, pp. 230–32).

When parents or guardians considered a marriage advantageous, threats, coercion, and force might be used to convince a child to marry the chosen person (or not to marry someone else). Antonio de Esquibel in 1702 vowed to his brother Ventura that he would "shame him publicly with curses and make him bite the dust (*morder la tierra*)" if he tried to marry Juana Lujan. Ventura boasted that he would enter the holy state of grace with whomever he chose, "for first comes my soul and I do not want the devil to take me." Unfortunately for Ventura's soul, he never married Juana Lujan, for his master, the governor of New Mexico, sent him to Parral to forget his love. Juana Lujan's mother was equally opposed to any union: "It is not my wish, nor the wish of Juana's relatives, for I want to marry my daughter to a man that knows how to work." Seventy years later, similar words of warning were issued by Doña Rafaela Baca to her daughter Barbara. If Barbara tried to contract marriage with Miguel Baca, forewarned Doña Rafaela, "I will tie a stone around her neck and throw her into the Rio del Norte" (AASF, DM 1702, no. 5, reel 60, p. 273; AASF, LD 1772, no. 4, reel 52, pp. 430–32).

Although it was technically contrary to canon law for a parent to force a marital partner on a child, the practice seems not to have been especially uncommon. Typical was the case of Vicente Luna, a resident of the Spanish settlement near Isleta. In 1774 Vicente told his father, Don Domingo Luna, that he wanted to contract marriage with Bitoria Chaves. Don Domingo ignored his son's request and instead arranged a matrimony with María Bárbara Chaves. Vicente accepted Don Domingo's choice because of "all the threats and grief my father expressed; I finally decided to marry María Bárbara against my will, only to please my father." Shortly after the betrothal, Don Domingo died, and Vicente immediately recurred to the ecclesiastical court to invalidate his engagement. Bitoria Chaves was the woman he truly wanted to marry and finally did (AASF, LD 1774, no. 2, reel 52, pp. 449–58).

Illustrative of the discord that occurred between parents and children over mate selection, and the compulsion that could be applied to reach an agreement, is a case related by Sebastiana de Jesus of Santa Fe. In 1715, when Sebastiana appeared to begin the matrimonial investigation so that she could be joined sacramentally with Gerónimo Ortega, she said:

> When the mother who raised me, whose name is Lucia Ortis, asked me about the marriage the first time I said no, I did not want to marry; but later, so that my mother would not be angry I said yes. But now, the desire to marry him does not spring from my heart . . . and having heard that the father of Gerónimo de Ortega has become a public ward in Santa Fe, I refuse to marry him. And if I marry him it will be only because my mother forces me to; I must do as she wishes, and will do it only to please her. . . . I do not wish to marry, it is not of my heart. . . . Before it was not of my heart and it is even less so now.

Because Fray Antonio Miranda was uncertain whether Sebastiana was being forced into matrimony, he ordered a new investigation and declaration taken. When Sebastiana appeared before the priest the second time, she stifled her former feelings and blankly stated that she now wanted to marry Gerónimo de Ortega "of my absolute liberty" (AASF, DM 1715, sn, reel 61, pp. 209–12).

Sexual Activity Outside Marriage

Although the social ideals of proper sexual conduct prescribed the segregation of nubile men and women, enough examples exist to show that some young women were able to escape the watchful eyes of elders. Only in upper-class households, where servants and retainers abounded and productive activities did not consume all familial resources, could time and energy be expended to see that a daughter was properly restrained. If a parent had been widowed or the family was particularly large, it was more difficult to be constantly attentive to a daughter's activities.

For the lower classes, scarcity and the work routine dictated the employment of every capable body at planting and harvest, and these seasonal activities provided occasions for mingling of the sexes and kindling of illicit love affairs. Desires sublimated under the heat of the sun might be inflamed in moonlight. Juana Carillo fell prey to just such passions. In 1712 she told her confessor that she had engaged in the carnal act with two men her stepfather had hired "when we were seeding." Miguel Carillo, her stepfather, complained of Juana's conduct, her unruliness and frequent disappearance on long horseback rides. How could parents be expected to instruct their children when the fourth commandment—honor your father and mother—was so blatantly ignored? Carillo's solution was to "catch and bind my children for their mischievous behavior and beat them" (AASF, LD 1712, no. 5, reel 51, pp. 735–58).

Domestic duties also provided an opportunity for love. In 1763 Manuela and María Paula Chaves, both domestic servants in Albuquerque, succumbed to the temptations of the flesh "while out tending to the sheep." Juana de Guadalupe was at home alone in Santa Fe grinding corn when her 1705 "frailty" with Antonio Belasques occurred. And "a jar of wheat" finally betrayed the true nature of the tryst between Inés García and Marcial Martínez of Santa Cruz de la Cañada. Antonio Montoya, in whose charge Inés had been left while her parents were in Santa Fe attending Holy Week services, reported that early on Holy Wednesday morning, 1736, Inés had run off to the house of Marcial Martínez to mill some wheat. When she delayed in returning, Montoya went in search of her and found that the door to the Martínez house was bolted from the inside. Montoya waited outside the Martínez home from ten in the morning until after four in the afternoon, when at last the door was opened and Marcial emerged. Inés followed carrying the container of wheat, "which was only cracked but not yet milled" (SANM, 1763, no. 574, reel 9, pp. 524–26; AASF, DM 1705, no. 21, reel 60, p. 428; AASF, DM 1736, no. 1, reel 62, pp. 183–90).

Recreational events provided another context in which love affairs could blossom. Juana Rodriques had "dry loves" with Bentura, her beau, while collecting pine nuts outside Santa Fe in 1705. Francisco Belasques saw Calletano Fajardo and his love "play, titillate each other amorously, and kiss (though they were only what is called dry kisses) . . . while going to see the *cañute* games in Analco." Joseph Duran y Chaves and María Miranda copulated on the day they went horseback riding together. "But I did not impregnate her," claimed Joseph, to the charge that he had snatched the flower of María's body and engendered a child. "Even if I were a cock I could not have made her bring forth a child so quickly." María gave birth in 1771, and because sex with Joseph had occurred only three months before, he was obviously not the father (AASF, DM 1705, no. 6, reel 60, pp. 276, 381; SANM 1771, no. 659, reel 10, pp. 634–57).

Aside from covert attempts to gain the affections of women, there were certain ritualized contexts in community life where the sexes could meet and intermingle with a minimum of supervision. These events usually marked major seasonal changes measuring the passage of time—rites of sowing and harvest, first fruits, religious feast days, or the celebration of a village's founding. During such rituals, when periods of public liminality and comity were activated and when the normative constraints of the social structure were lowest, egalitarian sentiments such as those of love, sexual passion, and physical attraction could be momentarily expressed without public sanctions or danger to the social order (see van Gennep [1908] 1960 for the classic statement; and Turner 1965, pp. 338–39; Turner 1969, pp. 94–130; and Turner, 1973, pp. 36–52 for a more recent and fuller development of the concept of "liminality"). The consumption of alcohol at these events of community solidarity also helped lower inhibitions; demure and listless young maidens became footloose and gay, and their consorts were transformed into bold and daring men. Stolen kisses might be less objectionable at a dance, and furtive groping or moments of intimacy might escape the notice of the merry mass. One popular proverb, which reminded New Mexicans of the occasion to adultery that celebrations provided, cautioned: "Keep your eyes off the wife of the guitarist" (WPA 5-5-17, p. 7).

Needless to say, many ignored the advice. Pedro Martín, for example, was already quite tipsy when he left the October 1812 Río Arriba fiesta dance to fetch Juana Baca. Juana's parents were at the festival and wanted her to join them. Pedro had to convince Juana to go with him, and hardly had they turned the hill near her home when Pedro "started caressing my breasts, touching my private parts, and saying that he wanted to enjoy me . . . he then unfastened his belt and took off his neckerchief." Unable to resist, Juana submitted (SANM 1812, no. 2464, reel 17, pp. 573–629).

The night of merriment for José Antonio Lucero, for his wife, María Manuela García, and for her mother, María Soledad Chaves, was not really over when they left the Alameda fiesta dance in 1819. Taking hospice in the house of José Perea, the three proceeded to climb into bed together. Estanislado Trujillo and his wife, who were sharing the same room with the three, were awakened by all the commotion. Estanislado reported: "The mother lay down in the middle, with the daughter at one side and Lucero on the other and such conduct made me extremely suspicious, so I remained awake most of the night observing what might occur there, and what happened was that shortly after they went to bed, the mother and son-in-law started caressing each other as husband and wife, and from there they led up to the ultimate extreme" (SANM 1819, no. 2842, reel 19, p. 911).

Don Ignacio Sánchez Vergara, the chief constable of Xemes jurisdiction, in 1819 used the authority of his office in an attempt to persuade María Chaves "to go with him to a dance at the house of Reyes Padilla. . . . He sent for two bottles of brandy . . . and tried to intoxicate me . . . he came looking for me later that afternoon . . . bringing me gifts—some of the wheat flour the soldiers were milling for their provisions, strings of chile, onions, beans and wheat." Foiled despite all his blandishments, Don Ignacio took to referring publicly to María as a "whore" (SANM 1819, no. 2842, reel 19, pp. 844–45).

The lurid and lusty behavior that prevailed at celebrations and dances provoked church officials to demand restraint. One priest exhorted women in an 1800 sermon on penance to refrain from dance because of the occasion to sin that a swiveling hip or bouncing breasts might create. These enticements were the work of the devil and tempted men to indulge in transitory pleasures of the flesh. He blasted: "You women, dancers of the devil, scandalous persons, you are the damnation of so many souls. Oh! What horror! . . . You provocative women, dancers of the devil, scandal, nets of the devil, basilisks of the streets and windows, you kill with your stirrings, with your ————." Fray Joaquín de Jesús Ruiz of Isleta believed that the sexual excess displayed at fiestas could be tempered only if constables performed their tasks more scrupulously. In 1774 he suggested that public lasciviousness would be curtailed if a night patrol were established to make sure that unmarried men were not roaming the streets engaging in sin. Don Bernardo Bonavía y Zapata, the commander-general of the Western Internal Provinces, took more drastic steps to curtail such licentiousness. In 1817 he outlawed all public dances because proper decorum and honesty were not being exhibited. This prohibition continued into the first years of the Mexican Republic and was achieved through the imposition of a heavy tax (AGN, Real Hacienda, 1800, vol. 291, exp. 9, fols. 3–6, dash in the original; AGN, Historia, 1774, vol. 25, exp. 39, fol. 337; SANM 1817, no. 2687, reel 18, pp. 804–21).

Periods of unconstrained liminality at festivals and dances held the potential for resolving conflict and acting as a cathartic release. Both of these possibilities had to be held in check by secular and religious authorities. Every official thus hoped that when the lights went out, the music ended, and a new day began, life would continue as before—regimented and hierarchically structured. The fiesta should be only a temporary suspension and release, necessary to dissipate internal community tensions.*

Love, Marriage, and the Church

The seeds of individualism and a sanctioned expression of love also existed in the doctrines of the Catholic church. In colonial New Mexico

*The potential for festivals to incite violence and/or to resolve conflict has been brilliantly studied by Ladurie (1979).

the egalitarian thrust of ecclesiastical teachings stood juxtaposed to hierarchical family honor concerns. Early in the history of the church, St. Paul had asked the Galatians to forsake their hierarchical traditions for the equality and freedom of Christ's salvation: "Baptized into Christ, you have put on Christ: there can be neither Jew, nor Greek, nor bond nor free, there can be neither male nor female, for you are all one in Jesus Christ" (Gal. 3:27–28). On the basis of this universalist message, the church over the centuries had protected the rights of individuals to partake freely of the sacraments. Because all souls were equal before the eyes of God, and earthly distinctions would be obliterated in heaven, personal salvation should take precedence over honor.

Doctrinal concerns found expression in marriage regulations, over which the church exercised exclusive jurisdiction until 1778. It was the duty of the church to establish the sacramental rituals and to determine who were and were not appropriate partners. Initially the church had accepted a whole spectrum of local customs, but increasingly after the eighth century, and particularly after Pope Gregory VII (731–41) elevated matrimony to the status of a sacrament, it determined that the rituals would have to be clerically supervised before they could be considered legitimate. Of much more importance historically, however, was the church's concern over the definition of appropriate and inappropriate conjugal partners, regulated through the prohibition of matrimony between persons found to have a canonic impediment (Epstein 1942; Goodsell 1934).

Impediments fell into two categories: dire impediments, which prohibited marriage, required papal or episcopal dispensation, and annulled a nuptial if discovered after it had occurred; and preventative impediments, which were of lesser severity, could be dispensed by the lower clergy, and infrequently undermined the legitimacy of the contract. The dire impediments of most importance were consanguinity, affinity, a solemn vow of chastity, religious orders, differences in religion, bigamy, polygamy, male impotence, crime, misrepresentation, and coercion (Escriche 1838, pp. 276–77; Mans Puigarnau 1951a, 1:152–73; Mans Puigarnau 1951b, pp. 1–84).

Before a marriage could be celebrated, it was the responsibility of the local priest to undertake a thorough investigation to discover any impediments to the proposed union. The *diligencia matrimonial*, as the matrimonial investigation was called, required that the potential bride and groom, as well as two witnesses on behalf of each candidate, appear individually to answer a litany of questions that had been formulated according to the canons of the Council of Trent. If no impediments were discovered during the process, then the nuptial could be celebrated. If, on the other hand, impediments had been found, a dispensation would have to be issued before any ceremony could take place.

Owing to the limited population pool from which marriage partners could be selected, the most common dispensations in colonial New Mexico were for consanguinity and affinity. Next in importance, at least for enforcement, was the application of the ecclesiastical principle that every individual had an absolute liberty to marry freely according to his or her will. This doctrine, stemming from the notion that all Christians had an absolute freedom to choose a vocation, be it in clerical or conjugal life, had been reinvigorated at the Council of Trent after the church fathers had decreed that clandestine marriages would no longer be considered either valid or legitimate. The canon authors argued that because salvation could be attained only through personal actions and intentions, ecclesiastical law had to protect, through its definition of force as a dire impediment, persons from being coerced into marriage (Tejero 1971, pp. 348–58).

Enforcement of a person's absolute freedom to marry was the sole responsibility of the local priest. When there was reason to believe that a marriage was being contracted without the full consent of the partners or was being discouraged under pressure, it was the duty of the friar to intercede and investigate the matter fully. The procedure was simple. Accompanied by a civil official, the priest would remove the prospective bride and groom from their homes and place them *en depósito* (in deposit) in the custody of a good Christian for isolation from parents and any pressures that might influence their decisions. After several days of solitude, the priest would return with a notary and take depositions concerning each person's desire to marry. If the priest was convinced that a person wished to wed, even against parental wishes, he was free to dispense with up to two of the three required banns so that the ceremony might be celebrated more quickly. If the child was being forced to marry against his or her wishes, the priest was obliged to prevent the ceremony.

In accordance with this law, Doña Lucía Gomes was, in 1697, taken from the Santa Fe home of her widowed mother, Doña Juana Ortís, and placed *en depósito* after Miguel Sandoval asked the ecclesiastical judge to intervene so that Lucía might exercise her free will. Miguel had asked for Lucía's hand in matrimony. Doña Juana Ortís "did not want to give her to me and because of that all of their relatives and in-laws have threatened me saying that if Lucía enters the state of Godly grace with me they will take her life as well as mine." Lucía, when asked in seclusion if she truly wanted Miguel for her husband said, "Yes, but my mother forbade it and threatened me, not allowing me to act according to my will." The couple was finally allowed to marry (AASF, DM 1697, no. 11, reel 60, pp. 40–45).

Because access to women and their sexuality was strictly guarded by most reputable families, it was usually the male who complained to the priest that a woman was not being allowed to exercise her will. Occasionally the opposite situation occurred. A woman might protest that a proposed union was being deterred by the groom's parents. Such was the case of Joseph Bijil and Petrona Martín, who in 1777 contracted marriage in Chimayo. Joseph had, with a promise of marriage, seduced and impregnated Petrona and at this point wished to free her from her "damnification" through the sacrament of matrimony. He solicited a dispensation of two banns to permit a speedy ceremony, for he knew that "my father will oppose it. And if he returns before the wedding he will impede it." Haste was not taken, and Christobal Bijil returned home before his son Joseph married. The wedding plans were canceled because Christobal Bijil did not approve of his son's choice of a mate. In anguish, the visibly rotund Petrona Martín petitioned Fray Silvéstre Vélez to intercede in her case. The friar ordered Joseph into *depósito,* "because it can be inferred that because of threats, the young man is denying what he truly feels, and his father is performing his duties with malice." In isolation, Joseph admitted his desire to take Petrona as his wife and was ordered to do so quickly (AASF, DM 1777, sn, reel 63, pp. 663–68).

Church doctrine and ecclesiastical practice regarding the scope of parental supervision over mate selection were perhaps more frequently at odds than can be gathered from the extant documentary evidence. On the basis of scriptural admonitions—"Call no man your father upon the earth: for One is your Father, which is in heaven," and "He that loveth father and mother more than Me is not worthy of Me" (Matt. 23:9; 10:37)—canon law placed limits on parental authority by protecting the right of children to follow the will of God and choose a vocation freely. The rationale for this policy was clearly understood by one New Mexican friar when he wrote in 1803 concerning an arranged marriage, "What sort of tranquility and regularity can we expect if they are forced to marry?" (AASF, LD 1803, no. 2, reel 53, pp. 489–90). Yet the discretionary powers of the lower clergy in New Mexico to interpret the law left room for a variety of practices. Some friars firmly buttressed parental prerogatives by maintaining that the natural law authority of a father over his children was in full accord with the will of God.

In 1710, for example, Joseph Armijo complained to Fray Lucas Arebalo that María Belasques was, against her wishes, being prevented from marrying him. Fray Lucas questioned María and quickly ascertained that she wanted Joseph as her husband. When the friar suggested that she enter into his custody so that the nuptial could be performed, María begged him not to remove her from her home. "I fear my parents, and so that they do not beat me or cause me other harm, do not tell them that I wish to marry but instead tell them that I do not wish to marry . . . that way I can escape from the house with greater safety." María fled to the convent the next morning and was placed in deposit. While there, she was visited by her *comadre*, Lucía Gomes, who asked her, "Do you really wish to hurt your parents by marrying that young man, a prospect that so displeases them that they are in total anguish? Do you think it impossible to find another good man, more to your parents' liking, with whom to contract marriage?" Moved by the emotion and tears of her gossip, María agreed that she would not marry Joseph if her parents promised not to subdue her so rigorously in the future. Gomes consulted María's father and returned with a message stating that he would marry his daughter to anyone he chose and that "in the future . . . would be even sterner with her." Later in the day, and without any explanation, María's father and Fray Lucas returned María to her parents' home. Had Joseph Armijo not been familiar with the law, his bid would have ended there. Instead, he appealed immediately to the provincial ecclesiastical judge, Fray Miguel Muñiz, saying that it had already been determined that María wanted to marry him "of her own free will." For Fray Lucas to act as he had and to say that "María had had a sudden change of heart" was highly irregular and "scandalous, for it is the work of various people, the product of bad advice which ignores the decrees of the Holy Council of Trent which prohibits this type of influence and excommunicates for such counsels" while a person is in deposit. Fray Muñiz agreed that Fray Lucas had acted inappropriately, ordered a new investigation, and finally married the couple after their true wishes had been reaffirmed. The conclusion that can be drawn from church doctrine, though not always from the practice of its clerics, is that it consistently attempted to protect personal and individual desires over familial ones (AASF, DM 1710, no. 24, reel 60, pp. 680–92).

Colonial Reform and the Process of Change

New Mexico's isolation from the rest of New Spain before the 1770s limited the extent of external sources of innovation and cultural change. Then, primarily to curtail Russian, Anglo-American, and French expansionist designs on the sparsely populated and poorly protected southwestern frontier, the Spanish crown undertook a series of military, administrative, and economic reforms to safeguard the area. The reforms, enacted by the Bourbon king Charles III, were part of a larger policy aimed at overcoming the crisis of production in the American colonies. Their result in New Mexico was to accelerate change in the pace and tenor of life. Centuries of neglect were reversed quickly. First a team of specialists, headed by the Marques de Rubi, was sent from Spain in 1765 to assess frontier defenses. The Spanish Royal Corps of Engineers accompanied the mission, mapped the area, and identified all its mineral and hydraulic resources. Charts were drawn to show the best routes of communication, and recommendations were made on the military reorganization necessary to safeguard the frontier. Additionally, California's ports were mapped for safer navigation in anticipation of increased dockings; Texas's water resources were surveyed for the feasibility of textile production; and methods for increasing livestock and agricultural production in New Mexico were proposed (Bannon 1970, pp. 143–90; Fireman 1977).

In 1776 the crown, on the basis of the expedition's recommendations, reorganized northern New Spain into one military and administrative unit called the Internal Provinces. New presidios were constructed to ward off foreign attack, and vigorous campaigns were launched to subdue the hostile Indian tribes that made trade and communication difficult. By 1774 an overland link between California and New Mexico had been established. With these initial changes complete, the frequency at which mule trains traveled to and from the regional market in Chihuahua increased, money began to circulate, and colonists from central Mexico began arriving. The crown believed that New Mexico could be protected from foreign encroachment only through its fuller integration into northern New Spain's market economy centered in Chihuahua. To achieve this aim, trade and travel restrictions were abolished. New Mexican products were exempted from paying sales taxes in Chihuahua. And agricultural specialists, veterinarians, and master weavers were sent to New Mexico, with their modern technology, to upgrade local production and improve the competitive position of the kingdom's products in Chihuahua (AGN, Historia, 1774, vol. 25, exp. 31, fol. 252–53; AGN, Historia, 1779, vol. 25, exp. 36, fol. 297; AGN, Californias, 1789, vol. 17, exp. 7, fol. 228; AGN, Californias, 1801, vol. 17, exp. 10, fol. 325–27; SANM 1777, no. 706, reel 10, pp. 931–33; SANM 1778, no. 832, reel 10, pp. 1020–37; Agustín Escudero 1832, pp. 37–38).

These incursions into New Mexico precipitated a period of change that was marked by the growth of a cash economy, the establishment of commercial agriculture, and the development of a wage-earning class. Increased communication and mobility, as well as the arrival and proliferation of socially autonomous forms of labor, presented New Mexicans with a variety of new values concerning individuals and their place in society.

The most important of these values for marriage was romantic love, which underscored the notion of personal autonomy and the importance of mate selection on the basis of individual desires.

Economic Development and the Transformation of Marriage

One source that provides a glimpse into and a history of changes in human sentiments in New Mexico between 1690 and 1846 is the *diligencias matrimoniales*. Whereas most of the questions the priest was required to ask at these marriage investigations seemed to evoke the pat sort of response one might learn at catechism instruction, unique answers occasionally emerged.

When New Mexican friars asked men and women why they wished to marry, the most common statements between 1690 and 1790 were of a religious or obligational nature. Christobal García said in 1702, "I want to put myself in the state of grace." "It is my goal to serve God and no other reason," claimed Gregoria Valverde in 1712. And "to better love and serve God," declared Andrés de la Paz in 1719, as did Doña Gertudes Durán in 1771 (AASF, DM 1702, no. 4, reel 60, p. 256; AASF, DM 1712, no. 5, reel 61, p. 68; AASF, DM 1719, no. 13, reel 61, p. 546; AASF, DM 1771, no. 1, reel 63, p. 24).

The first sign of any change in the reasons for desiring marriage appears in a record for 1798. José García of Albuquerque avowed that he wanted to marry María López "because of the growing desire (*voluntad*) that we mutually have for each other" (AASF, DM 1798, no. 7, reel 66, p. 18). The word *voluntad* had previously appeared in the marital investigations, but only to mean volition, as in the determination that free will was being exercised. María Durán gave the word *voluntad* this meaning (in 1795) when she said, "I marry freely and spontaneously, neither counseled nor coerced, but totally of my volition" (AASF, DM 1795, no. 16, reel 61, p. 220).

Beginning in 1800, a whole flurry of new responses appeared that stressed individualism and love as reasons for wishing to marry. Juan José Ramón Gallego, a resident of the small Spanish village at Xemes, said in 1810 that he wanted to enter the state of matrimony because "I fell in love (*me enamoré*) with Juana María, the daughter of Santiago Aragón," while visiting San José del Vado. José Rafael Sanches of Tomé was moved to take Gertudes Sanches as his wife in 1838 "because of the great love that I have for her." José Torres of Belén in the same year gave "the mutual love that I have with the said María Serafina Chaves" as his reason for wishing to marry (AASF, LD 1810, no. 7, reel 53, p. 759; AASF, DM 1822, no. 1, reel 68, p. 697; AASF, DM 1838 sn, reel 76, p. 842, 811).

The Varied Meanings of *Love*

Amor (love) as a verb or a noun appears in New Mexican colonial documents with two meanings. Reference to Christian love is made throughout the whole period 1690–1846 as a sentiment that must be displayed out of duty. Good Christians were commanded to love God, neighbor, and self. Thus Francisco Durán y Chaves said that he was marrying in 1713 "for love of God." Jacinto Mirado in 1771 expressed "the fatherly love" that he had for his adopted daughter. And María Loreta García in 1835 pleaded that her husband, who frequently mistreated her, "should love me as Christ loves his Church" (AASF, DM 1713, no. 4, reel 61, p. 85; SANM 1771, no. 659, reel 10, p. 634; AASF, LD 1835, no. 5, reel 55, p. 454).

Natural love, or love stemming from concupiscence, was the second meaning of the word *amor*. Before 1800 the word was used in this sense only to refer to illicit sexual contact, that is, seduction, concubinage, and adultery. Antonio Belasques claimed in 1705 that "as a frail man I happened to make love (*llegue a enamorar*) to the said Juana de Guadalupe after having known that she had an illicit friendship with Juan Antonio Ramos, Mariquita, the Indian Zhacambe, and many others whom I will not mention so as not to become burdensome." Josepha Sedano demanded from the ecclesiastical court a divorce from her husband in 1711 because she was tired of feeding him, clothing him, and "giving him money to play cards and *enamorar*." It is interesting to note that before 1800 the mention of concupiscent love in the ecclesiastical archives occurs only in the context of illicit sexual acts, and not as a reason for desiring marriage. After 1800 derivatives of the word *amor* are no longer used to refer to illicit acts, but are replaced with the more frequently used expressions *amistad ilicita* or *copula ilicita* (AASF, DM 1705, no. 2, reel 60, p. 365; AASF, LD 1711, no. 5, reel 51, p. 646).

As evidenced above in the statements children made concerning their reasons for marriage, by 1800 a love born of passion was judged sufficient reason for choosing a particular conjugal mate. "The urges of the flesh, human wretchedness and the great love which we have for each other," stated José de Jesús Romero in 1845, were his reasons for wishing to marry Doña Persiliana Salazar (AASF, DM 1845, sn, reel 79, p. 122).

Symbolism of the Heart

It was popularly believed that the heart was the physical organ from which concupiscence sprang. Writing the governor of New Mexico in 1805 concerning the frequency with which the Zuñi Indians engaged in fornication and adultery, Fray José de la Prada noted that "their customs and heathen friskiness have sunken very deep roots into their hearts." Another friar, in an 1837 sermon on sexual desires, blasted from his pulpit, "It is from the heart that we must displace this monster of sensuality" (SANM 1805, sn, reel 15, p. 617; AHH, vol. 291, exp. 8, fol. 1).

The heart as a natural symbol had a long history in New Mexico. In the physical symbolism of the honor ideology, it was through the heart that one's conscience was known. In it true emotions and intentions were felt. Marriage candidates frequently mentioned that a desire was heartfelt and therefore had to be reckoned with seriously. "The woman I elect with all my heart" is Bernardina Rosa Lucero, said Ventura de Esquibel in 1702. "I do it only to serve God and because it comes forth from my heart, without it being the result of any other motivation," responded Sebastiana de la Serna in 1715, when asked if she was being forced to marry by her parents. "I do not wish to marry, it is not of my heart. . . . I will do it only to satisfy my mother. . . . Before it was not of my heart and it is even less so now," claimed Sebastiana de Jesús in 1715. The wedding ring, the symbol of marital fidelity, was always placed on the fourth finger of the bride's left hand: folk wisdom held that a vein ran from that finger directly to the heart (AASF, DM 1702, no. 5, reel 60, p. 278; AASF, DM 1715, no. 14, reel 61, p. 214; AASF, DM 1715, sn, reel 61, p. 212).

The use of the heart symbol as a metaphor for love stemming from concupiscence became more frequently employed in New Mexico after 1800. Certainly this association was not a new one. Since at least the Middle Ages, popular consciousness had been familiar with the heart imagery employed by troubadours and courtiers singing of their impossible love for a married lady. But unlike courtly love, which was an idealized love that could not be realized because of the fact of arranged marriages at court, romantic love advocated the free expression of passion and attractions as the basis for marriage (Moller 1959, 1960; Hunt 1959; Moore 1979).

Love as a motivation for marriage was the selection of a conjugal mate on the basis of personal attractions. It was an irrational, whimsical, and spontaneous desire, oblivious to all earthly constraints. An 1830 New Mexican folksong described how the love-possessed person felt:

It was nearly midnight
When my heart desired you anxiously

For your love fair maiden
My soul shudders with pain.

Jesusita, please do not forget me
For my soul loves and adores you
To enjoy that sweet calm, oh
Sweet painful calm.

Since I met you I have walked about aimlessly
From that moment I have loved you
With burning frenzy.   [Campa 1933, p. 64]

Frederico Arellano of Santa Fe eloquently detailed the bewitching
powers of love in a poem that he composed in the mid-nineteenth century:

Lovely maid come to my arms
Your brow so pure, that ardent breast I would enfold
And if some day, maid of bewitching charm
I could kiss those ruby lips how happy I would be,
A kiss from those lips, a kiss I pray
One look from those lovely eyes I beg
I would see us in ardent embrace
In ardent and loving embrace I vow
Your fluttering heartbeats I would feel
As lip to lip I press you close,
Kiss for kiss of tenderest love.   [WPA 5-5-20, p. 8; my translation]

Love was considered a subversive sentiment because it made persons
oblivious to status and to generational and sexual hierarchies. It was an
emotion to be distrusted because it drove children to abandon all reason,
to ignore the matrimonial concerns of their parents, and to marry only on
the basis of attraction. An 1851 Mexican medical dictionary warned of the
dangers inherent in such uncontrolled human urges when it discussed aspects of sexual life:

DANGERS OF SEXUAL LIFE: Though the sexual life leads to
the highest virtues and even to sacrifice itself, and to sacrifice of self;
yet in it lies great danger. Unless properly checked it may degener-
ate into powerful passions and develop the greatest vices. When love
is permitted to become an unbridled passion it is like a fire that
burns and consumes everything. It is like a pit that swallows all—
honor, fortune and happiness. [Medicología 1851, p. 122; my
translation]

The conflict between honor and love considerations, between parents and children over nuptial choice, was frequently articulated in song. One songbook that has been in Truchas, New Mexico, since colonial times tells of a young man lured by love into forsaking all. In "The Errant Dove" a remorse-ridden man ponders his mistakes:

I lost my courage, I lost my honor
. . . everything I lost.
I lost my parents who loved me so
For having fallen in love with you.   [WPA 5-5-12, p. 20]

The "Bride" from San Miguel del Bado tells of her misfortune:

At first I was very anxious
to contract marriage with him.
Today I ask God
that I may be granted my freedom.

I was still so innocent
Oh, what luck befell me!
Because I did not obey my parents
God has brought this punishment upon me.

I was only eighteen.
Too young to comprehend.
Knowledge is what I lacked
to be able to understand.   [WPA 5-5-20, p. 36]

The ideals and proscriptions articulated by New Mexicans faced with social and economic change established boundaries within which the practice of nuptial-age children could be fashioned. Unfortunately, because of the less-detailed records on marriage produced by the secular judiciary, it becomes increasingly difficult as we turn to the beginning of the nineteenth century to document the strategies employed in the taking of a marital partner.

Changing Bases of Marital Choice

One index of the extent of change in the mode of matrimonial selection in New Mexico between 1690 and 1846 can be gained by examining the age difference between a husband and wife at marriage. The transition from familial honor considerations to personal love motivations should theoretically entail a shift in age differences between spouses at the time or marriage. A father seeking to expand a family's actual or symbolic capital through an arranged marriage would be oblivious to the age differences involved or, for that matter, to the preferences of the child. If, on the other hand, love was the motive for marriage, by necessity a person would want as a mate a compassionate equal. The chances of creating an egalitarian relationship would be greatest if the bride and groom were of approximately the same age. A situation in which a man was much older than his wife would establish him as a dominator in the union and reinforce aspects in the relation which would cause it to resemble that between a powerful father and a helpless child. The opposite situation would also underscore the age-status difference (Shorter 1977, pp. 154–55; Bell 1979, pp. 67–122).

Figure 1 shows the age differences between spouses for all first marriages in New Mexico between 1690 and 1846. The most obvious change that occurred during this time was a large rise in the proportion of persons

Figure 1. Age Difference at First Marriage between Husband and Wife in New Mexico, 1690–1846 ($N = 5,463$). Positive numbers indicate that the husband is older; negative numbers, that the wife is older. Compiled from AASF, DM 1690–1846, reels 60–79.

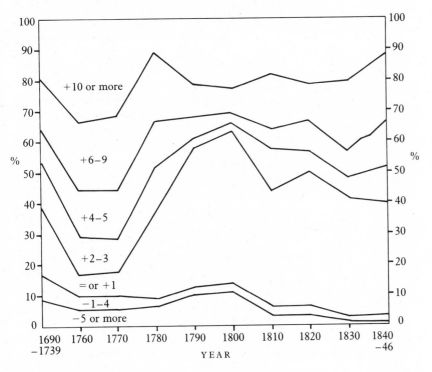

marrying someone of the same age or just one year older or younger. This increase began in 1780, rose to a high in the decade 1800–1809, when half of all people marrying took spouses of similar age groups, and then gradually declined, closing the period at 38 percent of all marriages. The conclusion to be drawn from Figure 1 is that the age difference between husband and wife decreased substantially after 1780. This change seems to have been due to the increasing importance of individual choice in matrimony.

Change in the manner of marital selection however, did not occur among all social classes. The numerically small New Mexican aristocracy continued to arrange marriages for its children throughout the period under study. Lower-class families engaged in the subsistence mode of agricultural production established at the time of the area's colonization also did not significantly alter their patterns of marriage selection. Merchants, artisans, wage workers, and other socially autonomous laborers active in the burgeoning capitalist mode of production were the people who openly expressed sentiments of love as their reason for marrying. The development of commercial agriculture in New Mexico in the 1770s increased social differentiation and, at a time of intense land pressures, accelerated the mobility of those persons requiring work opportunities. Once people were separated from parents and community, they appealed more often to personal and internal forms of authority to guide their actions. These actions were dictated by conscience and known through the heart. The pace at which love came to take precedence over honor considerations in marriage was accelerated by the arrival of Anglo merchants from St. Louis after 1820 and the occupation of New Mexico by the United States.

One example from Placitas, New Mexico, in the 1830s provides a particularly revealing glimpse of the ways in which changes occurred among those who entered the wage-labor sector of the economy. Placitas during the 1800s was a small mountain hamlet, fifteen miles north of Bernalillo, primarily dependent on subsistence agriculture. Young men and women began migrating from Placitas to Albuquerque, Bernalillo, and Santa Fe in the 1780s to take jobs as wage laborers.

Camilia Montaño left her family and Placitas in 1830 at the age of twelve to supplement family income by working as a domestic servant in the house of Don José Gonzales, Bernalillo's wealthiest *hacendado*. While employed there, she learned how to sew, weave, and dye bright colors into cloth. With this knowledge she started making her own dresses, frequently tapering the waistline and fastening them with colored sashes to accentuate the shape of her body. She also began combing her hair as the other women in Don José's employment did, forsaking the braids that maidens traditionally wore in Placitas. And finally, Camilia fell in love with Andrés, a trusted servant of Don José. When Camilia's parents observed all the changes in their daughter, they forced her to return home and married her to a man they chose. Life back in the community was difficult for Camilia. She longed for her Andrés, disliked her husband, and was constantly ridiculed as egotistical by other women in the village. They complained of her vanity, because of the brightly colored dresses she wore, her unconventional manners, the way she combed her hair. Camilia's unwillingness to conform to village norms was also a source of constant marital discord. One day she finally had enough. She packed her clothes, abandoned her children, and fled to Bernalillo to be with her lover. Once Camilia was reunited with Andrés, they went together to Chihuahua. Camilia's husband hunted her down and finally killed her, laying her head open with a stone machete for the adultery she had committed. Life as a domestic in Bernalillo so altered Camilia's values that she was no longer willing or able to conform to the traditional authority structure in the village. Had she not been exposed as a domestic wage earner to greater freedom and mobility, she probably would never have thought of abandoning her marriage and family. Placitas's residents recount this incident, even today, as an example of the way authority relations changed with market growth and the commercialization of their economy (WPA 5-5-49, p. 55).

The amount of physical mobility unleashed in New Mexico by the crown's attempt to integrate the area into New Spain's market economy is difficult to ascertain with any precision. An analysis of a bride and groom's place of residence at the time of first marriage indicates that before 1780 a relatively small proportion of all marriages were contracted between people residing in different localities. After 1780, the proportion of marriages to someone residing at a distance increased dramatically. This trend was most acute at central places in the marketing system—Albuquerque, the Bernalillo hamlets, Santa Fe, and Santa Cruz de la Cañada.

The acceptance of romantic love placed the sexes on more equal footing regarding the selection of a spouse. Although bourgeois and wage-earning women were in no way emancipated or given sexual freedom, they did increasingly come to have more individual control over the decisions affecting their lives. William Watts Davis, the U.S. attorney for New Mexico, in 1853 observed how such behavior manifested itself:

> I chanced to call at the home the same evening the letter had been received, and the mother, feeling unusually happy in view of the proposed alliance . . . descanting with considerable eloquence upon the advantages to arise from such a match—that the young man was *mui rico* (very rich) and *mui buen* (very good), with many other words of praise. . . . The mother was quite anxious for the alliance to take place, but told me, in a semiconfidential manner, that her

daughter was opposed to the arrangement—a perverseness that the
old lady could not understand. . . . I determined to know how the
matter stood with the daughter. . . . She told me, with great frank-
ness, that she did not love her suitor, and would not marry him. . . .
I counseled treason in the premises, and advised her to have her
own way in a matter which was of more importance to her than any
one else. She took this course, and the unromantic and unwooing
swain was obliged to look elsewhere for a housekeeper. A few eve-
nings afterward I saw the father of the young man at the house, who
had come to talk the matter over with the mother; but it did no
good, for the young lady had a mind of her own, and neither persuasion nor parental threats could induce her to accede to their
wishes. [Davis 1857, p. 280]

In nuptial formation women increasingly came to reject mates as
easily as they elected them. Fray José de Castro chastised María del Refugio Herrera in 1824 for breaking the promise of marriage she had given
to Juan de Jesús Rivera. When the priest asked María what reason she had
for changing her mind, she responded: "I have no reason except that previously I wanted to marry him and now I no longer do." Fray José asked
the constable of Santa Clara to punish María "as an example to other
women, so that they fulfill their contracts and do not promise so easily
things they do not plan to deliver" (AASF, DM 1824, sn, reel 69, p. 591).

One of the saddest stories was related by Felix Esquivel, recalling an
incident that occurred in northern New Mexico in the 1870s. Esquivel told
of a woman who freely decided to marry the man she truly loved. On the
day of the betrothal festivities the groom had too much to eat and drink.
After the party, while riding in a buggy to church for the celebration of the
nuptial, the flatulent groom cut air quite loudly. "Stop this buggy," said
the bride to her godfather. "Did you not hear that loud and gross flatus?"
When no one responded the angry bride said, "I will never marry such a
gross pig!" She called off the wedding and refused to marry the man for
whom she had once proclaimed so much love (Rael 1957, 1:88–90).

Of course, marriage for honor and marriage for love were not necessarily mutually exclusive options. For example, a young man and woman
aroused by a genuine love for one another and desiring matrimony, but
fearing that parents would object, might devise a ploy to maneuver an acceptable solution within the established limits of family honor preoccupations. A woman might allow her virginity to be taken, claim that her honor
had been sullied, and demand marriage simply as a way of forcing parents
to consider a mate that otherwise might never have been acceptable. The
discourse in such a case would be totally in the idiom of honor, but only

because there would be no other way of manipulating the parental value system. That this was an actual solution to a problem was confirmed by the bishop of Durango and his assistants: they expressed suspicions that the increased incidence of deflowered maidens and illicit coition in New Mexico between 1810 and 1825 was the result of youthful schemes "undertaken to facilitate" the celebration of unacceptable marriages (AASF, LD 1813, no. 4, reel 53, p. 790; AASF, DM 1806, sn, reel 66, p. 381; AASF, DM 1813, sn, reel 67, p. 43; AASF, DM 1811, sn, reel 66, p. 513; AASF, DM 1812, sn, reel 66, p. 621; AASF, DM 1813, sn, reel 67, p. 41).

Conclusion

In this essay I have tried to show the ideological components influencing marriage formation in colonial New Mexico. The most predominant of these elements was honor in both its status and its virtue meaning. The definition of the honor-status hierarchy at any particular time was largely the result of changing public political relations. In colonial New Mexico the juridically sanctioned ascribed honor of the conquistadores derived from Iberian Reconquest monarchical concern to assure the preeminence of those persons active in the expansion of the realm. Two centuries later, as the social structure of the colony became more differentiated, and personal achievement came to displace ascription as the basis of status, honor lost the meanings it had attained during the American conquest.

By the nineteenth century, New Mexican proverbial wisdom held that "money is social status," and "sir money is a powerful aristocrat." In 1834 Manuel Álvarez, the U.S. consul in Santa Fe, more perceptively discussed the nature of change in the value of honor. Writing in his ledger book, titled *Thoughts I wish to remember and have at hand . . .* , he scribbled, "The honorable poor man (if it is possible for a man to be poor and honorable at the same time) has a jewel in having an honorable wife." Dissecting Álvarez's comment, we note that honor was at this time no longer attainable through ascription. Intact, though, was the honor-virtue concept, a much older Mediterranean cultural value that antedates the status dimensions attached to it in Reconquest Spain.

Earlier I mentioned that honor-virtue had both corporate familial and personal definitions. Value reorientation in New Mexico is best understood as a shift in the relative importance of the ideological components delimiting behavior. Personal sources of authority, specifically, the conscience, came to take precedence over familial and parental concerns. The convergence of Christian doctrine and communal ideology with native conceptions of virtue dictated the idioms through which persistence and change in nuptial formation would be expressed.

Acknowledgments

I would like to thank Rachel Klein, Lynn Thomas, Ralph Bolton, and Hal Barron for offering criticisms during various stages in the production of this essay.

More complete details of the honor system in New Mexico will be found in Gutiérrez 1980, a work inspired by Verena Martinez-Alier's brilliant 1974 study of racial values and sexual attitudes in Cuba.

References

Agustín Escudero, José
1832   *Noticias históricas del estado de Chihuahua.* Mexico City: Juan Ojeda.
Álvarez, Manuel
1834   Ledger Book. Álvarez Papers. New Mexico State Records Center and Archives. Santa Fe, New Mexico.
Archives of the Archdiocese of Santa Fe, New Mexico. Diligencias Matrimoniales (AASF, DM).
Archives of the Archdiocese of Santa Fe, New Mexico. Loose documents (AASF, LD).
Archivo General de la Nación. Mexico City (AGN) Californias. Historia. Inquisición. Real Hacienda.
Archivo Histórico de Hacienda. Mexico City (AHH).
Bannon, John F.
1970   *The Spanish Borderlands Frontier, 1513–1821.* New York: Holt, Rinehart and Winston.
Bell, Rudolph M.
1979   *Fate and Honor, Family and Village.* Chicago: University of Chicago Press.
Campa, Arthur L.
1933   *The Spanish Folksong in the Southwest.* Albuquerque: University of New Mexico Press.
Caro Baroja, Julio
1965   "Honor and Shame: A Historical Account of Several Conflicts." In *Honour and Shame: The Values of Mediterranean So-*

ciety, edited by J. Peristiany, pp. 81–137. Chicago: University of Chicago Press.

Castro, Américo
1972   *De la edad conflictiva: Crisis de la cultura española en el siglo XVII.* Madrid: Taurus.

Davis, William Watts
1857   *El Gringo; or, New Mexico and Her People.* New York: Harper and Bros.

Epstein, Louis
1942   *Marriage Laws in the Bible and Talmud.* Cambridge: Harvard University Press.

Escriche, Joaquín
1838   *Diccionario razonado de legislación civil, penal, comercial y forense.* Valencia: J. Ferrer de Orga.

Espinosa, Aurelio
1926   "Spanish Folk-lore in New Mexico." *New Mexico Historical Review* 1 (no. 2): 149.

Fireman, Janet R.
1977   *The Spanish Royal Corps of Engineers in the Western Borderlands: Instrument of Bourbon Reform, 1764 to 1815.* Glendale, Calif.: Arthur H. Clark Co.

García Valdecasas, Alfonso
1948   *El hidalgo y el honor.* Madrid: Occidente.

Gluckman, Max
1955   *Custom and Conflict in Africa.* Glencoe, Ill.: Free Press.

Goode, William J.
1959   "The Theoretical Importance of Love." *American Sociological Review* 24: 34–47.

Goodsell, Willystine
1934   *A History of Marriage and the Family.* New York: Macmillan Co.

Gutiérrez, Ramón A.
1980   "Marriage, Sex and the Family: Social Change in Colonial New Mexico, 1690–1846." Ph.D. diss., University of Wisconsin.

Hunt, Moreton M.
1959   *The Natural History of Love.* New York: Knopf.

Ladurie, Emmanuel Le Roy
1979   *Carnival in Romans.* New York: George Braziller.

Mans Puigarnau, Jaime M.
1951a   *Derecho matrimonial canónico.* Barcelona: Bosch.
1951b   *Legislación, jurisprudencia y formularios sobre el matrimonio canónico.* Barcelona: Bosch.

Martinez-Alier, Verena
1974   *Marriage, Class and Colour in Nineteenth Century Cuba*. Cambridge: Cambridge University Press.
Medicología
1851   Biblioteca Nacional de México. Mexico City. Colección la Fragua, vol. 610, no. 7215.
Moller, Herbert
1959   "The Social Causation of the Courtly Love Complex." *Comparative Studies in Society and History* 1:137–63.
1960   "The Meaning of Courtly Love." *Journal of American Folklore* 73:39–52.
Moore, John C.
1979   "Courtly Love: A Problem of Terminology." *Journal of the History of Ideas* 40:621–31.
Oostendorp, H. T.
1962   *El conflicto entre el honor y el amor en la literatura española hasta el siglo XVII*. The Hague: Van Goor Zonen.
Pitt-Rivers, Julian
1965   "Honour and Social Status." In *Honour and Shame: The Values of Mediterranean Society*, edited by J. Peristiany, pp. 21–77. Chicago: University of Chicago Press.
Rael, Juan B.
1957   *Cuentos Españoles de Colorado y Nuevo Méjico*. Stanford: Stanford University Press.
Scholes, Frances V.
1935   "Civil Government and Society in New Mexico in the 17th Century." *New Mexico Historical Review* 10 (no. 2):71–111.
1942   *Troublous Times in New Mexico, 1659–70*. Albuquerque: University of New Mexico Press.
Shorter, Edward
1977   *The Making of the Modern Family*. New York: Basic Books.
Simmons, Marc
1968   *Spanish Government in New Mexico*. Albuquerque: University of New Mexico Press.
Spanish Archives of New Mexico. Santa Fe (SANM).
Tejero, Eloy
1971   *El matrimonio misterio y signo: Siglos XIV–XVI*. Navarra: Universidad de Navarra Press.
Turner, Victor W.
1965   "Betwixt and Between: The Liminal Period in *Rites de Passage*." In *Reader in Comparative Religion*, edited by William

Lessa and Evon Z. Vogt, pp. 338–339. New York: Harper and Row.

1969   *The Ritual Process: Structure and Anti-Structure.* Ithaca, N.Y.: Cornell University Press.

1973   "Variations on the Theme of Liminality." In *Secular Ritual*, edited by Sally Moore and Barbara Myerhoff, pp. 36–52. Amsterdam: Van Gorcum.

van Gennep, Arnold

1960   *The Rites of Passage.* Chicago: University of Chicago Press.
[1908]

Works Progress Administration, New Mexico Writers' Project (WPA). Santa Fe: Museum of New Mexico.

The Exploitation of Family Morality: Labor Systems and Family Structure on São Paulo Coffee Plantations, 1850–1979

Verena Stolcke

Coffee growing demands not the contribution of casual labour but, indeed, that of "well constituted" families, of at least three hoes.

Boletím do Departamento do Trabalho Agrícola, (São Paulo), ano 11, no. 72 (1932): # 11

It is now generally recognized that neither the nuclear family nor gender hierarchy was created by the industrial revolution or capitalism for the sake of capital accumulation. Despite the warnings and fears of the political right and some scholars like Lasch (1979), it does not seem either that we are to witness the family's early demise. Instead, the relevant question continues to be, what is it in advanced industrial society that accounts for the extraordinary resilience of the family and gender hierarchy? Though their forms may change, they remain basic social facts. How do we explain the paradoxical coexistence in class society of an ethos of individualism, self-reliance, and personal achievement along with the persistent mediation of the individual's place in society by family ties? As Barret and McIntosh have argued recently, there has been an "underemphasis of the extent of the cultural hegemony of familial ideology . . . 'the family' . . . is not only an economic unit, nor merely a kinship structure; it is also an ideological configuration with resonance far beyond these narrow definitions" (1982, pp. 129–30).

Accumulating evidence on the persistence of gender hierarchy, despite rapid and often profound economic change, requires a rethinking of the structural link between the economy and the family. We need to examine the "ideological configurations" referred to by Barret and McIntosh and to discover the way in which ideology and culture act upon, and interact with, processes of socioeconomic change. As I have suggested elsewhere (Stolcke 1981), the ideological constitution of personhood in class society (as free agent but at the same time the bearer of immutable essences) decisively shapes bourgeois family values and practice. However, no single model will suffice to explain the family in class society. Although bourgeois ideology typically seeks to universalize its own institutions and values, an explanation of working-class family structure and meaning must be sought in the particular relation between the working class and the bourgeoisie. There are at least two sides to the question of the persistence of the working-class family: namely, bourgeois class interests, both economic and ideological, in maintaining the nuclear family; and, equally significant, the forces and motives that account for working-class adherence to the family.

In the past decade, extensive research into the evolution of the working-class family and gender hierarchy in capitalist society has shown the contribution made to the cheap reproduction of labor power by the family and women's domestication (see, for example, Coulson, Magaš, and Wainwright 1975; Seccombe 1975; Gardiner 1975; Himmelweit and Mohun 1977; Hartmann 1976). Still, research has shown little awareness of the contradictions generated within the working-class family, and for women in particular, by capitalist development. Nor has it paid attention to the cultural forces and ideological processes that might mediate the impact of economic change on the family and modify the intrahousehold conflicts generated by that change.

A recent exchange over the political meaning of the working-class family's persistence under capitalism has made explicit the contradiction embodied in an institution that both constitutes a source of women's subordination and is able to offer support and solidarity to family members in the face of economic hardship (Humphries 1977; Hartmann and Markusen 1980; Sen 1980). This new perspective challenges the idea that the family is a collectivity of reciprocal interests, a pooling of efforts for the benefit of all members (Harris 1981; Whitehead 1981), and suggests that it is as important to detect the effect that economic change has upon power relations *within* the household as it is to trace historical linkages between economic process and family structure.

Assessing the effect of socioeconomic change on the condition of women is a central concern of the historical analysis of the family and gender hierarchy. However, research on the subordination of women during the expansion of capitalism in Latin America has displayed an underlying tension (for example, Young 1982; Deere and León 1982; Roldán 1982). At the core of this tension is a persistent uncertainty about the degree to which capitalist development, understood as the mercantilization of social relations, will undermine traditional links of personal dependence and subordination based on gender and enable women to enjoy the formal freedom that men are supposed to enjoy.

This article has two related aims: to trace the transformation of the social relations of production on São Paulo coffee plantations from the introduction of free labor in the 1850s to the present *and* to detect specific links and interactions among family ideology, gender hierarchy, the sexual division of labor, and the labor systems chosen by the planters. Central to this analysis is the idea that socioeconomic change does not occur in an ideological vacuum. On the contrary, the objective processes of material change are shaped decisively by the preexisting family ideology and gender hierarchy, from which the new conditions derive their meaning. Whereas much research into the subordination of women aims to measure women's relative access to once exclusively male privileges, I argue here that we can understand the effect of capitalist development on the condition of women only if we realize that subordination is a social and political relation, historically determined by the circumstances of men in relation to women in society. In this sense I am not making just another attempt to rescue women from their historical invisibility: I am endeavoring to write an anthropological history of which women are an active part.

Educating Labor for Intensive Work

The introduction of free labor into São Paulo agriculture is exceptional in that it rested from the very beginning on the preference of the planters for contracting labor in family units. The immigrant laborers were recruited by agents in Europe under a sharecropping contract. According to this contract, the planter financed the immigrants' transportation from their country of origin to the port of Santos, advanced the cost of transport from Santos to the plantation, and provided foodstuffs and tools until the laborers could obtain them with their own labor. He assigned them enough coffee trees to tend and harvest and granted a piece of land to produce food crops. The laborers were obliged to refund these expenses with at least half of their yearly returns from coffee cultivation. There was no time limit in the contract, but the amount of the debt incurred for transportation and other advances was clearly stated. Until that debt had been redeemed the immigrants could not move off the plantation (see Stolcke and Hall 1983 for successive changes in the contracts). Upon their arrival on the plantation the immigrant families were settled in often very poor individual houses, built, however, especially for them, separate from the slave quarters.

Why did São Paulo planters opt for the sharecrop~~~~~~~er than recruiting individual wage labor, why did they prefer whole families, and what effects did this labor system have on the immigrants' families? These are related questions.

Sharecropping in a situation of scarce labor is more efficient than wage labor; it is similar to a carefully negotiated piecework system. Both are forms of the incentive wage system, ways of securing extra effort from labor, of making laborers work harder and better for only a small increase in total remuneration over that of wage labor. Also, sharecroppers are typically recruited in family units, for one or more agricultural cycles. São Paulo planters usually explained their preference for family labor by arguing that immigrants accompanied by their families were less prone to abandon the plantations. This is at most a partial truth, for it hides the ideological notion of the family as an inherently solidary unit, a notion cherished by the planters themselves. To the planters it was inconceivable that a person would run away and abandon his family.

This notion of the family had material consequences for the planters because, in fact, the immigrants' families constituted a cheap labor reserve. A sharecropper would usually accept a division of the product that would not fully cover the potential market price of family labor, for if he did not, family labor would remain under- and unemployed; planters at times even prohibited immigrants and their families from working outside the plantation (Davatz 1941). The planter obtained this additional labor at a cost below that which he would have had to pay were he to contract it as wage labor. Coffee is a labor-intensive crop, requiring varying amounts of labor throughout the agricultural year; harvest requires a fifth more labor than cultivation (Ramos 1923, p. 358). The laborers' wives and children could make up this increased demand during the harvest.

The food plot assigned to the immigrant families was a way of reducing unit labor costs further. Crops were produced, primarily by women and children, when labor demands for coffee were low. The sharecropping family was expected to produce its own subsistence, without, however, neglecting the coffee groves, which were the planters' main concern. Foodstuffs were intercropped with coffee, planted in low-lying areas not suitable for coffee, or grown on virgin land that would later be planted in coffee.

The ideology of solidarity and cooperation within the family, as distinct from non-kin, was an important element favoring the planters' aim to exploit the whole immigrant family to the fullest. As one observer lucidly commented in 1877:

> The colonization that has really been useful for us has been that of Germans and Portuguese; the German *colono* [immigrant laborer] is

always hardworking and honest, and when he has a numerous family he offers an incalculable advantage. The head of the family attempts to demonstrate in practice the English proverb—that time is money—and with his family they turn time into their property in such a way that even when they are working in the coffee grove for the planter, they make use of the weeds that grow there to feed their pig and chicken, and when they return home, the children start to work; all of them go to school and when they rest they remove the maize kernels from the cob, build fences, cultivate the food plot, raise chickens and pigs and calves which are the source of subsistence. The wife and the daughters prepare the famous maize bread which is the basis of their food. [Domingos Jaguaribe Filho 1877, p. 19; my translation]

This ideology was shared by the workers themselves. One example is their reaction to the clause in the contract requiring all members of a family to be collectively responsible for the family's debt. This clause was especially resented because the Swiss communities of origin often forced families to take along non-kin —"people with whom they had nothing to do"—in order to rid the communities of burdens on their finances (Karrer 1886, p. 69; Natsch 1966, p. 176; Heusser 1857, p. 14).

Still, in the fifties and sixties, the majority of the planters were dissatisfied with the immigrants' assiduity in work. The initial debt, by reducing the laborers' expected share of the profit, discouraged effort in coffee cultivation. The immigrants systematically diverted labor to food production, where the product belonged to them directly. Productivity in coffee was low, and the planters lacked the means to impose the necessary labor discipline. Only after the 1880s, when the government assumed the full subsidization of the mass immigration that brought one million Italian immigrants into São Paulo agriculture over a twenty-year period, did labor productivity in coffee reach a satisfactory level. Subsidized immigration eliminated the initial debt, encouraged significant contract changes, and created the conditions for the constitution of a labor market. Initially one laborer tended no more than seven hundred trees throughout the year. In the eighties the average number was between two thousand and twenty-five hundred trees.

The sharecropping system, the labor-leasing contract that succeeded it, and the *colonato*—a mixed task and piece-rate arrangement that was to predominate in coffee cultivation in São Paulo until the 1950s—all presupposed the recruitment of labor in family units. Although the planters' choice was in part inspired by a specific family ideology, the labor system had an equal effect upon the laborers' family structure, morality, intrahousehold relations, and reproductive behavior, and on the sexual division of labor.

The family presupposed in the contracts was the nuclear family as a separate residential unit. The contract defined explicitly the functions of this nuclear household: joint labor in coffee cultivation and the growing of the food strictly necessary for the consumption of the family.

Retrospectively, it is difficult to assess the quality of intrahousehold relations. The *colonato* as a wage-incentive system put a premium on work commitment by, and cooperation among, family members and reinforced their interdependence. It strengthened the commonality of interests of the household. The allocation of family labor was decided by the husband or father, as household head, and followed a division of labor by sex and age (see Table 1).

The contract was always signed with the head of the family, who also received the family earnings. Children of either sex were expected to contribute their share in looking after small animals and participating in the harvest. The wife was primarily responsible for domestic tasks and the cultivation of the food plot, with the aid of the adult men when they had time left from their main task of tending coffee trees, which required several weedings. Men, women, and children worked together in the harvest.

Table 1. Allocation of Family Labor under the *Colonato* Contract during the Annual Agricultural Cycle

Crops/tasks	Family members	Period
Coffee: weeding	Men	Sept. to Apr./May
Coffee: harvest	Men, women, and children	May to Aug.
Food crops: cultivation and harvest	Women and children[a]	Oct./Jan. to Apr./May
Occasional wage work for plantation	Men	Occasional days throughout the year
Childbearing, child rearing, and domestic tasks	Women	All throughout the year

a. When corn or beans were intercropped with coffee, men weeded the crops simultaneously.

Significantly, the number of coffee trees assigned to women was usually about half that assigned to men.

The husband or father's preeminence and authority over family members derived in part from his relative autonomy to organize the labor process and allocate the family's labor. More difficult to assess are the material benefits he may have derived from this preeminence. There is no information on allocation of income and resources within the household or on decision making beyond the organization of work. As regards work effort, though the tasks differed by sex all household members worked from dawn to dusk in response to the incentives. The income the family received was family income and expressed not individual effort but that of all household members. At times food surpluses were sold, and men would work at odd jobs on the plantations for a day wage. There is no indication that these additional earnings were individually attributed.

At the level of meaning, however, there is a significant difference between tasks carried out predominantly by men and those carried out by women. Both the weeding of coffee and the cultivation of food crops were regarded as *serviço da gente* (that is, "our own job") by contrast with day-wage labor, which was regarded explicitly as work for the plantation. The coffee harvest paid at the piece rate was part of "our own job," but the product was for "the boss."

In the category of "our own job" a further distinction was made between coffee weeding and food growing. Coffee weeding was paid at a task rate per thousand coffee trees per year—that is, a kind of incentive wage. The number of coffee trees tended by a family depended as much on its work capacity, as determined by household composition, as on its labor intensity. The allocation of family labor was left to the husband or father, but labor intensity depended largely on family members' own will to work. Coffee weeding was, in fact, regarded as *trabalhar por conta* (to work of one's own accord); one stopped when one wanted, and there were no set times. Weeding was done mainly by men. A significant characteristic of this task was the degree of autonomy it allowed the worker. The workers perceived the fact that this relative autonomy was the precondition for high labor intensity but appreciated it as an opportunity to increase their income. Food growing, predominantly done by women, was seen by contrast as *trabalhar para a gente* or *plantar para a gente* (to work or grow food for ourselves).

Within the general category of "our own job," the task carried out by men was defined by the workers' autonomy it implied. Although women also worked of their own accord, their tasks were conceived to be work for the collectivity.

Analysts frequently have regarded the food plot given the workers under combined cash-crop and self-provisioning systems as a form of payment in kind (Palacios 1980; Kageyama et al. 1982; but cf. Sallum 1982). This is a double mystification. It obscures the labor input required to produce foodstuffs and the fact that self-provisioning reduced not only the money wage; the labor invested by workers in growing their own food also diminished the cost of reproduction of labor in absolute terms. The workers themselves, in this case predominantly women, invested part of their labor power in producing food for the family, a practice that allowed the planters to pay work in coffee at a lower price. Self-provisioning was thus an additional source of exploitation, specifically of the women. But the definition of food growing as "work for ourselves" indicates that this mystification was shared by workers themselves, both men and women. Only one woman among my informants pointed out that when she was weeding corn she was not earning anything.

Planters not only preferred families to single workers; they favored large families. The greater the proportion of workers to consumers in a family, the greater its productive capacity. Under the sharecropping system, the laborers' income depended directly on the intensity of their work in coffee. Under the *colonato* system, however, coffee cultivation was paid at a fixed task rate per thousand trees per year. Income thus depended not only on the number of trees taken by the family but also on the task rate set by the planters. Planters calculated the task rate by taking as a basis a family containing at least three adult workers. Thus, under the *colonato*, small families were even worse off than under the preceding system (Maistrello 1923). As one experienced planter rejoiced in 1877:

> These families are truly patriarchal both because of their size and their morality, solidarity and love of work. . . . The families from the Tyrol are still the most advantageous ones for the planter because of their size. This advantage is considerable: the greater number of workers, beyond accelerating emancipation of the *colono*, which is an edifying example, offers the planter a better guarantee, because the collective responsibility of all warrants the whole payment of the debt even if some family members are forgetful of their obligations. [Visconde de Indaiatuba (ca. 1878) 1952, p. 245; my translation]

The planters' interest in the size and composition of immigrant families influenced demographic behavior by placing a premium on high fertility. This emphasis, in turn, affected the sexual division of labor. Having a large number of children, although it might initially have meant a considerable burden on the mother and father, implied that after the first years the family's productive capacity would increase year after year. By contrast, a family with few children was disadvantaged throughout the family life cycle (Heusser 1857; Ozorio de Almeida 1977). A mother with a large number of children would be fully occupied with childbearing and rearing during a considerable period of her life and would have less time left for extradomestic activities. Domestic tasks were, however, recognized as essential and duly valued. As a French observer noted in 1879:

> The conclusion to be drawn is that . . . the more numerous a family is the greater the help it can offer its head to redeem himself of the initial debt. . . . The help and arms of his children constitute a natural aid, the more precious the more numerous they are, and the woman while she minds her own business, is also productive in the home, without her presence being indispensable in the fields, a thing that will become necessary if the family is composed of few members. [Turenne 1879, p. 451; my translation]

By allowing only those families with good productive capacity to redeem their debts and accumulate, the *colonato* had consequences for the wider social structure as well. The degree of exploitation to which the immigrants were subjected and the opportunities for upward mobility offered by the *colonato* are much-debated issues (Holloway 1980; Dean 1976; Stolcke and Hall 1983; Sallum 1982). With the beginning of mass immigration in the eighties, living and working conditions became particularly harsh. Restriction of output in coffee at an individual family level had been one form of resistance to the sharecropping arrangement. With increasing control over the labor process, strike action became more frequent. The largest strike occurred in 1913 and mobilized ten to fifteen thousand workers.

Politically, the family labor system was also relevant: the laborers

> did not adopt the system of head or leaders because this would have meant reducing to misery and persecution some of the most valuable members of this union. They acted in groups of four to five families in accordance with the friendship within these groups, having not one leader for this group but rather one family in charge of transmitting the thoughts of the secret collective leadership which was the one that solved all problems. ["Um Socialista," in Pinheiro and Hall 1979, p. 117; my translation]

Even so, there was a measure of upward mobility and social differentiation between the workers. Combined with other factors, such as movement to the newer coffee areas where planting rights were more favorable or marriage into a better-off family, family size and composition were decisive in enabling immigrants to move out of the plantations and establish themselves on their own (for a similar process see Deere and de Janvry 1981).

As the division of labor on the plantations increased, planters chose labor more consciously according to the laborers' family status and the specific requirements of the job. Single men were usually employed as *avulsos*, laborers recruited exclusively for the harvest or for special tasks, or as *camaradas*, workers in coffee processing and transport. *Camaradas*— a category that also often included young families—were resident wage laborers paid on a monthly basis. Large families were employed as *colonos* (Carvalho de Moraes 1870, p. 66; Bollettino UCICA 1903, p. 73; Domingos Jaguaribe Filho 1877, pp. 19, 32). Gangs of men contracted for specific tasks were called, significantly, *turmas de solteiros* (gangs of bachelors) (Ramos 1923, p. 120). Having a family was an advantage for employability. In addition, *camaradas* were less secure in their jobs (Dean 1976, pp. 170–71). This factor must have made marriage all the more attractive. The labor system had already affected marriage, in that the initial indebtedness, and the planters' efforts to recoup their investment, curtailed marriage choices. Women usually followed their husbands in marriage, and parents, fathers in particular, tended to intervene in their daughters' marriage preferences. A child left the family upon marriage to set up a separate household. In order not to forgo their investment, planters would prohibit marriage with a girl from another plantation unless the employer of the bridegroom was willing to pay off her debt (Heusser 1857, p. 48; see also Domingos Jaguaribe Filho 1877, p. 32).

The extraordinary coffee boom at the turn of the century is proof that subsidized mass immigration and the *colonato* system, resting in part on the capitalist exploitation of the family, was most successful in solving the labor problem that had been posed by the abolition of slavery. A Prussian agronomist observed at the time that the *colonato* was "the most perfect possible labor system," the product of São Paulo planters' "untiring effort and intelligence" (Kaerger 1892, pp. 333, 335).

Subsidized immigration continued until 1927, but planters recruited more and more national labor, generally from among those driven out of the Northeast by economic misery. At first national labor was contracted temporarily for specific tasks, but eventually whole families were employed as *colonos*. This change required some revision of the planters' traditional prejudiced view of the *caboclos* as idle, undisciplined, and immoral. As one contemporary observed:

> I still have to say what I have heard about the morality of the national laborer. It is good, very good. Well constituted families, mutual respect among the spouses, deference on the part of the chil-

dren toward their parents. . . . Isn't it remarkable that in the wild *sertoes* [backlands] and distant lands, where civilization arrives only rarely, an institution such as monogamous marriage should have been preserved. . . . Isn't it extraordinary that an institution which is justly regarded as the flower of Christian civilization should have persisted in the nature of such a race despite the wildness of the environment in which they live? [Papaterra Limongi 1916, pp. 365–66; my translation]

The Transition from Family Labor to Individual Wage Labor

The inordinate expansion of coffee growing generated the first over-production crisis at the beginning of the century. By the late twenties, government intervention and the recovery of the international market after the First World War produced a new coffee boom. The economic crisis of 1929 found coffee planters with the largest coffee harvest ever. Cattle, sugar cane, and cotton for the expanding textile industry were only gradually substituted for coffee, and large numbers of *colono* families were left out of work. An indication of the comparative profitability of the *colonato* system over straight wage labor is the fact that the remaining coffee continued to be cultivated under this labor system. Only in the late 1950s did the planters increasingly recruit casual labor for work in coffee.

Coffee enjoyed a new, though brief, recovery in the 1950s when it expanded into the neighboring state of Paraná and returned to the older coffee regions in São Paulo. New, more productive coffee varieties were introduced, and contour farming was used to prevent erosion. To increase the productivity of soil, coffee trees were planted closer together and organic fertilizer was applied to exhausted soils. Intercropping of foodstuffs became less frequent as coffee trees were planted closer together; intercropping was frowned upon also because it reduced yields on poorer soils, especially undesirable at a time of rising coffee prices. At the same time planters were increasingly reluctant to grant separate food plots—because they wanted to put those lands to other use but also because they hoped to increase the productivity of labor in coffee cultivation. Mechanization of coffee weeding, however, continued to be regarded as incompatible with the *colonato* system (*Agricultura em São Paulo* 1952).

Even the limited innovations listed above altered the traditional annual labor demand cycle, accentuating demand peaks during the coffee harvest. By this time planters recruited *colonos* mainly to meet the labor demand for coffee weeding, using additional casual labor for the harvest.

The *colonos* themselves, deprived of planting rights and without compensation in wages, abandoned the plantations for better opportunities either in other regions or in industry.

A new decline in coffee prices in the late fifties produced the eradication of almost half the existing coffee trees in the sixties and the unemployment of many *colono* families. Finally, President João Goulart's enactment of the Estatuto do Trabalhador Rural (rural labor statute) in 1963 produced the dismissal of the remaining *colonos*. This new labor law repeated in part the ineffectual 1943 labor legislation; in addition, however, it granted to the *colonos* indemnity in case of dismissal and security of tenure after ten years of work on a plantation. This statute was a mere palliative to deal with growing social conflict in agriculture. Nevertheless, the planters saw these rights as a serious challenge to their freedom of contract and as a first step toward the loss of their land at a time when the debate over land reform was becoming increasingly heated. The most effective way to defeat the law was to dismiss the remaining *colonos* with or without indemnity and thereafter to work their plantations with *pessoal de fora* (outsiders), that is, casual labor recruited by *turmeiros* (labor contractors).

Other categories of resident laborers were similarly affected by the statute. The new system made labor supply more flexible and freed planters from any of the obligations stipulated in the labor statute. By 1970, of a total agricultural labor force of eighteen million in Brazil as a whole, over six million were casual laborers. In São Paulo in 1971 about 25 percent of the agricultural labor force worked as casual wage laborers, the so-called *volantes* (flying workers) or *boias-frias* (cold food). Note, however, that about 50 percent of the agricultural labor force consisted of smallholders and their unpaid family labor. The laborers formerly resident on the plantations moved to the periphery of small towns in the interior of the state. In many of these towns homogeneous neighborhoods of little self-built houses or huts sprang up during the 1960s. Workers who received an indemnity under the new law managed to acquire plots to build houses, but the majority had to pay rent.

These workers no longer have land or the time to produce their own subsistence. The *volantes* recall the *colonato* as the "time of abundance." With the exodus from the plantations the "time of money" set in. Now it is only through the market that they can have access to use value, and they are entirely dependent on market forces. Because they are contracted individually on a temporary basis, economic uncertainty has increased. The end of the *colonato* produced the *turmeiro*, who recruits, transports, and oversees the laborers and serves as mediator between them and the estate. Laborers are typically recruited on a weekly basis, though they may work in the same gang and on the same estate for longer periods of time. Women and children from the age of about twelve, as well as men, have become casual laborers working in gangs. Roughly 25 percent of casual laborers are women, though women's participation rate varies regionally, depending on the supply of men and on alternative work opportunities for men. The additional burden of the rent and total dependence on the market for subsistence, coupled with the post-1964 wage freeze and inflation, have produced an almost continuous decline in real wages, even in regions such as Campinas, where employment opportunities exist for most of the year. Once again it takes contributions of all able family members to make ends meet. As one woman explained, "We have to work; [the husband's wage] is not sufficient because we have to pay rent. . . . Before when we lived with our parents [on the plantation] it was better . . . everybody planted food; before there was abundance, we raised small animals; now we have to buy everything; in my youth the plantations were full of people; now they are empty."

Proletarianization and migration to the towns have altered the quality of social relations. Looking backward, it is thought that the *colonato* enhanced solidarity not only within the household but between households. By contrast, individual wage labor has generated great uncertainty among the laborers and is thought to have strained interpersonal relations in the neighborhood, among kin, and particularly within the family.

Although these laborers have a keen awareness of their exploitation in a world that is seen as divided between "us," the "poor," and "them," the "rich," they are very skeptical about the possibility of joint action now, not only because of the adverse power relations in society at large but also because *união* (solidarity), the recognized prerequisite for any collective action, is felt to be lacking (Martinez-Alier and Boito 1977). Kin and friendship ties served as important links in the process of migration to the towns, and they persist in the new environment, though often with new content. Neighborhood relations are now tenuous, and conflict can break out over the smallest cause. As one older woman noted:

> Before it wasn't the same . . . it was everybody together . . . the families all together, not like now, one here and the other there; for me it was better before; everybody was united, neighbors also combined well; we lived all together, combined well; now it is difficult to find anybody to do anything together, there is mistrust; first, there was no mistrust; one day you would give corn flour and eggs to me, another day you trusted me and I would give to you; now nobody does anything together anymore; I don't know why this is so; first we were more united, now nobody gets on anymore.

In situations of rapid and profound change without any noticeable improvement it is not unusual to idealize the past. Life on the plantations was far from idyllic. The whole family worked from dawn to dusk. Relations between households were not especially harmonious. Particularly during the harvest, competition between families could be intense. Those families who managed to complete the harvest of their own coffee grove before the others could earn additional money by helping families that were behind. Those who were behind resented having to hire this help, for it meant that they lost part of the income from their grove.

On the other hand, there was also cooperation (*mutirão*) and the exchange of days of work between *colono* families. The homogeneity of working and living conditions, as well as self-provisioning, permitted exchange of food without monetary expense. Now it is *cada qual por si e Deus para tudos* (each one for himself and God for everybody). Although it is felt to be important to have neighbors, mutual aid and cooperation between neighbors is practically absent. Social relations have been totally monetarized, and nobody has enough to give another. Nowadays, as one woman exclaimed, "without money nobody is worth anything." Moreover, "in the village everybody is the same; it is impossible to help anybody with that miserable wage." Conversely, there is reluctance to ask for a favor for fear of being unable to reciprocate and thus losing face in a situation where self-esteem is at a low ebb.

Permanent economic insecurity in a profoundly unequal society in which manual labor lacks any social prestige has eroded self-esteem and has made casual laborers extremely sensitive to the slightest offense. Mutual accusations, quarrels, and even outright fights are not infrequent. In such a harsh and tense social environment it might be expected that the family and kin would function as the last, but essential, source of support and solidarity. But the circumstances under which the transition to wage labor has occurred have severely strained intrafamilial relations as well. The quality of these relations appears to be more distant than ever from what is regarded as the ideal. The family continues to be coterminous with the household: "The family are the people who live together in a house." There is a resonance of the past: "The family is a lot of people in a house, a crowd." People not belonging to the family or household are *gente de fora, homems de fora, os outros* (people from outside, men from outside, the others), as opposed to *alguem da casa*, (somebody of the house). But whereas *colonato* household members worked together, now family members are dispersed among different workplaces: "The family are those who help us to work, whose wages belong to us."

Households are predominantly two-generational, containing either both parents and their unmarried children or a mother and her unmarried children. Children are expected to remain in their parents' home until they marry and to contribute their entire earnings to the family income. Upon marriage they are expected to establish their own households. It is rare to encounter grandparents beyond working age within the family household. Married adults will attempt to live in their own households as long as they are able to earn their own livings, often until they die: "As long as one is able to work one will work." People regard going to live with their children as a very unattractive prospect.

If the necessity arises, however, it is the sons rather than the daughters who are expected to care for aging parents. The daughters have to look after their husbands, and the husbands generally are not willing to take care of parents-in-law. "The daughters' husbands don't like to work for *others*." A distinction is made between consanguines and affines: consanguines belong to one; affines are the others.

Relations with kin outside the nuclear family are quite fluid, and the boundaries beyond which any specific kin obligations cease are difficult to define. There is a certain amount of visiting between kin, usually between consanguines unless it is a joint visit by a married couple. Visits by or to neighbors are rare. As one woman remarked, "I don't use to go to my neighbor's house; I don't like to go to other people's houses." Relatives, usually up to the second degree, are expected to help in case of need, and it is resented when assistance is not forthcoming. These expectations and obligations are also extended to ritual kin, by baptism or marriage, who have been and continue to be chosen among kin or acquaintances—the latter ideally of the same class, although people certainly do not always abide by this rule.

Interaction between kin is not only determined genealogically; both geographical and social mobility have produced social distancing. Contact is maintained only among those relatives who live within reasonable distances. Travel is expensive and takes time, so that it is impossible sometimes even to visit one's own parents. The older laborers are illiterate; they do not write letters. Thus, contact is very easily lost.

In addition, social differentiation between kin is a perceived obstacle to sustained contact. Whereas it is precisely the better-off relatives who could be helpful, they are often regarded with a mixture of distrust and shame. As one woman, the only one still working in agriculture, said of her brothers, who live and work in town, "They don't pay any attention to me and I don't run after them; since my father died [eighteen years ago] I haven't seen any of them; they are better off than I, they have a car; I don't care if they don't come; let them stay there; when my mother and father were alive I would go there every week; when one has a father and a mother one has the obligation." Moreover, one would not know how to behave in the home of the better off and would feel awkward. Another woman confessed: "I'm ashamed to go to visit my daughter for lunch in Campinas; I'm ashamed to eat, to open my mouth, to cut the meat with a fork . . . my daughter is a *grāfina* [a fine lady]; her husband works in a bank; they have a car; they don't come to visit; the husband doesn't allow her to."

That is, social advancement tends to erode solidarity with parents, especially in the case of married daughters. Sons, as men possessing a status that can be shared with others, are more likely to maintain the ties with their family of origin and might even help their siblings to advance. Women, whose status is derived from their husbands, have no status to bestow on others.

As indicated, sons rather than daughters are expected to take care of their aged parents. This is also one of the reasons some parents adduce for preferring sons to daughters, who in addition are said to be more difficult to raise as respectable adults. This preference does not mean, however, that relations between parents and sons are more intimate than those between parents and daughters, provided they have remained at the same social level. Practical assistance tends to flow more frequently from mothers to married daughters than from mothers to sons. In the specifically feminine sphere of childbearing, a mother will assist her own daughter during birth but not her daughter-in-law, unless the latter has no female consanguines living close by. Such assistance, however, is rarely extended to childminding if the daughters work, because usually the mothers also work for a wage.

The nuclear family household constitutes a distinct social unit within which, ideally, effort and income are shared. Even in cases where married children continue living with their parents, or old parents reside with married children, each nuclear unit tends to have a separate economy with its own stove and shopping, cooking, and eating arrangements.

Another category of kin—children by adoption—bridges the boundary between the nuclear family and extrahousehold kin. Unlike married children, who are genealogically close but residentially separate, adopted children are usually more distant kin but now a part of the household. Although the expected family size has decreased, it is still not uncommon to raise someone else's child or children, usually the children of some dead female relative, with one's own. This is a moral obligation that, nonetheless, has material implications. In a situation of grave economic uncertainty no one can afford to invest effort without being sure of a return. Social relations with social equals, whether neighbors or kin, are governed by the imperative of reciprocity. Favors must be *reconhecidos* (recognized)—that is, acknowledged and repaid. Indebtedness means incapacity and inferiority and is feared also because it may mean no further help. Logically, the principle of reciprocity does not operate in the same way with social superiors. Favors do produce a feeling of obligation, but at least material repayment can always be relegated to a mystical agent: *Deus lhe pague* (may God pay you).

Kinship creates a moral obligation to offer help that may be canceled out by other social factors, but once given it must be reciprocated. An adopted child is expected to pay back the investment made in its upbringing as soon as it is able to contribute to the family income. Still, this right acquired by the household through teaching the child and caring for it is not uncontested. The surviving parent may reappear when the child has reached working age and, adducing parenthood, may claim it back to put it to work for him- or herself. In one such case a foster mother went so far as to go to court and was told by the judge that he would compute the cost of the labor she had invested in raising the child. The father was in no condition to pay, and the child remained with her. One way to prevent reclamation is to adopt legally, *com papel pasado* (handing over the birth certificate), a procedure that is said to *cortar o sangue* (cut the blood); but parents are not enthusiastic about this procedure. With married and adopted children, the articulation between kinship ties understood genealogically and material rights and obligations grounded in the household is often problematic.

From a formal point of view, the new socioeconomic conditions have not threatened the nuclear family as the typical household structure and unit of social reproduction. In practice, however, the household has lost one of the central attributes that gave it cohesion, joint labor. The family has ceased to be a labor and consumption unit to become a wage-earning unit. This transformation in the material content of intrafamilial relations appears to have menaced its very persistence as a viable unit.

Under conditions of declining real wages and increased economic uncertainty, everyday survival depends more than ever on the pooling of effort by all members of the household and reciprocity over time. Life was hard on the plantations, but subsistence planting protected the *colonos* against market forces even if it implied a high level of exploitation. Now it is more important than ever that all household members contribute to the family income, for capital has been able to depress wage levels below the cost of reproduction even of an individual female laborer. The *colonato* labor system enhanced family solidarity. The transition to individual wage labor at current wage levels makes cooperation imperative; on the other hand, it puts considerable strain on household cohesion by eroding the family morality that the *colonato* reinforced. Mutual dependence among family members remains, is perhaps even increased, but individualization of labor and individual aspirations often frustrate a consensus of needs. As one older laborer of Italian origin remembered:

As *colonos* the family worked all together; women and men did all the same work; where one went all the family went; the head, the father, contracted with the *fazenda*; the head received the money; it was he who arranged everything; the coffee *colono* is the same as the coffee *empreitada* [mixed task and piece-rate system]; the harvest was done by everybody together; it wasn't like at present that only women harvest the coffee; we were paid every sixty days; each pay covered one weeding; the payment was calculated per thousand coffee trees; the number of coffee trees contracted depended on the size of the family and these had to be tended all year round; the harvest was paid by the sack of coffee the same as now; the family worked together, not like now in the gang; the gang scatters everybody now; one goes in one direction, the other in the other; we [the men] also worked *por día* . . . women would go to weed rice, beans on the family plot; the *patrão* [boss] did not want to contract women *por día* in order to protect the family plot; only the men would go and work for the plantation directly; and it wasn't like now either, everybody earning the same; the weaker [families] earned less; that was already set down in the contract book; . . . at that time things were bad because there was no money; you worked and worked and had nothing; the family was more united everywhere because at that time it was the family head who commanded; what he said was done . . . also there was no fighting because there was little money, we bought few things.

Now each family member is recruited individually by the *turmeiro*. Men attempt to decide changes of gang for their wives and children, to arrange jobs for them, but in practice women make decisions for themselves and for the young children, who usually start working with their mothers. Ideally the wages of all family members should be pooled and administered by the husband or father as family head, but sons in particular are often reluctant to hand over the whole of the wage, paying instead only for their room and board. Wives and daughters do hand over wages, but the husband does not always administer the joint income. As one woman pointed out: "It is the family head who should control the money; in many places the head of the household is the man, in many it is the woman; if the husband is irresponsible, spends all the money on silly things, the woman has to take control." The one who controls the money is the household head.

As provider the husband should pay for the running expenses of the household, the *despesas*, that is, food, rent, water, and light bills. The wages of the wife and children should be used for occasional expenses such as clothes, a piece of furniture, doctor's bills, and so on. Husband and sons are entitled to spending money for cigarettes and drinks, and the girls should get something to accumulate a trousseau. The only one who is not entitled to any expenditure on herself is the wife or mother. Women constantly fear that husbands might divert more than their legitimate share to excessive drink or to other women, thus menacing the whole family's survival—"robbing the innocent children of their food," as they say.

It is generally accepted as an undesirable fact of life that both wives and daughters must work for a wage. Because they no longer work under the direct surveillance of the husband or father, their work is cause for new suspicions and new friction between spouses. One man voiced the concern of many: "The gang trucks have brought many novelties, they have brought the separation between husband and wife, quarrels between husband and wife, they have brought lack of respect; women have lost the fear of their husbands, they have brought the husband's distrust." The laboring gangs are regarded as places of dubious morality, inappropriate for respectable women. *Turmeiros* have a reputation, not unfounded, for taking advantage of their position to seduce women workers. Men's suspicion is enhanced by the belief that women who lack the protection of their men will easily succumb to other men's advances. Mistrust derives from traditional morals that gave men control over and exclusive rights to their wives' sexuality, and from fear of the possible consequences for the survival of the household of women's contact with *homems de fora* (men from outside).

In earlier times there was surely no perfect fit between an ideal morality and practice regarding women's sexual integrity. Planters and overseers seem to have been a considerable menace for the *colonos'* women, and cases of pregnant daughters' having to get married did occur. Still, living and working conditions must then have seemed less of a threat to the men's power to exert control over their women. Also, the material implications of, if not the ideological motivations for, control over women's sexuality seem to have shifted. During the *colonato* the procreative capacity of women was of prime importance to men and was duly recognized. Now procreation is far less important to men than is access to a woman's domestic and extradomestic labor. Some women suggest cynically that men no longer marry women for their beauty, but to have them working for themselves. A man can obtain a woman's labor without pay only if she is his wife, either legal or consensual, or daughter.

The husband's jealousy is a frequent cause of fights. Time and again stories are told of women who have run away with other men—stories that often have little basis in reality. There are constant complaints that the neighborhood is no place to raise respectable daughters, that morals are not what they were. Men's fears that women might run off with other men, or that unmarried daughters will present the family with additional mouths to feed, are far less founded than is women's mistrust; an important element in men's fears is the feeling of loss of control. Women are justified in their misgivings about male alcoholism, which is a major cause of family instability and violence, and when a man becomes involved with another woman, family income is diverted accordingly. As one woman, the lover of the husband of one of the women workers, declared emphatically: *Não so boba de dar o rabo de graça* (I am not a fool offering my backside for free).

At this point it is important to stress that it is by no means only the purely material consequences of the transition to individual wage labor— the generalization of commodity relations, declining real wages, and instability of work—that have strained intrahousehold relations. There is no immediate reason why economic hardship in itself should generate conflict rather than reinforce solidarity within the family or household. Rather, the meaning of socioeconomic change for those concerned is compounded of material changes, previous socioeconomic circumstances, and the ideological and cultural expectations implied in them. More specifically, the effect of economic individuation for household members has been mediated by a gender ideology that accorded specific attributes to the sexes, attributes that have been challenged materially and ideologically by the transition to individual wage labor. The *colonos* have experienced proletarianization not as autonomous individuals but as social beings enmeshed in specific social relations with specific reciprocal rights and obligations.

In order to evaluate adequately the effects and meaning of socioeconomic change as it affects gender relations, one must take into account at least three different, though related, levels of experience. There is the first, most objective level of immediately material change in the individual condition of women and men with regard to work. Secondly, there is a relational level. Gender is a social relation; therefore, any change in the circumstances of one of the terms of the relation will necessarily produce a transformation of the relation as such, a transformation that will in turn have an effect on each partner to the relation. And there is a third cultural level. As I suggested above, among the elements giving meaning to change are previous cultural and ideological expectations and norms of conduct. It is also this cultural dimension that in a very material way will shape the responses to change of those concerned.

Their transformation into casual laborers has affected women and men in fundamentally different ways. Men have been reduced to simple wage laborers. They have lost the relative autonomy to organize work. There is no longer any possibility of their deciding the allocation of their own or their families' labor power. In the process, they have also often lost the right to control the family income. This perceived loss of significant elements of men's social identity has undermined their authority, producing a profound feeling of insecurity and an erosion of self-esteem that makes men all the more distrustful of their wives and children. Job insecurity and low wages have made it increasingly difficult for men to fulfill their ideologically constituted role as breadwinners. In view of all this, the danger that their wives may leave them seems all the more real. The transition to wage labor has not affected women in the same way. During the *colonato* women worked both at home and in the fields, but they were excluded from wage labor for the plantation. They worked *para a gente* (for ourselves). Their incorporation into wage labor has meant not a reduction but an increase in women's obligations. There has been no transformation of the domestic sexual division of labor or of the traditional definition of women's work as subsidiary to that of men: "The one who has to maintain the family is the husband; the wife works to help the husband."

Men work to maintain their families; women work to help their husbands. Motivations for working for a wage also differ between men and women. Women work for a wage reluctantly, driven by necessity in a context of general poverty; men work because they are men. As a consequence of this interaction between material and ideological forces, men have a stronger commitment to work for a wage and are more directly affected by the conditions of the labor market—the lack or insecurity of work. They will endeavor to leave agriculture and work in the construction industry where wages are higher and working conditions somewhat better.

Work is available for women, but alternatives outside agriculture are less attractive. They could work as maids, but this work is regarded as undesirable because of long hours and greater dependence. Women do not only work in the fields. When they come home they still have to prepare food and do other domestic chores. When men come home, they change and either watch television or go to a bar. Women not only get up earlier now and work longer hours than men; their cultural definition as women makes them more submissive and less demanding at work, so that they accept any task. "Those who work for a day wage have to do what they are told; if they tell us to quarry stones, to dig a ditch, we go." This is also the reason why women nowadays usually do those jobs that are paid at a piece rate, like harvesting coffee or cotton. Working for a piece rate means working with greater speed and intensity than for a day wage. Men refuse to do such jobs. As a result, not only do women work longer hours than men, but often their labor intensity is greater.

The transformation of the whole family into wage laborers has affected the sexual division of labor in a complex way. For those women who do not go out to work, either because they are in the initial phase of the family life cycle and cannot leave their small children or because the husband has a better income and the wife does not need to work, the division of labor by sex has been intensified. For those women who work for a wage, the effect has been to redefine tasks by gender and create a new general division of labor between the sexes, with women doing the worst jobs. Agricultural tasks formerly done by men or by the whole family, such as weeding or harvesting coffee, are now done by women, and men are attempting, not always successfully, to move into new, better-paid, and exclusively male occupations—construction work, for instance. The redefinition of tasks by gender proceeds in three steps. Men move out of jobs for better ones; women succeed them in doing what are inferior and worse-paid jobs; finally, what have now become female jobs are typified as feminine on account of some alleged special female ability, such as the famous nimble fingers that seem to qualify women for the privilege of picking coffee and cotton. Men justify their advantages on the labor market ideologically.

Change has generated resentment in the women, and new misgivings toward men. As the women complain: "It is a good thing to find a man who does not allow one to work; but working, it is no use to have a husband"; "We marry for sport; the husband does not take care of the wife; we take care of ourselves." Two points need to be made, however. First, women resent having to work for a wage. The necessity is perceived as a result of the situation as a whole and as a failure of their husbands. Women *do not* resent the continuing responsibility for domestic duties (see Hartmann 1981 for a case where housework sharing is a source of conjugal conflict). Secondly, though in different respects, both men and women resent the transformation in their mutual relations brought about by proletarianization.

If they could, women would stay at home, but domestic work is not paid. In fact, domestic work is neither invisible nor regarded as inferior by these laborers, though some women think it more entertaining to work in a gang (probably a sign of growing social isolation in the home). With the transition to wage labor, domestic labor has lost its value in a relative sense. During the *colonato* a woman's work at home, and in the fields when feasible, was regarded as the proper and sufficient contribution by women to the family income. Now a woman has to work more than a man to fill family needs and expectations. It is in this sense that domestic work has been devalued. Paradoxically, while on the one hand "the woman always is useful in the field and at home, she always works more," on the other hand "the woman nowadays has no value anymore; before she had greater worth." In this sense also the incorporation into wage labor offers no more personal autonomy to women than did the earlier exclusion from it. Compared with men, women feel acutely that they have the worse lot now. All the same, men, when out of work, have nothing to fall back on and lose their male social identity; women, by contrast, not having been deprived of their essential attribute, motherhood, feel useful even if they do not work for a wage. Proletarianization has increased women's burdens, but it has not affected their social identity as women, that is, as wives and mothers.

Generalized wage work has affected family size, though again the situation is contradictory. During the *colonato*, having a numerous family was of positive value. Small children were taken along to the field and left sleeping in the shade of the coffee trees while the mother participated in the harvest or tended the food plot. Having several children of working age is still a distinct advantage for the family, for the more favorable the worker/consumer ratio in the family is, the better its economic situation will be. However, a mother with small children cannot take her children to the fields and work for a wage, and a single wage is absolutely insufficient to feed a wife and several small children. "For those who had many small children it was better before; those who had twelve, thirteen children could raise them easily . . . now, those who have only small children, for the father to work alone it is very hard."

Not surprisingly, expectations about number of children have dropped. "Nowadays nobody wants to have children anymore"; that is, ideally a person should have two or three, but not more. "The thing is to close the factory gate, close it and lose the key." Probably the most frequent method used to prevent conception is coitus interruptus ("you have to shoot and miss"), but some women, in particular the younger ones, take the pill or use the IUD, even though medical assistance is precarious.

The ideal number of children has diminished, but both men and women share the conviction that one should have children, and if one cannot have them oneself one should adopt them. One woman who had adopted a boy underlined the women's ideal of having children with the graphic proverb *bananeira que não da cacho merece ser cortada* (a banana plant that does not give bananas should be cut down). Motherhood is woman's essential attribute. Only by losing it will she cease to be a social being. Women's transformation into wage laborers has not threatened their procreative role, however. For men, the consequences of the trans-

formation in the relations of production, which deprived them of some of
their fundamental attributes and made their role as providers so much
more insecure, have been dramatic. One woman remarked ironically of
her husband, who had been unable to work for some time, "He was not
meant to be a man; a man should not like to stay at home; women must
like to stay at home; I don't like it. . . . God made a mistake." The husband revealed his own discomfort at not being able to work, which was
again the product of a combination of cultural and material considerations:
"If I was a woman, nobody would find it wrong that I stay at home; being
a man I think myself that people are starting to say, won't he ever get better?" This sense of uselessness is certainly intensified by seeing women
working for a wage.

   Women's greater versatility, while involving hardship, provides them
with special resources with which to confront life. As women themselves
often say, they have more "courage" than men. Still, this greater resilience
has contradictory consequences: women are stronger because they must
confront hardship, but precisely because of that greater strength they also
have a greater capacity to put up with it.

   As we saw earlier, drunkenness among men is frequent, an under-
standable reaction to their demoralization. Deserting their families is another response to socioeconomic hardship (see Hagerman Johnson 1978;
Kuznesof 1980, Roldán 1982). About one-third of the women I knew (seventeen out of a total fifty-seven) lived with their children without a man in
the household. Among those women who lived with their husbands, there
were instances where the husband was incapable of working and/or drank.
None of these women, however, thought of deserting their men. There are
ideological reasons that make it much more difficult and thus unusual for
women to abandon their families. Whereas men have to, literally, "earn"
their rightful place in the household, women's "natural" place is in the
home. Men might abandon the home when they feel they have failed. For
women, abandoning the family *constitutes* the failure: "Many women who
leave their husbands . . . did so with reason . . . and still people would say
that it was she who was wrong; women always get a bad name."

   A decisive obstacle discouraging wives and mothers from leaving
their homes is the special bond thought to link mothers and children. As
the saying goes, "Mother you have only one, father, nobody knows who he
is." The physiological difference between women and men in regard to
childbearing is ideologically marked to underline the special nature of
motherhood. It is also for this reason that fatherhood depends on co-
residence and exclusive access to the wife's sexuality, and that it is potentially more fragile. The maternal and paternal bonds are conceived of as
differing in quality and intensity. Children are expected to respect both

their parents, to obey them and not talk back. Yet their attitudes toward father and mother are different: "They must respect their father and even more their mother because the mother suffers more; also, the mother feels greater love for her children; a mother will go without food in order to give something to eat to her children."

Because the wife and mother is conceived of as the natural center and agglutinating force of the family, a husband and father's desertion is much less of a peril for the persistence of the household than would be that of the woman: "When the father leaves the home, the household trembles; when the mother leaves it, the house crumbles."

Although it is difficult for women with children and without husbands to reconcile their domestic duties with the need to earn a wage, nevertheless they will do their utmost to succeed. A widow of about thirty-five—four of her six children were alive and living with her, one of them working like her—commented disapprovingly: "On the truck a man said that if he were in my position he would have abandoned the children; love does it all; what do you think of that, when the father dies to go off; not me; I show them a happy face."

Just as men are judged the natural providers of the family's material needs, women are conceived to be endowed by nature with special abilities to care for and raise the children. But whereas this special ability of women is not necessarily incompatible with wage work outside the home, men are dependent on women for all domestic services. Thus, a man will make a great effort always to have a woman at his disposal: "A man does nothing; he has to pay for it; if he has a lot of money, he has a maid." It is rare, however, for a widow or a deserted wife to accept another man: "To get another man for him to do it even worse; I rather stay alone," said one deserted woman.

By challenging previous gender roles, the transition to wage labor has altered gender relations, eroding the authority structure within the family. The diminished power of the husband and father within the family and the new tensions that have resulted in the household contrast sharply, however, with the persistent need—perhaps greater than ever—for household members to stick together and, by pooling their efforts, to confront material difficulties. As members of *colono* families, married women were motivated to work outside the home by family needs rather than personal aspirations, just as they are now as casual laborers; then as now they had little control over their earnings. Men are committed to work because they are men, and in principle it is they who control the household budget—this often being a source of considerable anxiety to the women. Nonetheless, this greater degree of individuation of men, at least in relation to their control over the income (Whitehead 1981) and in work motivation, in fact obscures the consequences of the ideology of the male breadwinner in severely curtailing men's individuality. Casual laborers are probably the "formally free" laborers par excellence. But it is precisely these male laborers who reveal most clearly the contradiction between individuation on account of capitalist expansion and the ideological constitution of men as family providers (which is another facet of capitalist expansion, of course).

However, this male gender identity is not a historical residue. It is permanently recreated in advanced industrial society. The new economic circumstances have not produced new definitions of gender roles. Rather, one is impressed by the strength and good humor of the women in contrast to the defeated look of many of the men. Women resent the added burden they have to carry, blaming both the planters for not giving them subsistence plots and their husbands for not providing for them. Husbands blame the socioeconomic system as such for their difficulties, but frequently vent their frustrations on their wives and children. Domestic violence seems to have increased. Although it is difficult to know exactly, it appears that conjugal conflict ending in physical violence occurred also in the past. The new tensions, however, have certainly exacerbated conflict. As one woman complained:

> There are people who really hit; he [the husband] when his foot got bad, the beatings he gave me, and the children got bread only on Sundays; in the fields I ate only rice and beans; there were many people who felt sorry for me and would give me some bread . . . this village is a place of much confusion; I hit her [the husband's lover] because she made us starve; just think of it, to work the whole week and having to starve on Sunday . . . now the situation is much worse; now they [the men] are all scoundrels; when we lived on the plantation, some men were like that but not all by far.

The victims of intrafamilial physical violence are typically women and children. When men feel their inadequacy most keenly they attempt to reassert their authority and domination through the use of physical violence—that is, naked power. There are circumstances that are generally believed to justify beating, as when a child is disobedient or a woman has another man. But a woman gets the worst of both worlds: the husband is as likely to beat her up when he fears her reprimands for his infidelity as when she is suspected of being unfaithful. Drunkenness often precipitates physical violence and is justly feared by women.

Children, particularly sons, will usually come to the aid of their mothers in a fight. In one instance, a father shot his own son for trying to prevent him from returning to the bar where he had already got drunk (most men have small firearms or knives at home). In another case, a son stabbed his drunken father, who was trying to beat his mother. Another woman with a number of small children attempted suicide when she could no longer bear her husband's assaults. These are extreme cases. Still, they indicate one of the contradictions of a socioeconomic system that with one hand endorses and permanently recreates a family ideology and structure implying women's subordination to the power of men (who do not realize that they pay a dear price for their preeminence as the family providers) and with the other may undermine the family as one of its sources of profit by forms of extreme exploitation.

Conclusion

The transition from the *colonato* to wage labor was not a passage from an idyllic life of abundance, personal gratification, and happiness to one of misery and demoralization. Such an impression would be inaccurate. The *colonato* was a labor system based on the extreme exploitation of family labor, and as such it reinforced the nuclear family as a set of social relations and moral values. The *colonos* were aware of their exploitation and resisted it when they could. Under the present system of temporary wage labor, because of declining real wages, cooperation between family members is as vital as ever. On the other hand, the new relations of production, by individualizing labor and depriving the men of important attributes, have had a disintegrating effect on personal relations within the household and between households. These contradictory pressures are particularly felt against the background of the *colonato*.

The transition from the *colonato* system to temporary wage labor on São Paulo coffee plantations is only one instance of the more general operation in economic processes of detectable extraeconomic ideological and cultural forces. In this case, planters organized production on the premise of a specific family model and in so doing created material constraints that reinforced this family form as a set of social relations and values. The laborers' reaction to economic change is, in turn, mediated by their belonging to a family and by the social roles assigned to them within it. The contradictions that mark this process are the compounded result of economic pressures as they are experienced in the light of social values and expectations.

As *colonos*, the laborers knew how to cultivate coffee and food crops and had a significant amount of autonomy to organize the labor process. This was surely a source of self-esteem. Now people have to sell their labor and carry out whatever task they are told to perform. The trucks that take the laborers to work are called *pau-de-arara* (bird cages) in which they travel like birds sitting on a rod. The only thing expected of the laborers is that they work as hard as possible at the lowest wages that planters can impose.

There is an important political dimension to this transition. Wages are never determined exclusively by market forces. In countries like Brazil, political control is an especially visible factor in depressing wages. Thus, the incipient rural unions that grew out of the increasing mobilization of rural labor in the fifties were either taken over by the government or simply closed down after the military coup of 1964. The laborers are well aware of the forces that are at the root of their poverty and exploitation, but power relations are seen as essentially adverse. There is also constant reference to the absence of *união* (solidarity). On one's own it is impossible to achieve anything, and still people are not united. There are at least two reasons for this lack of solidarity. People cannot stick out their necks because they would be fired at once. But there is also the socially disintegrating and demoralizing effect of the transition to wage labor.

It has been shown that wage labor has affected women and men in different ways because the transformation in the relations of production was mediated by former cultural values regarding sex roles and the sexual division of labor. Women also perceive the roots of their present situation differently from men. They share men's general interpretation of their exploitation but also blame their husbands for the increased burden they have to bear. Women are keenly aware of their greater exploitation in comparison to the men. On the other hand, however, by demanding of their husbands that they fulfill the traditional role of provider, these women are endorsing those institutions—marriage, the family, and the sexual division of labor within it—that are at the root of their exploitation and subordination as women.

It could be argued that this attitude is an indication of the women's basic conservatism (not to mention that of the men, who resent having lost part of their power over women and children), one of the consequences of the penetration of the dominant family values into the working class. But this system of values—the aspiration to marry, the pressure on women to stay at home, the expectation that men will provide for their families, the demand that girls be respectable—coexists with a considerable tolerance toward those who do not observe the community values. There was one girl in the gang who was the lover of the *turmeiro*, became pregnant by him, lost the child, eventually had an affair with her mother's sister's husband, had a child by him, and went to live with him. Her aunt understandably was deeply affected by all this, but the women in the gang and the neighborhood did not discriminate against her in any way. Of another woman, who had five children by different fathers and now lived in poverty with her aged parents, it was merely thought that she had been silly in getting herself into such difficulties. Beyond purely ideological constraints there are material pressures that enforce the nuclear family as the appropriate form of social reproduction. In a society in which all aspects of life are structured on the premise of the universality of the nuclear family, alternative forms of living are difficult to envisage but even more difficult to put into practice. Also, in societies such as Brazil, where social inequality is so overt, the complex articulation of the family with the socioeconomic order is much more obscure than class antagonism and exploitation and the power relations that sustain them. Finally, emotional dependence among family members hides the underlying exploitation, but cannot prevent and even aggravates personal conflict.

There are a significant number of female heads of household. These women often have no desire to acquire new husbands. Even so, women do not often choose such households for everybody is aware that it is very difficult, at least materially, to get along without a male provider in the family. Both women and men are forced to live within an institution that is strained by deep conflicts and contradictions, and are unable to escape from it. The result is the extreme exploitation of women and the further demoralization of men.

As indicated earlier, capital organizes its strategies of accumulation on the basis of existing social institutions, such as the nuclear family. Yet it may change and, in times of extreme exploitation, undermine them. In this particular case (which is similar to the situation during the early decades of the English industrial revolution and to times of crisis of capitalism), generalized wage labor not only has uprooted and demoralized the laborers but has had a negative effect on the productivity of labor. In recent years individual planters and the Brazilian government have made attempts to reorganize the labor system to overcome the widely felt deterioration of productivity. Labor-intensive crops such as sugar cane and coffee require reliable and good-quality labor, not provided by the temporary wage laborers who now try to work with the least effort for the best pay, as a last form of resistance. One of the attempted solutions has been to resettle laborers on the plantations in order to revive the commitment to work that has been so greatly undermined by the general misery and disorganization of their lives.

Acknowledgments

The research on which this study is based was carried out between 1973 and 1978 as part of a wider study of the anthropology and history of labor relations on coffee plantations in interior São Paulo. The work was partially financed by a grant from the Ford Foundation.

References

Agricultura em São Paulo.
1952–   São Paulo: Boletím da Divisão de Economia Rural, Secretaria
present   de Agricultura.
Barret, Michèle, and McIntosh, Mary
1982   *The Anti-Social Family.* London: Verso Editions.
Bollettino Ufficiale della Camara Italiana di Commercio ed Arti in São
1903   Paulo, February 1903.
Carvalho de Moraes, J. P.
1870   *Relatorio apresentado ao Ministerio da Agricultura.* Rio de Ja-
           neiro: Ministerio da Agricultura.
Coulson, Margaret; Magaš, Branka; and Wainwright, Hilary
1975   "The Housewife and Her Labour under Capitalism—a Cri-
           tique." *New Left Review* 89:59–72.
Davatz, Thomas
1941   *Memoria de um colono no Brasil (1850).* São Paulo: Livraria
           Martins.
Dean, Warren
1976   *Rio Claro: A Brazilian Plantation System, 1820–1920.* Stan-
           ford: Stanford University Press.
Deere, Carmen D., and de Janvry, Alain
1981   "Demographic and Social Differentiation among Northern
           Peruvian Peasants." *Journal of Peasant Studies* 8:335–66.
Deere, Carmen D., and León, Magdalena
1982   "Producción campesina, proletarización y la división sexual del
           trabajo en la Zona Andina." In *Debate sobre la mujer en América
           Latina y el Caribe* 3 vols., edited by Magdelena León, vol. 2,
           pp. 115–132. Bogotá: ACEP.
Domingos Jaguaribe Filho
1877   *Algumas palavras sobre a emigração.* São Paulo.
Gardiner, Jean
1975   "Women's Domestic Labour." *New Left Review* 89:47–58.
Hagerman Johnson, Ann
1978   "The Impact of Market Agriculture on Family and Household
           Structure in Nineteenth Century Chile." *Hispanic American
           Historical Review* 58:625–48.

Harris, Olivia
1981   "Households as Natural Units." In *Of Marriage and the Market: Women's Subordination in International Perspective*, edited by Kate Young, Carol Wolkowitz, and Roslyn McCullagh, pp. 49–68. London: CSE Books.
Hartmann, Heidi I.
1976   "Capitalism, Patriarchy, and Job Segregation by Sex." *Signs* 1 (no. 3, pt. 2): 17–69.
1981   "The Family as the Locus of Gender, Class, and Political Struggle: The Example of Housework." *Signs* 6 (no. 3): 366–94.
Hartmann, Heidi I., and Markusen, A. R.
1980   "Contemporary Marxist Theory and Practice: A Feminist Critique." *The Review of Radical Political Economics* 12 (no. 2): 87–93.
Heusser, C.
1857   *Die Schweizer auf den Kolonien in St. Paulo in Brasilien.* Zurich: Bericht des Herrn Dr. H., an die Direktion der Polizei des Kantons Zürich.
Himmelweit, Susan, and Mohun, Simon
1977   "Domestic Labour and Capital." *Cambridge Journal of Economics* 1 : 15–32.
Holloway, Thomas H.
1980   *Immigrants on the Land: Coffee and Society in São Paulo, 1886–1934.* Chapel Hill: University of North Carolina Press.
Humphries, Jane
1977   "Class Struggles and the Persistence of the Working-Class Family." *Cambridge Journal of Economics* 1 : 241–58.
Kaerger, Karl
1892   *Brasilianische Wirtschaftsbilder: Erlebnisse und Forschungen.* Berlin.
Kageyama, Angela et al.
1982   "Diferenciacion campesina e cambio tecnologico el caso de los productores de srigol en São Paulo." Mimeo. Universidad Estadual de Campesinas.
Karrer, L.
1886   *Das schweizerische Auswanderungswesen und die Revision und Vollziehung des Bundesgesetz über den Geschäftsbetrieb von Auswanderungsagenturen.* Bern.
Kuznesof, Elizabeth A.
1980   "Household Composition and Headship as Related to Changes in Mode of Production: São Paulo, 1765 to 1836." *Comparative Studies in Society and History* 22 : 78–108.

Lasch, Christopher
1979   *The Culture of Narcissism: American Life in an Age of Diminishing Expectations.* New York: W. W. Norton and Co.
Maistrello, Guido
1923   "Fazendas de café—costumes (São Paulo)." In *O café no Brasil e no estrangeiro*, edited by Augusto Ramos, pp. 553–590. Rio de Janeiro: Santa Helena.
Martinez-Alier, Verena, and Boito, Armando Junior
1977   "The Hoe and the Vote: Rural Labourers and the National Elections in Brazil in 1974." *Journal of Peasant Studies* 4:147–70.
Natsch, Rudolf Arnold
1966   *Die Haltung eidgenössischer und kantonaler Behörden in der Auswanderungstrage, 1803–1874.* Zurich: Keller.
Ozorio de Almeida, Anna Luiza
1977   "Parcería a tamanho da familia no Nordeste brasileiro." *Pesquisa a Planejamento Económico* 7:291–332.
Palacios, Marco
1980   *Coffee in Colombia, 1850–1970: An Economic, Social and Political History.* Cambridge: Cambridge University Press.
Papaterra Limongi, J.
1916   *O trabalhador nacional.* Boletím do Departamento do Trabalho, no. 5. São Paulo.
Pinheiro, Paulo Sérgio de M., and Hall, Michael M.
1979   *A classe operaria no Brasil: Documentos 1889 a 1930.* Vol. 1. São Paulo: Editora Alfa Omega.
Roldán, Marta
1982   "Subordinación genérica y proletarización rural: Un estudio de caso en el Noroeste de México." In *Debate sobre la mujer en América Latina y el Caribe* (3 vols.), edited by Magdelena León, vol. 2, pp. 75–102. Bogotá: ACEP.
Ramos, Augusto, ed.
1923   *O café no Brasil e no estrangeiro.* Rio de Janeiro: Santa Helena.
Sallum, Brasilio, Jr.
1982   *Capitalismo e cafeicultura, oeste Paulista: 1888–1930.* São Paulo: Livraria Duas Cidades.
Seccombe, Wally
1975   "Domestic Labour—a Reply to Critics." *New Left Review* 89:85–96.
Sen, Gita
1980   "The Sexual Division of Labour and the Working Class Fam-

ily: Toward the Conceptual Synthesis of Class Relations and the Subordination of Women." *Review of Radical Political Economy* 12 (no. 2): 76–86.

Stolcke, Verena
1981 "Women's Labours: The Naturalisation of Social Inequality and Women's Subordination." In *Of Marriage and the Market: Women's Subordination in International Perspective*, edited by Kate Young, Carol Wolkowitz, and Roslyn McCullagh, pp. 30–48. London: CSE Books.

Stolcke, Verena, and Hall, Michael
1983 "The Introduction of Free Labour into São Paulo Coffee Plantations." *Journal of Peasant Studies* 10: 170–200.

Turenne, P. de
1879 "L'immigration et la colonisation au Brésil." *Revue Britannique* (February): pp. 437–461.

Visconde de Indaiatuba
1952 "Introdução do trabalho livre em Campinas." In *Monografia*
[ca. 1878] histórica do municipio de Campinas. Rio de Janeiro.

Whitehead, Ann
1981 "'I'm hungry, mum': The Politics of Domestic Budgeting." In *Of Marriage and the Market: Women's Subordination in International Perspective*, edited by Kate Young, Carol Wolkowitz, and Roslyn McCullagh, pp. 88–111. London: CSE Books.

Young, Kate
1982 "Formas de apropiación y la división sexual del trabajo: Un estudio de caso de Oaxaca, México." In *Debate sobre la mujer en América Latina y el Caribe* (3 vols.), edited by Magdelena León, vol. 2, pp. 55–74. Bogotá: ACEP.

Marriage, Property, and the Position of Women in the Peruvian Central Andes

Fiona Wilson

This essay focuses on women in order to examine gender relationships at the level of the family. The term *gender* is used to emphasize that it is the socially constructed categories of masculinity and femininity that are under discussion and not divisions that can be deduced from biological differences. The aim is to show how an understanding of gender relationships is essential for analysis of the way in which families are constituted and respond under situations of socioeconomic change.

This is a broad topic and could be approached from a number of perspectives. Here I examine one important expression of gender relationships in an agricultural society by asking what rights women possess over property and how women's rights differ from those of men. The discussion is restricted to a single historical case: relationships to property within families belonging to the dominant social class in the province of Tarma in the Peruvian central Andes during the latter half of the nineteenth century.

Gender Relations in the Family and Kinship System: Some General Points

The conceptual framework used by Schneider and Smith ([1973] 1978) to compare family organization in middle and lower class in the United States can be taken as a useful starting point for the discussion of gender. Their central argument is that it is necessary to dissolve family and kinship roles into their constituent elements as a prelude to analysis. The attribution of universal significance to "the family" can be avoided when questions are asked about the units constituting the kinship system in a particular culture, in order to determine how those units are defined and differentiated and how they are related to other cultural domains. Schneider and Smith write, "It is our contention that what are normally thought of as family and kinship roles are actually compound or conglomerate roles which are analytically separable into 'pure' kinship elements, sex role elements, and elements derived from the system of status and class differentiation" (p. 7).

The "pure" kinship elements (cultural assumptions about blood, the obligation to stick by relatives regardless of circumstances, and the like) are widely held across classes in American society and are imbued with ideas of "natural" behavior and "natural" morality. At a lower level of specification, kin are culturally constructed as persons with combinations of attributes (sex role, age, status, and class, as well as kinship) that define the manner in which action can take place. What these authors term the sex-role domain contains two opposing sets of meanings: one expressing complementarity, interdependence, and unity and thus coinciding with the dominant symbol of sexual union within the kinship domain; the other emphasizing the separateness and opposition of the sexes.

This analytical scheme departs most from feminist writing on kinship and the family (for example, Mackintosh 1981; Harris 1981) in the place and importance accorded to gender inequality. Though Schneider and Smith recognize that they are dealing with a culture in which men are held to be superior to women, gender inequality is not treated as integral within the constitution of the family and kinship system. Instead, inequality is introduced as an exogenously determined feature of the whole system. It is not part of the cultural definition of pure kinship elements, but it does give different values to the sex-role meanings with which it interacts: inequality becomes a residual where unity is the cultural message, and has an equal stress where differences are uppermost.

The deconstruction and separating out of elements contained in family and kinship roles and the appreciation of the various conceptual levels in which kinship systems can be specified are important clarifications. But once gender inequality and women's subordination are taken to be central within a culture, then a different formulation is required of the position and meaning of family and kinship in society and the interrelationships among the constituent elements. The position adopted here is similar to that taken by Verena Stolcke when she writes:

> The crucial issue is to understand the ways in which the institutions of marriage and the family lend support to, and serve to perpetuate, social inequality and relations of power, and the particular way in which the subordination of women is one of the pre-requisites for the maintenance of social relations of domination. I would argue that while class oppression and the social division of labour have their origins in unequal access to the means of production, it is social reproduction, i.e. the perpetuation of class relations and domi-

nation—mediated directly by the institutions of marriage and the family and inheritance—which requires (and thus determines) both women's primary assignment to domestic labour and the under-valuation of this function. [1981, p. 34]

Just as the kinship characteristics isolated by Schneider and Smith are imbued with ideas of "natural" behavior, so have biological theories been invoked to legitimize women's subordination, as well as the role of marriage and the family in class and society.

Women and Property in Tarma: An Apparent Paradox

This discussion of women's relationships with property in Tarma can begin with an apparent paradox. According to customs governing the transmission of property in the Peruvian central sierra during the nineteenth century, daughters and sons belonging to the families of the property-owning elite inherited equal shares of parental property. Ownership of large haciendas was closely associated with high status and prestige for both men and women, although only for men did property ownership open the door to positions of political power and authority. Only men could hold political office; only men could vote for and take office in the Provincial Council, the most important local government institution in a period of regional autonomy. Ownership of land, the most important means of production, brought men economic power and considerable cash wealth, especially in the latter half of the century, whereas the effective rights of women over property appear to have become ever more restricted.

It is not my intention to inquire into women's rights according to law (see Lewin 1981 for a discussion of changes in women's legal position as owners of property in Brazil). Republican governments were primarily concerned to institute a free market in land. They passed legislation freeing property owners from all encumbrances and attempted to remove the distinctions between European and Indian owners. Interpretation of the law was in the hands of the dominant white property-owning class, a matter that obviously had a bearing on how much notice was taken of reforms trying to improve the lot of the Indian. The interpreters were also men, a factor that in turn must have influenced how women's rights were perceived and defined in practice. What concerns me here, therefore, is not the legal basis of property rights but the subtle ways in which a male-dominated society regulated women as property owners.

An example of this domination is to be seen in the data sources available to historians. Male mayors and prefects compiled reports and engaged in voluminous correspondence on local affairs; the male "intellectuals" produced newspapers and wrote pamphlets and articles on matters they considered interesting. Data sources are not only class-specific: they are largely sex-specific. I discovered only one local archive in which a few women of the elite felt themselves free to record their views: the notarial or lawyers' records. In wills and in various types of contracts (mostly concerned with the sale or rental of property), women, far more commonly than men, departed from the dry legalistic prose to describe in their own words what they were doing and why they were doing it. Why women should have taken greater pains than men to set down for posterity the reasons for their actions regarding property is in itself an interesting question. The subject matter of these occasional entries and the manner in which they are expressed form the basis of my analysis.

The Rules of Class and Family Membership

In Tarmeño society, membership in the elite class rested on two principal attributes: ownership of hacienda property and European blood. The elite was composed of families. Family members, both men and women, shared the same blood and status, and this sharing was symbolized in the equal division of inheritance. Membership in the dominant social class was denied to those branches of the kin group which permanently lost access to large properties or prestigious positions, though many were still recognized as family members—with an inferior status—so long as they continued to serve their "superior" kin.

Because social inequality was also perceived as a matter of racial difference transmitted genetically (by European as opposed to Indian or mestizo blood), inheritance was seen to follow the dictates of heredity. As Stolcke notes in the case of nineteenth-century Cuba: "The perpetuation of class supremacy depended not only on the transmission of property according to the prevalent rules of inheritance but equally on the preservation of racial purity through control over heredity" (1981, p. 42). And as in the case of nineteenth-century Tarma, this preservation was achieved "through severe control by upper class men of the sexuality of the women of their class and women's consequent domestic seclusion. A woman's purpose in life was ideally to bear legitimate, i.e. racially pure, children to her husband" (Stolcke 1981, p. 42).

If women transgressed the strict rules governing their behavior—in particular, if they were felt to have compromised family honor—they risked ostracism from both family and class. Men, on the other hand, could openly live with and father children by women of inferior race; they risked ostracism from family and class only if such alliances were legalized through marriage. Women were to be sheltered and protected by fathers and/or brothers while they remained unmarried, and were handed over into the care of husbands on marriage. As dependent beings deprived of control over essential areas of their selves and their lives, women took on some of the attributes of property themselves. If the cultural definition of the relationship between the genders carried with it the data that women were the property of men, how could women as property, in this instance, at the same time be considered as the *owners* of property in another? The answer is that they were not.

Although women were granted equal shares of the inheritance, it did not follow that men and women were therefore considered equal. The fact that women were eligible for property shares says nothing about what kind of property women inherited (and whether it was different from men's); about what property represented for women (and whether it represented something different for men); and about what women were allowed to do with property once they got it (and whether men were subject to far fewer constraints). Furthermore, although women's rights of inheritance conferred high status and expressed their membership of class and family, it did not give women the right of entry into other cultural domains, as it did men. This essay contends, therefore, that in order for elite families to reproduce themselves socially, not only did women's property differ from men's, there was a fundamental inequality in the rights and powers that property conferred.

But reality does not always conform to the ideals that guide the actions of a social class. At a lower level of specification, as Schneider and Smith indicate, kin are culturally constructed as persons with combinations of attributes. Differences in people's age, marital position, and access to wealth become relevant. At this level of analysis, despite the overriding necessity for gender inequality and the subordination of women for the perpetuation of class domination, the real situation in which Tarmeño women found themselves was highly complex. Contradictory demands were placed on them as property owners, and at times they were needed to act as trustees for family property. Women themselves were not always wholly compliant and cooperative in conforming to societal ideals that emphasized their subordination. The economic transformations of the late nineteenth century, whereby the province became progressively incorporated into the world economic system, and capitalist relations of production spread to certain zones, radically altered the opportunities open to women as property owners. And the precise definition of gender roles among the Tarma elite varied in response to the impact of new ideologies formulated largely by an urban bourgeoisie.

In the discussion so far, questions have been posed at a number of levels of analysis. In order to suggest some of the answers, I examine here material taken largely from notarial archives. As conditions were not static in this period of economic transformation, the main trends are outlined. The questions for which data have been selected are the following:

1. How did female inheritance differ from male inheritance in actual property rights and in what that property represented? What constraints limited women in the exercise of rights over property? To what extent could men appropriate women's property?

2. What contradictions can be discerned in the role women were expected to play with regard to family property, either because of conflicting demands placed on women or in response to women's efforts at gaining a greater measure of independence?

3. What light is shed by an analysis of property rights on the content of gender relationships within the family and kin group and on how families were constituted, especially in the allocation of roles and the values placed on them? In particular, did female property carry with it specific implications of women's roles in reproduction of the family?

Before these questions can be answered, it is necessary to outline the nature of the production system in which the elite families were embedded.

The System of Production

In the province of Tarma, as elsewhere in the Andean region, families of European descent had amassed properties located in environmentally distinct zones. Each extended family group had accumulated a congeries of complementary properties: livestock and arable haciendas, silver and copper mines, small irrigated holdings in the valley floors surrounding the town of Tarma, and extensive land concessions in the recently re-colonized subtropical *montaña*. Extended families were composed of several branches, each represented by a nuclear family group. These branches usually owned one large hacienda or mining property as well as various smaller agricultural properties and houses.

Until the late nineteenth century, most large properties could be defined as haciendas, in the sense that they were worked by resident Indian families under a rental system. On the predominantly arable haciendas,

Indian families were allocated plots of land on which to produce their subsistence; in return they were obliged to work on the landlord's part of the property, in his town house, and in his other enterprises. Under this system, though technology was extremely primitive and productivity and output remained very low, the resident labor force produced some surplus year after year, no matter what was happening in the world outside the hacienda. The system possessed considerable strength and durability.

After the end of Spanish rule, Peru was submerged in political and economic chaos. The two overall effects were economic recession and political fragmentation. Long-distance trade routes were cut, and the cash economy became far more restricted. Throughout the country, regions such as Tarma became largely autonomous, with local political power passing entirely into the hands of property owners. Under these conditions of regional isolation, the property-owning elite were forced to depend to a far greater extent than before on products from their properties. Their congeries of properties supplied a wide range of foodstuffs, cloth woven on the haciendas, leather, wood, turfs for fuel, mules, and so on. Small amounts of cash derived from the sale of silver and wool paid for a few luxury goods available from the external economy. The various branches of a kin group living in the provincial capital of Tarma tended to establish internal circulation systems to exchange and redistribute products produced on family property, a system that strongly favored solidarity within the exchanging, extended family group.

For much of the nineteenth century, property owners lived as rentiers in their town houses or were absent from the province for years at a time, and needed to play only a minimal role in the management and investment of their property. Always, a few had chosen to tinker with agricultural improvements, but only in the latter half of the century did prevailing conditions allow radical transformation of the social relations of production. As Tarma was drawn again into the wider economy and society, property owners became increasingly motivated to produce a larger surplus for cash sale to a burgeoning home and export market. Over time, Tarmeño property owners supplied larger quantities of wool, silver, copper, and coffee for the export market, and livestock products and alcohol distilled from sugar cane for consumption in other regions of Peru.

Under these conditions, rentiers were pressed into becoming entrepreneurs and into transforming unproductive mines and agricultural haciendas into commodity-producing enterprises. Production for the market became the principal force in the reorganization of the productive system. The most dramatic indicator that a new economic era had begun was the *aguardiente* (cane alcohol) bonanza gathering momentum in the Tarma *montaña* in the 1860s and dominating much of the regional economy from the 1870s on. Sugar cane was grown on recently colonized properties, and the alcohol distilled on these estates was transported up to the sierra. It was purchased largely by Indians with cash generated by the mining sector—slowly recovering from its collapse at the end of Spanish rule.

As the native population of the *montaña* was killed or expelled, owners of the concessions had to play an active entrepreneurial role if land was to be cleared and planted and if any product was to be forthcoming. At the start, Tarmeño owners relied on supplies of labor, food, and cash from other family property located in the sierra; *aguardiente* production initially formed a part of the hacienda economy. As a result of what seemed enormous cash returns, commodity production in the *montaña* broke free from the constraints of the hacienda economy. At the same time, it gave greater opportunities to outsiders not connected to the old Tarma elite to acquire land, labor, and necessary inputs.

As the *aguardiente* economy expanded, producers were faced with two major problems: labor supply and investment capital. No longer could enough workers be found in the adjacent highlands. Entrepreneurs set up plantations worked initially by slaves (Chinese coolies or captured Amazon tribesmen), and later found contract workers through a system of labor recruitment known as *enganche* and through debt servitude. Expansion also led to a growing social division of labor in which certain ethnic or social groups took over specialist functions servicing the *aguardiente* sector; for example, land clearing and long-distance trade in basic goods were handled largely by Chinese; the luxury trade tended to be conducted by Italians; local trade in foodstuffs was run by Indian peasant producers; and the transport and sale of alcohol to consumers was managed by Indian and mestizo muleteers.

Tarmeños' access to investment capital was progressively hindered by the underlying ideology concerning property of the class to which they belonged. By the turn of the century, a crisis had developed concerning who had the right to make decisions about the utilization (i.e., immediate consumption or investment) of cash earned on family property. Property was seen fundamentally as a collective resource belonging to a family group, not as the private property of the person named in the title deed. Thus, although Tarmeño producers had considerable advantages in the early phase of the bonanza through their privileged access to family resources, in a later phase they were far less able to compete with immigrant entrepreneurs. By the end of the century, many Tarmeño families had been forced to withdraw from the *montaña*, and *aguardiente* production was largely in the hands of European immigrants, aided by the major merchant and moneylending houses run by Italian immigrants (see Wilson 1982 and forthcoming for fuller discussions of the economic transformation and the property ideology of the Tarma elite).

The General Position of Women from the Tarma Elite

Women belonging to the rentier class possessed certain advantages over women from other classes and at other time periods. The elite had access to various forms of wealth and could lead comparatively comfortable lives. Neither men nor women were obliged to undertake manual work in connection with their properties. Through their access to servile labor, these women were relieved of the burden and drudgery of domestic work. Servants cooked food, washed clothes, and looked after the children.

Childbearing and rearing were primary activities of women in property-owning families. Reconstruction of the genealogies of the leading families shows that a high fertility level was desirable. Families of ten to twelve children were not uncommon, though as a rough generalization, only about half could be expected to survive to adulthood. A comparison of family fortunes indicates that those with more children tended to move into positions of power and preeminence because they were able to establish larger congeries of properties and to place sons in important posts. Women from this class spent much time pregnant and rearing children in the family's Tarma town house. However, given the minimal involvement rentiers needed to have in the management or labor processes on their properties, women's responsibilities for child rearing do not explain why women's rights should have diverged from men's rights, though biological arguments were often invoked to explain why this should be so.

Women from this rentier class had advantages that, at least in theory, might argue for the existence of a greater equality between the sexes. A detailed case study of women belonging to the most privileged class is important at a theoretical level to pinpoint and underline some of the bases on which gender categories are constructed and perpetuated, as well as the contradictions implicit within them. It does not support simplistic conclusions about other classes.

From a cursory glance at the evidence, it is clear that the extent to which women could acquire and control property varied in the course of their lives: at certain periods, women were more free to acquire and manage property than at others. Thus it would be wrong to proceed with an analysis on the assumption that "women" represented a single undifferentiated category. By far the most important classificatory basis for determining a woman's role and expectations as a property owner was the position she was accorded within the kin group. According to this classification, distinctions can be drawn among women largely with respect to their primary relationship with a male. Thus the broad category of "women" can be broken down into subdivisions: daughters, sisters, wives, and widows.

The role or status of women within the family was made real by association with differential access to, and rights over, property. As the evidence presented below demonstrates, women in their role as daughters inherited property, and as sisters they were expected to give it up. But the association of kin role and access to property went far beyond this point, for while women were considered daughters and sisters, the dependence of their position was emphasized by society and they had little or no chance of purchasing their own property or administering property they had inherited. In this matter, women were far more circumscribed than men. Though a man's position as son and as brother affected his inheritance expectations, once he was an adult he was not subject to any restrictions preventing him from acquiring property or from managing what he owned.

The following case studies show that the categorization of women according to their identity within the family, and the association of this categorization with property rights, acted as the principal means by which society controlled women's rights over property.

Daughters and Their Inheritance

The inheritance custom adopted in republican Peru meant that all legitimate sons and daughters were entitled to inherit equal shares of the parents' property. The transmission took place at the death of the parent; there is no reference in notarial archives to daughers' being endowed with the inheritance portions at the time of marriage.

Information on the ownership of some ninety haciendas in Tarma province was discovered in local archives, principally, the Departmental Property Register now located in Huancayo, local Tarmeño newspapers of the period, and notarial archives. Of these, ownership dates were more or less complete in the case of some forty major properties in the sierra and *montaña* in the nineteenth century. Throughout the nineteenth century, ownership of all these properties went through periodic subdivision among co-heirs and a slow process of reaccumulation by a single male heir. Then at his death the pattern was repeated. These data show conclusively that women always relinquished their inheritance shares except in the case specifically mentioned in the text.

By the twentieth century, though some properties continued to exhibit the same ownership patterns, a growing number were changing hands through the market. Subsequently, those families which had managed to retain their hacienda property set up registered companies in which each heir was named as a shareholder. This adaptation did safeguard collective rights to property, but economic costs were high. The formation of family companies severely impeded the process of agricultural modernization and transformation in the Andes because decision making tended to rest with the family group and not with an individual owner/manager. Family members (most of whom lived in Lima) were far more interested in using cash earned from the property, or loans raised on its security, for urban property speculation or urban commercial ventures than in investments in the Andes.

Case studies have been selected to illustrate various aspects of a daughter's rights and expectations concerning her inheritance.

Reunification of a Single Hacienda Divided by Inheritance

The major families of the Tarma property-owning oligarchy were composed of several branches, and in general each branch owned one major hacienda and other smaller properties. By far the most common pattern throughout the nineteenth century was for ownership of the major property to be temporarily divided on the death of the male owner. The widow received half of the property, and the children received equal shares of the remaining half. Only very rarely did kin other than the widow and children inherit shares.

Normal procedure was for one son to take on the role of "heir apparent" of the hacienda and then to acquire the inheritance shares of his mother and siblings. There is little evidence to suggest how the choice of male heir was made, though generally it appears to have been the eldest son. Material on hacienda division and reunification was found for more than fifty cases in the Departmental Property Register, and only in comparatively rare instances did sons fail to reach a compromise and hence enter legal conflict. The main problems interrupting the peaceful transmission of property were encountered when owners died intestate, or when there were children from more than one marriage named as heirs, or when illegitimate offspring claimed portions of the inheritance. Generally, illegitimate children claimed cash in lieu of a share of the father's property; in one case illegitimate children made claims on their mother's estate.

The reunification of a hacienda divided through inheritance usually took a very long time—as much as twenty years. The children inherited additional portions following the death of the widow, and then the heir apparent had either to persuade brothers and sisters to sell their shares for a cash payment or to appropriate the portions inherited especially by his sisters, thus risking family conflict and possibly a costly legal dispute. Given the nature of the production system, the temporary division of ownership had little impact on the economic functioning of the hacienda in the precapitalist stage: resident serf families continued to pay rent regardless.

This inheritance pattern represented a compromise between two conflicting needs. On the one hand, all members of the family could look to property to provide status, security, and a means of survival for part of their lives. Most heirs continued to have access to the product from the parental property until some alternative source of income was found or until they were faced with some desperate need for cash—for example, to pay the legal costs in a court case. The pattern also allowed the heir apparent time to accumulate cash in order to buy out his co-heirs. On the other hand, from the point of view of the continuity and power of the families, it was essential that haciendas remain intact as enterprises. Ownership rights might be divided periodically, but the viability of the estate was not to be threatened through any permanent physical division of the property among its heirs.

Thus, within this system, although daughters apparently were given the same inheritance rights as sons, in practice their expectations were very different. A single daughter could never expect to be named as heir apparent; it was understood that the large, prestigious haciendas on which family status (as well as economic survival, especially in the early republican years) depended would be inherited by a son.

Sons took precedence in every case recorded in the Departmental Property Register and notarial archives, save one. This single exception is of particular interest because it demonstrates that women did not always conform to the social precepts controlling their behavior. Following the death of Bernardo Alvariño, owner of hacienda Calla, an intense struggle broke out between the heirs in the course of which Calla was put up for public auction in 1869. In this case, Mercedes vda de Benavides, the widow, favored the claims of her three daughters over those of her sons. The daughters handed over their inheritance shares to Mercedes, who was then in a position to purchase the rest of the property by offering a larger amount than the eldest son, José María Alvariño. In 1871 Mercedes gave back the property to her daughters. The following year a younger son, Cipriano, sold his share of the inheritance to his sisters, who, as far as is known, continued to hold the property jointly until their deaths. Deprived of his patrimony, José María later recorded that his wife gave him her jewelry, which he used to purchase land elsewhere in the province.

Ownership of Several Properties

Some major property owners possessed more properties than heirs at the time of their death. One would assume that parents would have preferred to hand on properties intact to their heirs to avoid possible dispute. But whereas sons often inherited whole properties, daughters did not. To take one example, following the deaths of Domingo Santa María and Petronila Cárdenas, his wife, their surviving heirs (one son and one daughter of a total of eleven children born) stood to inherit sizable properties. In an agreement made in 1892 between Máximo Santa María and his sister, Elvira Rosa Santa María de Demarini (who was married to an Italian immigrant), each inherited individual smallholdings, but the ownership of the two large livestock haciendas, Apaicanchilla and Huaylahuichan, was divided between them. In time, Máximo bought out his sister's shares and became sole owner.

The Problem of Female Heirs

Although most wives bore large numbers of children, child mortality was high. Sometimes only daughters survived. The most notable example in these records was the Otero family. Francisco de Paulo Otero, formerly a mule trader from Argentina and a general in the Liberation army, settled in Tarma and acquired land by marrying Petronila Aveleira, daughter of a property-owning family. Otero accumulated many properties in all parts of the province and was actively involved in their management. But the only son died young and the property was inherited by three daughters, only one of whom was married. The ownership of the properties was split, with Isadora and her Italian immigrant husband, Benito Cajigao, inheriting the largest livestock hacienda, Cachicachi, with thirty thousand head of sheep, while the sisters Melchora and Dominga were joint heirs of the other properties, including silver mines in Cerro de Pasco. But none of the daughters was expected to take charge of these properties. The heirs appended a clause to their mother's will in 1867 stating that Benito Cajigao would administer all the Otero property. Melchora and Dominga agreed to hand over their shares (with the exception of their part of the town house in Tarma and some cash) to their brother-in-law on the condition that he pay them the fixed sum of eighteen hundred soles in cash each year and support them while they all lived together "as a family." The sisters faced a crisis when Benito died prematurely. Isadora then married a kinsman, Martín Otero, who in turn took charge of the management of the sisters' property.

The Sexual Division of Inheritance

For daughters, the inheritance share of the parental property virtually always represented a cash endowment made at a later date. This practice was not sex-specific, because sons other than the heir apparent also received the value of their inheritance portions in cash. However, there was a difference between the sexes in that daughters had neither other expectations nor alternatives. In their dependent role as daughters, women were effectively barred from acquiring property, a prohibition that certainly did not apply to sons. Thus there was a profound discrimination in practice that constituted a very real division in how the inheritance portion could be used.

A necessary precondition for the functioning of this pattern of inheritance in the nineteenth century was the possibility of outward expansion of the hacienda or estate sector. Evidence from the Departmental Property Register suggests that sons who relinquished their shares of the parental estate to the heir apparent did have ample opportunity to acquire other properties in the province. Most notably they could acquire abandoned mines or vacant land in the *montaña* or establish new estate properties by dispossessing Indian communities no longer protected by the state. Acquisition of these types of properties became increasingly attractive as commodity production gained momentum.

Younger (or noninheriting) sons could use the cash received in lieu of their share of the parental hacienda to help acquire or invest in these properties. Thus, for these sons, the sale of an inheritance portion for cash could easily be reconverted into property—and highly productive property at that. For daughters, no such possibility existed. A daughter's inheritance portion was realizable only in cash, unless of course she was married.

The wills in the notarial archives make clear that two forms of property in particular were considered "female property." Not only did women usually own the families' houses in Tarma and Lima, they had often financed their construction. For example, Catalina Benavides de Chávez recorded in her will, written in 1861, that the family house in Tarma was her sole property. She had built it on a plot inherited from her parents, using money she had raised by selling land and a shop she had owned and by borrowing from an aunt.

Mothers could settle these forms of property on their daughters in addition to the inheritance shares of land. Jewelry in particular may have served as a form of dowry (though not exclusively: daughters sometimes gave jewelry received from their mothers to their fathers to purchase property). Some women made special provisions for daughters in their wills; Catalina Benavides's will can be used as an illustration. She had inherited a number of properties that her husband, Agustín Chávez, from the coastal province of Moquegua, managed. In her will she divided her property among her three sons and two daughters but made the following recommendation: "Using the powers that the law gives me, in addition to the fifth portion of the property, I give to my daughters my house as well as my jewelry because they are of weak and unfortunate sex, and I beg my sons to respect my decision on this." (This is one of several references in the notarial archives in which women describe themselves in a highly self-deprecating way.)

But in a later codicil, Catalina altered the distribution of her property, an amendment indicative of the conflicts she felt in providing for her children as individuals. She later elected to benefit one son so that the product of two irrigated *chacras* she owned would finance and clothe him while he attended the Military College in Lima. The protection and endowment of daughters was not to conflict with a mother's determination to see her sons well placed. This is only one of several wills that emphasize women's acute preoccupation with the welfare of their children. In contrast, men never made special recommendations in their wills stipulating that property should be divided to accord with the needs of children as individuals.

The Selling of Property Rights to Brothers

By selling their inheritance portions of major haciendas, sisters did not automatically give up all rights to the property. At least in the sierra, sisters continued to receive some share of the hacienda product, though these customary rights were no doubt being eroded in the course of the nineteenth-century rise of commodity production and sale to an external market. In addition, sisters might retain other rights. For example, the sisters Carmen Llavería vda de Allende and Sofía Llavería de Arroyo sold their shares of hacienda Maco to their brother in 1897 to raise money to finance a legal dispute. But the contract drawn up entitled them to keep their cattle and sheep on the hacienda free of charge.

Sons in the process of reuniting the ownership of a hacienda did not always respect their parents' wishes. Cash payment to co-heirs could be an excessive burden when sons were trying to raise investment capital. One illuminating example of such a dispute is revealed in the will of Mariana Aza de Briceño, written in 1900. She had inherited a share of the large livestock hacienda Quiulla, some nine hundred head of sheep, and twenty cattle. She claimed that her brother Manuel had falsely sold her inheritance share to their older brother Alejandro, who was attempting to unite the ownership and change the system of production on the hacienda. She also complained that Alejandro had robbed her of her livestock by selling without her permission and failing to reimburse her.

The injustice was compounded in her eyes by the fact that she had taken the responsibility for bringing up her younger brother and sisters, who were still children. She needed the cash that her inheritance represented, not for herself but to provide for her siblings. She wrote that Alejandro "had not fulfilled the sacred duties which were placed on him through his double obligation as executor for and guardian of the minors, on account of which I saw myself bound to take on the role of mother to my brother and sisters, giving Carlos, Josefa and Elisa food, clothing and education." This example, corroborated by other evidence, suggests that entrepreneurs from this social class increasingly begrudged the customs surrounding the transmission of property, especially the obligation imposed on them to reimburse their sisters. Clearly they were pressing for a different philosophy toward property rights, one that allowed private rights over land as opposed to the collective rights of a kin group.

The conclusion to be drawn from this discussion of daughters and sisters is that women were clearly discriminated against as owners of property but at the same time did possess rights to a share in the hacienda product and to reimbursement in cash for the inheritance portion forgone. Although the discussion of women's rights is incomplete, it can be suggested that this cash did not pass automatically or necessarily into male hands; women might finance their own lawsuits with the proceeds and use the cash as they wanted to support their children. Though society obliged women to take prime responsibility for the children, access to cash that the inheritance represented allowed women some freedom of action within what was defined as their sphere.

The implication is that if women were deprived of access to an inheritance portion of the family hacienda through a change in the way that property was transmitted, or if the family gave up most of its property and became part of the urban bourgeoisie, a woman's right of access to goods and cash could well be curtailed. In an urban setting, women from this class could be forced into a more dependent relationship with male providers.

The Rights of Married Women over Property

Contradictory propositions can be put forward concerning the property rights of married women. On the one hand, propertied families closely controlled their daughters' marriages; and husbands not only took care of their wives, they also took charge of their wives' property. Women's rights to property thereby passed into the hands of their husbands. On the other hand, implicit in previous discussions on the categorization of women according to their role within the family is the suggestion that married women were freer to acquire property than they had been as daughters or sisters. The implication of the first proposition is that marriage led to an appropriation of women's rights over property, whereas the implication of the second is that once she was accorded the status of wife, a woman was allowed by society some independence as a property owner and the possibility of playing a role complementary to that of her husband in the *sociedad conyugal*. The validity of these two propositions in the Tarmeño case is explored in this section. But first some comments are in order on the marriage strategies followed by Tarmeño families in the period.

Marriage Strategies

The choice of marriage partners for their daughters was obviously a matter of great importance for property-owning families. Perhaps the most powerful force governing the selection of affines was a negative one. By the middle of the century, society in Tarma had become divided into rival factions. Visitors to the town lamented the violence of the feuding and plotting among opposing family groups. Factionalism within regional oligarchies was characteristic of the period throughout the Andean zone (as Favre 1965 has shown for Huancavelica and Jacobsen 1978 for Azangaro).

It is possible to link inheritance patterns with the explosive relationships among the leading families, and it can be argued that each extended family group felt itself bound to maintain an identity separate from rival families in order to ensure its survival. The all-pervading feeling of threat strongly influenced marriage strategies. Marriage to children from rival families was to be avoided at all costs. This taboo may have been based on the fear that if intermarriage were permitted, a son-in-law might take on the role of heir apparent to his wife's family's property and reunite ownership in his name.

For most of the century, the families therefore demonstrated a clear preference for "foreigners" as affines. Following the Independence Wars, some Spaniards elected to settle in Tarma and to marry heiresses, as did several Argentinian mule traders whose commercial enterprises were brought to a halt by the end of the Spanish colony. In later decades, a number of Italian, French, and German immigrants seeking new lives in Peru were co-opted into the oligarchy. Some of these immigrants enchanced their families' positions by contributing wealth and connections in Lima; others were penniless adventurers. The alternative strategy was to marry daughters to kin; cross-cousin marriage became increasingly prevalent toward the end of the century.

These marriage strategies and the marriage taboo are indicative of a wife's rights over property. To some extent at least, women were vehicles through which property passed between men. An immigrant without social or kin links in Tarma province was attracted to marriage with a daughter of a property-owning family because of the opportunity to acquire land and other resources that such a marriage afforded. For example, by marrying Isadora Otero, the Italian immigrant Benito Cajigao became a very rich man. Indeed, for the first half of the century, until a market for land had developed in the province, most immigrants found it extremely hard to gain access to land by any other means.

The Rights of Wives within the *Sociedad Conyugal*

For much of the nineteenth century, a husband and wife were recognized as forming a joint property-owning partnership, the *sociedad conyugal*, which lasted until they died. Both partners contributed properties they already owned to this common fund, and after marriage, property could be purchased jointly in both their names. Especially when daughters married foreigners, the institution of the *sociedad conyugal* allowed a husband the right to take control of his wife's property. Also, in the early period a wife's family frequently assisted the son-in-law in gaining access to a hacienda or mine in the province, so that the branch could become established as part of the extended family group able to share in the intrafamilial circulation of goods and cash. Though a husband could appropriate rights of control over his wife's property, the institution did set limits on how far this appropriation could go. A husband might manage his wife's property during his lifetime, but he was not granted the right to dispose of it; formal ownership remained with the wife and reverted to her at her husband's death.

Evidence from the notarial archives suggests that the transfer of property from a wife to a husband was more a loan than a gift. Wills written by men often record in detail the cash, jewelry, livestock, and land wives had donated, and the purposes to which they were put in financing particular properties. From the wording of many wills, it seems that these donations were treated as debts for which reimbursement might be made before the husband's death or in the disposition of his property. For example, in his will made in 1880, Lorenzo Aza recognized a debt to his wife, Carmen Puch; she had earlier given him 252 cattle inherited from her parents. Lorenzo later reimbursed her with 100 cows and 400 sheep and paid for improvements undertaken on her irrigated *chacra* near Tarma town.

Wives as Owners of Property

By far the most common way for wives to own property was in partnership with their husbands. In many cases where property was purchased jointly, it was the wife who put up the major share of the cash. As noted above, the opportunities for buying property expanded greatly over time, but this trend was to have highly deleterious effects on wives as owners.

In the *montaña*, for instance, during the early expansion phase of the 1860s and 1870s, the majority of new properties were bought jointly by married couples, or by unmarried men. With the upsurge in *aguardiente* production and the formation of plantation enterprises, property ownership in the *montaña* was altered. No longer were these capitalistic enterprises owned by the *sociedad conyugal*; instead, most were the property of business partnerships established by males, in which a division was recognized between the partners who provided capital and the partners who undertook the management. Whereas the administrative partner was usually a member of a Tarmeño family, capitalists were drawn in from outside; usually they were men with other financial interests resident in Lima. Thus, as capitalist relations of production spread in the *montaña*, wives were squeezed out of their former position as co-owners, for the finance a wife could contribute was no longer sufficient to sustain the commodity-producing estates. As a result, wives came to forfeit their rights as joint owners.

Elsewhere in the province, similar changes were taking place in the ownership of properties expanding output for the market. There was, however, one type of property in the sierra increasingly identified as "women's property": the small arable holdings located near Tarma town. These irrigated plots of former Indian land, often described as *huertas* (gardens), produced crops of vegetables, fruit, and alfalfa all year round and supported dairy cows, chickens, and mules. The purpose of these properties was to provide subsistence for family consumption. Thus, over time, women's property tended to become restricted to those holdings producing use values, whereas men took control of cash-earning enterprises.

Wives as Managers of Property

There were three principal property-management options open to property owners in the latter half of the nineteenth century. First, owners might make little change in the way a hacienda was run, and continue to leave *mayordomos* and *caporales* in charge of the organization of work on the property. Second, a property could be rented out under a contract stipulating a fixed rental paid in cash or in a combination of cash and goods. Third, owners could become entrepreneurs and take over the management directly. When family branches owned only one major enterprise, the male family head could easily assume control. But serious problems could arise when a family owned a number of important properties in different parts of the province and/or wished to combine other activities, such as trading, with property ownership. When individual estates were rented out, owners lost access to a large part of the proceeds earned from cash sales. Yet many owners chose this option. The other possibility was to allocate responsibility for management among family members—to wives in particular. Women faced serious problems, but they were not insurmountable. The notarial archives reveal that a few wives successfully took over the management of important commodity-producing enterprises.

The case of Beatriz Benavides de Alvarez is a good example. In the 1870s Beatriz mortgaged her property in the sierra to raise cash to buy and operate the *aguardiente*-producing estate of La Libertad in the *montaña*. This "loan" cost Beatriz her property; in 1879 she was forced to sell it to pay back the debt. Her husband, Manuel Alvarez, wanted to establish a trading empire, bringing food and other consumer goods into the *montaña* for sale to the plantations and distributing *aguardiente* in the sierra. He made La Libertad his headquarters, but was often absent. In 1878 Manuel ceded full ownership of La Libertad to Beatriz, and she took over its management. She exercised far more than token control over the property, as shown by the contracts and deals she made with various neighbors. She managed the property for almost twenty years and in 1897 rented it to her sons.

The example of Beatriz Benavides demonstrates that wives could become independent, successful entrepreneurs managing commodity-producing enterprises. Yet very few did so. Apparently it was more common for wives from the peasantry than from the elite to have an active part in the family trading and farming enterprise.

Widows and the Chance of Independence

It was generally expected that wives would outlive husbands. Men married younger women (as much as thirty years younger). Furthermore, many younger men perished in the civil wars of the nineteenth century and in the War of the Pacific (1879–84), when Chilean forces occupied much of Peru, including the province of Tarma. But women of the property-owning families rarely married twice, even when widowed at a young age. The few known exceptions married relatives. The limitation imposed by society on women's second marriages was closely connected with the concern felt by the family group for safeguarding the transmission of the property. This concern is exemplified by the action of José Cárdenas, who in 1884 bequeathed his *montaña* plantations and property in the sierra to his daughter-in-law, Juana Alvarez, widow of his only child, Ricardo, and her seven young children, on condition that she did not marry again.

The primary responsibility of widows was to hold family property in trust for the heirs. On the death of the male family head, widows were entitled to a half share of property held by the *sociedad conyugal*. Furthermore, in cases where the children were minors, the widow took over their rights and acted on their behalf until they reached maturity. In some cases widows could play a decisive role in selecting the heir apparent and so could help ensure that the difficulties inherent in partible inheritance were circumvented. Thus, for some period of time, widows were given the opportunity to take on the role of the deceased husband, with the duty of keeping family property intact.

Widows as Entrepreneurs

The socioeconomic changes of the later nineteenth century placed mounting pressure on widows acting as trustees of family property. With the development of commodity production and the monetization of the economy, a widow had to ensure that property was managed and thus could no longer remain a passive rentier. During the interregnum of power she had to become actively involved in management, to find male kin *de confianza* (trustworthy) to fulfill the demands of administration, or to rent out the property until a son was old enough to take charge of it. Some widows embraced the opportunity given them to manage the property, but others shrank from the task.

The most outstanding example of a successful female entrepreneur was María Gálvez vda de Lara. Because this case illuminates many of the problems women had to face, it is explored in detail even though neither she nor her husband were Tarmeños. María Gálvez was born in 1831 in the small town of Izcuchaca, department of Huancavelica. She married Colonel José María Lara, thirty years her senior, the officer in command of the fort at San Ramón built to protect the colonization area against the Amazon tribes. Together they bought the land concession of El Milagro in 1855. But in 1860 Lara died, and María, left with a baby daughter, took over the property. At the time of Lara's death very little of the concession had been cleared and a large part had been usurped by an Argentinian immigrant, Antonio Araoz, on the pretext that it was vacant land. María immediately took charge of the legal case against Araoz in the Lima court, but the court decided in favor of Araoz's claim and María had to pay a considerable sum to get back her land. This money she raised by mortgaging the portion of El Milagro where ownership was not in dispute.

Between 1863 and 1873 María organized the clearing and planted sugar cane to produce *aguardiente*. In 1873 she came into conflict with another neighbor, a Prussian immigrant named Juan Ihmer. It appears that Ihmer took advantage of the fact that his opponent was a woman: María claimed that Ihmer had insulted and personally threatened her and had ordered all the workers from his estate to invade El Milagro. But Ihmer's attempts at intimidation failed. María won the subsequent court case, and Ihmer was ordered to pay damages. Such border fights were common in the *montaña*, but the incident demonstrates the toughness and resiliance that women in this frontier colonization had to possess to survive.

María continued to invest in El Milagro and purchased additional land in the *montaña*—small plots on which to grow food for the plantation labor force—as well as land in the Tarma sierra and a town house in Lima. In the late 1880s she found herself in conflict with yet another neighbor. To power the cane crushers El Milagro was dependent on water from a stream flowing through the neighboring estate of Huacará. Earlier, when Huacará had also been owned by a widow, Mercedes Hereza vda de Piedra, the two women had reached an agreement that allowed María to build a culvert to carry stream water to El Milagro. Then Mercedes was forced to sell Huacará owing to indebtedness. It became first a business partnership and then the property of Esteban Santa María, the most powerful Tarmeño property owner. After lengthy negotiations María and Esteban reached a new agreement, but it ended when Pablo Santa María inherited his father's property. In 1890 Pablo cut off the water supplies and brought the cane crushers to a standstill. Once again María appealed to the law, and won the case in 1891.

María Gálvez continued to manage the estate personally until her death in 1903, by which time El Milagro was one of the leading *aguardiente*-producing enterprises in the *montaña*. This biography (like that of Beatriz Benavides) shows that despite the problems and limitations imposed on women by society, it was still possible for some women to succeed as property owners and managers, win legal battles, withstand aggression from neighbors, and keep properties intact for many years.

There are several other examples of widows active in property management, although less is known about them. Dionesia Cerradell, widow of a Spaniard without children, managed the important livestock estate of Cacaracra, and large holdings of irrigated land at lower altitudes, until she was over seventy years old. Only then did she give power of attorney to a distant relative. Petronila Cárdenas, widow of Domingo Santa María, noted in her will that she had administered all the properties she inherited following the death of her husband (with the exception of one livestock hacienda), had paid all her husband's debts, and had bought several additional properties. But although there are many instances of widows succeeding as entrepreneurs, no tradition of female control over property was being formed. Both María Gálvez and Petronila had daughters, yet in neither case was the daughter allowed to follow in her mother's footsteps.

The Disposal of Family Property by Widows

In the later years of the nineteenth century, an apparently larger proportion of widows chose to sell property soon after the death of their husbands. Often they described their reasons for selling in some detail in the notarial archives. Two cases can be noted as examples. In 1880 Generosa Garra vda de Yramategui sold the *montaña* estate Masayacu to German immigrant Francisco Baumgarten. She explained that the sale was forced upon her "as much on account of my condition as a woman foreign to managing the work of cultivation as for a lack of capital." In 1910 Concepción Villaizan vda de Limailla sold her *estancia* in the sierra, noting that this was because "of being a woman alone and not able to look after it and also because I am greatly in need of money."

These two examples contain two points of interest. First, why should these women feel the need to provide reasons for selling their property? The notarial records contain no similar explanations by men. Maybe widows felt a need to exonerate themselves in the face of possible criticism for their failure to act as trustees for their children. Second, the primary reason given in each case is gender. Simply describing themselves as women, alone, seems to have been considered a valid reason for their action. Yet why should gender take precedence over the need for cash, especially in a period when both men and women from the Tarma oligarchy were facing a greatly increased need for cash? The need to raise cash from their properties may well have been greater for women than for men, partly because women were barred from holding cash-earning offices and jobs. Therefore, why was the need for cash given as a secondary and not the principal cause of the decision to sell? Widows might have been coming increasingly under the influence of an ideology in which they perceived themselves as unable to take on the "male" role of property manager.

Widows as Renters of Their Property

Many widows responded to the situation following their husbands' deaths by renting out their property. Some appointed male kin to take control, but the evidence suggests that it was becoming more difficult for widows to find suitable relatives who had the time to manage their property. With agricultural development in the central sierra, many Peruvians and immigrants were attracted to the province in search of land. Many were willing to rent land until they accumulated sufficient capital or had the opportunity to purchase. Widows found plenty of willing applicants to rent their land—an option taken by many male property owners as well as widows. Experience varied over time, and there was a growing divergence between the *montaña* and the sierra, largely because of specialization in commodity production in the *montaña*.

In the case of properties in the sierra, widows could generally demand payment of rent in cash and kind (as they had done for decades). For example, Elvira Guido vda de Santa María, who had been left with eight young children, elected to rent out her many properties—livestock haciendas in the highlands and rich arable farms in the temperate zone. The contract she signed with the Italian immigrants Francisco Ferro and Luís Gestro was for eight years, and it stipulated not only that rent was to be paid in cash but that the renters supply free of charge 25 sacks of potatoes, 150 sheep, 20 sacks of maize, and 6 sacks of barley each year; 4 loads of wood and 2 cheeses each week; the milk from 2 cows every day; and the permanent use of 5 mules. In addition, Elvira demanded that she keep her own 500 sheep and 25 cattle on the largest hacienda of Huaymanta.

Through this type of rental contract, a family could meet its basic subsistence requirements and also earn a little cash income. This family retained its property, and at a later date Elvira and her adult sons engaged in extremely profitable property speculation when the Central Railway was constructed across their land. With the proceeds they formed a very profitable commercial venture, Mercantil La Oroya. Elvira's success in keeping the family property intact can be attributed to a number of factors. First, the bulk of the rental was paid in goods, most of which had little market value at that date. Hence renters were not so motivated as they would otherwise be to sell these goods instead of supplying the widow and her family. Second, the Santa María family was the largest and most powerful in Tarma at the time and had the means to enforce adherence to the contract. Finally, as the later evidence shows, Elvira was a strong and able administrator, not a vulnerable widow whom renters could easily deceive or defraud.

The experience of widows renting out *montaña* property was generally very different. *Montaña* plantations were specialized in commodity production, and there was little possibility of making a contract with rent payable in subsistence products. Furthermore, there was keen competition for land among prospective entrepreneurs. One obvious strategem was to rent land from a widow and then force her to sell. The case of Juana Alvarez vda de Cárdenas illustrates the problems faced by young widows in the *montaña*. As noted above, she and her seven young children had inherited *aguardiente* estates from her father-in-law, José Cárdenas. Initially, she rented them to a partnership composed of her brother and two capitalists. For reasons unknown, the partnership came to an end in the 1890s, and she then rented them to a German immigrant, Emilio Bhorn, for a fixed cash sum. After signing the contract, Bhorn not only neglected the property, he paid no rent for a period of eight months. According to Juana, as she had no alternative source of cash, she was forced to sell the estates to pay for her children's food and education. The purchaser was an Italian trader, Pedro Buraschi, who was rapidly accumulating *aguardiente* estates and who very probably had been working in collusion with Bhorn, for Bhorn stayed in the *montaña* and purchased a large coffee estate soon after.

This example demonstrates the acute dependence of some widows on their properties to provide for their children. After a lapse in rental payments of a mere eight months, Juana had been forced to sell. Unlike the Santa María family, the Cárdenas (the most prestigious Tarma family at the end of the colony) had fallen on hard times, partly on account of demographic hazard: small numbers of children born at a crucial period and a shortage of male heirs owing to the untimely death of sons. There were no longer any powerful male kinsmen to protect the interests of the widow.

This case also illustrates the relative powerlessness of the old Tarma families when pitted against the rising entrepreneurs, who combined commerce and moneylending with an aggressive search for land. Widows were particularly vulnerable during times of family crisis, but this was part of a far more general process in which the old, established property-owning class in the sierra was increasingly challenged by immigrant entrepreneurs and merchants.

Concluding Remarks

In conclusion, I return to the questions set out at the beginning of the Tarma case study in order to draw together some of the findings that have emerged relating to the introductory discussion.

1. How different was women's property from men's property?

The bundle of properties that women stood to inherit had always been somewhat distinct (e.g., houses and jewelry were handed down from mother to daughter), but in the course of the nineteenth century differences between women's property and men's property tended to widen. For example, whereas in the earlier period wives were generally named as co-owners of large properties acquired by the *sociedad conyugal* in the sierra and *montaña*, in later years this practice ended. The properties that women normally inherited as whole units, or that they purchased in their own right, were small irrigated plots in the sierra valleys that produced subsistence goods for family consumption. Over time, therefore, women's property was increasingly restricted to holdings producing use value, while men took charge of enterprises producing exchange value.

The distinction between what property represented for women and what it meant for men has been explored in the discussion on hacienda division and reunification. Although women were legally entitled to inherit an equal share of property, this share was transmitted in the form of cash, which in practice could not be used directly by women for purposes of production. Social ordinances prevented unmarried women from acquiring their own property. And in earlier years, wives handed over some proportion of the cash and other resources they inherited to their husbands to buy and invest in property.

But such loans made to the *sociedad conyugal* during the husband's lifetime were not supposed to interfere with what was regarded as women's principal obligation: the financial support of children and other dependents.

Although many forms of male appropriation of female property were considered legitimate, such as the effective right of husbands to control their wives' property, or the right of male kin and affines to manage property belonging to unmarried women, there was one form of appropriation that became increasingly prevalent and was fiercely resented by women: the attempts of brothers to deprive their sisters of their inheritance shares. Women were listened to with some sympathy when they complained of injustice at the hands of their brothers; entrepreneurial property owners found themselves utterly frustrated by customs requiring the distribution of inheritance shares among large numbers of co-heirs.

2. What contradictions can be discerned in the role women were expected to play with regard to family property?

Although women might generally be considered vehicles through which property passed between men, there were occasions when the survival of the family as a property-owning unit and the perpetuation of its place in the dominant social class depended on the ability of particular women to act as trustees of family property. It was asked earlier how these different demands on women could be accommodated and represented in ideology. To meet these obligations, widows were given greater opportunity for independent action as property owners and managers. They could assume the powers of their deceased husbands over family property, although widows' powers did not extend to other important spheres of male life. However, a widow's independence could not be emulated by or transferred to other categories of women, precisely because other women were unable to escape from the paternalism and protection of fathers, brothers, and husbands. By and large, only widows were in a position to challenge the rules that governed women's access to land or deprived them of such access.

There does appear to be a moment during the development of commodity production and the spread of capitalist relations in the province when accepted rules governing gender relations were shaken. A few wives and widows, especially in the relative social and economic freedom of the *montaña* frontier, were able to confront male supremacy and to participate successfully as entrepreneurs. But the moment was short-lived. By the turn of the century wives and widows faced increasing restrictions on their behavior, both because of the diminishing economic opportunities they could grasp and because of the reinforcement of an ideology emanating from the urban bourgeoisie that emphasized women's weak and dependent position.

3. What light is shed by an analysis of property rights on gender relationships within the family?

Time and time again, entries in the notarial archives show that women took prime responsibility for providing for their children and other dependents. Though men were expected to feel (rather nebulous) "sacred duties" toward their families, it was up to women to secure food and clothing and to find the cash sums necessary to give sons an education. Over time, the level of cash expenditure this support demanded rose rapidly on account of progressive monetization of the local economy, changes in consumption patterns (a larger proportion of the family's needs were purchased from external sources), and the growing preoccupation among families of the regional oligarchy with giving sons a higher education in order to maintain their class position in a national context.

Women's rights to property reflect the division of gender roles within the family: women were responsible for reproduction, and to safeguard this role, their rights were protected. Any move that threatened a woman's access to her inheritance, such as a brother's attempt to dispossess his sister, was not tolerated by the social class as a whole. However, because of the definition of the "women's sphere" as responsibility for reproduction, women were at the same time effectively barred from accumulating capital for investment in productive activities. The growing need for cash to provide for their children meant that women were not generally in a position to accumulate capital for investment in their own independent economic activities.

It would appear to follow that men, having escaped the burdens and responsibilities involved in family reproduction, could accumulate and transform the social relations of production on their properties (in line with what immigrant entrepreneurs were doing). Although freer with regard to capital accumulation, Tarmeño entrepreneurs confronted a basic cultural element of family organization of that dominant social class: the rules governing the transmission of property. And these were far more resistant to change.

References

Favre, Henri
1965   *La evolución y la situación de las haciendas en la región de Huancavelica, Perú.* Serie Mesas Redondas, no. 1. Lima: Instituto de Estudios Peruanos.

Harris, Olivia
1981   "Households as Natural Units." In *Of Marriage and the Market: Women's Subordination in International Perspective,* edited by Kate Young, Carol Wolkowitz, and Roslyn McCullagh, pp. 49–68. London: CSE Books.

Jacobsen, Nils
1978   "Desarrollo económico y relaciones de clase en el sur andino." *Análisis* 5:67–81.

Lewin, Linda
1981   "Property as Patrimony: Changing Notions of Family, Kinship and Wealth in Brazilian Inheritance Law From Empire to Republic." Paper presented to a conference on Theoretical Problems in Latin American Kinship Studies, Ixtapan de la Sal, Mexico.

Mackintosh, Maureen
1981   "Sexual Division of Labor." In *Of Marriage and the Market: Women's Subordination in International Perspective,* edited by Kate Young, Carol Wolkowitz, and Roslyn McCullagh, pp. 1–15. London: CSE Books.

Schneider, David, and Smith, Raymond T.
[1973] *Class Differences in American Kinship.* Ann Arbor: University
1978   of Michigan Press. [Englewood Cliffs, N.J.: Prentice-Hall.]

Stolcke, Verena
1981   "Women's Labours: The Naturalisation of Social Inequality
and Women's Subordination." In *Of Marriage and the Market:
Women's Subordination in International Perspective*, edited by
Kate Young, Carol Wolkowitz, and Roslyn McCullagh, pp.
30–48. London: CSE Books.
Wilson, Fiona
1982   "Property and Ideology: A Regional Oligarchy in the Central
Andes in the Nineteenth Century." In *Ecology and Exchange in
the Andes*, edited by David Lehmann, pp. 191–210. Cambridge: Cambridge University Press.
forth-   "The Generation of Commodity Production in an Andean
coming   Province during the Nineteenth Century." *Latin American
Perspectives*.

Glossary

afilhados (Portuguese): godchild

aguardiente (Spanish): cane alcohol

alforriado (Port.): liberated slave

amancebado (Sp.): used in fifteenth century to describe a man living with a woman to whom he was not married according to Catholic sacrament

anaco (Quechua): woman's woven garment made of one piece of cloth

avulsos (Port.): laborers recruited exclusively for the harvest or for special tasks

ayllu (Quechua): the local kinship and social unit that constituted the basic cell of Andean social structure

caboclos (Port.): Brazilian Indian; also, a Brazilian of mixed parentage

cacique (Sp.): political boss; used to designate local ethnic headmen

camaradas (Port.): resident wage laborers paid on a monthly basis

caporal (Sp.): resident hacienda foreman

casco (Sp.): physical core of a hacienda, including houses of the owner, the administrator, and the permanent laborers.

chacara (Old Sp.): individually assigned agricultural plots

chacmeo (Quechua): preparing fallow land for cultivation

chacra (Sp.): farm; usually small and intensively cultivated

chicha (Quechua): maize beer distributed on ceremonial occasions

chuño (Quechua): dehydrated potatoes

coamil (Mayan): plot of hilly land worked by hoe (*coa*)

colonato (Port.): a mixed-task, piece-rate wage incentive system that predominated in Brazilian coffee plantations during the first half of the twentieth century

colono (Port.): immigrant laborer

comadre (Sp.): term used reciprocally by the mother and godmother of a child

compadrazgo (Sp.): the relationship between the parents and godparents of a child; the system of compaternity instituted by such a relationship

compadre (Sp.): term used reciprocally by the father and godfather of a child

confu man (Afro-Guyana): sorcerer

criollo: person of Spanish descent born in the Americas

Cristero Rebellion (Mexico, 1926–30): rebellion in retaliation for the vigorous anticlerical measures of President Plutarco Elías Calles. The church suspended religious ceremonies and approved, and possibly sponsored, the rebellion.

curaca (Quechua): local ethnic authority

de confianza (Sp.): literally trustworthy, usually associated with a real or created kinship tie

ecuaro: plot of land producing for domestic consumption. Used in areas of Tarascan influence: Michoacan, Jalisco, Guanajuato and Queretaro

ejido (Sp.): communal holdings of public lands

encomendero (Sp.): agent or commissioner; a Spanish colonist given authority over an Indian territory

enganche (Sp.): a system of labor recruitment by which workers from the sierra of Peru were found for capitalist enterprises and major construction works. Employers forwarded money to intermediaries who advanced cash or goods to recruits which had to be paid off by a specified period of work.

engenho (Port.): a mill, usually sugar mill

estancia (Sp.): farm, ranch or estate. In the Peruvian Andes often used to distinguish a smaller property from a hacienda

exposto (Port.): foundling

fazenda (Port.): plantation or estate

forro (Port.): freed slave

godparenthood: spiritual relationship created between sponsors and initiate at baptism and confirmation as well as at various nonsacramental rites of passage

habilitación (Sp.): outfitting, equipping, financing. Also used to mean grain given to a sharecropper by the landowner, both for seed and to feed the family before harvest time

hacendados (Sp.): landowners, ranchers

huaca (Quechua): local shrine; the deity worshipped in such a shrine

huerta (Sp.): small field producing fruit and vegetables

jacal: hut

latifundio (Sp.): vast rural estate

lavrador de cana (Port.): cane farmer

liberto (Port.): freed slave

madrinha (Port.): godmother

mati (Guyanese): mate, group member

mayordomo (Sp.): overseer or resident adminstrator

mestizo (Sp.): person of mixed Spanish/Indian descent. Also refers to acculturated Indians (*ladinos, cholos*)

mezcal: alcohol distilled from the *agave* plant of that name

mit'a (Quechua): Andean institution whereby an individual was obliged to perform work by turns; adopted by Spaniards

mitimae (Sp.): Spanish for Quechua word *mitmaq*, a people permanently removed from their home and placed in other areas to exploit local resources, man fortresses, or control conquered populations

montaña (Sp.): highlands, mountainous region; the *"ceja de montaña,"* or the subtropical zone of hills and valleys lying at altitudes of about 700 to 1,000 meters to the east of the Andean Cordillera above the plains of the Amazon basin

municipio (Sp.): Administrative unit consisting of a main town and subordinate hamlets

obeah (Afro-American): sorcery

oligarchy: dominant economic and political class

padrinho (Port.): godfather

pardo (Port.): person of mixed race

parientes: kin of all sorts

quipucamayoc (Quechua): specialist in using the *quipu*, the colored, knotted strings used as counting devices

ranchero (Sp.): Ranch owner. In Mexico the term has two connotations: it points to a rural middle class, a buffer between the *hacendado* and the peasant, but also to a subculture of *mestizo* and *criollo* independent farmers and livestock raisers.

rancho (Sp.): A land unit not as big as a hacienda but big enough to operate at a profit. Also refers to the set of houses where the families of the owner and workers live

senhor de engenho (Port.): plantation owner

sitio (Port.): place, locale

sociedad conyugal (Sp.): the marriage partnership with respect to property

taata (Afro-Guyanese): father

tambo (Quechua and Sp.): way station

tienda de raya (Sp.): hacienda store

tío (Sp.): uncle

tomin (Sp.): coin of small denomination (eight *tomins* equal one *peso*)

yanacona (Quechua): servant attached to the household of ethnic lord or an Inca; after 1532, permanent servants of Europeans

yunta: a yoke of oxen

Contributors

Jack Alexander is an applied anthropologist who currently is working for the New York State Department of Correctional Services. His work focuses on the social and cultural analysis of prison classification systems and applications developed from the analysis. He has published several articles on the cultural analysis of kinship in the middle-class Jamaican family and has completed a book-length manuscript based on his research in Kingston, Jamaica. He obtained his doctorate in anthropology at the University of Chicago.

Ruth C. L. Cardoso obtained her Ph.D. in anthropology from the Universidad de São Paulo in 1972 and is now a member of the Departamento de Ciencias Sociais at that institution. She has carried out research on Japanese immigration to Brazil, social movements in São Paulo, patterns of political mobilization, and the impact of electoral campaigns on social movements, as well as studies of family organization in the poor areas of São Paulo.

Stephen Gudeman is professor of anthropology at the University of Minnesota. His major fieldwork was carried out in rural Panama where he studied peasant economy, kinship, and godparenthood. His publications include "The *Compadrazgo* as a Reflection of the Natural and Spiritual Person" (1972), *Relationships, Residence and the Individual* (1976), and *The Demise of a Rural Economy* (1978). Currently he is working on metaphors and reflexivity in the construction of economic models.

Ramón A. Gutiérrez is assistant professor of colonial Latin American and Chicano history at the University of California, San Diego. His book *Marriage, Sex and the Family: Social Change in Colonial New Mexico* has been accepted for publication by Stanford University Press. Gutiérrez, who is the recipient of a MacArthur prize, will be a fellow at the Center for Advanced Study in the Behavioral Sciences during 1983–84, where he will undertake research on the ideological construction of gender in colonial Latin America.

B. W. Higman is professor of history at the University of the West Indies, Mona, Jamaica. He spent 1981–83 as senior research fellow in the Research School of Social Sciences, Australian National University. His book, *Slave Population and Economy in Jamaica, 1807–1834*, won the Bancroft Prize in American History in 1977. He has published many papers on the historical demography of slave populations, and his new book, *Slave Populations of the British Caribbean, 1807–1834*, is to be published by Johns Hopkins Press in July 1984.

Larissa A. Lomnitz is professor of anthropology at the Universidad Nacional Autónoma de México. She has carried out research on both upper- and lower-class family life in Mexico and has written extensively on such varied topics as economic development and social change, political organization and concepts of trust among the Chilean middle class. She studied anthropology at the University of California, Berkeley, and has been a visiting scholar at Berkeley, at the Institute for Development Studies at the University of Sussex, England, and at the Hebrew University, Jerusalem. Her book *Networks and Marginality* was published in 1977.

Enrique Mayer is a Peruvian anthropologist who has worked extensively in the Central Andes of Peru studying economic exchange, traditional Andean agriculture, and the social organization of peasant communities. He has edited and contributed articles to *Reciprocidad e Intercambio e los Andes Peruanos* (1970) with Georgio Alberti, and with Ralph Bolton, *Andean Kinship and Marriage* (1977). He has taught at the Catholic University in Lima, was head of the Research Department of the Interamerican Indian Institute in Mexico City, and is currently a member of the faculty of the Department of Anthropology and the Center for Latin American Studies of the University of Illinois at Urbana-Champaign, where he continues his work on Andean agriculture.

Juan M. Ossio is head of the Department of Social Sciences and director of postgraduate studies in anthropology at the Catholic University of Peru in Lima. He studied at Oxford University, where he took the D.Phil. in social anthropology. His work has concentrated on the analysis of social structure, myth, religion, and ideology in Andean communities.

Guillermo de la Peña is director of the Centro de Estudios Antropologicos at El Colegio de Michoacán (Zamora, Mexico) and has previously taught at the Universidad Autónoma Metropolitana (Iztapalapa, Mexico City), at the Centro de Investigationes Superiores del Instituto Nacional de Anthropologia e Historia, and at the University of California at Santa Barbara. He is currently visiting professor at the University of Texas at Austin. He studied social anthropology at the University of Manchester in England and is the author of *A Legacy of Promises: Agriculture,*

Politics and Ritual in the Morelos Highlands of Mexico (1982), *El Aula y la Ferula: Aproximaciones al Estudio de la Educatión* (1981), and numerous papers on themes related to regional development and the anthropology of education.

Marisol Pérez-Lizaur is a Ph.D. candidate in social anthropology at the Universidad Iberoamericana and is working on a study of the entrepreneurial activities of a Mexican upper-class family.

Stuart B. Schwartz is a historian of colonial Latin America and has concentrated his research and writing on Brazil. Educated at Middlebury College and Columbia University, he has been teaching at the University of Minnesota since 1967. His particular interest is social and economic history. Among his publications are *Sovereignty and Society in Colonial Brazil* (1973), *A Governor and His Image in Baroque Brazil* (1977), and as co-author, *Early Latin America* (1983). He is presently completing a study of sugar and slavery in Bahia (1500–1830) to be published by Cambridge University Press.

Raymond T. Smith is chairman of the Department of Anthropology at the University of Chicago. He studied social anthropology at Cambridge University and has taught at the University of the West Indies, the University of Ghana, McGill University, and the University of California at Berkeley, as well as at Chicago. He has carried out research in various parts of the Caribbean, in Ghana, and in the United States. Currently a Guggenheim Fellow, he is completing a book on kinship, class, and race in the Caribbean.

Verena Stolcke was born in Germany and studied social anthropology at Oxford. She has lived and worked also in Argentina, Cuba, and Brazil. At the moment she is engaged in writing a book on women agricultural workers in São Paulo, and teaches anthropology at the Universidad Autónoma de Barcelona. The author of *Marriage, Class and Colour in Nineteenth Century Cuba* (published in 1974 under her married name, Martinez-Alier), which is a study of sexual values and racial attitudes, she has also published articles on the connection between racism and sexual hierarchies and is active in women's groups in Barcelona.

Fiona Wilson is a guest researcher at the Centre for Development Research and edits publications in English at the International Work Group for Indigenous Affairs, Copenhagen, Denmark. Her main research has been on economic and social change in the Peruvian Andes and at present she is preparing a book on this theme. Recent publications include "Property and Ideology: A Regional Oligarchy in the Nineteenth Century" in *Ecology and Exchange*, edited by D. Lehmann (1982); "The Generation of Commodity Production in an Andean Province," *Latin American Perspectives* (forthcoming); and "The Effect of Recent Strategies of Agricultural Change on the Position of Women: A Review of Literature on Latin America," Centre for Development Research Project Papers, 1982.

Index

Acculturation, 17

Adoption: and the definition of kinship, 196, 200; and socialization, 197; frequency of, 200; and the creation of kinship, 202; and cultural factors, 202; and reciprocal obligation, 279–80; and infertility, 286

Agrarian reform. *See* Land reform

Amacueca: description of, 212–13; and regional transformation, 215–18

Andamarca: description of, 120

Arranged marriages. *See* Marriage: transactions

Baptism: meaning of, 35; records of, 39–40; and contradiction with slavery, 41–42; of adult slaves, 51–52, 55. See also *Compadrazgo*; Godparenthood

Baralong boo Ratshidi, 23

Bilaterality: of kinship terms, 77; and *compadrazgo*, 137–38; of descent, 200; and kin group boundaries, 225; and ideology, 228; and social change, 229

Braudel, Fernand, 14

Capitalism: changes in, 6, 25–26, 205; and noncapitalist forms, 205; and persistence of working-class family, 265; and subordination of women, 265. *See also* Economic change

Capitalist enterprise: and kinship, 18, 186–89, 191–92, 223–25; and women's rights, 315; female management of, 316

Catholic church: and family authority, 24; and godparenthood, 37, 39, 42, 119; and marriage, 121, 123–24, 244–48, 250; and baptism, 121, 127–28, 136–38; and family ideology, 210; and matrimonial investigation 241, 245–48, 250

Ceremonial kinship: types of, 120–22; and generational continuity, 132; and affinity, 132–35. See also *Compadrazgo*

Child labor, 217, 219; and education, 217

Children: as basis of family, 198–99

Ciudad Guzman: description of, 223–24

Class: and race, 168–73, 300; and family life, 169–71, 225, 298; origins of Jamaican middle, 177; conflict, 208; and honor, 238; and subordination of women, 298; in Peruvian Andean society, 300. *See also* Kinship; Family

Class interests: and Jamaican nationalism, 177–78; and means of production, 205; and kinship, 205

Class strategy: and kinship, 206; and cultural definition of need, 207

Coffee cultivation: changes in, 274; and patterns of labor demand, 274–75

Collective representations: nature of, 148–49; and kinship, 148–50

Community studies, 18

Compadrazgo: and deep structure, 20; constituent parts, 118–19; differing views of, 119; occasions for, 121; and kinship terminology, 122, 133; and affinity, 122–23; and marriage rituals, 123–24, 126; and gift exchange, 124; and calendrical feasts, 125; and house roofing rituals, 125–26; and dichotomous nature of human be-